A Citizen's Guide to City Politics

A Citizen's Guide to City Politics

James Lorimer

photographs by Myfanwy Phillips

James Lewis & Samuel
Toronto 1972

ISBN   cloth   0-88862-026-8
        paper   0-88862-027-6

Design and layout   John Williams
Diagrams and maps   Lynn Campbell
Editing   Wayne Lawson
Photographs   Myfanwy Phillips
Typesetting   Chuck Cassity

James Lewis & Samuel
35 Britain Street
Toronto 229

Printed and bound in Canada

4 3 2   74 75

Contents

Preface

In a way, I have been working on this book since I went to a public meeting in the east of Parliament area of Toronto in January 1967 and heard from area residents that city hall was about to expropriate the area and turn the land over to private developers for high-rise apartments. In the end that did not happen, though our efforts in the local residents' association did not prevent gradual redevelopment of the area by middle-class higher-income renovators, who persuaded many working-class home owners to sell their properties and who pushed out even more of the tenants by buying up houses from absentee landlords.

I began publishing what I suppose amounts to a documentation of that neighbourhood and of city government with a short book entitled *The Real World of City Politics*. A collection of articles that had first appeared in the Toronto *Globe and Mail*, the book offered snapshots of city hall in action and recorded the efforts of several city neighbourhoods, many of them working-class areas like east of Parliament at the time, doing their best to defend themselves. In the introduction to that book, I said that two subjects touched on there I hoped to develop in future books. One was older central-city areas with predominantly working-class populations. To people who do not know it from personal experience, working-class life in Canada has been almost completely inaccessible. Not only did the rest of us know nothing about the real impact of government policies like "slum clearance," expropriation and urban renewal on the residents of areas where they were being carried out, but we had very little information about the general shape of working-class life, whether in its family and social aspects, its economic aspects, or its political aspects and little was understood about the specific characteristics of the political and economic circumstances which underlie working-class life in Canada. In 1971 Myfanwy Phillips and I published *Working People*, an account of life east of Parliament Street and our attempt to provide an overall picture of a Canadian working-class neighbourhood.

In the summer of 1971 I took up the other task that seemed required to fill out the reports of encounters between neighbourhoods and city government that I had written in *The Real World of City Politics*. This was the job of analysing why the civic political system works the way it does. Even though I made a specific point of saying in the introduction to *City Politics* that I was well aware that such an analysis was required, and that I hoped at some point I would be able to write it, two or three critics have complained that I published an account of city hall in its dealings with some neighbourhood groups without attempting an analysis of the causes of the events described there. I felt in writing *City Politics* that even the simple job of documenting some of the ordinary workings of city hall would be considered valuable by many people, and from the reception accorded the book that seems to have been the case. Nevertheless it has always been clear to me that we must understand why city hall works as it does, why neighbourhoods are constantly being sacrificed to developers, why city politicians so often seem to have business interests in real estate and development, and why citizen groups are able to make so little headway in their protests at city hall if we are going to have real success in the fight to change city government.

This book is an attempt to deal with those questions, to explain how the civic political process works and why it operates as it does. I have discovered that it is necessary to extend the investigation well beyond city hall, to the complex of businesses and professions (which I have labelled the property industry) involved in real estate and land development, and to examine the connections of both city hall and the property industry to the federal and provincial governments. I have, in other words, attempted to analyse city politics in its political and economic context. This book has become a citizens' guide to city politics because the explanations I have arrived at are explanations that people in the citizens' organizations that have sprung up to challenge city hall in virtually every Canadian city are likely to find useful. It is also a citizens' guide because people like city politicians, most city bureaucrats, and particularly people in real estate and land development are definitely not going to regard it as useful, accurate, or even-handed. They will not like the explanation and analysis of city government offered here, and I expect they will lose no opportunity to try to discredit what I say here. By calling this a citizens' guide and not a politicians' or a developers' or a real estate investors' guide to city politics, I hope to advertise the fact that this is a book for people involved in citizens' groups,* as well as for the many people who are interested in and sympathetic to the efforts of these groups and to the city hall citizen opposition generally. At the same time, I hope I am making it clear that developers and real estate investors won't find what they like to see in these pages.

Again I find it necessary to issue a disclaimer about the kind of book this is, although my experience suggests that if you write one kind of book and critics feel you should have written another kind of book, they are not in the least discouraged from taking you to task even if you demonstrate that you were quite well aware of what you were doing and what you weren't. This book is not a manual for citizen groups on how to fight city hall. It is rather an attempt to explain the nature of their opponents, in this case the property industry and city hall. Hopefully that information will be of assistance to citizen groups when they are making their decisions about how to defend their interests and attack the opposition. But this book does not explain how citizen groups can be organized, what role

* The term "citizens' groups" is the proper one for organizations of citizens, but it is awkward to pronounce and seems usually to get shortened — in conversation, at least — to citizen groups, no *s* and no apostrophe. In this book, I adopt the spoken version of the term and refer to these organizations as citizen groups.

community organizers can play, how groups should make decisions about internal structure and external tactics, and so on. Unfortunately there is no good manual of this kind available which makes use of the wide experience citizen groups have had across the country. But my own experience would not qualify me to write such a book, and so I have not tried to write it here.

Many people have helped me in researching and writing this book, and I owe them all a great deal, particularly Peter Akehurst, Paul Barber, Meyer Brownstone, Jeremy Carver, Donald Gutstein, Brian Iler, Wayne Lawson, Jim Lemon, Alan Samuel, Jim Sellner, John Sewell, and Grant Sinclair. While waging a continuous war against the mounds of newspapers I am always collecting without clipping, Mif Phillips has helped me immensely with this enterprise and has provided many fine photographs to accompany the text. She says it is time I dedicated a book to her, and I agree.

Ironically, this foreboding building is called a "Holiday Inn."

CHAPTER 1

The real business of city government

"Let's face it: the developers run city hall."

In most Canadian cities, that is fighting talk — but it is also the conclusion more and more people have come to out of bitter experience. It is not an insight that has arisen from the research of academics or the reflections of civic administrators. Rather it has developed out of the experience of citizen groups where people have taken an interest in civic affairs and tried (more often than not without success) to persuade city hall of their point of view.

Getting to the heart of the realities of city politics means, in part, finding the explanation for the power that people have come to realize developers have. We might start by looking at the connection between the functions and powers of city hall and the concerns of the land development and real estate business.

Servicing and regulating property

The connection, as it turns out, is a much stronger and closer one than we might think. When you look closely at the functions of city government, it becomes quite apparent that almost everything city hall does is related to real estate. In fact, the real business of city government *is* property.

The activities of city hall fall into two main categories. The first is servicing urban property, providing the necessary services and facilities that are required in order for a piece of land to be used for urban purposes.

The list of services starts with roads, sidewalks, sewers, water, utilities. It includes maintaining these facilities and providing garbage collection, fire protection, traffic control, public transportation, and public health measures. Often through trial and error, each of these has been discovered to be necessary in order for cities to exist. In some cases, some of the basic services are provided not by city hall but by private companies with profitable local monopolies. This is still true of gas utilities in many cities, even though electricity is usually provided by a public agency. Municipal officials are well aware that city hall's services to property are virtually indispensable to property owners — a fact neatly demonstrated by the veiled threat of Vancouver's

Who does what:
servicing and regulating the property industry at city hall

	Toronto (City of)	Winnipeg	Vancouver
Departments Servicing Urban Property	Fire Public health Public works Parks & recreation	Fire Police Works	Fire Health Police Engineering (Board of Parks)
Departments Regulating Property	(City Planning Board) Development Buildings	Environment	Planning Building Electrical
Internal Housekeeping Departments	City clerk Finance Personnel Legal Audit Purchasing & supply Real estate Property Surveyor	City clerk Finance	City clerk Finance Law
Other Departments			Social services Family & children's court Civil Defence Museum Auditorium

Notes:

The departments categorized for Toronto are those of the City of Toronto. A number of city government functions, like police, are carried on by the second-tier city government, Metro Toronto.

In a few cases, city government boards with independent staffs have been included in the list in order to cover essential functions. They are listed in brackets.

Dog control under study

Sun Staff Reporter

BURNABY — Burnaby is going to the dogs — literally.

For the second time in as many weeks, municipal council Monday received complaints about dogs running at large.

Municipal manager Melvin Shelley said in a report to council the municipality will proceed with legal action if complainants will come forward to identify the owners of dogs running at large.

He said consideration is also being given to stronger means of control and enforcement, including an increase in impounding fees and possibly charging a boarding fee as well.

Vancouver Sun 8 Mar. 1972

City politics: mainly trivia?

City hall deals with an enormous range of matters, many of them small, some laughable. The impression given by the news media is that there is no particular logic to this jumbled collection of concerns. Nevertheless there is a basic pattern. Dog-catching, water delivery, and storm sewers are all services which people have discovered are necessary for urban land use. Deciding whether bingo can legally be played commercially and permitting the installation of machines selling contraceptives are within municipal jurisdiction because,like decisions about whether a building may be used for offices or housing, they amount to regulating real property and the way it is used.

News reports of this kind reinforce the notion that nothing of much importance goes on at city hall. What has to be remembered is that a city council which argues about dog-catching for an hour can spend five minutes making a simple zoning change which can mean a million-dollar profit for a developer.

CRESCENT BEACH COMPLAINTS

'Wild' dogs, cats stir wrath

By PAUL KNOX

Dogs, cats, horses, garbage, motorcycles.

A lack of toilets, drinking fountains, law enforcement and village maintenance.

That's a partial list of the complaints aired at Surrey Municipal council Monday by the Crescent Beach Property Owners' Association.

David Oppenheimer, chairman of the association's public works committee, told the council the group has been trying for years to get action on what he called "grievances which you have neglected to have rectified."

The lack of action, he said, is threatening to ruin the recreational value of Crescent Beach and make it an unpleasant place in which to live.

The stray dogs, he went on, "are running wild, fighting, biting and spreading garbage," and the cats, "breeding prolifically, are running wild, continuously prowling and fighting at night."

Vancouver Sun 2 May 1972

City police 'raid' bingos

Inner City police have "raided" 24 community centres in the last week because the centres don't have licences to operate bingos, an official of the Winnipeg Association of Community Centres said Wednesday.

Floyd Williston, vice-chairman of the association, made the charge at Wednesday's special meeting of city council, while discussing the East Elmwood community centre auditorium project.

He said he used the term "raided" because that was the impression people in the community clubs got from the police visits. He said he didn't know of any instance where the police "shut down "a game in progress. The police entered, identified themselves, took names, questioned people, checked the premises and told the organizers they would be hearing further about the situation, Mr. Williston said.

Mr. Williston said in an interview it is ridiculous for the city to charge the licence fees to the centres.

Winnipeg Free Press 3 May 1972

city council to strand the provincial government's new downtown 55-storey office building by not providing it with city water and sewer service if the province wasn't a bit more co-operative about its development plans.

Besides servicing urban property, the other main function of city hall is regulating urban property, controlling (usually in minute detail) every aspect of the way every piece of land can be used: what sort of building can be erected, how big it can be, how it must be constructed, and how its occupants may use it. Regulating urban property includes city planning, of course, but it also involves the system of zoning bylaws, bylaws regulating construction of new buildings, bylaws about minimum standards and fire standards of existing buildings and so on. Regulating property use is a complicated business, and occupies the attention of a considerable chunk of the city hall establishment.

These two basic activities of servicing and regulating urban property make city living and the property industry possible; in a sense, they *create* the value of urban land, a fact many municipal politicians are well aware of.

In carrying out the functions of servicing and regulating property in its jurisdiction, city hall requires a considerable amount of internal housekeeping. Separate civic departments — accounting, auditing, legal, city clerk, personnel —

provide this administrative support.

Exceptions to the rule?

Many city hall responsibilities that at first glance seem to have no connection to servicing and regulating property in fact do. When you think of parks, for instance, your first thought is likely to be of oases for city residents, facilities not for property but for people. Obviously, however, acquiring and administering parks is a real estate management matter. More important still, parks are generally understood at city hall to be a service to property and, like other services to property, an influence on the value of privately-owned pieces of land. A given quantity of private property requires a certain amount of public land set aside for park purposes just as it requires public land for roads, sidewalks and schools. Though we might like to think that the function of parks is really a lot more complicated and subtle than that, there is no doubt that at city hall parks are turned into one more civic service to privately-owned property.

City police services also appear at first glance to have little connection to the job of servicing and regulating urban property. The police are organized to enforce laws of all kinds, only some of which are directly concerned with

MUNICIPAL SERVICES, THEN AND NOW: One of the services provided by city hall is drinking water in public places. The brass fountain on the left, which stands on the sidewalk by the edge of the street, is an example of how this service used to be provided. The large trough on the street side is for horses; on the sidewalk side, there is a drinking fountain at the top which can also be used for filling pails. Note also the cat and dog trough at the bottom on the sidewalk side.

In contrast to this convenience is the "modern" park water fountain. Its sole use is for people who want a drink of water. Note how, in order to make the fountain usable by children as well as adults, a special stone step had to be included.

real property (like trespassing). Yet the major functions of city police forces are very much property-oriented. The police devote considerable effort to keeping buildings and their contents secure, protecting real property from damage, and administering the transportation system through traffic control. They also spend a lot of time in the old-fashioned-sounding job of "keeping the peace," which means breaking up noisy and sometimes dangerous family quarrels and stepping in when people are beating each other up on the street. These duties might seem to be mainly for the benefit of the directly-involved participants, but usually, in fact, it is neighbours who call police to complain that these disturbances are keeping them from the "quiet enjoyment" of their own property.

Despite the predominant property orientation of most of the activities of city hall, clearly there are some civic activities that are not services to or regulations of urban property. For instance, city governments are still involved in welfare policies, in providing what used to be called relief to the poor. This includes welfare payments, care of the aged in institutions, the provision of hospitals and similar matters. Gradually, however, city halls have been losing more and more of these welfare matters to provincial governments. Usually all that is left of city hall's responsibility for welfare payments, for example, is the actual hiring of social workers (paid mostly out of provincial and federal funds) to pay out welfare payments (on a schedule largely determined and financed at federal and provincial levels).

Independent city hall initiative in this field has been severely narrowed (though not to the extent that all debate at city hall on welfare has ended). City government is mainly reduced to retailing services provided wholesale by the province. In some provinces, much of the direct assistance to welfare recipients is paid by the provincial government itself.

City hall also has a role in cultural matters, for example in giving grants to local theatre groups and administering libraries. But the area of culture has also of late become the domain of federal and provincial governments and their agencies like the Canada Council. City hall is reduced mainly to awarding occasional small grants and to providing some of the necessary physical plant like concert halls and hockey arenas. Only when it comes down to these real estate jobs is city hall allowed to carry on.

Cities and provincial power

Why is city hall almost exclusively in the business of servicing and regulating urban property? It is not because at some mysterious point in the past, the citizenry gathered together and decided to have a local government that would do nothing but that. It is not the will of the people that has determined what city hall will do; it is the will of provincial governments. The provinces, armed with the B.N.A. Act which gives them authority over property rights, amongst other things, have set up local municipal governments to exercise some of this authority in their specific localities.

THE NECESSITY OF MUNICIPAL SERVICES: this is a rare case where a municipality and a developer ended up in a bitter fight. When this building was started in 1959, the Metro Toronto borough of East York was opposed to it because it didn't fit in with their planning policy and zoning. When the developer went ahead with construction, East York refused to service it with sewer or water. Metro Toronto refused to allow the developer to put in adequate road access. The result: the developer decided city hall was serious, and stopped construction with the building only partly completed. He and East York went to court and, thirteen years later, they were still fighting it out. Meanwhile the building stands incomplete and vacant.

Vancouver's Pigeon Park before its proposed "beautification."

PARKS AS A REAL ESTATE OPERATION: The saga of Vancouver's Pigeon Park illustrates how city parks can operate as a boon — and sometimes, at least in the eyes of local property owners if not park users, a handicap — to business districts. Note that owners of area stores, not city hall, were to pay for the proposed "improvements" in the park. Property owners aren't going to invest their own money if they don't think it will make their locations more attractive, and hence their property more valuable. Note, too, that people using the park received little attention compared to the businessmen-property owners.

Pigeon Park ordered to be flattened

City council made it official Tuesday — Pigeon Park will be flattened, literally.

Three weeks after turning down an administration proposal to spend $54,000 on new seating, lights and landscaping for the Hastings Street triangle, council voted Tuesday to eliminate the benches and remove the planter walls at the site.

These will be replaced by a ground-level planted section and a rebuilt sidewalk area.

A special four-man committee recommended the change after meeting with local merchants, who came up with a set of 36 photos depicting a typical day at the park. The pictures showed men and women drinking, fighting and sprawling on the ground.

The report also noted the merchants' fears that the presence of derelicts and drunks might make any beautification useless and it requested the police commission to see that special attention is paid to the area following the alterations.

Council also approved a recommendation urging provincial and municipal agencies to expedite the implementation of treatment services to deal with alcoholics.

In a brief debate before the latest beautification proposal was approved, Ald. Marianne Linnell said the city's park board is upset at the idea of council deciding the future of the park.

Ald. Harry Rankin, who opposed the plan, said more important should be placed on the social dilemma of the park inhabitants, but this is not done because it would cost money.

He suggested that members of the merchants advisory committee, while protesting against the derelicts, probably include the pawnbrokers who strip them of their possessions and the storekeepers who sell them bay rum.

Vancouver Sun 19 Apr. 1972

Stores won't back plan until derelicts bounced

City council reacted unfavorably Tuesday to suggestions that Hastings Street merchants will not take part in a $118,000 beautification scheme unless the city cleans skid road derelicts from Pioneer Place.

A delegation representing the Improvement of the Downtown East Area Society (IDEAS) told council that Pioneer Place, also known as Pigeon Park, is a "sore" in their midst.

Council was asked to renovate the park in such a way that would not attract congregations of alcoholics and other persons from the skid road area.

Vancouver Province 29 Mar. 1972

Of course there are often tremendous arguments and fights between city politicians (and sometimes ordinary citizens too) and provincial governments about exactly what the powers of city hall should be, but the point is that in Canada they are the province's to bestow and to take away.

Not only do the provinces have the authority to decide what powers city hall will have; they also have the authority to make all decisions about the structure of city government. It is the provincial governments, for example, that decide whether city hall should have the authority to license bicycles, and what the fee should be for this service. They decide how many aldermen there will be, and how often elections will be held.

Most provinces have set up intermediary boards between the provincial government and the municipalities which have the power to act as watchdogs over city councils and to enforce uniform provincial policies when they review specific civic decisions. In both Manitoba and Ontario, there are municipal boards performing this function. In British Columbia, the "supermayor" minister of municipal affairs keeps all this power for himself. Where there are review boards, provincial governments can still step in and turn a city hall decision into the decision the province wants.

This local government system is not as unique a governmental device as it might appear to be. One of the common practices of governments, both federal and provincial, is to exercise some of their specific powers by setting up government agencies with a narrowly-defined area of responsibility. Provinces, for instance, have the power to regulate the securities industry, and generally they do this by setting up a provincial securities agency. The federal government has the power to regulate the national transportation industry, and it has established the Canadian Transportation Commission to regulate this industry while the federal Department of Transport also does some regulating and also services the industry. Provinces have the power to carry out social welfare measures and as part of this responsibility many have set up provincial housing agencies like the Ontario Housing Corporation to provide public housing. In cases like these, the people with the ultimate authority to run the agency are almost always appointed by the senior government. The members of the Canadian Transportation Commission, for instance, are appointed by the federal government. The board of directors of Ontario Housing Corporation is appointed by the Ontario cabinet.

The provinces have the power to regulate and to service the urban property industry — the business of owning real property and of providing new land and buildings for urban use — and they have dealt with this power by setting up city governments to carry it out. The only departure from the usual practice in this case is that in city government the people with ultimate authority over the agency — in this case, the members of city councils — are not appointed by the province. Rather they are elected by people in the jurisdiction that they govern. At one time, of course, only owners of property in the jurisdiction could vote in municipal elections, and until more recently certain decisions — like money bylaws — were made by votes of property owners only. Lately it has become the usual practice to let any resident in the jurisdiction participate in these elections, on the grounds that all are users of urban property and so are paying for it and for the functions of city government.

Tenants given go-ahead

City council gave final approval Tuesday to allowing tenants voting rights on Vancouver money bylaws.

The legislature amended the city charter in March to give council the power to extend the vote, previously restricted to property owners, to tenants. Council unanimously passed the necessary motion.

Tenants now have the right to participate in all city-wide votes. Local improvement issues in specific neighborhoods will be restricted to property owners only.

Vancouver Province May 1972

Even so, the continued link between property and city government is made clear by the fact that someone who owns property in a city but lives elsewhere can usually vote in civic elections, and that people who own property in more than one ward in a city with a ward system often get to vote more than once.

This departure from the usual practice of governmental agencies does not change the basic situation: city government is the regulatory and service agency set up by the provinces for the property industry. Clearly the property industry needs both basic services and considerable regulation in order to function as it does now. City government is the way in which the provinces have arranged for these services and regulations to be provided.

This analysis of what the real business of city hall is proves to be a very helpful one, because for one thing it reveals the logic behind the set of powers which provincial governments delegate to city hall and those which they keep for themselves or for other administrative agencies. It also establishes how important an understanding of the property industry is for an understanding of city government. Obviously, if city hall is the regulatory and servicing body for the property industry, it is necessary to be familiar with the industry in order to understand properly what city hall does and why.

Many people have learned from their own experience that at least some elements of the property industry, for example land developers, exercise great influence over city hall. We will see in later chapters that it is not just land developers but the property industry as a whole that is influential with city government. In fact, it is more than just influential; the industry has captured control of city hall. The attention given wishes of land developers is just one expression of this situation. In the next chapters where

we examine the property industry, then, we will be looking at the business which city government has been established to regulate — and we will also be looking at the industry which, as we will see in Part II, has captured effective political control of its own regulatory agency.

PART 1
The property industry

CHAPTER 2
An introduction to the urban property industry

Reprinted with permission San Fransico Bay Guardian Books

The urban property industry, as defined here, encompasses all the businesses and professions involved in supplying accommodation in cities. Accommodation includes housing and all other kinds of urban shelter — office space, shops, factories, etc. The businesses, industries and professions that make up the urban property industry are quite familiar to us. What is not so familiar is the idea of lumping them together into a single category, a kind of superindustry, which emphasizes that they all have in common the fact that they make money out of accommodating people in the city.

We need to spell out the organization of the industry, but before doing so we have a basic question to consider: why can people make money owning and building urban property? As we all know, investing in urban real estate has always been a popular thing to do. The main reason for this seems to be that it is an easy and almost foolproof way to make money. A few people have got very rich indeed, just by owning and dealing in urban property. Many more very rich families have got a great deal richer by investing their money in real estate. Though the question is a simple one and the answer may seem obvious, it helps clarify the nature of the property industry to ask: why?

Why you can get rich on real estate

Investors make money by owning urban property because people need accommodation of various kinds, and usually the only way most people get this accommodation is by paying either to buy or to use a building — a house, office building, shop or whatever. Generally people have to pay handsomely. They can almost always be persuaded to pay enough for the use of a building for its owner to recover the cost *of its construction* within five, ten, or perhaps at the most fifteen years of the time it was built. But of course a building goes on providing accommodation much longer than that, and the owner can collect rent from users (often in ever-increasing amounts) as long as the building stands. That is why urban property owners make money, and why real estate is a profitable business.

Key to the way the property business is organized is the fact that a building requires a site to be built on, and for urban accommodation a site in the urban area is necessary. *The fact that a piece of urban land has to begin with a price — usually a pretty hefty price — attached to it reflects the surplus that the landowner can receive over his costs if he puts a building on that land and rents it out.* The bigger that surplus is, the more valuable the land is.

Confidential report for CMHC

Housing called 'almost a byproduct of making money'

A confidential report prepared for a Central Mortgage and Housing Corp. task force on low-income housing says housing is "almost a byproduct" in an agglomeration of builders, developers and financial institutions committed to the routine of making money.

And CMHC. the federal housing agency, is also oriented to market interests, rather than consumer interests, the report says. The private sector of the industry is "involved in low income housing only insofar as the delivery of this housing corresponds to the objectives of the influential members of the industry."

The report, written by Melvin Charney, a professor of architecture at the University of Montreal, and Serge Carreau and Colin Davidson. also from the University of Montreal, is one of six prepared for the CMHC task force. None have yet been made public by CMHC.

Globe and Mail Mar. 1972

Errors and successes in Don Mills

Some of the facts and figures provided by the three Canadians seemed to astonish their U.S. counterparts. Mr. Diamond's announcement that Erin Mills land sells for $13,000 a single family lot with a 50-foot frontage and $20,000 for a lot for a pair of semi-detached units, for example, drew gasps from the audience.

In the United States serviced land in cities comparable in size to Metropolitan Toronto sells for between one-half and one-third of the Erin Mills prices.

Mr. McClaskey, after providing the background of Don Mills and listing his mistakes and successes, told the audience there was only one thing he could add to the history of the development, but stressed that it was a most important point: "We made money."

Globe and Mail May 1972

There are many factors that affect the size of the income flow a property owner receives, and consequently the value of his property and particularly its land component. As incomes go up, for instance, people have more money available and can be persuaded to pay higher and higher prices for accommodation. This is especially true if the supply of accommodation is regulated, which of course it is in every city. Also as a city's population increases, specific pieces of land produce larger cash surpluses for their owners because they are accessible to more people, and relatively better located. The surplus produced by a specific piece of land depends greatly on how intensive and desirable a use it can be put to according to the regulations governing land use. If a downtown lot that can be used only for a two-storey house suddenly gets recategorized so it can be used for a 90-storey office building, and if the owner puts up the office building, then the lot is likely to produce a much larger surplus over costs for the owner and to be worth far more.

This is a simplified summary of a difficult subject with many complicating factors. Economists have developed extremely complex theories to explain the general level of land prices and local variations in prices in a city. What is important to remember is that the high value of urban land is a result of the fact that property owners can make more money out of their buildings than is necessary to pay the costs of erecting, maintaining and repairing those buildings.

Making money from real estate in Boomtown

Commercial property zoning in the City of Toronto is governed by the following density categories: V1 — permits a floor area of three times the area of the lot; V2 — permits a floor area of five times the area of the lot; V3 — permits a floor area of seven times the area of the lot; V4 — permits a floor area of 12 times the area of the lot.

A zoning change to allow 12 times coverage in place of three times coverage should increase the value of land from $10 per square foot to $50 per square foot.

To calculate the residential equivalent, consider that prime apartment land in Toronto is worth between $3,000 and $5,000 per suite. Land which allows only one times coverage — as much floor space as land area — can be bought for $3 to $4 per square foot. If the permitted density of this apartment land is doubled, the value is more than tripled to $10 per square foot. Similarly, if two-and-a-half times coverage, the highest residential density, is applied, the value of the land may increase to $12 to $15 per square foot.

City planners encourage the concentration of apartments around subway stations. *So, if you can manage a rezoning from R.2 Z.3, which allows one times coverage, to R.2 Z.5 which allows two-and-a-half times coverage, you could quadruple your money.*

Donald Kirkup, *Boomtown.*
Toronto: Toronto Real Estate Board, pp.66-8

Property rights and property profits

It takes a whole set of circumstances to create the situation where owners of real urban property, buildings and land, can exist in the first place and can then make enormous profits on what they own. One basic circumstance is that pieces of land in urban areas can be privately owned. A second is that owners can charge whatever they can get when they sell their property or rent it to other people to use. A third is that people need to have accommodation, and both land and buildings are necessary in order to provide it. A fourth is a tax system which lets property owners keep most (often all) of the profits they make selling or renting accommodation.

There is an enormous body of law concerning the way urban property may be used in Canada, and the rights of property owners and other people. Often the claim is made that all this law and public policy is based on the principle that land and buildings should be privately owned by individuals, and that private property owners should be able to do whatever they want with their property free from interference from government, from other property owners, or from anybody else. It is absolutely clear that this is not in fact the principle that lies behind federal and provincial legislation and the general body of property law. The ways in which a property owner can use his property are strictly limited and regulated in many ways. In part these regulations protect the interests of other property owners, who could be adversely affected by what is done with neighbouring land and buildings. But they reflect many other concerns as well. When Victoria's city council imposes a height limitation of 14 storeys on high-rise buildings (not that 14 storeys is that low), its decision reflects aesthetic concerns and reservations about the kind of accommodation people should have to live or work in, not an attention to the rights of nearby property owners. There are also many different kinds of situations in which the ordinary ambitions of government, such as the desire to build a new road or to provide a site for a new downtown Eaton's store, can completely extinguish the rights of a property owner and lead to his forcible eviction from land that was his own.

For small property owners, who occupy and use the property they own either for their business or their home, the right to be able to continue to own and use that property means one thing. We have all learned from the experiences of people living in old central-city residential areas threatened with expropriation for urban renewal projects how important a home is as a familiar place to live in in a familiar spot, and as an asset that makes it possible to live a decent life on tiny old age pensions, because there is no rent to pay and because there may be a little money coming in from boarders.

For property investors, however, who invest in real estate and make money by renting it or selling it to other people to use, the right to be able to own property, to control who uses it and to charge whatever price can be obtained for it means something quite different. It amounts to a license to make fortunes at the expense of the people who have to pay the prices property investors charge. Property investment of this kind, with all the economic activities that accompany it, is a device for extracting large amounts of money from the pockets of people who have little enough money as it is, just because they have to have accommodation. Whenever they buy a house built on a lot where developers and speculators have made capital gains of $5,000 on a piece of land selling for $7,500, whenever they rent an apartment or a house from a property investor who can charge them a price quite unrelated to the cost of that accommodation, they may be getting the accommodation they need, but they are being forced to contribute to the profits of property investors and speculators.

For small property owners occupying and using the property they own, there are reasonable expectations that they can keep their property as long as they want and live in it free from interference. But there is also a good chance, in fact an ever-increasing risk, that they will at some point be deprived of the use and ownership of their property by a government or public agency who wants their land for itself or who wants it in order to turn it over to some large developer. The rights that go along with property ownership, for owners of this kind, amount to a certain measure of security and financial independence, but this is steadily being eroded in favour of the interests of big government and big corporations.

For large property owners, the significance of the legal situation in which they now operate is that by means of investing in real estate they have open to them a remarkable, easy, and almost sure-fire way of making large amounts of money. Nor is the money they make created out of thin air; it is taken directly out of the pockets of ordinary people who need to buy or rent the property the owners control because they need accommodation. As we will see in later chapters, the present arrangement for big property owners is such that they can make enormous capital gains, and extremely high profit rates on their investments, and pay little or no taxes on the money they make. Small property owners who possess property so that they can use it themselves receive small comfort and attention in the existing situation; large property owners who possess property for no reason other than the desire to make money are making very large amounts of money indeed, and are·receiving lots of desirable protection from government.

The opposite side of the coin — of the large and increasing profits made by property investors — is that the cost to consumers of housing has been rising rapidly for many years. Rents and house prices move in one direction only: up. Part of the explanation for the increase in the cost of *new* housing is that construction costs have been increasing. But this increase is small in comparison to the increase that has occurred in the cost of urban land. And, while higher construction costs are passed on in part in the form of higher wages for construction workers, higher land costs benefit a small and already well-off group: land speculators and developers. The third increasing cost item is the higher cost of borrowing money, something which most house buyers are forced to do in order to finance their purchases. While house construction costs increased by 48 per cent in Canada from 1961 to 1971, land costs increased by 88 per cent — almost twice as much. But mortgage interest rates increased, and so the cost of borrowing money for housing purposes increased by the greatest amount of all during the period — by 98 per cent. Property developers and speculators are doing pretty well — but mortgage lenders, the big insurance companies, trust companies and other large corporations, are doing very well too.

Increases in the cost of existing housing as opposed to

Average Metro home buyer can only afford vacant lot

A vacant lot is all the average Metro Toronto family can afford at current housing prices, John Hurlburt, Toronto Home Builders' Association president, s a i d yesterday.

He appeared before a convention of the Ontario Association of Architects at the R o y a l York Hotel with charts showing an income of $625 a month would only permit a family to carry payments on a mortgage of $15,600.

He said the average lot in Metro costs that much, leaving the average family with only a vacant lot for the money it has available for shelter.

Even if such a family were subsidized by $44.31 a month down to a 6½ per cent m o r t g a g e (current rates are 8¾ to 9¼) repayable over 35 years, a house selling at $22,211 is all the family could afford.

"Where can you buy a house in Toronto for $22,-211?" Hurlburt asked.

House prices in Metro average $31,537.

Toronto Star   Feb. 1972

new have been just as large, reflecting the careful way in which the housing market is controlled in Canadian cities. The supply of new housing is carefully limited, making it possible for builders and developers selling to prospective homeowners to charge high enough prices to cover their higher costs *and* to make increasing profits on land. As this happens, prices of existing houses are driven up as well.

Rents on new and existing housing also increase, reflecting the same tight control over the housing market. Developers and real estate investors can charge high enough rents for new buildings to cover the steadily increasing costs of construction, to justify the higher and higher values attributed to the land they are built on, *and* to pay the higher interest rates on money borrowed to cover building costs and land price. Owners of existing buildings find they can increase their rents too, thereby making new profits.

The property business as an industry

There is no difficulty in seeing the wide range of businesses that are involved in owning, managing, servicing and building urban real estate in one way or another, or in identifying the professionals who service these businesses. But it is not common to think of all of these interests together as the property industry, and in fact there are some problems about labelling it an industry in the first place.

Land speculation and housing costs

Developers always object when people label them "speculators" and complain about the enormous profits they make on the vacant land they buy up when it is farmland and sell as suburban building lots. They argue they are not profiteers, but rather responsible and respectable companies trying to do something about the housing problem.

A good specific example which shows the enormous profits developers make on land was given in a *Toronto Star* article written by Walter Stewart.

Stewart described the case of an Oakville family, Marg and Bill Hammond, who bought a new house in 1971 in a subdivision in Oakville 22 miles from downtown Toronto.

The Hammonds paid $22,350 for their house, quite a low price for the Toronto area housing market.

Of this price, $6,900 was for the land.

The cost to the developer of servicing the land and turning it from farmland into a building lot was $3,000. This is higher than in many parts of the country, and reflects the high requirements laid down by the municipality.

In effect, the Hammonds paid $3,900 for land and $3,000 for services. But the developers purchased the land — in this case from the municipality of Oakville — for only $612. In other words, the difference between the price the developers paid for their land and the price they sold it for was $3288. If the Hammonds had not been forced to contribute to the developers' profit, they could have bought their lot for $3612, almost half what they actually paid. That would have reduced the cost of their house by 14 per cent.

But the total cost of the Hammonds' land to them is much more than $6,900. That is because they had to borrow the money they used to pay for their lot and house on two mortgages, one a 25-year first at 9 7/8 per cent and the other a 7-year second also at 9 7/8 per cent. Over those 25 years, the Hammonds will end up paying $15,866 for their lot. The total cost to them of house plus lot plus interest on mortgages is over $50,000.

So one major factor contributing to the high cost of this typical suburban home *is* the profiteering by developers on land.

Another major factor is of course the extremely high cost of borrowing money to use to buy a house. *The Hammonds will pay more in interest over the 25-term of their mortgages than they paid for the house itself.* If they had had to pay 5 per cent instead of almost 10 per cent for the money they borrowed, the cost to them of their housing would have been about $150 a month instead of the $225 they were playing. If their lot had cost $3612 instead of $6900, that would have nocked another $20 or so a month off the monthly cost of their house.

Data from Toronto Star 29 Jan. 1972

COST INCREASES FOR NEW HOUSING 1961–1971

100%

50%

CONSTRUCTION COSTS

LAND COSTS

MORTGAGE INTEREST COSTS

SOURCE: CANADIAN HOUSING STATISTICS 1971/TABLES 108,112

The viewpoint from which these businesses appear to be an industry is this: there are all sorts of different kinds of businesses, professions and industries whose activities all go towards producing urban accommodation. While there is a significant market for buildings where people buy a house or a store and then use the property they own themselves, there is a larger and faster-growing market for rental accommodation which people buy from businesses which are in the accommodation field as suppliers. Accommodation is what everyone in the property industry produces, though it comes in different forms and on different terms. That is this industry's output, just as the real output of both the auto industry and the airlines is transportation.

But there are some differences between this "property industry" and the auto industry or the toy industry. Only a portion of the industry actually produces a flow of real physical product, analogous to the toys produced by the toy industry and the cars produced by the auto industry. The building industry sector produces new buildings of various kinds, with the participation of the construction industry, the building materials industry and so on. The rest of what I have labelled the "property industry" services, maintains, manages and deals in the stock of *existing* buildings which are standing and are going to continue to stand no matter what happens to the banks, insurance companies, or real estate speculators.

For some purposes, this distinction between the service sector of the property industry and the production sector is extremely important. For our purposes, and for the purpose of understanding the housing market in Canada, what is important to emphasize is what they have in common: the fact that together they are supplying all the available urban accommodation. They also share a common regulatory agency which, at least in the first instance, makes many of the decisions of detail about how the industry will operate as well as providing it with necessary services. That agency is city government.

The industry, the home owners and small businessmen

Another question arising from the concept of the property industry is this: should everyone who owns urban property, for whatever reason, be classified as part of the property industry? Specifically, can people who own the house they are living in be lumped together with developers who are making their money building apartments and renting them out? And what about small businessmen who own the property they use for their business?

Owner occupiers account for a considerable fraction of the housing stock in most Canadian cities, though their share is diminishing quite rapidly in some cities as more and more people find themselves forced to remain tenants. Owner occupiers are quite different from other property owners *because their primary motive is not investment for profit*. They are not putting their resources into a house because they think it is the best way for them to make capital gains and profits. Usually they are doing it because they find it is the best way for them to provide themselves with shelter. As a result, usually the housing aspect of the house they own or are buying — whether they like it as a place to live, whether it suits them, whether it is on a street and in a neighbourhood they like, whether their friends and acquaintances live nearby — looms far larger than the investment aspect. The profit-making possibilities of home

Emotional problems

Illustrating difficulties land assemblers often face, Toronto area development company director Gordon Gray mentioned the assembly for the Erin Mills and Meadowvale new towns outside Metro which are only now beginning to be developed.

"We assembled 13,000 acres of farmland in 1954 and 1955, mostly from farmers whose father's father's father had bought the land from the Indians," he said. Mr. Gray described how one holdout had been dealt with by Brian McGee, now chairman of the board of A.E. LePage Ltd. and president of Markborough Properties. "Mr. McGee went out with a suitcase full of money." He then counted out the several hundred thousand dollar purchase price the farmer was being offered for his land, in $10 bills. "The farmer still wouldn't sell," said Mr. Gray. "I consider this a real emotional problem." Later he said it was not unusual to take unwilling vendors suitcases full of money in hopes of persuading them to sell.

Globe and Mail 21 Mar. 1972

ownership may be one matter that receives consideration or it may be ignored; rarely is it pre-eminent in a home owner's mind. Usually though not always owner occupants act quite differently from the way a property investor would act in their place. When Toronto home owner Kate Burgess, an old lady who was a long-time resident of a street where a developer called Greenwin was assembling property, told the money-laden agents for the developers: "I won't trade greenbacks for memories," she was the living antithesis of the property investor, for whom profits and capital gains are the only consideration. Development enthusiasts condemn the Kate Burgess mentality as "emotional" and they hate it, probably because they encounter it so often. Home owners own property, but by their actions and in their interests they are not at all part of the property industry. Occasionally, of course, there are people who look like owner occupiers but act like real estate speculators, buying and selling the houses they live in as soon as they see a quick profit. Such people are at the small-time end of the property industry, and are not at all typical home owners.

The same sharp distinction that exists between people who own houses for their own use and people who own them for profit does not exist between businessmen who own property for the use of their own business and businessmen who own commercial and industrial property as an investment for profits. More often than not, businessmen who own the real estate in which they do business treat their real estate holdings as a second kind of business they have got into alongside their main business. A florist may regard himself as being partly in the flower business and partly in the real estate business through owning the shop he operates from. Decisions about his real property holdings are likely to be made at least in part from a property viewpoint.

The bigger a business is, the more likely this is to hold true. Developers worry least about big corporations when they assemble land. "National corporations don't see themselves standing in the way of progress," Toronto real estate

BUSINESSMEN AND PROPERTY DEVELOPERS: The refusal of developers of the Bloor-Yonge corner in Toronto to offer Britnell's bookstore a deal whereby the bookstore could sell their existing store and relocate in the new development on terms which the business could carry was what prevented the new project from swallowing up the north end of the block.

Another example of businessmen dealing with developers is tailor Lou Casaccio. The apartment building erected behind his store in the controversial St. Jamestown project appears to be bent in especially for Casaccio's building. Casaccio was prepared to sell to the developers for a reported $100,000. The developer, the Meridian Group, refused to go quite that high and Casaccio was left holding the bag instead of making a killing.

agent and development company director Gordon Gray told a meeting of would-be developers I attended. "Commercial deals usually don't involve emotional problems." In other words, businessmen usually look at real estate propositions like other investment decisions, and act just as any other property investor would. Businessmen of this kind are part of the property industry in exactly the same way as property investors who own buildings they rent out to others. Small businessmen sometimes take a different attitude towards the property they own, particularly when it is a relatively small matter compared to their principal line of business. But in a rapidly-growing city like Toronto, where tremendous profits are regularly made from real estate deals, every variety store owner and beauty shop operator sees himself as a big-time giant-killing million-dollar real estate speculator. This is so even though many small businesses are ruined when they lose premises they leased or owned to redevelopment projects.

The property industry in outline

The structure of the property industry, shown in the accompanying diagram, involves two main sectors. The first owns, manages and services the existing stock of urban property. The second, the building industry sector, adds to this stock. Many businesses are involved in either one sector or the other, and a number of very important and powerful businesses are intimately involved in both.

At the heart of the sector that provides accommodation from the existing stock are property investors, who own urban real estate for profit. Included in this category are many small-time property investors, whether in the business as a sideline or as a principal activity. All together small-time investors appear to hold quite a large portion of the urban property under the control of the property industry, but in spite of this they do not loom nearly so large politically as the relatively few big-time property investors who have large and extremely valuable chunks of urban real estate. Each city has its own set of major property owners, though some of the same names turn up in city after city. Some big property investors like Cemp and Fairview, real estate investment trusts of the Bronfman family, are into property investment as their major activity. Others, like Eaton's and the CPR, are in real estate in a big way as well as being in a number of other businesses simultaneously. Usually real estate is a very important corporate money-maker to investors of this kind.

Servicing the property investors who hold all the urban property that is operated for a profit are a range of professional groups and a few major industries. Pre-eminent amongst all of these is the property financing business, which lends property investors the money they need to finance their transactions. The big mortgage lenders in Canada are life insurance companies, trust and loan companies, and chartered banks. These corporations are of course tremendously powerful as well as wealthy. A second major service industry to property owners is the property insurance business, made up of the insurance companies that insure real property against fire, theft, damage and so on. A third is the urban utilities industry, providing basic services to urban property — gas companies, oil heating companies, hydro suppliers and phone companies. The professions servicing property investors include real estate agents, lawyers, and insurance agents.

Many of these same businesses and professions are also involved in the other major sector of the property industry, which adds to the stock of urban property by construction and new development. Property investors sometimes provide the necessary land, financial institutions provide the necessary funds, and real estate lawyers and real estate agents service the operations. Also involved in the process is another major group of businesses: the construction industry, the construction materials industry and the construction equipment industry. There are also a number of building industry professionals: architects, engineers, surveyors. Construction workers' unions stand somewhere between construction workers and the construction industry.

Many businesses that are heavily involved in the property industry are involved in other activities as well. Banks, for instance, are part of the property industry through their activities as lending agents for residential mortgages, for short-term financing of other real estate transactions, and for home renovations and repairs; but the property industry is only one of the businesses they are involved in.

In spite of the tremendous range in the activities of different parts of the property industry, it is useful to see the common thread which runs through all the businesses in it and their common involvement in the business of supplying urban accommodation. Together they amount to a large, strong industry with some clearly-definable and imporatnt basic common interests.

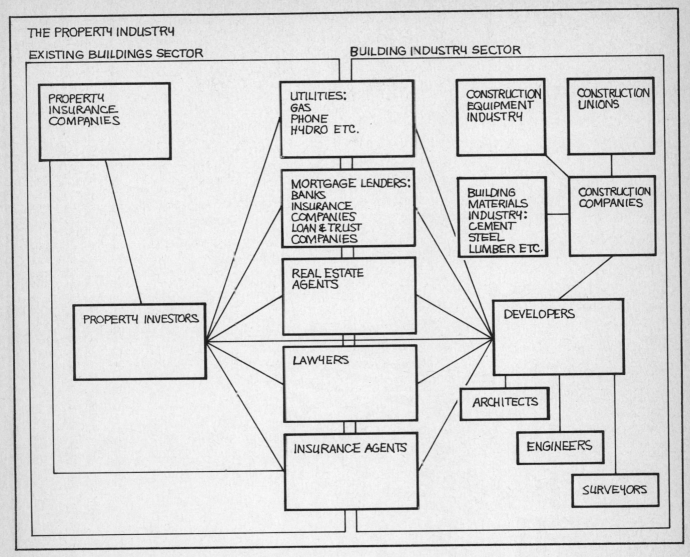

THE PROPERTY INDUSTRY

EXISTING BUILDINGS SECTOR   BUILDING INDUSTRY SECTOR

PROPERTY INSURANCE COMPANIES

UTILITIES: GAS PHONE HYDRO ETC.

CONSTRUCTION EQUIPMENT INDUSTRY

CONSTRUCTION UNIONS

MORTGAGE LENDERS: BANKS INSURANCE COMPANIES LOAN & TRUST COMPANIES

BUILDING MATERIALS INDUSTRY: CEMENT STEEL LUMBER ETC.

CONSTRUCTION COMPANIES

REAL ESTATE AGENTS

PROPERTY INVESTORS

DEVELOPERS

LAWYERS

ARCHITECTS

INSURANCE AGENTS

ENGINEERS

SURVEYORS

This diagram is a simplified picture of the property industry. Lines indicate the main relationships amongst businesses and professionals involved in the industry.

Many other relationships could be noted — for instance, insurance agents who sell property insurance and deal mainly with owners of existing buildings also deal with developers and are linked to property insurance companies; they are usually linked to life insurance companies as well. Lawyers who do real estate work provide services for a large number of businesses in the industry. The building materials industry sells materials mainly to construction companies, but some of their business is in materials for maintenance and repairs which may go directly to property owners or to property owners through construction companies.

There are other businesses and professions which are involved in the property industry, though to a less important extent than those mentioned. A tiny but quite important industry, for instance, is the real estate market information business, which provides property owners, developers, real estate agents and others with data on the real estate markets in Canadian cities. There is also the trade magazine business, which is tied closely to the industry as well as promoting the image the industry likes to have of itself.

Also important to note is that, as the whole industry integrates vertically and horizontally, single firms take on several quite distinct functions. Many development companies have their own construction subsidiaries. Many are both developers and major owners of existing properties. Some life insurance companies like Manufacturers' Life are developers, property owners and mortgage lenders.

CHAPTER 3
Owning, financing and servicing urban property

Equipped with a basic source of government statistics like *Canada Year Book*, you can like a shot discover the total value of the country's raspberry production last year ($3,545,000) or the number of tons of cargo shipped through National Harbours Board ports (74,099,525 in 1969). It is not nearly so easy to get figures on the total value of urban property in the country.

The figures involved are certain to be stupendous. One estimate of the total value of all land and facilities in Metro Toronto alone in 1970 puts the figure at $50 *billion* That is about $25,000 worth of real estate for every man, woman and child who lives in Toronto. New house construction across Canada amounted to $3.2 billion in 1970, 4.2 per cent of total national production that year. Yet that produced only 176,000 new houses, an increase of 3 per cent to the total stock of existing houses. The total value of the urban housing stock in Canada in 1961 was about $37 billion, and by 1971, with new construction and the increasing value of the existing stock, it must have at least doubled to $75 billion.

The property owning business

In the property owning business — the business of owning land and buildings — the most important people are a city's large property owners, who control great chunks of real estate worth millions of dollars. There are always some around, but their identity may not be well known. Nevertheless, identifying them is important to understanding the power structure in the property industry, and in tracing industry links with city hall.

Details of the extent or the value of the holdings of these major property owners are difficult to come by. Assessment records are a source of clues and some information, but it is not hard for a property owner to cover his tracks with a maze of lawyers, holding companies and other devices. Still, a simple list of a city's 10 or 20 biggest property owners in terms of the assessed value of their holdings would be useful and interesting information.

You can find many of the same names turning up on lists of big property owners in almost every Canadian city. First, look for the CNR and CPR. The railways tricked, swindled, stole and — rarely — purchased large quantities of urban land from government in their heyday, and had considerable amounts simply thrust upon them. They have parted with very little of it. Second, look for Eaton's and the other large department stores. Large chunks of downtown land are valuable in any city, and one of the fortunate accidents of the department store business, if you happen to be in it, is that you usually find yourself owning land of this kind. Eaton's has large land holdings in most cities where it operates in a major way, and often other department stores like Simpsons in Toronto and The Bay in Winnipeg do too.

In a search for major city property owners, look carefully for evidence of holdings by major local businesses and especially local wealthy families. The rich usually put at least some of their money into land in their home town. That is part of the explanation, no doubt, for the extent of the Eaton family's holdings in downtown Toronto, where they control a tract of eleven acres right in the main shopping area. The Richardsons, probably the wealthiest local family in Winnipeg, own an important piece of the city's downtown, where they have built the Richardson Building as a symbol of their importance to the city.

There are now a number of major real estate firms that have substantial land holdings in a number of Canadian cities, in addition to continuing with development work. They often figure as important local property owners. In many cities, for instance, the Bronfman family-owned firms, Cemp and Fairview, have very important interests. Other local property owning firms may have important holdings in their own city but nothing outside. Kitchener-Waterloo, for example, has a local development and property owning firm called Major Holdings, which is large in Kitchener-Waterloo but has no major properties elsewhere.

Another important category of major property owners to watch for is institutions and governments. Universities, for instance, always have extremely valuable property holdings and often figure in the top ten local property owners (though of course not among the top ten municipal taxpayers because they pay no taxes on their property). In provincial capitals like Toronto and Winnipeg, provincial governments own large amounts of urban real estate and are often involved in major development projects to satisfy their constantly-growing demand for accommodation. Finally, city governments themselves are always major local property owners because of their ownership of all public lands like roads, sidewalks, lanes, parks and so on. In any

Trying to find Toronto's largest property owners

I started at the statistics division of the assessment branch of the provincial Department of Municipal Affairs. The province now handles property assessment in Ontario, a function which of course increases its potential power in deciding on land use policies and planning matters. 'No,' said the man I talked to, 'we don't have a list of the 10 largest property owners in Toronto. The two biggest are Meridian and Cadillac (local high-rise apartment developers). The city clerk's office has a list.'

So I called the city clerk. 'No,' said the man I talked to, 'we don't have any such list. I can't think of anything anyone would use it for. Besides, it would be almost impossible to draw up accurately, because property owners don't hold all their land under the same name. Some of them like Eaton's and Simpson's you'd know right off, but I don't know how you'd actually get a list.'

Then I tried the Info-Pak lady at the Development Department. Info-Pak is a collection of documents put out by the Development Department boasting about all the wonderful development going on in Toronto. She had never seen a list, but she suggested the statistics division in the city planning board.

'There would be no such list available to you, Mr. Lorimer,' said the man in the planning board. 'You're not in city government, are you?'

'You mean to say that such a list does in fact exist?' No, I've never seen it. We have thought of doing it here, but there are tremendous conceptual problems about how to do it satisfactorily, and it's hard to see how anyone could use it.'

Getting nowhere with the public authorities, I thought I'd try A. E. LePage, the biggest real estate agents in Toronto who have a sizeable research department and churn out many reports on city real estate. 'No,' said the researcher I talked to, 'I don't know of any such list. How would you ever draw it up? But try Municipal Affairs, or the city clerk's office. Maybe the planning board would have something.'

I gave up.

The St. Jamestown apartment development, owned by the Meridian Group which may be one of Toronto's largest property owners.

large development project, city hall almost always turns out to be a co-venturer with the private developer because of the land sales and exchanges that the scheme involves.

A final and very important group of major landowners in any city consists of the firms who own large tracts of vacant land just beyond the built-up area of the city, where new development will be located. Evidence recently collected by Central Mortgage and Housing Corporation (CMHC) researcher Peter Spurr suggests that in many Canadian cities a small group of speculators — sometimes just one firm — controls enough of the supply of vacant suburban land to dominate the market and to control prices. Often firms in the vacant suburban land business are in other branches of the property business as well. Sometimes they are controlled by one or more of the local wealthy families with other substantial property interests. This is a particularly important part of the property market, partly because there is so much money to be made from developing vacant land for new urban development and partly because controlling the supply of new vacant land affects prices for all property in the city and pushes housing costs up for everyone.

Taken together, the total holdings of all the major property owners in a single city might amount to 20 or 30 per cent of the city's property by land area, and a higher percentage of the total value of urban property. In most cities most urban property is still in the hands of medium-sized and small property owners, who measure their property by the square foot or by lots, not by acres and full city blocks. Amongst these smaller property owners, the most important distinction to be made is whether they are basically profit-oriented in their property operations or whether, like many home owners, they have other concerns and motives that are more important to them.

Though small property owners still own a very large percentage of a city's real estate, there is an obvious and extremely important trend towards concentration of property ownership in the hands of a few large property owners. The faster a city is growing, the more development and redevelopment it is experiencing, the more quickly this concentration is occurring. Small property owners are being squeezed out by public redevelopment schemes, by private developers, and by the trend towards renting rather than buying by families and businesses both. The pace is speeded up because small property owners suffer greatly from not having the same political force and not being nearly so well organized as large property owners. Even though this shift in the pattern of urban property ownership is perhaps the single most important change occurring in Canada's cities, however, I know of no useful data that reports how much of it is happening and how quickly. Perhaps people responsible for collecting data about cities feel that this is one set of statistics it would be better to leave uncollected.

Profits of property investors

There is virtually no reliable publicly-available information on the profits that property investors make on their money. The usual figures quoted tend to sound substantial but nevertheless reasonable — like 10 or 15 per cent a year, a hefty return on investment but still not all that much more than you make if you put your money into government bonds. Public real estate companies with a substantial portfolio of buildings show reasonable rates of profit on their capital invested. Rarely is the word "profit" used by these companies, you understand; they prefer the more "human" term, "income." Profits as published by these companies for 1970 ranged — after taxes — from $3,039,000 for Campeau Corporation and $2,684,000 for

---

Gifts to the Railways

NORTHERN RAILWAY SUBSIDY JOBBERY: As for subsidies procured from the larger municipalities, the Northern Railway scandal, revolving around the issue of Toronto City bonds in aid of that project, revealed the methods often used to get municipal subsidies.

In 1850 the City of Toronto, or rather its officials, voted a gift of £25,000, a valuable site for a station, and the right of way, to aid this enterprise. The next year the City of Toronto was prevailed upon to loan £35,000 more to the Company, under conditions making it virtually a gift. One of these conditions was that certain parts of the road had to be completed before these sums were available. Despite the fact that they did not comply with the required conditions, the contractors, in the very act of "scamping," had the assurance to ask for the full subsidy. Mayor John G. Bowes had been a director of this same railway company.

An illegal by-law was thereupon passed to hand over £60,000 to the Railway Company. Advised by "eminent counsel" that this by-law was in fact an illegality, the contractors and their confederates quickly hit upon a plan of circumventing it. A Bill was hurried

through Parliament. This Bill was apparently innocent and modest-looking; its sole ostensible object was to allow Toronto to issue a loan of £100,000 of bonds for the purpose of consolidating the City's debt. But it was in the fifth clause of the Bill that the "little joker" cunningly lay. Notwithstanding the fact that the subsidy railway debenture bonds voted by the City's officials did not mature for twenty years, this clause compelled Toronto to pay *at once* to the contractors the debenture bonds *at their face value*. Prime Minister Hincks rushed this Bill in all of its stages through Parliament in a few days, and it became law. None or few of the legislators knew that a few weeks previously Hincks and Bowes had personally bought those very bonds at four-fifths their face value.

Soon revelations were forthcoming that Bowes and Hincks had been in secret partnership, and that they had bought from the Northern Railway contractors, at a large discount, a batch of the identical bonds issued by Toronto to aid that Company. By certain bank manipulations, it appeared, they did this without having to spend a cent of their own money.

Gustavus Myers, *History of Canadian Wealth*.
Toronto: James Lewis & Samuel, 1972, pp.192-3

Cadillac Development Corporation on down. For Cadillac this is a return of about 10 per cent on the capital put up by shareholders in the company plus retained earnings.

An interesting insight into how these published figures understate the real situation is given by the fact that Cadillac in 1970 charged itself an expense of $1,292,607 for "depreciation" of its buildings. Yet there is very little reason to think that the buildings were in any sense "wearing out;" and indeed, quite separate from the value of the land they stood on, Cadillac's buildings probably rose in value rather than declining during the year. Eliminating the fictitious "expense" for depreciation adds $1.3 million to the admitted $2.7 million profit, raising the total for 1970 to $4.0 million.

Another important consideration is that, while the value of Cadillac's buildings is probably going up, the value of the land on which they stand certainly is increasing as land prices generally increase. Cadillac's land is, however, valued at the price the company paid for it, and nowhere in the balance sheets does the company count as real or potential profit the increases that have occurred that year in the value of the land it owns. Estimating the value of land owned by Cadillac in 1970 at $35 million (one fourth of the total value of land plus buildings owned by the company)

and assuming that its value increased by 10 per cent during the year (a modest assumption, given the rate of increase of land values in Toronto, where most of Cadillac's holdings are located), we should add another $3.5 million to profits. We are now up to $7.5 million.

Yet another factor to be taken into account is that Cadillac and other companies in the same business count income tax as an expense, *yet in fact they pay virtually no income tax because their tax payments are "deferred" courtesy of the federal government and a tax dodge.* The tax dodge is, basically, that the government allows Cadillac to count depreciation as a business expense and to depreciate its buildings at an even faster rate for tax purposes than the company does on its own balance sheets. Eventually, though, you might think, that deferred tax will have to be paid. But it will not have to be paid while Cadillac continues to expand. If it expands fast enough, it can defer paying any income tax almost indefinitely. Income taxes counted as an expense by Cadillac but not paid by the company in 1970 were $2,342,000. Assuming that the company's directors will be clever enough to postpone paying these taxes indefinitely, we can add the amount deducted by Cadillac for income tax — $2,342,000 — to its profits. We are now at $9.8 million.

EATON'S IN VANCOUVER: This new downtown Eaton's store in Vancouver sits on part of a city block known as Block 52. Note how the forbidding exterior of the new building creates a situation where shoppers would far rather walk through the store than around it on city streets.

A similar downtown development has been proposed by Eaton's for its land holdings in Toronto. The Toronto project would bring Eaton's together with Fairview, one of the two partners it worked with in Vancouver. Also to be involved in Toronto would be Victor Gruen, a U.S. architect who is an associate architect for the Vancouver store as well.

Actual cash investment by shareholders in the company in 1970 was $15,000,000. Retained earnings (profits left in the company rather than being paid out as dividends to shareholders) amounted to another $10 million. Our figures of real profits of $9.8 million suggest that the real profit being earned by Cadillac on the combined total of shareholders' capital and retained earnings was closer to 35 per cent than to the admitted figure of about 10 per cent. On shareholders' investment alone, *it was exactly 65 per cent.*

Cadillac is not an unusual case amongst companies investing in real estate for a business. Its admitted profits of $2.7 million are close to the "official" industry norm of about 10 per cent. There is every reason to think that other property investors are making the same kind of money Cadillac is making — 65 per cent a year on their money.

Other evidence also suggests that 35 to 50 per cent a year is a lot closer to the truth than 10 per cent for the profit that real estate investors actually make. Obviously conditions vary from city to city, and if real estate values are not rising quickly one important avenue for profit is cut off for the investor. Nevertheless, the figures indicate that property investors are making a lot of money indeed from their tenants.

The property financing business

Completely intertwined with the property owning business is the property financing business — the business of lending money to finance new construction and the buying and selling of existing land and buildings. Property financing is just one of the businesses of the country's large financial institutions — the chartered banks, life insurance companies, and trust and loan companies.

One of the problems of running a business like a life insurance company is to find profitable ways of lending the money you accumulate. Obviously you can't make money as a life insurance company if you simply take in the cash people pay for their life insurance policies and keep it in your vault, waiting for the insured to die or for their policy to become due so you can pay the money back to them. The way you make money is by taking in this money and lending it out at a higher interest rate than the rate you are paying your customers. The problem is to find ways of lending the money which will pay you a good high interest rate and where you are pretty sure of getting your money back.

Lending money to people who want to own real estate is desirable in many ways from the point of view of a financial institution. Borrowers can be persuaded to pay higher interest rates than, say, governments will pay when they borrow money from private sources. And the risk is very low, because you get a foolproof claim allowing you to take possession of the borrower's property if he doesn't pay the money back, and you are always careful to lend him a somewhat smaller amount than his property is worth. There is of course an incredibly elaborate legal system worked out for this kind of lending — for mortgage lending, as it is called. A mortgage is simply the legal contract setting out the arrangement between the borrower (who owns some property) and the lender who gets the right to claim that property if the borrower doesn't pay back his loan.

Most people who want to own real estate find they have to borrow money to do so, because the cost of urban property — an ordinary suburban house, for example — is so much greater than the amount of savings they have. People commonly find they have to pay three or four times their annual income in order to buy a house to live in. No wonder they need to borrow money. Bigger property owners also borrow money to finance their transactions, often because they don't much want to tie all their own money up in their property when they can get hold of other people's money for that purpose.

WHO OWNS WINNIPEG: Statistical data which would show who is the largest property investor in Winnipeg is unavailable. But one very reliable indicator is simply looking around and seeing who owns the tallest building in the city. The Richardson building, shown above, is owned by the Richardsons, the most prominent family in Winnipeg's economic elite. The Richardsons are involved in the brokerage house of James Richardson & Sons as well as many other enterprises. One family member, James Richardson (rudely labelled James Richmanson by a Winnipeg opposition newspaper) is a federal government cabinet minister.

Continued on page 30

TABLE 3-1   INDICATORS OF CONCENTRATED OWNERSHIP

URBAN AREA	OWNER, NOTES ON LAND MARKET, OR NUMBER OF OWNERS	ACREAGE	AREA STARTS 1970	SOURCE
Toronto, Metro	Bramalea Consolidated Developments Limited	6,365		CREA
" "	The Caledon Mountain Estates Limited	2,401		" "
" "	Markborough Properties Ltd.	3,716		" "
" "	S. B. McLaughlin Associates Limited	5,345		" "
" "	Pinetree Development Co. Limited	1,564		" "
" "	(5)	19,391	30,521	
Kitchener	Buildevco Limited	1,000		CREA
" "	Major Holdings and Developments Ltd.	2,040		" "
" "	(2)	3,040	3,075	
Calgary	Nu-West Homes Limited	3,600		CREA
" "	Quality Construction Ltd.	1,500		" "
" "	(2)	5,100	6,740	
" "	less competition, large developers dominant			UPP
Ottawa	Campeau Corporation Limited	3,000+		CREA
" "	Canadian Interurban Properties Ltd.	3,200		CREA
" "	Minto Construction Ltd.	710		CMHC
" "	Costain Estates Ltd.	1,400		CMHC
" "	Nepean Carleton Development Co. Ltd.	800		CMHC
" "	(5)	9,110	8,204	
" "	few large speculators control market			UPP
South Pickering Twp	One developer	2,200		OAPADS
Oshawa	Twelve developers	1,240	1,302	OAPADS
Whitby	Seven developers	1,000		OAPADS
Winnipeg	Four large developers			UPP
Hamilton	Most land owned by developers			UPP
London	Five major developers			UPP

In each urban area listed, the holdings cited could provide one-half of the 1970 housing starts for at least the next ten years.

SOURCES:
CREA — The Canadian Real Estate Annual, 1970
UPP — Appendix "B" Chapter 5, Urban Policy Paper
OAPADS — Oshawa Area Planning and Development Study, Report #Two, Volume #1, p. II-51
CMHC — Review of Ottawa Vacant Lands, CMHC, A & P Division
AREA STARTS — CHS, 1970, TABLE 7

From Peter Spurr, *"Land and the urban policy paper."* Unpublished CMHC research paper, 1971 (?)

Investment properties may return from 10 to 35 % a year

By TERRENCE BELFORD

Some forms of real estate are as nearly inflation-proof as any form of investment open to the general public, according to Walter Keyser, vice-president of Gairdner and Co. Ltd., Toronto.

Speaking to a seminar entitled Financial Management Against Inflation at the University of Toronto Business School, Mr. Keyser said the return on investment properties can, depending on the type of property, amount to between 10 and 35 per cent a year.

Based on his own tabulations of net cash flow return on properties he is acquainted with through his position at Gairdner, properties acquired between 1961 and 1967 for an unleveraged 6 to 7 per cent rate of return now return 10.1 per cent to 11.2 per cent a year on original cost plus improvements.

(He characterized these properties as low-rise apartment houses, 10 to 15 years old, containing 85 to 100 units and situated in lower middle-income areas of Toronto).

The return rises to between 13.1 and 20.3 per cent when the annual increase in property value is added to cash flow. When leverage is applied—Mr. Keyser adds that all of these properties were financed at mortgage rates considerably below those prevailing currently—rates of return on invested capital range upward from 35 per cent a year.

Discussing the single-family house as an investment, he relied on Toronto Real Estate Board figures on the average resale price for houses since 1953. The annual compound growth rate in resale prices was 5 per cent. This compares with a 7.25 per cent growth rate for the Dow

BUILDING AND REAL ESTATE

Jones industrial average and the Toronto Stock Exchange industrial index.

For the passive investor—the one who wants a long-term investment with no management responsibility—Mr. Keyser recommended a long-term land lease with frequent rent reviews and rent pegged to changing land values.

"This provides the landlord with rent from a tenant who has built an improvement on the land at his own expense and who risks losing his improvement for failure to pay land rent."

Rent would be calculated as a percentage of market value of the land and adjusted as land values increase. At the end of the lease, the landlord can enter a new lease, assume the improvements, redevelop or sell.

For the active investor, Mr. Keyser suggested a retail-commercial revenue-producing property, leased to an established retailer on a long-term basis for a fixed minimum rent plus a percentage of sales.

"Using Bloor Street in the Avenue Road-Yonge Street section as an example, an actual lease signed 20 years ago called for a rent of $3 a square foot plus 4 per cent of gross sales exceeding the base amount.

"This lease is currently providing a rental rate equal to $14 a square foot. In the meantime, land values have increased tenfold to approximately $125 to $150 a square foot."

Mr. Keyser explained that leverage can "make every good aspect of an income property better".

His advice was that if a leveraged investment was to be as inflation proof as an unleveraged investment, then the term of mortgage should be as long as possible.

"To make your income property investment a true hedge against inflation, make your financing for as long a term as possible and your lease rents as net-net as possible."

There are, however, some unforeseeable factors in property investment, he warned. Government action is one, citizen group opposition is another.

"Government planners will dictate more frequently the location of development and the type of land use permitted.

"Through fiscal and monetary policies or outright price controls, the federal Government might artificially reduce money costs, which would have an adverse effect on some types of income property, temporarily at least."

Globe and Mail May 1972

The figures produced by the investment firm executive whose speech is reported in this article show that a property investor who puts his cash into a down payment on an existing apartment building can expect to make "upward from 35% a year" on his investment.

An important contributor to this return is "leverage", the term for using a small amount of your own money in tandem with a lot of money you are able to borrow from elsewhere for a real estate deal.

TABLE 3-2   REAL ESTATE INVESTMENTS OF LIFE INSURANCE COMPANIES

COMPANY	1969 MORTGAGE HOLDINGS (IN MILLIONS)	1969 TOTAL ASSETS
Nominally Canadian-owned		
Sun Life	$ 1,123	$ 3,498
Manufacturers' Life	631	1,915
London Life	1,149	1,533
Great West Life	549	1,400
Mutual Life	551	1,164
Canada Life	475	1,231
Confederation Life	282	748
Crown Life	330	682
North American Life	260	667
Imperial Life	181	478
Total, Canadian firms	$ 6,039	$ 14,441
Nominally British-owned		
Standard Life	294	708
Prudential	84	262
Norwich Union	21	62
Total, all British firms	$ 402	$ 1,098
Nominally foreign i.e. U.S.-owned		
Metropolitan Life	504	1,146
Prudential Insurance	455	681
Total, all foreign firms	$ 1,035	$ 2,247

SOURCE: *Report of the superintendent of insurance for Canada, 1969 Vol. I*

Trizec: A Canadian real estate giant

Sam Hashman   Peter F. Bronfman   Edward M. Bronfman

James A. Soden, President of Trizec Corporation Ltd., announces the appointment to the Trizec Board of Directors of Messrs. Sam Hashman, Peter F. Bronfman and Edward M. Bronfman following the acquisition by Trizec of control of Great West International Equities Ltd.

Mr. Sam Hashman is President, Mr. Peter F. Bronfman is Chairman of the Board and Mr. Edward M. Bronfman is a Director of Great West International Equities Ltd.   *

No one knows for sure who is the biggest property owner in Canada. It could be the CPR, it could be Eaton's, or it could be the Bronfman family (through their investment trusts Cemp and Fairview). We do know who is the biggest real estate investment company with publicly-listed stocks: Trizec. It owns property which it values on its balance sheet at $352,000,000 (1970 figures). In addition it owns a controlling interest in two other major public real estate companies, Cummings Properties Ltd. and Great West International Equities. Great West's real estate holdings are valued at about $60 million. Cummings are valued at $110 million. That puts the total for Trizec and its subsidiaries at $522 million. These balance sheet estimates, of course, underestimate the real value of the company's holdings because properties are valued at their purchase price, not at their current market value. So Trizec's real estate holdings are probably worth $600, $700, or $800 million dollars. They may not be far off from their first billion.

Enormous figures like this are hard to comprehend. The lists of the Trizec group's properties gives a better idea of how large their holdings really are. To cite some of the more notable: in Montreal, Place Ville Marie, the BCN buildings and many others; in Calgary, the Royal Bank

Property acquisitions stressed

By TERRENCE BELFORD

Trizec Corp. Ltd. of Montreal, Canada's largest public real estate company, is not likely to opt for growth through the acquisition of other companies, its president, James Soden, told the Toronto Society of Financial Analysts yesterday.

"While it is our intention to maintain our momentum in the future, I would be inclined nonetheless to anticipate that future acquisitions would more likely be in the nature of purchases of individual properties as distinct from the acquisition or merger of other companies," he speculated.

Trizec doubled its assets in 1971 to more than $500-million through the acquisition of two Calgary-based development companies, Cummings Properties Ltd. and Great West International Equities Ltd.

Mr. Soden told his audience his company will more likely spend a little while "digesting and integrating" the operations of the two western units and consolidating its position.

"We will be inclined more toward the development of our own properties and the purchase of existing properties under selective circumstances and less toward the acquisitions of corporate organizations, although this will be c o n s i d e r e d where appropriate."

He added: "However, this doesn't rule out the latter possibility altogether."

Mr. Soden did not venture much new information to the analysts, sidestepping questions in Trizec's financial participation in Montreal's Place Bonaventure complex and comparisons of financial return on the company's various activities.

In answer to the query about Place Bonaventure, he said Trizec had a five-year management contract for the centre, which gave the company an annual fee plus equity, but refused to specify the size of either. To the question on comparative profitability of various projects, he answered they all compared "favorably".

He did forecast a 10 per cent growth rate for the company compounded annually if for some reason Trizec froze its portfolio today. He did not, however, offer any predictions about 1972 p r o f i t or revenue.

The Trizec chief told the analysts he preferred to use his time with them to explain his company's history and philosophy of development, which basically was to acquire quality buildings that are well located and have the potential for growth in revenue generated.

He suggested any increase

in revenue and profit would come from a variety of areas. The first of these would be the current development program.

Trizec has $139-million of new construction under way, which will result in 1,262,000 square feet of income-producing office space, 1,677,000 square feet of retail space, 1,732 hotel rooms, 349 residential units and one retirement lodge.

Trizec can also expect to benefit from rent increases on its properties as leases come due, Mr. Soden said.

"With office leases, for example, this situation provides us with the opportunity to renew the lease of existing tenants, or re-let the space of new tenants, at improved rentals on a continuing basis."

S h o p p i n g centres have b u i l t - i n revenue growth through frequent roll-over prospects, as do residential buildings: both have short-term leases. Nursing homes and hotels and their high turnover offer the advantage of almost immediate price increases if necessary, he added.

Trizec is 60 per cent owned by Star (Great Britain) Holdings Ltd. Since its incorporation in 1960, gross property interests have increased from $30-million to $480-million.

Revenue has increased from $4,194,000 to $77,517,000 and earnings have increased from a loss of $2,877,000 to a profit of $4,529,000.

"We attach a great importance to the quality of our income which to a very substantial degree is made up of committed lease income from major Canadian corporations. This affords us a good downside protection."

Mr. Soden also told the analysts that the Hashman Construction Ltd. unit contributed about 7 per cent of profit in the 10 months ended Oct. 31. Hashman Construction is currently doing $75-million of construction work for Trizec and has another $43-million of projects in addition.

Discussing financing for the companies portfolio, which was carried at about $425-million at Oct. 31, Mr. Soden told the analysts Trizec had mortgages on its properties amounting to $275-million with an average interest rate of about 7.5 per cent and a term of about 15 years.

The company has also issued $30-million in senior debentures and has general corporate debt amounting to $55-million. Of this about $32-million is convertible into equity between 1975 and 1980 at prices ranging from $15 to $22.70 a share. Equity base is about $100-million.

Globe and Mail

building, the Glidden Building, the Texaco building, Calgary Place, Macleod Mall; in Edmonton, the CN Tower, the IBM building, the Centennial Building; in Halifax, the Halifax Insurance Building, the Halifax shopping centre, and the Centennial Building; in Toronto, Yorkdale Shopping Centre, Hyatt House hotel; in Vancouver, the Regency Hyatt House.

Along with its office buildings, hotels and shopping centres, the Trizec group owns a number of apartment buildings and "retirement lodges" with space for 2574 old people.

Trizec is constantly expanding its real estate investment portfolio, and is in the midst of several large development projects. It manages Place Bonaventure in Montreal and may have plans to acquire the building; it is "acting as consultant" in the development of 170 acres of Scarborough; it is developing a square block of downtown land on the south-west corner of Portage and Main in Winnipeg.

Where did Trizec come from? It was originally set up by U.S. real estate developer William Zeckendorf in partnership with British insurance company interests to cash in on profitable Zeckendorf developments in Canada. When Zeckendorf's empire began to collapse his British co-venturers took over the company. It is now controlled by Star (Great Britain) Holdings Limited and its subsidiaries, who own 61 per-cent of the outstanding stock. Star Holdings is related to the Eagle Star insurance group. Appropriately, then, Canada's largest public real estate company is foreign-owned.

One of Trizec's recent acquisitions, Great West International Equities, was formerly called the Great West Saddlery Limited. Its real estate operations were set up in 1969 by an amalgamation of the real estate interests of Calgary developer Sam Hashman and a Bronfman family company.

Another recent Trizec acquisition, Cummings Properties, was owned by the Cummings family and was a Calgary-based development and real estate company.

The Canadians involved in Trizec's direction appear to be mainly local representatives of British interests or spokesmen for minority shareholders.

Among these Canadian directors is Lazarus Phillips, a Montreal lawyer who was a key local boy in William Zeckendorf's manipulations to get hold of the CN land on which he built Place Ville Marie. Phillips is a senior member of Montreal's Jewish financial circles. He is also involved in Bronfman real estate firms as a director of Cemp Investments, and perhaps represents the Bronfmans on Trizec's board.

Another Canadian director of Trizec is E. Jacques Courtois. Courtois is senior local boy for Eagle Star, as vice chairman of Eagle Star Insurance Co. of Canada. He sits on the board of a number of Quebec gas utility companies, and he is on the board of the Bank of Nova Scotia. He also sits on the board of another large public real estate company, Bramalea, in which Eagle Star has a 14 per-cent interest, apparently the largest single block of shares.

Another Canadian director of Trizec is F. B. Common, a Montreal lawyer with ties to British insurance interests.

Two Cummings family members, their firm having

been taken over by Trizec, appear on Trizec's board and on the board of Star (Great Britain) Holdings Ltd.

Trizec also has on its board S. E. Nixon of Montreal's Dominion Securities Corp. He has some other impressive directorships, including Canadian Pacific Investments.

Another Trizec director and resident of Montreal has widespread property industry interests. He is Caryl Nicholas Charles Hardinge, the Right Honourable Viscount Hardinge of Lahore(!). Hardinge is chairman of Greenshields Inc., a Montreal investment house. He is also chairman of Ritz-Carlton Hotel Co., and a director of Markborough Properties, Phoenix Assurance, and Acadia Insurance.

A final Canadian director of Trizec represents the property industry financial elite of the Atlantic provinces. He is lawyer Frank Covert, chairman of General Mortgage Corporation of Canada, and director of Acadia Insurance, Phoenix Assurance, the Royal Bank, Eastern Telephone & Telegraph Ltd., Nova Scotia Light and Power, Bowaters, Sun Life. Mr. Covert is also member of the board of directors of Dalhousie University.

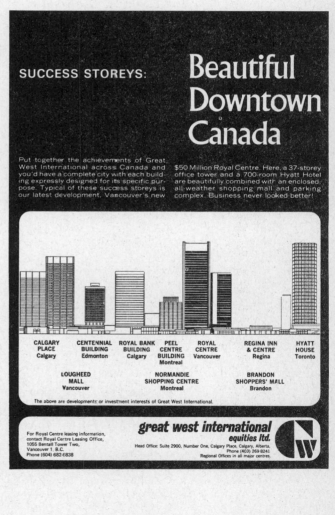

In the property financing business, the biggest operators are the life insurance companies. In 1969 all the life insurance companies operating in Canada had a total of $7.47 *billion* lent out on property. These mortgage holdings amounted to something less than a half of their total assets of $17.78 billion. Together, the three biggest life insurance companies — Sun Life, Manufacturers' Life, and London Life — had $2.9 *billion* lent out in mortgages. That is a lot of money, even for life insurance companies. Supposing that the life insurance companies' mortgages yielded an average of 7 per cent in interest, that would produce an annual income for them of $523,000,000.

Trust and loan companies operate much like banks in many ways, but differ from banks in that a far higher percentage of all the money deposited with them is lent out for real estate mortgages. The total of their mortgages outstanding in 1969 was $5.772 billion, not much less than the life insurance companies.

The third kind of financial institution involved in the property financing business is the chartered bank. Banks are strictly regulated in many aspects of their operations, and only recently have they been allowed by the federal government to lend money on real estate. They are limited to National Housing Act (N.H.A.) mortgages, mortgages for housing only, which are guaranteed and insured against loss by the federal government's agency in the housing field, CMHC. The banks' real estate lending amounted to $1.464 billion in 1970, and in addition the banks owned real estate used for banking premises that they valued at $436 million. These figures, while enormous by ordinary standards, amount to a relatively small percentage of the total assets of the chartered banks, which at that time were the staggering sum of $47 billion, about $2,000 for every man, woman and child in the country.

Along with these privately-owned businesses that are involved in property financing, the federal government has an agency, Central Mortgage and Housing Corporation, which regulates many aspects of the housing market, insures and guarantees mortgages, and lends some money itself directly. Most of CMHC's lending goes for the construction of new housing, though some of it is to finance purchases of existing housing. In 1969, it had $3.9 billion of its own money outstanding in mortgages.

There are, of course, other sources of property financing. These include other kinds of lending institutions like Quebec savings banks and mutual benefit societies, credit unions ($4.1 billion outstanding in 1969), and estates, trusts and agency funds of trust companies ($2.5 billion lent out in 1969). There are also small-time lenders, who operate particularly in the lower-cost end of the housing market, lending money at high rates to working-class purchasers of old houses, providing second and third mortgages at scandalous rates, and generally making money out of the unwillingness of major lenders to let out money on kinds of property they disapprove of (such as houses in old, central-city residential areas).

Taking all this lending together, CMHC estimates that there was a total of $24 *billion* in mortgages on real estate in Canada in 1970. That is about $1,000 for every Canadian citizen. That investment, if the average interest rate being paid is 7 per cent (a low figure by current standards), produces an income of $1,680,000,000 every year for the owners of that money. Considering that virtually all you have to

do to make money on a mortgage is wait for the cash to come rolling in, $1,680,000,000 every year is not a bad income for the mortgage lenders of the country. People who own property may think that property ownership is a good way of making money, but obviously owning money (or controlling other people's) and lending it out on real estate is also a pretty profitable enterprise. While banks, life insurance companies, trust and loan companies and the others all have other ways of making money besides financing property, these figures indicate that they're into mortgage lending in a very big way indeed.

Property insurance

Just in terms of the sheer amounts of money involved, none of the other businesses that service property owners comes close to matching the property financing business in size or importance. But there are some other businesses closely allied to property ownership that are important enough to the people involved in them.

Real property insurance is insurance of buildings against fire, theft and other kinds of risks property owners run. Property insurance firms differ from life insurance companies in that most of the money they take in during the course of a year they pay out in the form of claims made by people who had fires, thefts and so on. Property insurance companies do not have the same opportunity as life insurance companies to build up enormous reserves of cash, though it should be added that many companies that are in one part of the insurance business are in the other part as well.

One very important part of the property insurance business is the selling end. Insurance of this kind is usually sold by independent agents who make their money on commissions on premiums paid by customers for their insurance. The insurance business is pretty well organized by the insurance companies, which manage to charge more or less identical prices. Agents can offer friendly, helpful service to

Continued on page 34

Insurance firms switch from mortgages to bonds

Life insurance companies made a sharp switch out of mortgages into corporate bonds in 1970.

Statistics released by the Canadian Life Insurance Association covering investment transactions by companies with 80% of the invested assets of life firms in Canada show that net acquisitions of corporate bonds totaled $161 million, vs only $13 million in 1969.

Mortgage acquisitions in 1970 totaled $108 million, down from $232 million the year before.

The association says mortgage commitments increased sharply during the first half of 1971.

Net acquisitions of stocks in 1970 totaled $71 million, compared with $108 million in 1969.

Financial Post 13 Nov. 1971

Nalaco and the property industry: how directors interlock

Corporations in one part of the property industry are usually linked via their boards of directors to other property industry firms, as well as to corporations outside the industry. Linked directors sometimes result from shareholdings, where for instance a company which holds a substantial number of shares of another company arranges to have one or more of its directors elected to the board of the company in which it owns shares. Linked directorships also relate to business interests. Life insurance companies are linked to people who need their money, who are customers of the life insurance companies, and in whom the life insurance companies have invested their assets.

This analysis of the directors of North American Life Assurance Company (Nalaco) shows that its directors appear on the boards of many other large corporations in the financial fields, and on the boards of a number of corporations in other divisions of the property industry.

There are other kinds of connections between these companies as well, of course. Nalaco owns shares in many; it owns the bonds of many more; and presumably it holds mortgages of others.

Nalaco's strongest single set of links is to other financial institutions: other life insurance companies, banks, and trust companies. Nalaco's directors sit on the boards of three of the major chartered banks, and have four bank directorships in total. Nalaco's directors have five seats on the boards of five trust companies, and one on the board of a mortgage company. Two Nalaco directors sit on the board of another insurance company, Eagle Star. As well, there are links to property insurance companies.

Like Nalaco, these other financial institutions are deeply involved in the property industry. But Nalaco has links to other sectors of the industry as well. Four of its directors sit on the boards of building materials supply firms. One of its directors is the president of a large construction company, Pigott Construction. Another Nalaco director, J.H. Taylor, is chairman of Bramalea Consolidated Development, a large land development and property investment company. A third Nalaco director also sits on the boards of two Toronto-based developers, Markborough and Cadillac.

A few of the 17 members of the Nalaco board are responsible for most of these links to the rest of the property industry. John H. Taylor, for example, has one seat on a trust company board (National Trust), one on an insurance company board (Eagle Star), one on a fuel oil firm (Canadian Fuel Marketers), and one on a property investment and development firm board (Bramalea, where he is chairman).

Another important director is G.P. Osler, chairman of UNAS Investments. Osler sits on the board of two building materials firms, North Star Steel and Lake Ontario Steel, as well as on the board of the Toronto-Dominion Bank.

A third important director is D.W. Pretty, executive vice-president of Nalaco. Mr. Pretty sits on the board of Eagle Star insurance, two property insurance firms (Scottish Canadian and General Accident), and on the board of two property investment and development firms (Cadillac and Markborough).

As life insurance companies go, Nalaco is relatively small and not particularly important. Its total assets in 1971 were $748 million, placing it well below the large and middle-sized firms in the industry. Its role in the property industry through mortgage lending was not enormous either, with mortgages worth $280 million in its portfolio at the end of 1971. That represented a net additional investment in mortgages during 1971 of $9 million. A more important life insurance company would have a broader and denser web of connections to other firms in the property industry. Nevertheless Nalaco is a good example of the pattern in the property industry. Links are numerous, and they express associations arising from shareholdings, investments and business dealings.

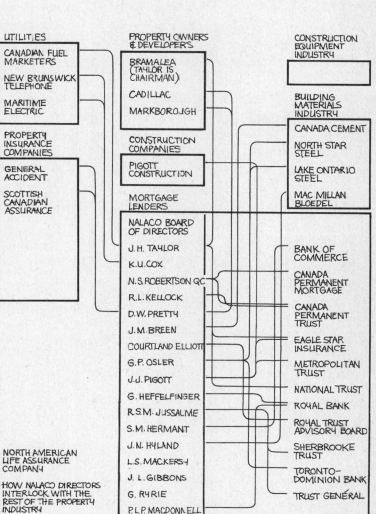

NORTH AMERICAN
LIFE ASSURANCE
COMPANY

HOW NALACO DIRECTORS
INTERLOCK WITH THE
REST OF THE PROPERTY
INDUSTRY

UTILITIES
CANADIAN FUEL MARKETERS
NEW BRUNSWICK TELEPHONE
MARITIME ELECTRIC

PROPERTY INSURANCE COMPANIES
GENERAL ACCIDENT
SCOTTISH CANADIAN ASSURANCE

PROPERTY OWNERS & DEVELOPERS
BRAMALEA (TAYLOR IS CHAIRMAN)
CADILLAC
MARKBOROUGH

CONSTRUCTION COMPANIES
PIGOTT CONSTRUCTION

MORTGAGE LENDERS

NALACO BOARD OF DIRECTORS
J.H. TAYLOR
K.U. COX
N.S. ROBERTSON QC
R.L. KELLOCK
D.W. PRETTY
J.M. BREEN
COURTLAND ELLIOTT
G.P. OSLER
J.J. PIGOTT
G. HEFFELFINGER
R.S.M. JUSSAUME
S.M. HERMANT
J.N. HYLAND
L.S. MACKERSY
J.L. GIBBONS
G. RYRIE
P.L.P. MACDONNELL

CONSTRUCTION EQUIPMENT INDUSTRY

BUILDING MATERIALS INDUSTRY
CANADA CEMENT
NORTH STAR STEEL
LAKE ONTARIO STEEL
MAC MILLAN BLOEDEL

BANK OF COMMERCE
CANADA PERMANENT MORTGAGE
CANADA PERMANENT TRUST
EAGLE STAR INSURANCE
METROPOLITAN TRUST
NATIONAL TRUST
ROYAL BANK
ROYAL TRUST ADVISORY BOARD
SHERBROOKE TRUST
TORONTO-DOMINION BANK
TRUST GENERAL

The London Life caper

Model showing how to reconstruct a downtown city block.

Jack Diamond on the importance of privacy.

Calgary Mayor Sykes on home ownership.

Why the private lot is coming to an end.

"Where we live"

FROM THE HUMAN JOURNEY SERIES

This thought-provoking London Life special focuses on *practical* solutions to Canada's housing problems—and reveals what people *really* want in a home of their own.

You'll hear opinions from Jack Diamond of the architectural firm of Diamond and Myers, Mayor Rod Sykes of Calgary, Moishe Safde designer of Montreal's Habitat, Toronto developer Charles Watson, and other experts as well as private and condominium home owners.

You'll see a model of a totally new concept in city re-development; designed especially for the program, a Nova Scotia co-operative building their own homes, and a fascinating private home in British Columbia.

Free! An informative booklet "*How to Buy a Home (and save yourself grief)."* It contains many useful tips. Write: London Life Insurance Company, Dept. B, Box 5560, London, Ontario.

London Life

Much of the new money invested by life insurance companies in real estate mortgages goes for the construction of high-rise apartments. This fact was emphasized in the summer of 1971 when residents of the Toronto neighbourhood called South St. Jamestown demonstrated outside the offices of London Life. London Life, a major mortgage lender, had provided the first mortgage funds used to finance the St. Jamestown apartment development, a massive high-rise redevelopment project built in east central Toronto in the mid-1960s. The Meridian Group, the developer involved, was assembling land in the neighbourhood to the south for an extension of St. Jamestown. Local residents, fighting against the redevelopment plans, wanted a commitment from London Life that it would not provide more mortgage money to Meridian for the proposed expansion.

The St. Jamestown development has become the touchstone of everything that Toronto residents do not like about high-rise redevelopment. Making public London Life's involvement in the project was probably an embarrassment to the company.

But there was no obvious reaction from London Life to the picketing. Later it emerged, however, that a London Life official had written a letter to Meridian as a result of the demonstration. The contents of the letter were unknown, but it appeared to have upset Meridian officials.

Nine months later, London Life turned up as the sponsor of a powerful and well-reviewed TV documentary arguing against high-rise redevelopment and proposing alternative ways in which cities can be improved and rebuilt. Not only did London Life continue to sponsor the program once it learned its content, as a Toronto TV reviewer reported in surprise; it went out of its way to advertise the program and its content.

While sponsoring this TV program, however, London Life continued its normal activities lending funds across the country that make more high-rise buildings financially possible.

CIVIC DESIGN AND LIFE INSURANCE: Life insurance companies who build themselves head offices are unusual because they don't have to design their buildings to suit an outside mortgage lender. They can fund their buildings for themselves, so in design terms they are free to do what they want.

These two buildings illustrate the architectural preferences of two Winnipeg life insurance companies. Both Great West Life and Monarch Life have built absolutely conventional office buildings for themselves. The only deviation from standard is that they are more expensively done than usual.

The two snapshots show houses that were torn down by Monarch Life to make way for its new head office. Clearly since this is the sort of thing that life insurance companies do for themselves, citizen groups are going to have a hard time persuading them that they shouldn't allow their developer friends to demolish fine old houses to make way for new high-rise buildings.

their customers, but there isn't that much room for price cutting or price competition. So people choose their insurance agents on vaguer grounds, and for an agent the most valuable commodity he has is contacts with people who own or control real estate and buildings that need insurance. Insurance agents are a long way from the upper reaches of high finance, from the management and boards of directors of property insurance companies, but they are certainly clever enough to understand that the more property there is in their locality and the more valuable it is, the more business there will be for property insurance companies and the more commissions there will be for insurance agents. They are an important part of the property insurance business.

Property utilities

Another important industry servicing urban property is utility companies, which provide gas, electricity, cable TV and phone services to the city. Sometimes these are privately owned and sometimes they are public utilities. The utility business uses very large amounts of capital, and private utility companies consequently have large investments in real property — phone lines, gas mains, phone exchanges and so on. They pay property tax on these installations, and loom large as property taxpayers.

Urban growth ensures expansion of utility services, and for the utility companies this means finding the capital necessary to finance expansion. The amounts involved are large: the capital investment of telephone companies, for instance, increased from $2.4 billion in 1960 to $5.9 billion in 1970. Along with this capital, utility systems have to be designed with future expansion in mind. Municipal land use and planning policies are consequently very important to these companies.

Dominating the telephone business is Bell Canada, along with its subsidiaries, including Maritime Telegraph and Telephone Co. (Bell has a 49.4 per-cent interest) and New Brunswick Telephone Co. (Bell owns 50.5 per cent). Bell's total assets in 1970 were $3.3 billion; its profits before taxes were $260 million. British Columbia Telephone Co., serving most of British Columbia, had assets of $625 million in 1970, and profits of $19 million after taxes. B.C. Tel is owned 50.24 percent by Anglo-Canadian Telephone, which is in turn a 100 per-cent-owned subsidiary of General Telephone and Electronics Corp., a U.S. firm.

In the gas utility business, still dominated by privately-owned, profit-making companies, the giants are Consumer's Gas, Gaz Métropolitain, Union Gas, Northern and Central Gas, and Greater Winnipeg Gas Co. Northern and Central owns 99.6 per cent of Greater Winnipeg, 81.6 per cent of Gaz Métropolitain, and has a number of other subsidiaries. Power Corp., controlled by Paul Desmarais and Jean Parisien, has a substantial stake in Northern and Central.

Real estate agents

There are a few other middle-class professionals servicing the property business besides insurance agents. One such group is real estate agents, who make their money on commissions when property is bought and sold. Real estate brokers and agents operate at many levels; the business ranges from large and extremely important firms offering clients a wide range of services to one-man offices where the agent spends most of his time showing people through houses he hopes he will be able to sell them.

The real estate agent business is organized on a city-to-city basis. Every city has its real estate board or a similar organization to which most real estate agents belong, which sets common fees for agents, does some work at regulating the business, often helps organize the market by providing a multi-listing service whereby any member agent can sell any property listed for sale in the locality, and sometimes does basic research and data-collecting on the local market.

Every city has its two or three important real estate firms which dominate the market or a particular segment of it, like the market for downtown office space or the market for industrial buildings. A dominant firm like A.E. LePage Ltd. in Toronto is in a key position in the property business because, as well as acting as agent for people selling or renting accommodation, it provides advice for prospective builders, developers and mortgage lenders about the potential profitability of new developments. If A.E. LePage says that a proposed development is not likely to be successful because there is already too much vacant space of the kind it would be providing, chances are the builder won't be able to find mortgage money and the building won't get built.

Politics and life insurance

Our corporate name "Manufacturers Life" was chosen in 1887 in honor of the Company's first president, Sir John A. Macdonald — who also happened to be Canada's first Prime Minister at the time. Sir John wanted his young country to become a strong manufacturing nation, and our "arm and hammer" symbol was designed to express the rugged pioneer spirit of Canada's early manufacturers.

Links between life insurance companies and government are a very old story, as this publicity handout from Manufacturers Life shows. Sir John A., as well as being Manufacturers Life's first president, was involved in railway companies and trust and loan companies as well. In spite of the tone of innocent wonder adopted by Manufacturers' copywriter, these links had the same function then as links between development companies and city councils have now.

Senior company members are, of course, very valuable people to have involved in development companies, and it is common to find senior partners and company directors of these real estate agency firms on the boards of directors of development firms.

Lawyers

Another service for the property business is provided by lawyers. Lawyers are involved in almost every transaction involving real estate. Even in the simplest transaction, like buying a new house, the seller usually has his lawyer who takes care of his interests, and the buyer is forced for his own protection to hire a lawyer to take care of his interests and to deal with the incredible complications involved in these transactions. The lawyers make money both coming and going.

Not all lawyers are involved in real estate, but it is a very important source of income indeed for a large number of members of the legal profession. Not enough is known about the way the law operates in Canada for us to be sure exactly what proportion of the income of lawyers is produced by real estate, but it is probably second in importance only to corporate work. As a rule of thumb, any lawyer who is not heavily involved in corporation law or who is not known to be a specialist in some other type of law can be expected to make a considerable portion of his income from real estate transactions. Small-time lawyers, the men who are not employed by the corporate law factories found in every major Canadian city, usually depend heavily on the money they make servicing the property business. Being close to the business as they usually are, many lawyers make money both from commissions on the sales and mortgages they negotiate for their clients and from their own investments and speculation in real estate.

There are many other businesses and some other professions that are also involved in servicing the property owning business, though none of them is as important as the ones just listed.

There is, for example, the outdoor sign business, which involves building and maintaining billboards, an activity that is very closely regulated by city hall. Or there is the business of providing information and statistics on real estate transactions. Most cities have one or two firms which make their money from this activity. Far larger in size and importance is the property management business with all its related activities. The office cleaning business provides a specialized kind of property management service. There is also a small industry that manufactures and sells the equipment and supplies used in building maintenance and management.

For our purposes here it isn't necessary to try to develop a complete and exhaustive list of all the businesses and occupations involved in one way or another in servicing the property owning business. The point to keep in mind is that many apparently diverse businesses *are* involved in one way or another, and when we are looking at the links between the property industry and city hall we need to remember that these are not limited to the short list of businesses that are most heavily and completely tied in to the property owning business.

TABLE 3-3   PROPERTY INVESTMENTS OF MAJOR CANADIAN LOAN COMPANIES

COMPANY	MORTGAGES AND SALE AGREEMENTS HELD (IN MILLIONS)	TOTAL ASSETS
Canada Permanent Mortgage	$ 545	$ 687
Huron and Erie Mortgage	488	607
Kinross Mortgage	209	221
Eastern Canada Savings	133	146
Nova Scotia Savings and Loan	65	68
Fidelity Mortgage and Savings	18	25
International Savings	7	11
	$ 1,483	$ 1,784

(A number of firms, all smaller than the last company listed, have been omitted from this list.)

SOURCE: *Report of the Superintendent of Insurance for Canada, 1969 Loan and Trust Companies.*

Though there are only four large loan companies operating, they hold real estate mortgages about equal in amount to all the chartered banks which have in total, of course, far greater assets than loan companies. The large loan companies are closely associated with specific chartered banks. Kinross, for instance, is controlled by the Canadian Imperial Bank of Commerce.

CHAPTER 4
The development and construction business

Senior executives of Four Seasons Hotels Ltd., as portrayed in the company's 1971 Annual Report. The company owns hotels in Toronto, Belleville, London and Israel, and it is involved in new developments in Calgary, Vancouver, and Toronto. Four Seasons was the developer who proposed building high-rise apartments and a hotel on the edge of Stanley Park on waterfront land. After months of bitter opposition from Vancouver citizen groups, the project was finally killed by a refusal of the federal government to let Four Seasons have certain Ottawa-controlled lands necessary for the project.

The sector of the property industry described in the last chapter is the one which makes money from the existing stock of urban property: owning property, lending money to people who are buying and selling it, insuring it, and providing property owners with a wide range of services.

The other big sector of the property industry which involves many of the interests we have already identified as well as a whole range of new ones, is the business of adding to the existing stock of urban property, that is, producing new buildings of various kinds.

This sector is the leading edge of the property industry — and in many ways the cutting edge. We begin to get some idea of the immense power of the industry and of the tremendous amounts of money involved when we look at the process of how new buildings are built and how land is developed and redeveloped. Look at Vancouver's Pacific Centre, where three Eastern-based property owners — Eaton's, Cemp Holdings (a Bronfman family company) and the Toronto Dominion Bank — are covering two downtown city blocks with about one million square feet of department store, shops and offices. When these companies encountered a little difficulty in the shape of property owners in the two blocks in question who didn't want to sell out, they were able to turn to Vancouver's city council and get the aldermen to expropriate holdouts.

Look at the Winnipeg city council's obliging attitude towards wealthy firms building big new downtown high-rise office buildings. For a new development to be built by Trizec on the south-west corner of Portage and Main, Winnipeg city council has agreed to expropriate the existing small property owners, to rent the land at an unbelievably low figure compared to its market value, and to use public money to build the underground parking garage which will serve the new development.

Look at what Toronto's city council is prepared to do for the CPR (a corporation well-known for its penury) and the CNR. When the railways announced that they wanted to build a project called Metro Centre on land just to the south of the existing downtown now used for rail tracks and the Union Station building, the city politicians and officials rushed to sell the railways a parcel of city-owned land crucial to the whole development. Using city officials' own figures on the values of the land parcels involved in the deal, Toronto alderman John Sewell has estimated that the city was selling its land to the railways for at least *$42 million less than it was worth.*

Countless examples from every Canadian city testify to the power of the interests involved in land development and construction, to their ability to get their way with politicians, and to the immense profits that are regularly made in the business. Usually attention gets focussed on the developers involved in these projects. In recent years people have learned from hard experience about the political power of developers, and of the ruthless tactics they regularly use in going about their business. They are in many ways the central figures in this part of the property industry, but their power is a direct reflection of the power, wealth and importance of the property industry as a whole.

Developers

Developers are the people who put together projects for new buildings which make money for everyone involved. The importance of the developers stems from the way they put together all the elements necessary to get a new building constructed. A developer operates in the property market by looking for a market for a particular kind of accommodation that isn't being met by existing buildings. In most Canadian cities, for instance, there is a continuous demand for more housing accommodation. In some cities there is a strong demand for high-cost downtown office space, and this is reflected by relatively low vacancy rates in these buildings once they are built and perhaps by rent levels which are rising more quickly than increases in costs appear to warrant.

A developer looks for land that he can buy at a price that will enable him to put up a building that will make money, and where he can get the necessary zonings and approvals from city hall that will keep the project profitable.

He then has to put together all the necessary elements of the project: land, a suitable building design, professional services like those of architects, engineers, surveyors and so on, a construction firm, the necessary short-term funds to get the project going, a long-term mortgage to pay off the contractor, and the city hall permissions and approvals necessary for the building to be built.

What is required to be a developer is the ability to get these various elements together. There is no need for the developer himself to have any money, or to put up his own money if he has any, and many relatively small-time local land developers work on this basis. He may be able to get his land simply by signing up the owners for an option to buy their land at a later date for a specified price. If he can't get these options for nothing, he probably won't have to pay much for them. Usually he can get real estate agents to work for him for nothing, assembling the properties on the gamble that the project will go ahead, at which time the agents will get their commissions on the sale. He can probably find architects and engineers to work on the same basis. And, though it is against the official rules of the legal profession, he can probably also get free or almost-free legal services from a lawyer who gambles that the project will come off, in which case he will be well-paid for his work.

There are no rules about how a developer goes about putting the elements of his project together. If he has to harass or intimidate property owners in order to get them to agree to sell, he will probably do it if he can get away with it. There are lots of documented examples of the vicious blockbusting techniques developers have used in assembling properties in residential areas. In fact there seem to be some developers in every city who specialize in taking on difficult projects and using a wide range of tactics including lying, confidence tricks, harassment, physical violence, arson and intimidation. No holds are barred, and these methods seem to be taken for granted in the business.

Continued on page 44

The developers 1

Two Canadian developers, as described by newspaper reporters. The articles illustrate the entrepreneurial function of a developer who puts together land, money, architecture and political skills at city hall to create a development.

Developer makes it big in Calgary now he eyes tough Toronto market

By MACK PARLIAMENT

Although the Toronto area's developers outnumber its innumerable parking lots, there are not too many to discourage outsiders from trying their hand at making fortunes, despite the competition.

Latest to invade Toronto is Paragon Properties Ltd., which made it big in Calgary and is flush with funds and ideas to repeat its western success story here.

The company has established branches in Toronto and Montreal in rapid succession. Its first Ontario contract, from the Ontario Housing Corporation, is for senior citizens' apartments in Thunder Bay.

Headed by lawyer-turned-developer Charles C. Smith, 42, the company has erected more than 100 buildings with a value exceeding $50 million in British Columbia, Alberta and Manitoba since formation in 1963.

Smith, who intends to have dual Toronto-Calgary residence, is already investigating a few multi-million-dollar projects here, including a 220-suite apartment building, a shopping centre and more Ontario Housing contracts.

He is also pursuing mobile home park opportunities in Ontario and Quebec and intends to break new ground in the field with a Calgary pilot project. It would combine a mobile home park with the condominium concept, making it easier for balky municipal councils to accept mobile home projects.

Paragon is now a public company, but the pair own 80 per cent of the 947,000 outstanding shares. "We went public at the proper time, so if we needed money we could get it. We didn't want to part with any more of the company than we had to," Smith says.

Smith, a grocer's son, doesn't believe in reticence. "I'm a visionary," he declares.

His aims are "to cover the total housing market spectrum and expand involvement into any area of real estate which is economically viable."

Last year Paragon was involved in construction of 1,265 apartment units. Flagship of its projects is the 600-suite twin-towered Place Concorde in downtown Calgary, which is being sold.

"There is no room in a publicly-owned company for sentimental attachment to bricks and mortar," Smith asserts. The firm retains ownership of only a few of its projects.

He is not claiming to bring anything new to Toronto. "This area is not going to stop growing and there is room for more real estate entrepreneurs — of which there are a very few good ones. What is needed is a rare quality and I think we have it."

Toronto Star 8 Mar. 1972

Campeau plans consolidation, 4 major jobs

By TERRENCE BELFORD

Campeau Corp. Ltd. of Ottawa has a new president, but that doesn't mean Robert Campeau, founder of the giant development company, is about to retire.

That's what Jean Paradis, the man who has succeeded Mr. Campeau in the presidency, says in response to questions on the subject. Mr. Campeau remains as chairman and chief executive officer.

"Bob had been away ill for the best part of a year and came back to us just about a year ago. He's fully recovered now and in good shape but he doesn't want to remain for the last 15 years of his business career chained to a desk from 8 to 5," Mr. Paradis said in an interview.

"My role will be that of chief operating officer. He will be looking more to long-range planning. I, of course, will always be involved in long-range planning but if the earnings are down at the end of 1972, then the buck stops here."

The role isn't really new to Mr. Paradis. It has been accepted by the industry for almost 20 years that Mr. Campeau and Mr. Paradis are the two halves of the force that has made Campeau Corp. click as a builder.

Anchor man

Mr. Campeau has been the promoter. He has the flamboyance and natural flair, plus the dream. Mr. Paradis has been the anchor, providing the detail, the financial expertise and the management base.

"I started with Campeau way back in 1954 after having been with Central Mortgage and Housing Corp. for about eight years," Mr. Paradis said.

"I had been transferred back to Ottawa as the Ottawa branch manager in the late Forties and that's when I met Bob Campeau.

"He approached me to come with him and his brother and brother-in-law who were at that time really the company. I moved back to Montreal as supervisor of the Quebec region in 1953 and he kept on suggesting I join him. I finally agreed in the summer of 1954.

"At that time it was Campeau Construction Co. Ltd. and had a contributed surplus value of about $250,000. I came in as a director, general manager and company secretary."

Surplus value

What Mr. Paradis brought Campeau was a knowledge of mortgages—how to get the most out of the National Housing Act and CMHC, says a friend of both men: "Jean was fantastic with mortgages, especially the NHA ones. After eight years with CMHC he knew all the ins and outs of the system. Bob probably would have made it big eventually, but with Jean getting the money for him that made everything a lot easier."

Mr. Paradis notes that the serviced land situation can change drastically, depending on the whim of the local municipal council, which must approve any registered plan of subdivision.

He expects one such plan to be approved this spring, and when it is, Campeau's serviced land inventory will almost double.

Globe and Mail 23 May 1972

The developers 2

This article is a report on a two-day seminar for people in the specialized branches of the land development business who wanted to learn more about the techniques of development. Conference participants, who paid $150 each, were mainly architects, planners, engineers, and civil servants.

This report on what seminar speakers said gives another view of how the land development business works.

Newspaper reporters were to be excluded from the seminar, so I enrolled as a university professor. By a slip-up, the hired organizers did invite the press and there were some short news reports on what happened. I was spotted sitting in the audience early the first day, and speakers from Toronto city hall did some fast revisions to the speeches they had intended to give. But real estate agent and developer Gordon Gray, the most interesting participant, didn't seem to pull any punches in his account of how you go about a major development project.

The Gothic Avenue house shown in the photo is part of a land assembly carried out in Toronto by Cadillac and Greenwin. It is scheduled for demolition to make way for Toronto's controversial Quebec-Gothic redevelopment project.

People who object to the activities of developers in Toronto often complain about tactics some developers use: block-busting, intimidation, lying, dummy companies established to disguise their real intentions.

In the last big battle at Toronto's buildings and development committee over the Quebec-Gothic area, for example, one woman complained she had been duped by a real estate agent who persuaded her to sell at much too low a price by telling her the land was to be used for triplexes. As a result, she said, she had agreed to a price that proved to be only half the average paid in the land assembly and only one-third of the price per square foot received by Mrs. Ben Grys, wife of the Toronto alderman, for two houses in the area she sold to developers.

It is one thing for local organizations to complain, after the fact, about the tactics of a developer. It is another to encounter people in the land development business specifically recommending these techniques to colleagues.

That was one of the interesting aspects of the Development 72 seminar sponsored by the Canadian Institute of Quantity Surveyors and the University of Waterloo. Speakers described in detail the logic to a developer of many of the tactics people complain about. Taken for granted was the fact that these are the tactics most land developers use.

The most interesting panelist was Gordon Gray. According to the 1971 Directory of Directors, Mr. Gray is president of a number of land development companies and a director of many others, including Markborough Properties Ltd., one of the firms which holds large tracts of vacant land suitable for development outside Toronto. He was responsible for assembling the seven-acre downtown site for the Toronto-Dominion Centre and was involved in the Eaton Centre project.

Mr. Gray described how to go about assembling land for redevelopment in Toronto. He was, as he said himself, "reasonably frank."

One crucial point about successful land assembly, he said, is that it must be kept secret. "In the Toronto-Dominion Centre project you couldn't walk up and say, "I'm Gordon Gray and I'm representing a billion-dollar corporation.' If we'd done this there would have been no T-D Centre. The situation usually is that we have a willing buyer and an unwilling, even reluctant, seller."

He complained that developers in Ontario cannot rely on help from government expropriation powers, even to complete the last 5 per cent or 10 per cent of an assembly. "In Ontario, you can spend millions of dollars, acquire 99 per cent of the land you want and be completely frustrated. So embarkation on a land assembly is a rather gutsy move."

Illustrating difficulties land assemblers often face, Mr. Gray mentioned the assembly for the Erin Mills and Meadowvale new towns outside Metro which are only now beginning to be developed. "We assembled 13,000 acres of farmland in 1954 and 1955, mostly from farmers whose father's father's father had bought the land from the Indians," he said. Mr. Gray described how one holdout had been dealt with by Brian McGee, now chairman of the board of A. E. LePage Ltd. and president of Markborough Properties. "Mr. McGee went out with a suitcase full of money." He then counted out the several hundred thousand dollar purchase price the farmer was being offered for his land, in $10 bills. "The farmer still wouldn't sell," said Mr. Gray. "I consider this a real emotional problem." Later he said it was not unusual to take unwilling vendors suitcases of money in hopes of persuading them to sell.

Before embarking on an assembly, said Mr. Gray, considerable preliminary work is required. Along with normal information about services, zoning and past attempts at assembly, he recommended obtaining details on the owners' original purchases of their holdings.

He also suggested investigating each owner's financial circumstances. Asked where he would go for this information and exactly what he was looking for, Mr. Gray said banks and credit agents. "Generally in the real estate business," he added, "you get leads on where to find out about people.

"You should also know which owners know each other." This makes it easier to estimate what each vendor will know about prices offered other property owners.

Generally you don't expect to encounter any difficulty in land assembly in dealing with international corporations or large firms. They don't see themselves obstructing progress, said Mr. Gray. It is small businesses and individuals that are likely to give you trouble. Family-run restaurants are a special difficulty because so much of their business depends on the goodwill and clientele they build up.

Once you embark on a land assembly, you try to wrap it up as quickly as possible. This prevents people from discovering too much about what is going on and holding out

for h gh prices.

How much you pay depends on what a study of the project shows you can afford. "We used to say that for every square foot of office space in downtown Toronto you could afford to pay $6 for land."

But land prices have risen well above this ceiling. "We are now paying as much as $25 for every net square foot of office. That is four times as much as our rule of thumb from only 10 years ago."

One major problem in an assembly is dividing the total you can pay among various owners and parcels. "Once you overpay for one parcel, you may be stuck for the rest of the assembly." To avoid this you generally keep holdouts to the end. "In spite of trying to keep the project quiet, word of it is bound to get out."

Depending on your project and your resources, you either buy properties outright or get an option. Usually options cost 2 per cent to 5 per cent of the purchase price on the option. Mr. Gray warned that it is essential to provide for several extensions in an option.

One difficulty in information about prices leaking out is that owners start demanding the highest going price for every piece of land in the assembly. Things get awkward when the developer has to buy a piece of land and register the sale. On registration, an affidavit is required setting out the price paid. "It is becoming increasingly difficult to suppress on registration the prices that have been paid." Once a sale is registered, it is possible for anyone to discover the price involved. "This means you must try to proceed very quickly indeed."

Mr. Gray warned of the implications of including public lands, such as a city lane, in a redevelopment project.

He noted that sometimes real estate agents get involved in speculative land assembly projects, where they earn their commission only if the whole project goes through. He talked about one unsuccessful assembly in west Toronto where his firm got control of about 275 of 325 properties, and then got nothing because the project fell through. "We wouldn't undertake it unless it looked promising," he said. "If it's successful we're well paid. We tend to be gutsy."

Asked when public participation should come in to a redevelopment project, Mr. Gray said it would be his recommendation to reveal intentions to the mayor and executive committee of the city after the assembly was underway but before it was complete. "The city inevitably becomes involved in the project, and informing them is fair ball. Also it helps you determine high level political attitudes to your project."

Mr. Gray indicated the city would usually be informed when the land assembly was complete except for holdouts.

One condition often laid down by companies selling commercial buildings is that the buildings be demolished immediately rather than be occupied and used.

This demand stems from the tax advantage which it confers on the seller, because he may claim the purchase price of the property was solely for the land and that his building was worthless. When a building has been depreciated by its owner for tax purposes to a very low value, this ploy prevents him from having to pay back taxes on recaptured depreciation.

"This situation comes up 75 per cent to 85 per cent of the time in commercial assemblies. You should not object to alloting the money you pay for a property to the land and not the building. But the view that the tax authorities take on the transaction will depend on what actually happens after the sale. If five years later the building is still there, then you can't argue you sold only the land. Often a corporate vendor will want to demolish its building itself, before or after the closing."

'Cruel' but 20 houses must go

By IAN URQUHART
Star staff writer

The Meridian Group will go ahead this summer with evictions in 20 houses south of the St. James Town apartments despite community objections, Meridian executive vice-president Phil Roth said yesterday.

"It may sound cruel, but those houses are coming down," Roth told about 70 residents at a meeting of a committee set up to sort out the future of the South of St. James Town area.

SEWELL MOTION

The committee, which includes representatives of eight neighborhood groups in the area bounded by Carlton, Sherbourne, Parliament, and Wellesley Sts., was asked by Alderman John Sewell to approve a motion calling on Meridian to delay evictions and demolition until it is ready to build new apartments.

Meridian, which owns about half of the 400 houses in the area and plans to build high-rise apartments on the land, is waiting for completion of a study of the area by city planners before undertaking development.

But Roth told the committee it did not matter what motion it approved because Meridian will evict its tenants and tear down its houses when it pleases.

Toronto Star 11 June 1972

Unfriendly five visit holdout, Jaffary says

The holdout roomer of 123 Bleecker St., who claims he is "guarding the house to prevent others from wrecking it" needed some protection himself yesterday.

Five unidentified people arrived uninvited while David Starbuck and four friends were watching the Grey Cup game on television.

The results, according to Alderman Karl Jaffary, provided evidence that more than words were exhcanged.

"The telephone had been torn out. The TV set was thrown out and there was evidence of a good fight inside. But from all accounts the serious stuff was outside," he said.

Globe and Mail Dec. 1971

The dirty business of land assembly

These articles all refer to events in Toronto's South of St. Jamestown area. The Meridian Group, developer of the enormous St. Jamestown apartment complex just to the north, has assembled parts of the area and is attempting to demolish the houses and to get permission from city hall to build more high-rise buildings.

Meridian is being opposed by a small but tenacious group of tenants who have been involved in this battle since 1970.

In late 1971, Meridian was trying to evict tenants in houses it owned or to persuade them to leave in order to demolish them. No city regulations prohibit a property owner from demolishing a house he owns, even if he has no development plans approved for the site. As a result, demolition becomes a very effective weapon in the hands of developers who want to ensure that an existing neighbourhood is redeveloped, overriding any objections from residents or neighbours.

One of Meridian's tactics in late 1971 was to offer tenants cash gifts ranging up to $1500 if they agreed to move out and give possession of their house to Meridian. For many of the tenants who had very low incomes, this offer was hard to refuse.

When one South St. Jamestown family, the Watsons, decided to leave their home, they did not succeed in evicting the roomer who had been living with them. The roomer, David Starbuck, was temporarily locked out of the Watson house but managed to find his way back in again.

Because Starbuck has not been successfully thrown out, Meridian did not pay the Watsons their promised cash.

The upshot of this was that, several days after the Watsons left, Starbuck was beaten up. He had been watching the Grey Cup game on TV when some men came looking for him.

Six months later, Meridian had succeeded in tearing down several houses in the area but was still being resisted by South of St. Jamestown tenants. More important, area homeowners who had previously supported Meridian's plans were changing their minds. Apparently they recognized that Meridian's land assembly tactics were not going to give them the windfall profits they were expecting when they sold their houses.

In mid-1972 Meridian was using the same approach to the tenants, warning them again that they would be evicted so that the houses they were living in could be demolished.

Meridian director and front man Phil Roth, watching Toronto city council from the gallery.

All these houses are located in Toronto's South of St. Jamestown ares where Meridian, the developer of the massive St. Jamestown high-rise development, wants to put up more high-rise apartments.

Meridian owns most of the houses in the largest block in the area. Faced with opposition sparked by an organization of tenants living in houses it owns, Meridian has tried to make high-rise development inevitable by demolishing its houses. This policy has two added advantages: first, it reduces the number of tenants living in the area, and hence the number of people who oppose Meridian; and second, it frightens remaining area home owners and helps force them to sell out to Meridian.

Virtually all the houses in the area were in good basic condition before Meridian moved in. Many still are, but they are rapidly being demolished. As this happens, the chances are reduced of implementing some alternative plan for the area — like simply renovating the existing houses, or combining renovation with new construction of housing on a new street opened up through the very deep back yards of the existing houses.

The important thing to remember about developers is that they themselves often have very little independent power or wealth. Their ability to operate depends completely on their success at lining up other people's services and capital. A developer who couldn't persuade anyone to lend him mortgage money couldn't continue to operate. A developer whose projects were so controversial that no insurance company and no construction company were willing to work with him would have to give up and leave town.

People often graduate into the developer business from one branch or another of the property industry. They often are former real estate agents, former real estate lawyers, former construction engineers, or former contractors. All they are really is operators. They depend completely on the other elements of the property industry, and nowhere is their dependence more complete than in their reliance on the tremendously respectable and (it is said) public relations-conscious financing firms, chartered banks, trust companies, and life insurance companies.

Real estate corporations

The land development business has, however, been changing rapidly in the last several years. Many developers have transformed themselves from fly-by-night, shady operators into more respectable operations. They have formalized and systematized their links to the crucial elements within the property industry that are required to carry out a development project. They have sold shares in their companies to wealthy families and corporations, and have boards of directors reflecting these connections. Robert Campeau, at first a local Ottawa developer, made his Campeau Corporation a public company and for a time it was controlled by the extremely powerful Power Corporation controlled by Paul Desmarais and Jean Parisien.

At the same time, some wealthy families and corporations have set up important development companies, which are responsible for a large share of all new construction. The Bronfmans set up Cemp and Fairview, major operators across Canada in the development business. The Eatons are involved in a number of specific development projects like Vancouver's Pacific Centre. British-based insurance companies also got into the business; the Eagle Star group, for instance, owns 61 per cent of Trizec, Canada's largest development corporation.

Tracing the links and alliances of small-time local developers to other parts of the property industry is often difficult because little information about their operations is publicly available. With larger private real estate companies and with all the public companies, the job is much easier. A lot of information can be pieced together from lists of directors, information on file with the provincial securities commission where the head office of the company is located, financial newspaper items, company prospectuses, and details published in trade organs like the magazine *Building and Development*. Overall, the industry is quickly becoming much more centralized and integrated, with a few large groups taking up a dominant position. This integration and concentration in the industry is a result of extremely powerful financial institutions like banks and life insurance companies as well as wealthy families taking over control of an industry where large profits can be made and where their capital is essential.

As this happens, the importance and function of development firms is changing. A small-time local developer may have had very little power or wealth of his own, but it is quite a different story with development companies like Trizec or Fairview, which are subsidiaries of extremely powerful corporations and which have all the power and weight of their corporate owners. When you tangle with Marathon Realty (the CPR's land development subsidiary) or Cadillac Property Management (affiliated with the Acres group, which includes Guaranty Trust and Traders Group), you are taking on a very powerful opponent. When you challenge the power of development firms like this to do what they want with Canada's cities, you come face to face with the enormous power of some of the biggest corporations in the country.

Financing

As this change in the structure of the business proceeds, the way that developers operate is changing. By far the most important consequence of a development firm's being owned partly or completely by sprawling holding companies like the Power Corporation or the Acres group or by a wealthy insurance company like the Eagle Star group is that the links of access to capital, land and the other elements required for development are formalized and rendered secure. Trizec can be certain of a supply of necessary capital for profitable projects from the Eagle Star group. Cadillac can presumably count on access to the funds of Guaranty Trust and the Traders group.

As the projects of these developers as well as those of small-time developers are completed, firms which started off as entrepreneurial groups putting other people's land and money together begin to become major property owners in their own right, because often they retain title to the buildings they develop. In the residential field, this is a remarkable change from the situation 20 years ago, when most new housing was sold to individual purchasers. Now firms that build new housing, particularly high-rise apartment housing, keep title to the property themselves. Instead of letting people buy housing for themselves, the developers have their tenants paying off the mortgage through their rents, and so buying the building for the developer.

The financial arrangements in the property industry are such that rents in a new building are kept up to the level needed to cover all maintenance costs for the building, all taxes, and all the payments on the building's mortgage. The developer manages the building, but his expenses for doing so are covered. As well, he can expect to earn an immediate cash return of perhaps 12 per cent of the little bit of money he may have raised himself to put into the building. At first his stake in the building is worth almost nothing; he owes almost as much on his mortgages as the building cost. But gradually over the years the value of his equity increases as his tenants pay off his mortgage. And there is an additional increase in the value of his equity because he is able to push rents up faster than maintenance costs increase, so that the building becomes worth more and more money. At the end of the mortgage period, perhaps 20 or 25 years later, he owns the building outright, and it is probably worth much more than it cost to build originally. The developer wins three ways: by the increase in value of the land and building, by the continuously increasing rents he is able to charge and get away with, and by having his tenants pay for

Blockbusting

1. Developer selects an area for development, perhaps 10 years before he expects to develop it.

2. Developer begins purchasing property as it becomes available, through the use of a real estate agent. First purchases are made usually by cash.

3. Developer tries to consolidate a few holdings by picking up bits of blocks here and there: usually this happens because one person will own two or three properties, and wants to sell as a unit.

4. Developer has these houses taken over by a manager who selects tenants and is responsible for repairs. In many cases the manager is not directly employed by the developer. The manager selects tenants who are easy to control, who do not ask that repairs be made. These people are often roomers, or people on welfare who are used to getting kicked around. Units are usually rented as furnished.

5. These properties begin to deteriorate, as few or no repairs are made. Tenants, of course, when they see that this landlord is no different than the others they know (that is, repairs aren't made, the landlord can never be reached, appears only to collect rent), begin to actively destroy the house.

6. Homeowners see the area deteriorating. The real estate agent begins to call on people unasked, and begins to get people to sign options, or alternatively, buys and gives a mortgage back to vendor, so that the cash outlay is minimal. Owners move out, and the developer turns the property over to the manager for deterioration.

7. As the process of deterioration continues, fire insurance companies begin to get worried about the area. Fires start occurring as tenants cause fires, both because of alcohol and carelessness, and because the condition of the house itself makes it prone to fires. Fire insurance policies aren't renewed.

8. As owners find they can't get insurance, that the area is deteriorating, and that the developer seems to be offering a lot of money (it seems like a lot of money because most owners haven't been trying to buy a house for 15 or 20 years) they sell.

9. As the developer begins to pick up a majority of properties, he finds he has to change his tactics. Prices get higher, as he picks up key properties. The developer rips down a few houses to scare people. Real estate agents begin to tell people that if they don't sell, then the developer will build around them.

10. By this time, people who have recently bought in the area for speculative purposes become apparent. It becomes clear that they too have been part of the process of deterioration of the neighbourhood. The developer then must bargain with them, and *they* get a lot of money for their properties.

(John Sewell provided this list: thanks.)

Pollution Probe, *Rules of the Game*. Toronto: 1972, p.39

his building.

The result of this situation is that the ownership of urban property in Canada is being concentrated more and more into the hands of a few large property owners — and it is all happening by financial manipulation, *with the new property owners actually having to put up almost no money of their own*. The key to the system, however, is continued control of the accommodation market so as to keep rent levels high enough to cover all the costs of maintaining and running the building and to cover both interest and principal payments on the mortgage. Should rent levels fall below this level, the developer-owner would have to contribute some cash out of his own pocket to buy his building, and that change — however fair it might appear to be — would spell an end to this incredible situation where the tenants of high-rise office buildings and apartments are providing all the money necessary to allow developers to buy up and eventually own outright large portions — perhaps the largest portions — of our cities.

In constructing new buildings, the developer or the development corporation is right at the centre of the process, bringing together the various necessary parts of the property industry that have to be combined in a construction project. The image of the developer as an entrepreneur, an adventurer, a creative operator making millions out of nothing, suggests that he does all this by skill, by persuasion, almost by sleight of hand. Accounts of the land development business in other countries (we have no boasting autobiographies or respectful biographies of our own recent land developers in Canada) make a lot of this image of the developer as creator. More and more important in the development business, however, are the development corporations, where the entrepreneurs and operators are hired hands, employees of the representatives of big money like Manufacturers' Life, Eaton's, the Power Corporation or the Bronfmans. They operate at the centre of a corporate structure that incorporates sources of mortgage money, short-term financing, real estate services, construction companies, and construction supplies and materials firms.

Construction

The construction industry performs a job distinct from the development business. It organizes labour and materials and builds buildings from the architects' and engineers' plans. As an industry, construction is a very big operation indeed. Production in the industry in 1971 was $14 billion, about 20 per cent of the total value of all goods and services produced that year in Canada. The industry's profits are correspondingly large. BACM Industries, a Winnipeg-based construction firm, declared profits of $3.5 million after taxes on sales of $99 million in 1970. Construction is also an important source of jobs; 575,000 men were employed by the industry in 1970.

Though there are very good statistics on the construction industry as a whole, there is very little information available on the big firms in the industry. A morning of fruitless telephone calls to industry organizations and trade magazines failed to yield even the simplest information such as a list of the top 10 or 20 firms in the industry. There are some very large construction firms in Canada, but the industry is still characterized by a huge number of firms of all sizes, from tiny operations producing two or three houses a year to enormous international firms doing commercial, residential and industrial buildings across the country and in other parts of the world. Construction is also a chancier business than many others. New firms are always coming onto the scene; small firms grow quickly; large firms diminish in size; and some firms including large ones collapse and go bankrupt.

In spite of its complicated and diverse structure, though, the construction industry is very well organized indeed. Every city has its local construction association; every province has a provincial association; and at the national level there is the Canadian Construction Association. These organizations are obviously very important as organized lobbies working to promote the industry's interests, but they have other important functions as well. They co-ordinate information about the local market; they often organize bidding for jobs; they pressure government at all levels; and they provide employers with a mechanism for bargaining as a group with construction unions.

The industry has a whole network of subdivisions. As well as general contractors, there are sub-contractors in every specialized field of construction. Each of the trades in the industry is organized separately, and even taken on their own they are important industries.

There is no sharp line dividing the construction industry from the rest of the property industry; quite the contrary. Most developers have close ties to specific construction firms, often because the people owning the development company own the construction company as well. One of the obvious reasons for this is that developers are the customers of construction companies, and if a developer is providing $100 million in business every year for construction companies, clearly it is to his advantage to own the construction companies he uses and to make the $10 million profit on that $100 million in construction as well as the profits he makes as a developer. Often the ties are open and boasted about. Says S. B. McLaughlin Associates Ltd., a firm that owns 4,000 acres of land in the Mississauga area, which is rapidly being built up as a suburb of Toronto: "We at McLaughlin are proud of the people of our various Divisions — Construction, Land, Residential, Industrial, Commercial and Sales. People engaged not only in the construction of the heart of Ontario's New City of Mississauga, but to be found throughout southern Ontario at work with McLaughlin projects. . . ." This integration is boasted about because it is a source of greater strength to the company, a way of increasing the profits they are making in the property business, and a means of increasing their control and power as a corporation.

Building materials

Another section of the building industry is the construction supplies and materials business. This includes the whole range of lumber companies, cement companies, steel companies, manufacturers of plumbing, heating and electrical supplies, etc.; a comprehensive list would by very long. Many corporations in this business are in other businesses too; the Steel Company of Canada, for instance, sells a substantial portion of its output to the building industry, but it is also very heavily involved in other businesses, like equipment manufacturing and the auto industry.

As for the construction industry, there are many formalized links between construction supplies companies and the rest of the property industry. Often construction companies own at least some of their suppliers. Contractors and developers in Toronto, for instance, own many of the local ready-mix concrete companies. Corporations in the supplies and materials business are often subsidiaries of large corporations like the Power Corporation which also own real estate and development companies. At a minimum, links such as common directors exist between many of these suppliers, construction firms, and development firms.

Architects, engineers and others

Servicing the building industry is a range of middle-class professionals whose specialized skills are used in this field. Many of the professionals like lawyers, real estate agents and insurance agents who service the property-owning business also service the building industry, but the building industry has an additional group of professionals it uses. Most important of these are architects and engineers.

Architects do not have their hand in all new construction; far from it. Small construction projects are usually handled without their services, and standardized large projects often are too. The high-rise apartment business, for instance, now seems to be so automatic in cities like Vancouver, Montreal and Toronto that you can buy plans off the shelf just like you can buy cheap plans off the shelf for a hundred different models of suburban bungalows. The most that is required is a draftsman who can make a convincing sketch of "your" off-the-shelf building on the site for which zoning and planning permission is required. Larger projects, more complicated ones, or one-of-a-kind buildings are the ones which involve architects. Their fees for the work are supposed to be reckoned not on the amount of work they do, but on a percentage of the final construction cost of the project. Obviously that creates a professional vested interest in large projects, and to a certain extent at least in expensive building. Architects can do more than just design new buildings; they can, for instance, plan renovations and rehabilitation of existing buildings. There is a certain amount of work of this kind carried out by the profession in Canada, but most of its money-making

Collusion charged in cement bidding

Identical bids from two cement suppliers drew accusations of collusion from Inner City councillors Tuesday, who decided to report the matter to the federal combines commission and award the contract based on the alphabetical order of the bidders.

The identical tenders came before the Inner City subcommittee on improvements, and drew criticism from Councillors Alan Wade (NDP — Weston), Joseph Zuken (LEC — Cathedral), Robert Taft (ICEC — Riverview) and Roy Parkhill (ICEC — Tuxedo Heights).

The subcommittee is recommending the contract be given to Canada Cement La Farge Ltd., alphabetically ahead of Inland Cement Industries Ltd.

Coun. Zuken said identical tenders have been submitted year after year, although the companies have a different number of employees, different machinery and different ways of doing business. The companies thought the business would be evenly split between them, Coun. Zuken explained.

"I have done everything to get them to sue me, because then I could get to look at their books," Coun. Zuken said.

Coun. Zuken also said union officials had approached him, saying jobs would be lost if both companies did not get the business. "I'm all for unions, but I'm not for the unions supporting collusion," Coun. Zuken retorted.

Winnipeg Tribune 8 Mar. 1972

This ad says a lot about the roles of architects in housing design. It suggests that people think architecture amounts to even fancier than usual dressing-up of ordinary buildings (look at the house with its crazy Mansard-style roof). It suggests that when architects get involved buildings are usually expensive. And it implies that architects usually have nothing to do with ordinary suburban house design for average-income families.

Ready-mix firms fined $245,000

Twelve firms that admitted conspiring to prevent or lessen unduly competition in the production, manufacture, sale or supply of ready-mixed concrete between 1961 and 1968 were fined a total of $245,000 by Mr. Justice John Osler yesterday.

In total, the fine is the largest so far imposed in Ontario for breach of the Combines Investigation Act—considering the number of firms involved and the fact that all are first offenders. Heavier fines have been imposed in the past on other corporations, but they involved companies that operate in more than one province or across Canada.

Mr. Justice Osler said the fines must be paid on or before May 30. He also issued an order prohibiting the companies from repeating the offence.

All the firms operated in the Metro Toronto area or elsewhere in the judicial district of York.

The heaviest fines—$35,000 each—were imposed upon St. Marys Cement Co., Dufferin Materials and Construction Ltd., and S P & M Materials Ltd.

Two firms, Lake Ontario Cement Ltd. and Richvale Ready Mix Ltd., were fined $30,000 each, and Kilmer Van Nostrand Co. Ltd. $20,000.

King Paving and Materials Ltd. and Teskey Ready Mix Ltd. were fined $15,000 each. Four firms, A B C Ready-Mix Ltd., Custom Concrete Ltd., General Concrete Ltd. and McCowan Mobile Mix Co. Ltd., were fined $7,500 each

Mr. Justice Osler said the offences were committed over

7½ years, and that not all the firms were in existence for that time or had participated in the combination for the whole period.

Representatives of the offending firms met often and discussed prices, Mr. Justice Osler said. All followed the lead of Dufferin Materials and Construction Ltd., which published new price lists, and the meetings decided on discounts to be allowed buyers.

Mr. Justice Osler said he agreed in the main with Crown counsel Patrick Duffy's submissions on the fines he might consider imposing.

Robert Loudon, counsel for Kilmer Van Nostrand, had argued that a large part of its orders went to so-called "locked-in" customers, and that the proportion it supplied to the open market was relatively small.

Mr. Justice Osler recalled the testimony of Kilmer's president, Max Tanenbaum; that much of the firm's output of ready-mixed concrete went to related corporations or to companies owned by him or his family and other affiliates.

Kilmer Van Nostrand did not enter the ready-mixed concrete business until 1965, Mr. Justice Osler said. He said the firms had co-operated with investigators, and that the results of the conspiracy did not involve undue increases in the prices charged.

Globe and Mail 22 Apr. 1972
Reprinted with permission

work is straight new construction.

Engineers have a somewhat broader range than architects. They do work for new urban construction, of course, but a civil engineering background also allows them to work on highways, pipelines and a whole range of jobs not in the urban building field. As well as new building, engineers do a lot of work designing the basic services required for urban land use: roads, sewers, subways, airports, etc.

As in the case of the property owning business, there are many other smaller professions that also service the building industry. Amongst these are land surveyors, quantity surveyors, and construction management consultants. They all live off the industry either completely or in part, and of course that creates a basic set of common interests which they share with the rest of the industry.

Construction unions

One final part of the building industry which should be noted is in some respects completely different from all the others. This is the construction unions, the organized segment of the very large labour force employed by the building industry. Of course there is a fundamental conflict of interest between workers in construction and their employers. Workers have an interest in being paid what their labour is worth, in steady and secure employment rather than uncertain jobs with the constant threat of unemployment and a drastic drop in income, and in safe working conditions even though safety costs money. These interests conflict to some extent with those of employers, who want to pay as little as possible for their labour in order to maximize their profits; although in the construction industry, where contractors often simply add 10 per cent onto their costs in bidding for work, higher industry-wide costs like higher union wages actually serve to increase the size of this 10 per cent bite. Construction workers have other interests as well, though these have not yet been clearly defined and articulated by workers and their unions. Obviously they have an interest in seeing that their work creates buildings that are genuinely useful to themselves and people like themselves rather than to the corporate owners. They have an interest in building decent, cheap housing for workers rather than in substandard, inadequate housing for the majority and luxurious, extravagant housing for the few.

Some of the immediate interests of construction workers are clearly opposed to those of the construction industry. Their long-term interests in many ways conflict with the economic system that puts them to work building high-rise apartments for low-income, working-class, public-housing tenants and lavish Holiday Inns for American businessmen and their Canadian shadows. To the extent that the organizations of construction workers reflect the true interests of their members, therefore, there are many points where these groups are at odds with employers.

But on some points the immediate interests of construction workers coincide with those of the construction industry. The industry's interest in the largest possible volume of business, for instance, coincides with the workers' interest in being employed rather than unemployed, and having steady work rather than occasional jobs. Measures that threaten the status quo in the construction industry, and in particular that propose a reduction in the amount of new building and development, threaten the interests of con-

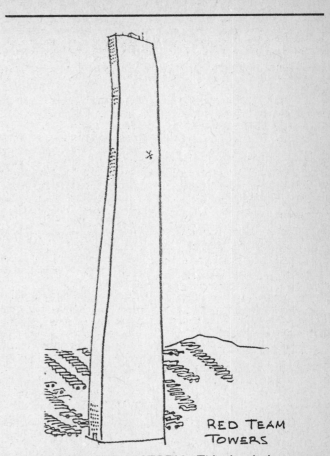

RED TEAM
TOWERS

105 STOREYS FOR VICTORIA: This sketch shows a proposal for the redevelopment of downtown Victoria made by a team of architects headed by Joe Baker at the annual convention of Canadian architects in 1972.

The Baker scheme is for a 105-storey building, large enough to hold everyone living in Victoria. The team proposed that the rest of the city be razed, and that everyone be accommodated in their tower. People of Anglo-Saxon origin were to live on one side; ethnics would live on the other side.

Baker's scheme was too close to the actual practices of Canadian architects for their comfort.

struction workers as well.

It is also crucial to remember that construction unions, like many other organizations, are a long way from expressing accurately and completely the real interests of their members, or from helping their members come to a more complete understanding of their situation and of their interests. Most unions have a highly centralized organization, with power firmly concentrated at the top and entrenched there. Individual union members have very little control over the actions of union bureaucrats. In these circumstances, it is very easy for union leaders to cosy up to the construction industry and to begin to think that what is good for the construction industry is much the same as what is good for construction workers.

In many cities the situation is even worse than that.

Stop Everything protestors hurting employment: union

By ALDEN BAKER

Minority groups in the community were blamed by representatives of organized labor yesterday for a Stop Everything m o v e m e n t in Metro Toronto and setting the stage for an ugly winter of unemployment.

The Laborers' International Union of North America, Local 183, in a brief to an unemployment conference at the King Edward Sheraton Hotel declared that a small but vocal and well-organized group, operating with a high degree of success since killing the Spadina Expressway, have elected representatives afraid to approve the building of even a bird's nest.

The Stop Spadina Movement, said the union, has turned into a Stop Everything Movement. The result is that politicians are fearful of some new citizen groups springing up like mushrooms under the name "People Power."

The union, representing laborers in the building construction industry, recalled that "this so-called People Power" is quoted often in "a little book widely distributed in Oriental countries." The reference was to a book by Chinese leader Mao Tse-tung.

Representatives of the Ontario Federation of Labor, Canadian Union of Public Employees, Metro Toronto Apartment Builders Association and Buildings Trade Council were reluctant to endorse Local 183's proposal that the province appoint H. Carl Goldenberg as a one-man royal commission to review the need for expressways, subways, highrise apartments and to determine the type of residential development s u i t a b l e for Metro Toronto.

"You can't be serious," declared Patrick O'Keefe, the Canadian Union of Public Employee's national representative.

Mr. O'Keefe said Metro Toronto was facing an unemployment disaster and what was needed was a federal-provincial Government winter works program to give employment and not a royal commission that would examine urban problems and unemployment over the next three or four years.

Mr. Gallagher replied that it makes him ill to see the amount of spite and hate generated at City Council meetings.

"That sort of thing has to be cleaned out," he said.

Mr. Gallagher's reference was to the apparent relationship between some council members and Alderman John Sewell. It also was a reference to, the council members considered to be establishment or old guard and the reform group that has expressed concern about environmental and social problems as they relate to highrise apartment development, expressways and other projects.

The mayor said a number of projects on the drawing board—a St. James Town extension, Harbor City, the Metro Centre and others—could provide 130,000 men with at least a year's work.

"The Eaton Centre project appears to be balancing precariously on the tip of Holy Trinity Church. I don't know which way it's going to fall."

Mr. Gallagher said the laborers' union wants jobs now. "It looks like some people are going to have a lousy, rotten, stinking Christmas," he told the conference. He said some men are already threatening violence. "They could be forced into crime if there is no employment."

The New Democratic Party sent Hugh Peacock, MPP for Windsor West, to the conference. Daniel De Monte, MPP for Dovercourt, represented the Liberals.

Mr. Peacock said the NDP would consider buying out the interest of the St. James Town developers and stop the trend of developments like St. James Town across the city. He suggested that townhouses and modular-style housing could meet residential needs without having to resort to towering structures.

Globe and Mail 1 Oct. 1971
Reprinted with permission

Construction union leaders are bought off, either by straightforward corruption or by a great show of respect and deference by the industry. Union men are tamed, and show up everywhere in the city as token representatives of labour, talking just like the businessmen who surround them.

Whatever happens, of course, construction workers are an important part of the building industry and figure in an important way in the industry's operations and in its politics. In many cases, however, construction union leadership has been in bed so long with management that it is hard to tell them apart in many of their political activities and attitudes except when they sit across from each other in wage negotiations.

With this description of the building industry complete, we now have the outline of the property industry complete. Many important facts about the industry are missing: we can't say, for instance, how much of the country's GNP is accounted for by this industry. We don't really know what percentage of national income is devoted to paying for urban accommodation of all kinds. We don't know what the total is of the capital gains made each year by all the owners of urban real estate. We don't even know on a national basis who are the biggest urban property owners, how much they own, or how much they earn from their holdings.

We do know, however, that in using the concept of the property industry we are grouping a number of familiar businesses and industries which together account for a large chunk of total economic activity in the country each year, and which appropriate a very large proportion of our income in the form of what we pay directly and indirectly for urban accommodation of all kinds. We know the property-owning business, the mortgage-lending business, the property insurance business, and the construction business separately. We are familiar with the activities of lawyers, real estate agents, insurance agents, architects, engineers, etc. But putting them all together and labelling them the property industry because of the common link that they make money from owning urban property, creating more of it, and servicing these activities establishes the common element of all these different people and businesses.

How useful this is, we will see in the following chapters. Now that we have established what the property industry is, we can look to discover its common interests — the basic interests everyone in the business shares. We will pay special attention to the common interests that relate to the activities of city hall, and we will find that the powers and functions of city government are absolutely crucial to the property industry as a whole. Once that is established, we can go on to trace the fascinating network of links that exists between city government in every Canadian city and the property industry. In those connections is the key to understanding what city hall is all about, and why it acts as it does.

Canada's major public real estate companies

	Total assets		Rev. from rentals	Rev. from sale of land, houses	Other revenue incl. brokerage	Total revenue	
	1970	1969	1970	1970	1970	1970	1969
					$'000		
Investment							
Cadillac Development Corp.	227,500	197,813	22,796	6,602	649	30,047	28,872
Cambridge Leaseholds Ltd.▶	30,929	27,191	3,792	—	97	3,890	3,112
Cdn. Allied Prop. Inv. Ltd.	17,246	15,180	1,510	—	33	1,543	1,489
Cummings Prop. Ltd.	117,733	103,474	14,229	—	450	14,678	10,695
Douglas Leaseholds	8,060	7,856	714	—	94	808	817
Great West Int.'l. Equities .	77,573	76,121	—	—	—	26,946	29,443
Imperial Gen.'l. Properties .	24,729	22,512	1,885	—	80	1,965	1,304
Int.'l. Land Corp.	6,124	4,459	926	—	19	945	600
M.E.P.C. Cdn. Prop.	80,027	70,007	7,910	—	—	7,910	6,311
Sussman Properties Ltd. . . .	11,516	10,750	—	—	1,006	1,006	708
Trizec Corp.	259,599	253,707	40,360	—	1,312	41,672	37,774
Y&R Properties Ltd.	43,743	40,124	9,016	—	273	9,289	7,813
Land diversified							
Bramalea Consol. Develop.	80,736	66,057	3,084	10,465	14,077	27,626	36,248
Campeau Corp*	272,247	111,199	26,643	33,691	2,474	62,808	56,887
Cdn. Equity & Developm't**	41,923	38,702	2,703	1,255	272	4,230	3,617
Cdn. Interurban Props. Ltd.	108,849	107,879	14,552	3,536	556	18,644	19,476
Dawson Development** . . .	25,355	12,977	239	8,775	6,403	15,417	14,876
Great N. Cap. (incl. mfg.)	60,710	44,540	925	9,781	21,699	32,405	25,898
McLaughlin S. B.■	—	51,500	—	—	—	—	4,999
Markborough Prop.	59,764	58,864	4,754	4,002	295	9,051	11,515
Orlando Realty Corp.	28,083	21,816	2,414	2,019	7,293	11,726	8,607
Paragon Properties*** . . .	19,437	13,945	513	5,708	171	6,392	4,003
Western Realty	67,116	54,040	3,888	10,743	1,114	15,745	11,464
Housing							
Cons. Building Corp.▲	19,623	20,492	2,977	4,530	280	7,877	10,717
Richard Costain (Can.) Ltd.	22,113	15,915	—	13,259	426	13,684	16,132
Headway Corp.	15,392	11,722	453	14,205	—	14,658	9,631
Nu-West Homes Ltd.	28,825	18,939	529	26,958	735	28,222	18,481
Sifton Properties Ltd.	20,423	15,461	—	3,917	1,552	5,469	6,128
Peel Elder Ltd.	28,513	25,430	3,328	1,716	273	5,317	6,163
Brokerage							
Block Bros.●	54,758	55,037	4,555	390	8,620	13,565	15,060
Gt. Nat.'l. Land◀	8,400	8,181	229	215	1,673	2,117	1,708
Melton Real Estate	7,128	6,598	251	159	2,547	2,957	3,020
Wall & Redekop♦	25,226	21,966	1,400	4,516	8,581	13,497	13.185

▶Year ended May 31, 1970. *14 months ended Dec. 31, 1970. **Year ended Oct. 31, 1970.
***Year ended Nov. 30, 1970. ▲Year ended Feb. 28, 1970. †Excl. spec. items.
●Year ended Jan. 31, 1971. ◀Year ended Apr. 30, 1970. ♦Year ended July 30, 1970.
■1970 figures n.a.

Financial Post 5 June 1971

CHAPTER 4 APPENDIX
Cadillac: anatomy of a land development company

Cadillac Development Corp. is one of the half-dozen largest developers in the Metro Toronto area. Its high-rise apartments, town houses, office buildings and shopping centres are scattered through Toronto, not to mention a few in Hamilton, Ottawa and Thunder Bay. As well as building on vacant land in residential subdivisions, Cadillac is active in redevelopment projects, where it assembles existing neighbourhoods, demolishes the houses, and puts up high-rise buildings in their place.

There is nothing special about Cadillac's operations. What makes it more suitable than most for study as a sample land development company is that it is a public company. Cadillac first offered shares to the public in Novem-

ber 1968, almost four years after it was formed as an amalgamation of 29 different companies owned by the same set of owners. As a public company, Cadillac was compelled to prepare an initial prospectus providing details of its business. It must publish its balance sheet and an annual report, and it has annual shareholders' meetings where owners of shares can question company directors. A certain amount of public disclosure and public scrutiny is the price real estate companies like Cadillac pay for access to the capital funds they can raise by selling their shares to investors.

Cadillac's properties

All together Cadillac owns exclusively or jointly 37 apartment buildings in Toronto, one in Hamilton and one in Ottawa. Most are owned outright. Cadillac calculates that it owns 11,746 individual apartment suites. Another 1,822 were under construction at the end of 1971.

Most of these properties are standard high-rise apartment buildings. They vary in their exterior finish, in the way the entrance lobby is decorated and in the landscaping of the grounds, but beyond that each building is much like the others, and very like the buildings put up by other developers.

The "$1 million" home of Joseph Berman, executive vice-president of Cadillac Development Corp. Ltd.

Along with its residential properties, Cadillac has moved into the office building field and completed its first office building in 1970. Interestingly enough, the prime tenant for this first building was the Ontario Housing Corporation, which uses the building (at 101 Bloor Street West, Toronto) as its head office. OHC is a customer of Cadillac's because the company has built a number of apartment buildings that it has sold to OHC for use as public housing. No doubt OHC's willingness to follow the common (but peculiar) practice of Ontario government agencies in leasing its office space rather than occupying a government-owned building — and in this case to become a prime tenant for an inexperienced office developer — was very helpful in allowing Cadillac to get into this new area of the development business.

Development and construction activities

The main thrust of Cadillac's activities is not that of owning and managing real estate. It got into the ownership and management business when it discovered that it was far more lucrative to retain the buildings it put up than to sell them to some other investor who could then make substantial profits out of them. Over time, Cadillac has been accumulating a larger and larger portfolio of real estate. But it is still very much a development company.

Cadillac's best-known development operations are land assemblies in Toronto neighbourhoods. Cadillac puts together a land assembly, gets an architect's plans for a high-rise project on the site, and goes to city hall to get rezoning and necessary permissions. It lines up financing, carries out the construction itself through its contracting division, and then rents out the apartments.

In mid-1972, Cadillac's officials claimed that they were moving away from the high-rise apartment business in Toronto. The explanation given for this by Cadillac president A.E. Diamond at the May 1972 annual shareholders' meeting was the opposition to residential redevelopment projects from citizen groups. Another explanation, however, was suggested in the 1971 annual report, where it was noted that prevailing rent levels in Toronto were not earning the company their accustomed rate of profit. "Rental rates in newer residential properties," said the report, "have not caught up with increasing costs." But as developers slow up the pace of new construction, rent increases can be expected, which would improve the company's profit position. "We expect," said the report in its rather careful language, "that there will be a decreased rate of starts of rental apartments in the Toronto area and this will bolster the rental market." Cadillac expected to have its cake and eat it: not only was it anticipating higher rents and higher profits, but it was also expecting to be able to shift the anger of its tenants for these increases away from itself and on to citizen groups.

In spite of its claim that it is getting out of the apartment business, Cadillac had at least two projects in the works in Toronto in mid-1972 — Pacific-Glenlake and Quebec-Gothic.

Quebec-Gothic created much unfavourable publicity for Cadillac in 1971-72. A good deal of the trouble resulted from the fact that the project was located in the High Park area of Toronto, where a large number of high-rise apartments have already been built. Objections to the new project came from tenants in the existing apartments, home owners in nearby houses, and people living in the houses on Quebec and Gothic scheduled for demolition. The houses themselves were obviously large, roomy and in very good condition. The developers could not argue that they were slums about to fall down.

A more serious source of problems for Cadillac came from dealings with one of the Quebec-Gothic property owners. Cadillac had joined with another major Toronto high-rise developer, Greenwin, for the Quebec-Gothic project. The Cadillac-Greenwin consortium indirectly arranged to purchase two houses in the redevelopment area which just happened to be owned by the family of the local ward alderman, Ben Grys. Mr. Grys, a former baker, later a partner in a bakery, and more recently an insurance agent, used to live in the area. He and his wife bought one house there in the 1950s, and added a second house to their holdings in the early 1960s. The two properties cost them $31,150. In early 1971, they sold the houses to companies representing the Cadillac-Greenwin group for a total price of $195,000, of which $60,000 was in cash. The Grys family held a mortgage for $135,000.

A few months later, the project was at city hall for approval by the politicians. Moving approval for the development — and moving that the developer be given more than the city's planning board had recommended — was Alderman Ben Grys, who happened at the time to be chairman of the city's building and development committee.

A few weeks later, Toronto alderman John Sewell revealed that Grys had taken this action on the Cadillac-Greenwin project while his family still held the $135,000 mortgage on their properties. Clearly the land would not be

worth anything close to that if high-rise rezoning were not allowed by city hall. At first Grys ferociously denied any conflict of interest in his actions, but eventually did admit the conflict — apparently in a vain attempt to avoid having the courts rule, as they eventually did, that he did indeed have an illegal conflict of interest.

A group of people — I was one of them — who bought single shares of Cadillac in order to attend the 1972 annual meeting of shareholders nominated Grys for membership on the company's board of directors at that meeting. Company president A.E. Diamond ruled the nomination out of order on the grounds that it was frivolous, but we were able to argue that Grys's dealings with Cadillac in the Quebec-Gothic development had made him very familiar with the company's affairs, and had showed him to be enthusiastic in promoting its interests. He would, we said, make an ideal director. When Diamond continued to refuse to allow Grys's name to stand, we challenged his ruling — and lost by a vote of 6,000,000 to 2.

As well as building high-rise apartments and office buildings, Cadillac, through a division of the company, is involved in building houses in residential subdivisions. Also, Cadillac and Cemp Investments Ltd. (a Bronfman family trust) together own Canadian Equity and Development Co. Ltd. This company is developing Erin Mills, a "new town" style residential development northwest of Toronto.

Another Quebec-Gothic area house threatened with demolition.

Financial logic of the company

Each of Cadillac's activities interlocks with the others

A house in Toronto's Quebec-Gothic area, scheduled for demolition to make way for Cadillac high-rise apartments

either by providing cash or by using it up.

Cadillac's tenants paid it rent totalling $26,494,929 in 1971, an average of $2,200 each. Slightly less than half of this amount went to pay property managers, municipal taxes, repair costs, water bills and so on. Cadillac was left with $14,500,000. Of this sum, a further $8,903,088 was paid in interest on the mortgages on these buildings. As well as payments on interest, Cadillac repaid $1,577,941 in principal on these buildings and invested a total of $166,514 in capital expenditures on equipment and building improvements. That left it with a cash surplus of $3,927,267 from its rental operations to use in financing its other activities or to pay out to its shareholders.

The home-building division of the company also contributed cash to its operations in 1971. Cadillac sold houses and land for $7,312,639. The cost to Cadillac of these sales, which includes both the cost of constructing the houses and the cost of the land they were built on, was $6,104,674. So home-building produced a total cash inflow of $7 million, and a surplus of cash over costs of $1.2 million.

Cadillac's construction business, which does general contracting for customers, also generates profits and cash for the company. In 1971 it completed a 220-suite apartment building contracted by an insurance company in Ottawa, and a 235-unit residence for a Toronto hospital. This work plus some other small items produced a profit for the year of $933,008.

Cadillac uses the cash its activities generate in various ways. First, it has general administrative expenses, which amounted to $658,629 in 1971. Presumably this includes the $452,296 the company paid its directors in salaries in 1971, an average of $34,792 each. Then it has other expenses for interest on money it borrowed that it does not charge against specific buildings, amounting to $462,752 in 1971. During that year Cadillac's profits made it liable in theory for income tax of $2,731,506. But only $20,000 of this was actually paid, and the rest was "deferred" — perhaps indefinitely. So, unlike many other corporations — and most people — Cadillac did not have income tax as a real expense during 1971. Together all the real expenses cost Cadillac $1,143,891. It was left with about $5.5 million to play around with.

But Cadillac has other ways of getting hold of cash besides the money its own business activities generate. In 1971 it floated a debenture on the capital market, selling company securities to investors which provided it with $1 million in cash. Also it sold a bit of its holdings in other companies, which yielded $335,283 in cash. It persuaded its customers to pay their bills a bit more quickly, yielding a net inflow of funds during the year of $1.2 million, because at the end of the year its customers owed Cadillac $1.2 million less than they did at the beginning of the year. On the other hand, Cadillac managed to persuade its creditors to allow it to pay its own bills more slowly, and at the end of the year Cadillac had in effect borrowed an extra $3.7 million from its creditors. Cadillac also borrowed an additional $2.8 million from the bank during 1971, which left it owing a total of $13.4 million to the bank at the end of the year. Cadillac also raised a tiny bit of money — $113,400 — during 1971 by selling some more shares in the company.

One other major source of cash for the company during the year was money it obtained from mortgage lenders for mortgages on new buildings it was putting up. Cadillac received a total of $25,966,973 from mortgage lenders during 1971. This was, of course, possible only because it was continuing to put its money into new land and buildings.

All together these borrowings yielded Cadillac approximately $35.6 million in 1971. This sum adds to the $5.5 million in cash Cadillac's own activities generated.

How did it use all this money? Most of it, of course, went towards constructing new buildings and buying land.

A total of $34,783,054 went for land and construction costs for new income-producing properties, most of which were high-rise apartments, which Cadillac was building not to sell but to rent.

A much smaller amount, $3,346,433, was used to increase Cadillac's total investment in housing and condominium projects where it was building to sell. Obviously in this part of its business there is a continual turnover of cash, with customers paying cash to buy new houses at one end and Cadillac putting cash into building more at the other. During the construction period, Cadillac is able to borrow some money on its land and partly finished houses,

Many Quebec-Gothic houses, like this one, are occupied by tenants who have been active in the fight to stop the demolition of the houses and their replacement with high-rise apartments.

but in 1971 it put in $3.3 million of its own cash as well, in addition to what it had invested in this business in previous years. At the end of the year, Cadillac had a total of $22 million invested in houses and condominiums it was planning to sell.

Cadillac used a bit of its money, $469,421, to invest in 1971 in the company it owns in partnership with Cemp Investments, Canadian Equity and Development Co. Ltd., which is building the Erin Mills new town project.

Cadillac also used $1.5 million to pay off some of the loans it had received in previous years from other lenders. It paid off $350,000 worth of debentures. And it redeemed $57,625 in preference shares held by shareholders.

And, to cap it all off and to reward them for all their time, trouble, and investment, Cadillac paid its shareholders a total of $640,042 in dividends in 1971. That was about 7 cents for each of the 9,111,962 shares outstanding.

Profits

As we saw in Chapter Three, the question of how much profit Cadillac made in 1971 is not answered by simply adding up all the money it took in, or the surplus of money it took in over money paid out, or even by looking in the annual report to see what the company itself claims its profits to have been.

Some parts of the profits Cadillac makes are simple and straightforward — like the $933,000 it made selling its services as a general contractor. Others are more difficult, as is explained in Chapter Three, where Cadillac's profits are examined in some detail. For instance, every year the value of the land and apartment buildings that Cadillac owns is increasing because of the general rise in real estate values in Toronto. This increase doesn't yield Cadillac any cash unless they sell those buildings, so they don't actually see the money rolling in every day, but nonetheless it is a real profit that they are making. Taking all these factors into account, the previous chapter concludes that the profit Cadillac actually made in 1971 was about $9.8 million.

The company's shareholders have actually invested $15.2 million in the company by their purchase of 9 million shares. So in 1971 they made about 65 per cent on the cash they collectively had put into the company. In

addition Cadillac has retained profits which could have been paid out to shareholders in the form of dividends amounting to $12.8 million. If this amount is also counted as shareholders' investment in the company — even though it was never paid out of their pockets into Cadillac — the rate of profit for the year becomes 35 per cent.

For ordinary investors looking at the company, profits of $9.8 million a year in 1971 and the prospect of much

MORE DEMOLITION: These houses, in Toronto's Pacific-Glenlake area, are owned by Cadillac and are boarded up, apparently waiting for demolition for another high-rise apartment project.

higher profits in future years make the company worth quite a lot. At the end of May 1972, shares were selling for about $10 each. With 9,111,962 shares outstanding, this puts a value on the whole company of $91 million. For a $91 million company, of course, profits of $9.8 million would be quite usual.

But the point is that Cadillac itself has received just $15 million in funds from shareholders who purchased those stocks originally from the company. That is all the money it has had to work with from its shareholders. To make its shares worth $10 each, it has to have been making profits in the order of from 35 to 65 per cent a year. When someone bought a share in May 1972 for $10, the $10 was not going to Cadillac. It was going to an investor, who was getting a price reflecting the fact that he had been smart enough to invest in a company that was able to make profits like 65 per cent a year on the money invested in it. So when Cadillac's directors protest — as they are bound to — that Cadillac is really not making 65 per cent a year in profits, the simplest response is that it must be, because otherwise no one would be foolish enough to pay $10 for a single share in the company.

Who is Cadillac?

Who are these people who own Cadillac by owning its 9 million shares? That information isn't given in the company's annual report, but it isn't difficult to get some facts.

The most useful source of information about shareholdings is company prospectuses. Cadillac's most recent, issued 19 January, 1971, contains a lot of information on who owns Cadillac's shares.

Executive vice-president and director Joseph Berman and his wife together own 1,823,927 shares.

Jack Daniels, another vice-president and director of the company and his wife and children also own 1,823,927 shares.

So do A.E. Diamond and his wife and children.

Gordon Shear, the third vice-president and director of the company, and his wife own 552,983 shares.

Acres and Canadian General Securities, two related companies, owned 1,519,933 shares at the time the prospectus was issued, but they were about to sell them.

In mid-1972 the shares owned by Berman, Daniels and Diamond were worth about $18 million each.

Together the four officers of the company who have

LANDLORD AND TENANT: On the left, lawn chairs informally set out on the terrace beside the outdoor swimming pool at the home of Joseph Berman. On the right, the sidewalk in front of a Cadillac building. Note the similarity between the street lamps at the Berman home and the lamps in front of the apartment.

large shareholdings in Cadillac own 57 per cent of the outstanding shares, and so they would appear to control the company outright. But the issue of ownership and control does not end there.

Two major outside corporations have a certain amount of control over Cadillac and interest in its operations. The first of these is North American Life (Nalaco). From the January 1971 prospectus it appears that Cadillac has borrowed about $6.6 million from Nalaco in the form of debentures, at an interest rate of 8.5 per cent. Nalaco in return gets two seats on Cadillac's board of directors, and has the right at any time up to 1987 to buy shares representing 15 per-cent interest in the company for $4.20 a share. If Nalaco had exercised its option in 1972, it would have been paying only 40 per cent of the market price for shares it bought, a nice extra profit to add to the 8.5 per cent interest it is collecting on its loan.

Cadillac also has links to the conglomerate of companies controlled by Acres. The Acres group includes Canadian General Securities, Traders Group, Guaranty Trust, Frankel Steel, Aetna Factors and a large number of other insurance companies. As of 1972 Acres no longer held a large block of Cadillac shares (as it did before January 1972) but Traders still held a $1.6 million Cadillac debenture renewable in 1974 at 1 per cent above the current bank prime interest rate. The debenture comes due in 1979. Cadillac is repaying it at the rate of $17,172 per month.

Senior management of Cadillac with their majority of outstanding shares have agreed to vote their shares so that seven of the 13-man board will consist of them and their nominees, two will represent North American Life, one the underwriters of the company (McLeod, Young, Weir), and one Traders Finance.

Power in Cadillac

In the make-up of the board of directors, Cadillac formalizes its links to other corporations and its major shareholders gather to decide how the company will operate. Cadillac's board indicates the alliances and relationships Cadillac has with Nalaco, Acres, and the other businesses which supply it with necessary loans and funds, mortgages, and so on.

First, there are the Acres directors.

One of these is Gordon Sharwood, president of Acres Ltd. Sharwood has a large number of directorships in other companies where Acres has an interest, many of which are in one area or another of the property industry. Sharwood's directorships include: Guaranty Trust, Traders Group, Canadian General Securities, Canadian Insurance Shares, Aetna Factors Corp. (property insurance), Traders Homeplan Ltd. (loans for home improvements, etc.), Traders Mortgage Co., Traders Properties (Church St.) Ltd.,

Top, a covered walkway with arch in the Joseph Berman home. Bottom, the covered walkway at the Thunder Bay Mall owned by Cadillac.

Toronto General Insurance Co. (property insurance), and Frankel Structural Steel.

The second Acres director is D.W. Naylor, president of Canadian General Securities Ltd. Naylor's directorships include Traders Development, Traders Group, Toronto General Insurance Co., Canadian Equity and Development, Guaranty Trust, and Canadian General Insurance.

The second group of Cadillac directors are the two North American Life representatives. One is T.H. Inglis, vice-president and treasurer of North American Life. Inglis's other directorships include Algonquin Building Credits.

The other North American Life director is D.W. Pretty, executive vice-president of Nalaco. Pretty is also a director of General Accident Assurance (property insurance), Scottish Canadian Assurance (also property), Canadian Pioneer Insurance, and Markborough Properties (a large Toronto-based development company).

The third group of Cadillac directors are those representing the executives of the company. The executives themselves are directors, and so is their lawyer Eddie Goodman.

The executives who are directors are Joseph Berman, J.H. Daniels, A.E. Diamond, and G.J. Shear. Berman, Daniels and Shear have no other important directorships; Diamond is a director of Eagle Star (an important property investing insurance company).

Eddie Goodman is an interesting figure on the board. As Cadillac's chief lawyer, he represents the firm in many of its dealings with city councils, the Ontario Municipal Board, and the Ontario government. No doubt he is a chief political strategist of the group. When Cadillac was unexpectedly confronted at their 1972 annual meeting with a group of us who had bought single shares in the company in order to participate in the meeting, Goodman was the only person from the management side of the company who was able to come up with a creative strategy to deal with the issues we were raising about their operations. He gave advice to company president and meeting chairman A.E. Diamond on whether to accept our nomination of Toronto alderman Ben Grys for the board of directors, and on whether to accept a motion requesting the board to consider at its next meeting the question of whether the company should make election campaign contributions to city politicians in 1972. He also made an unsuccessful attempt to deflect our criticisms when he proposed a meeting between company officials and the executive of CORRA, the federation of Toronto ratepayers' groups.

Goodman is extremely well suited for his role in Cadillac's operations. He is part of the powerful group of Ontario Conservatives who run the provincial government, and he has strong links to the federal Tories as well. He is a former chairman of the national Progressive Conservative party, and is often described as a senior party bagman, fixer, and campaign fund-raiser. He has long been closely associated with Toronto city politics, and was for instance one of the chief fund-raisers for Mayor Philip Givens, a Liberal, when Givens was running for re-election in Toronto in 1966.

Goodman's other directorships include Baton Broadcasting (the Bassett-Eaton family broadcasting company that

---

Cadillac's major shareholders and directors do not live in the high-rise apartments they build for other people to live in.

Executive vice-president Joseph Berman, for example, the owner of 1.8 million Cadillac shares worth in excess of $20 million, lives in a largish house in the expensive Toronto Bridle Path area.

The Berman house is worth $1 million.

It is often opened to social and charitable functions, one of which was a party sponsored by the Canadian Women's Opera Guild held in the summer of 1972.

The house itself has a central mall arrangement, passing between large rooms to the right and left. The night of the party, doors to these rooms were left open but small barricades erected so that people could look inside but not actually enter the rooms, the arrangement often made in furniture stores.

The house includes two apartment-building size swimming pools, one indoor and one outdoor. There is also a tennis court, and a small Japanese garden with a miniature Japanese-style temple.

Cadillac director (and former national president of the Progressive Conservative Party) Eddie Goodman, known as "Fast Eddie" to his friends.

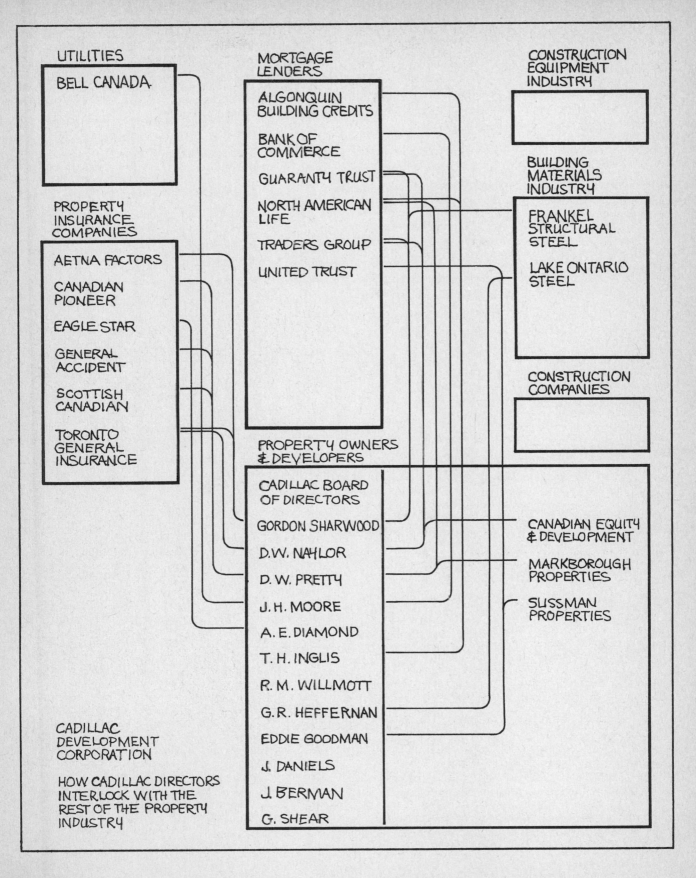

UTILITIES

BELL CANADA

PROPERTY
INSURANCE
COMPANIES

AETNA FACTORS

CANADIAN
PIONEER

EAGLE STAR

GENERAL
ACCIDENT

SCOTTISH
CANADIAN

TORONTO
GENERAL
INSURANCE

MORTGAGE
LENDERS

ALGONQUIN
BUILDING CREDITS

BANK OF
COMMERCE

GUARANTY TRUST

NORTH AMERICAN
LIFE

TRADERS GROUP

UNITED TRUST

PROPERTY OWNERS
& DEVELOPERS

CADILLAC BOARD
OF DIRECTORS

GORDON SHARWOOD

D.W. NAHLOR

D. W. PRETTY

J. H. MOORE

A. E. DIAMOND

T. H. INGLIS

R. M. WILLMOTT

G. R. HEFFERNAN

EDDIE GOODMAN

J. DANIELS

J. BERMAN

G. SHEAR

CONSTRUCTION
EQUIPMENT
INDUSTRY

BUILDING
MATERIALS
INDUSTRY

FRANKEL
STRUCTURAL
STEEL

LAKE ONTARIO
STEEL

CONSTRUCTION
COMPANIES

CANADIAN EQUITY
& DEVELOPMENT

MARKBOROUGH
PROPERTIES

SUSSMAN
PROPERTIES

CADILLAC
DEVELOPMENT
CORPORATION

HOW CADILLAC DIRECTORS
INTERLOCK WITH THE
REST OF THE PROPERTY
INDUSTRY

owns Toronto's CTV television station, CFTO), United Trust (a firm of real estate agents and a trust company operation), Sussman Properties Ltd. (now Corporate Properties Ltd., a Toronto-based developer), and John Labatt (the brewery company, controlled by the small-time Canadian multinational corporation Brascan).

Cadillac also has on its board of directors C.P. Keeley as the representative of McLeod, Young, Weir, Cadillac's underwriters and hence the source of much of its financing arrangements.

In addition to these directors, Cadillac has two directors who appear to be outsiders. One is G.R. Heffernan, chairman of Lake Ontario Steel. Heffernan does not have any other important directorships. Lake Ontario Steel is in the building materials business.

The second outside director, J.H. Moore, is another matter entirely. Moore is president of Brascan, on whose board Eddie Goodman also sits. Brascan, with assets in 1970 of a little more than $1 billion (expressed in U.S. dollars, an interesting indication of where it aims its financial reports), has very large holdings of public utility companies in Brazil. The company used to be called Brazilian Light and Power Company. Ownership of the largest block of shares in Brascan is in the hands of a company called Jonlab Investments, which owns 11 per cent of the outstanding shares.

Brascan's Canadian interests include 34 per cent of the shares of John Labatt and a 6 per-cent block of Hudson's Bay Company. Brascan appears to control Labatt.

Mr. Moore's directorships include the Bank of Commerce, Bell Canada, BP Canada, and Hudson's Bay.

Taken together, then, Cadillac's board of directors represents control of the company by a coalition of business interests that include the executives who now run the company, the Acres group, and North American Life. Through its board, Cadillac has links to many firms in other sectors of the property industry, which presumably are the basis for alliances and business relationships. These links provide Cadillac with the access to capital which, as we have seen in our analysis of the finances of the business, are essential for its land development activities.

Cadillac and the competition

The conventional theory about how business works is that companies in the same kind of business compete vigorously with each other, regard each other as rivals and adversaries, fight for customers, and in the process keep prices low. In land development, one implication of this view would be that developers would be competing with each other in many ways, including keeping rent levels as low as possible.

The situation is in fact quite different. Cadillac has a number of long-term alliances and associations with its "competitors" in the land development business, and we might surmise that the big developers in Cadillac's market have learned how to live with each other, co-operate with each other at least to a limited extent, and to prosper without doing so at each other's expense.

The widest set of links between Cadillac and other big development companies is through Modular Pre-Cast Concrete Structures Ltd. This company is a joint venture of five of the big Toronto high-rise developers. They have got together in this company with Wates Ltd., a big British development and construction firm, to fabricate systems-build-

Developers form consortium

Housing plan worth $79 million

Five Toronto-based developers have formed a consortium to build $79-million worth of housing in Bramalea.

The group will erect about 3,500 units on 200 acres of land owned by Ontario Housing Corp. in Chinguacousy Township during the next five years.

Members of the joint venture include Consolidated Building Corp. Ltd., Bramalea Consolidated Developments Ltd., Cadillac Development Corp. Ltd., Del Zotto Enterprises Ltd. and Victoria Woods Development Corp. Ltd.

Consolidated will act as the operating arm of the group and will look after construction of the housing units.

Plans are not completed as far as types of housing are concerned, and approval has not been received from Chinguacousy planning officials, but Consolidated says it is planning a construction start this spring.

Financing for the development has also not been arranged, but the consortium expects that its drawing power will provide mortgage funds. If OHC wants to participate, that is a matter for negotiation, according to one of the principals.

The consortium will be responsible for all planning and construction, subject to local approvals.

Globe and Mail 1 Dec. 1971

ing style concrete units that can be assembled to make apartment buildings. Modular Pre-Cast is using a system developed by Wates and used by that company in Britain.

The five Canadian developers owning Modular Pre-Cast are Belmont, Cadillac, Greenwin, Heathcliffe, and Meridian. All but Cadillac are privately-owned companies. The sixth owner of the company is Wates.

A second source of links between Cadillac and its competitors comes about through joint ventures on specific development projects. The controversial Quebec-Gothic development, being built by a partnership between Cadillac and Greenwin (another big Toronto-based private development company, also involved in Modular Pre-Cast), is one example of this pattern. Of the 39 apartment buildings that Cadillac owned in 1971, 10 were joint ventures of this type with a number of different partners.

A third link between Cadillac and other land development companies exists through Canadian Equity and Development. Cadillac has joined with Cemp Investments, a Bronfman family firm, in Canadian Equity. Cadillac owns about 40 per cent of this company, and Cemp about 30 per cent. Cadillac has an agreement with Cemp not to sell the bulk of its shares in Canadian Equity without Cemp's approval, so the two are bound up together in the firm. Cemp's real estate investments across Canada are enormous, but details are difficult to discover because the company is a private company, a trust for Samuel Bronfman's family. Canadian Equity has a number of projects going, the most important of which is Erin Mills new town being built northwest of Toronto.

Financing Erin Mills

"On the financial details side, the executives explained that the development of Erin Mills did not require an exorbitant amount of front money. The province provided much of the access transportation system and the main trunk sewers necessary for development."

ERIN MILLS: these photos, taken from the 1971 annual report of Canadian Equity & Development Co., a company jointly owned by Cadillac and Cemp Investments, pay as much attention to the countryside which is being eaten up by this new town development project as to the houses and high-rise buildings that are being put up.

Also featured in the report is Ontario premier William Davis, who is quoted as congratulating the developers on their "very real social conscience". Living in Erin Mills, according to Mr. Davis, will be "a truly human experience."

These are the publicly-known direct links between Cadillac and its competitors. There are other indirect links, for example, the director (D.W. Pretty) Cadillac shares with Markborough Properties and the other director (Eddie Goodman) Cadillac shares with Sussman Properties. And there may be other direct links which are not public. Gossip in Toronto, for example, has suggested that representatives of all the large Toronto high-rise developers meet together regularly, but when asked about this at the 1972 annual meeting company president A.E. Diamond denied that any such meetings took place.

In addition to business relationships, there are other connections between Cadillac and other developers. Most important of these is their political lobby, the Urban Development Institute, to which most Canadian land developers belong. UDI regularly makes public statements on political matters affecting development companies, and lobbies politicians at all governmental levels.

Cadillac and the property industry

Cadillac's business operations, the apartments it builds, the way it finances them, and the sources of its capital, are typical of the land development industry. No doubt all land developers manage, like Cadillac, to avoid paying much income tax. All of them are building apartment buildings that are being bought for them by their tenants, at no cost to the company. Cadillac is able to do this not because it is smarter than other companies. It has managed it because the property industry has set itself up so that things operate this way.

Looking at these operations from another angle, we should expect that all reasonably competent developers can make real profits of from 35 to 65 per cent a year on the money they actually put into their development operations.

Also typical are the formal business links with both competitors in the same business and companies in other parts of the property industry whose services are necessary to a land development company. Key to the land development business is having reliable links with sources of funds who will lend either directly to the company or with the security of the properties it owns.

Seen this way, it is clear that land development companies are really servicing operations for property owners and property investors, finding ways of making land yield higher profits to its owners, and finding ways for mortgage lenders to lend their funds on secure investments at high interest rates in large chunks so that the whole operation produces nice profits and no trouble.

Where development companies are vulnerable

This investigation suggests a number of points where Cadillac and other land development companies are vulnerable. Citizen groups have already discovered many of these points while attacking the redevelopment operations of land development companies. They have made land assembly more difficult, they have tried to block city hall rezonings which make redevelopment possible. Evidently there are other points of vulnerability.

Developers need bank loans, debenture financing, and mortgage money. If the supply of funds to a developer dried up, he would at a minimum have to stop his new development projects and he might have to sell off the properties he owns now. Developers usually use one bank where they borrow money, they have established links with certain mortgage lenders whom they usually rely on for funds, and if they are public companies they probably have both investors who are interested in their debentures and underwriters who arrange this for them. All these financial businesses are vulnerable to greater or lesser degrees to the kind of public pressure that citizen groups can bring to bear. No doubt at least some of them would have second thoughts if they knew that lending more money to a specific land development company was going to produce unfavourable publicity and public criticism.

With public companies, there are a few rights that minority shareholders have which can be used to put pressure on the companies. Embarrassing questions and motions at an annual meeting can produce unfavourable publicity for the company, and might lead financial analysts to urge ordinary investors to steer clear of such controversial shares. Shareholders might be able to bring to light suspicious company practices, like campaign contributions to politicians that are disguised as company expenses. The price of admission to shareholders' meetings is low — for Cadillac in 1972, $10 — and the ticket you get is good forever, a lifetime admission to meetings and a lifetime subscription to company reports.

6 million to 2 developer over people power

By IAN URQUHART
Star staff writer

"People power" came to the annual meeting of Cadillac Development Corporation yesterday and was overwhelmed by the power of shares, about 6 million of them.

Seven citizen activists, each holding one recently-purchased share in Cadillac, attended the meeting at the Royal York Hotel and nominated Mrs. Pat Adams, a west-end housewife and ratepayer leader who opposed Cadillac's apartment development north of High Park, to the 14-man board of directors.

She lost having only two votes. Thirteen incumbent board members and one new member, a Cadillac executive, were elected with the votes of more than 6 million shares each.

Mrs. Adams voted for herself and also received the vote of James Lorimer, a University of Toronto professor of planning who is a leading critic of high-rise development. The other five citizen group leaders registered their shares too late to vote.

Toronto Star June 1972

How to buy into land development companies

Anyone can buy shares in any public company in the property industry. One easy way to do it is to ask your local bank to buy it on your behalf. Often share owners and traders don't like dealing in single shares, but if you are firm you can buy only one. If you ask that it be registered, you will get a lovely engraved share certificate with your name on it to frame. The cost of buying the share is the price of the share itself, plus a few dollars for brokerage and bank fees.

How to investigate land development companies

This analysis of Cadillac is based on information from a number of sources. Cadillac itself provides certain basic information: first, in its annual reports; second, in the most recent company prospectuses. These documents are available on request from the company.

Newspaper clippings libraries are a further source of information about a company, and often contain facts that are not to be found in official reports.

There are several basic sources of information on Canadian corporations. The *Survey of Industrials*, published annually by the *Financial Post*, gives basic facts on all large public Canadian corporations regarding profits, sales, assets and debt financing. Directors are listed, and sometimes details of ownership given. The *Canadian Real Estate Annual* provides much the same information about a wider range of companies in the property industry. The *Survey of Invest-*

ment Funds, also published annually by the *Financial Post*, provides information on investors and their investments that is helpful in tracking down sources of funds for corporations. The annual *Directory of Directors*, also a *Financial Post* publication, lists the more important directorships of most important Canadian company directors. Finally there is *Intercorporate Ownership*, published every two years by the Dominion Bureau of Statistics. It is an enormous collection of data on the shareholdings companies have in other companies. Like all these other sources, this book is helpful but it is not complete in its information. Nowhere is there a reliable and complete source of data; what you have to do is put together all the information from all the sources that you can lay your hands on.

CHAPTER 5
The political program of the property industry

"... I've called this emergency meeting, gentlemen, because we've just received some rather desperate news... Hamilton is growing toward Toronto faster than Toronto is growing toward Hamilton... I realize you will appreciate the gravity of this situation...."

Reprinted with permission of the Toronto Star

People in the property industry have a remarkable enthusiasm for getting together into groups and associations of all kinds. The long list goes from the Appraisal Institute of Canada (for property appraisers, people who judge how much a piece of real estate is worth) to the Urban Development Institute (the organization for developers).

There's a very good reason for all these business organizations: people in the property business have certain common interests arising from the way they make their money. They get together into groups in order to protect these common interests and to promote them. Architects organize themselves into a national body, the Royal Architectural Institute of Canada, and provincial bodies in order to prevent price competition by setting common fees for all architects, to control the number of people coming into the profession and so prevent it from getting overpopulated, and to lobby with government for measures that will give architects more work, more powers and more responsibilities. General contractors get together for similar reasons. So do people in every sector of the industry.

Obviously the property industry is an important one, just in terms of its size, the number of people it employs, and the profits it earns from investors and entrepreneurs. Obviously too it has organized itself very well to work out its common interests and then to put pressure on government at every level to have those interests recognized and promoted. In order to look for the connections between the industry and politics (particularly city politics), we need to know what these common interests are. To people inside the industry, they are probably so clear and logical that it is rarely necessary to spell them out. To outsiders, however, the common interests of the property industry may be a bit more obscure.

Common interest 1: protecting property values

The most basic common interest of the property industry is *protecting the present value of urban property*. This means simply ensuring that property that is worth $1 million today will be worth at least $1 million tomorrow and next year.

When you consider how much wealth is tied up in property ownership, it is easy to understand why this common interest would be so obvious to people who own urban property as a business that it would go without saying. Think of the disappointment to Canadian Pacific if suddenly all the land they own in Canadian cities, now valued in the billions of dollars, were to plummet in value tomorrow. Think of what would happen to CP stock.

If the value of property in a city like Winnipeg decreased by 25 per cent over the next year, people in the property owning business would be extremely unhappy. So would corporations in the property financing business, because their investments in properties mortgaged for 90 per cent of

their market value a year earlier would suddenly become extremely shaky indeed. Property owners would often find it cheaper to default on their mortgages and buy buildings at the new low prices, rather than continue paying on the basis of the old higher values.

The ripples caused by a serious decline in the values of urban property would spread to other segments of the industry. Property insurance companies would see their income decline as property owners reduced the amount of insurance they carried. Insurance agents would suffer. Commissions to real estate agents on individual sales would go down because the average price of a property had declined, though far more important would be the question of whether total volume of sales went up or down. Everyone in the construction business would be adversely affected if the slump in values had the effect which it often has (though it need not have) of leading to a halt in all new construction because there is no money in building new buildings. Only real estate lawyers would soldier on, taking in fees from mortgage foreclosures and all the new transactions the reduction in property values produced. But what they made in fees, they would probably be losing in the decline of the value of their side investments in real estate.

Uniting the entire property industry, then, is this first basic common interest: protecting the present value of urban property. Property values are, as they would put it, sacred.

What this means. This rather abstract-sounding general interest has a lot of very specific and important implications in regard to how the property industry itself operates, how governments make policy regarding land and buildings, and in particular how city government acts.

One implication is that the *supply of land for new buildings must be very carefully regulated*. If it isn't, and an abundance of land becomes available for new buildings to be constructed on, the price of this new land will decline. But so will the value of land that existing buildings stand on.

Take as an example a suburban house lot costing $3,623 (the average national price in 1969). Let's suppose that the value of this piece of land is $500 if the only permitted use of it is farming, so it costs $500 to take the land out of farming and another $1,500 to pay the costs of all the necessary services to make the land into a building lot. If absolutely all regulations were removed about the supply of new building lots, people in the business might find that they could cut their price below $3,623 and still make money. They'd be inclined to do that. The price of a building lot would go down, and the profit made by a developer selling an individual lot or selling land where development is permitted would decline. To some extent the price of existing houses would also go down, because the price of newly-constructed houses will be going down as lots get cheaper.

So, for the property industry, the *supply of land for new buildings must be controlled if property values are to be protected at present levels*. This means much more than just regulating the supply of undeveloped land for new houses and factories at the edge of the city. There are all kinds of different markets for different kinds of land in the city. There is land for houses, land for high-rise apartments, land for low-density office buildings, land for high-density offices and so on. "New land" in any of these specific markets means additions to the supply of land where this specific use is permitted. It therefore includes additions to the supply of land where city policies would permit re-use and redevelopment. Rezoning a street of old three-storey houses for high-rise apartments is adding "new land" to the supply of land for high-density residential buildings. So all the powerful interests in the property industry have a stake in ensuring that the supply of new land for development and redevelopment occasioned by opening up vacant land or by rezoning land to permit re-use is carefully regulated at city hall, in order to protect the value of existing properties.

A second implication of the property industry's basic common interest in maintaining property values is that *high land prices, once achieved, should never be allowed to decline.* This is particularly important in cities where land costs, building prices and rents are very high. In Toronto, for instance, the average house lot in 1969 cost $9,533 compared to the national average of $3,623, and prices have continued to rise since then. Once land prices have reached this level, many very powerful interests in the property industry have an important stake in keeping them there. Land prices aren't like strawberry prices where you may pay 69 cents a basket in early spring, but with the knowledge that every summer prices eventually get down to "normal," 29 cents a basket, say. Every new high in land prices is automatically defined as "normal" by the industry. Property owners and property financing firms have huge investments towards making each new high a minimum, a floor price, and preventing any decline.

The property industry's stake in protecting existing property values also means that *restrictions should be enforced against innovations and new techniques that would reduce the construction costs of new buildings.* If innovations were developed that suddenly made it possible to build new office buildings at a third of the former cost, one immediate effect would be to depress the value of existing office buildings because new ones would be so cheap to construct. Such a development would greatly disturb office building owners and mortgage lenders. If the innovation meant new construction methods, perhaps even new trades or economies on labour inputs, the development would be very much contrary to the immediate interests of construction unions. It would also offend the construction industry, since the industry seems to operate on a cost-plus profit system, which means its profits would be reduced by two-thirds if costs went down by two-thirds. The innovating construction companies and the developers they were tied in with would stand of course to make huge profits through any such change, but their weight would be far less than the weight other property industry interests could pull against any such changes. So the array of building standards, construction codes, and mortgage company regulations about minimum construction techniques and fire regulations, which help to rule out any cost-reducing innovation in the construction industry, protect the industry's stake in protecting existing property values.

Protecting property values also means *supporting civic growth and expansion in general.* Booming business conditions help ensure a steady market for all kinds of existing accommodation as well as attracting new city residents who in turn create new housing demands. Slow-growth or no-growth cities do not attract new businesses or people; rather, a slow growth rate threatens to depress local pro-

perty values. One of the reasons banks and trust companies don't like separatism in Quebec is that it drives head offices and corporate executives out of Montreal, which has damaging effects on Montreal property values and drastically reduces new development and construction. Remember those long, sad newspaper stories in the late 1960s that told how difficult it was getting to be to sell a $50,000 executive's house in Montreal?

The property industry's fundamental interest in protecting property values has a direct link to the question of municipal property taxes. *Property taxes should be at the lowest possible level that provides adequate city services.* This in turn means that municipalities should make reasonably efficient use of the money they collect. Low taxes are not much good to the property industry if the sewage system in the city doesn't work properly.

The property industry's interest in low property taxes is somewhat different from that of home owners and tenants who can't afford to pay big taxes and meet all their other bills as well. The industry's interest in low taxes is a result of the way the property tax system works.

A municipal property tax is a kind of wealth tax: every year you have to pay a small percentage of the value of the land you own in taxes. The percentage you pay varies from city to city. Often it is in the range of from 1 to 1.5 per cent of the value of the property. Thus the taxes on a $25,000 house might be $250 a year, 1 per cent annually. From the point of view of an investor in the property industry, the effect of the property tax is to reduce the income a property would otherwise produce. If you own an office building worth $1 million and your net income from the building every year after you pay all your maintenance expenses is $100,000, you will have only $90,000 left after you pay property taxes of 1 per cent. If you had to pay only $5,000 in property taxes, the building would yield an annual income of not $90,000 but $95,000. This would make the building worth more to an investor. When previously he would have been willing to pay $1 million for it, he would now be willing to pay about $1.05 million.

Property taxes reduce the value of properties for property investors from what they otherwise would be, and other things being equal the lower the rate of property tax, the more existing buildings are worth. But a fine balance is required between the need to keep property taxes (and municipal expenses) low on the one hand, and the need to provide an adequate level of municipal services (which are paid for by property taxes) on the other. The more efficiently a city government uses its property tax revenues, therefore, the happier the property industry will be.

Common interest 2: maximizing property values

The basic concern of the property industry to protect the present values of existing urban property is taken very good care of most of the time. This allows the industry to concentrate on a related, but secondary, common interest: *ensuring the greatest possible increase in the value of existing properties,* maximizing their value. Just as before, this rather abstract-sounding concern leads directly to a number of specific government policies.

Obviously property owners are interested in maximizing the values of their holdings. Increases in the value of an existing property make the owner wealthier without his having to expend any effort whatsoever to come by the

CALGARY MAYOR TELLS TEAM:

Civic heads 'too lazy' to fix housing problem

By HALL LEIREN

Municipal politicians are to blame in large part for the housing crisis facing low and moderate income families in Canadian cities, Calgary Mayor Rod Sykes said Wednesday.

They have been too lazy, too uncaring and too cowardly in the past to do an adequate job in solving the problem, he told the annual meeting of The Electors Action Movement (TEAM) in Plaza 500.

And he said a major shift in thinking on the issue of providing public housing is required if the situation is to be met.

if you can't get a job and if you can't afford a decent place to live?'' he asked.

Municipalities have the power to do a great deal to solve the problem, he said.

One of the first things municipalities should do is to begin forcing private developers to provide a percentage of low-income housing in every development — say 20 per cent — Sykes said.

"Private industry is capable of providing it if it wants to but it's too busy doing what industry wants most, maximizing profits."

Sykes said that in Calgary private developers have learned that unless they pro-

municipal business more efficiently, we'd have more money to provide the things people need most without taxing them to death."

Sykes said that factory-built houses — evolved from mobile homes — can be produced at far less cost than conventional houses and last year comprised 25 per cent of new housing units in the United States.

But because mortgage money for this type of housing is not available it is being denied people of low income who cannot afford conventional housing, he said.

Sykes also called for much smaller housing units than CMHC standards now call for, on smaller lots, with planned communal recreational facilities, and for making mortgage money available to finance them.

Sykes also took a swipe at city planners, whom he accused of too often using people as guinea pigs in their experts' laboratories."

He said their mistakes have been made at enormous costs to the community in terms of opportunities lost, resources wasted and even human suffering.

Planning policies have been created that attempt to influenced development of public or high-density housing toward what the planners consider the least desirable neighborhoods.

Sykes said planning and development policies appear deliberately designed to separate people from their jobs by distance — making travel necessary and imposing enormous costs on the community for transportation needs.

He accused planners of fomenting serious neighborhood unrest and protest over "the

constant flow of plans to punch traffic arteries through settled residential neighborhoods with all that means to the esthetics of the home and the safety of the children — and · also all it discloses with respect to the foresight of planners."

Planning and development policies militate against low-cost mobile home parks and little attention is paid to maintenance of older neighborhoods while more prosperous ones get extravagant manicurings, he said.

And he accused planners of "a general lack of liaison and co-ordination and frequently a poor working relationship between municipal planning and other departments. which leads to increased costs, delays and frequently serious errors and embarrassment in the carrying out of public business."

He predicted planning and planners will lose their power as neighborhood people and local residents demand more say in their affairs and refuse to have policies dictated that they have had no part in formulating.

"Planning policy will increasingly come from below in future, from the people whose lives will be directly affected by the decisions, communicated to their elected representatives." Sykes said.

Vancouver Sun 23 Mar. 1972
Reprinted with permission

CITY POLICIES FOR CHEAPER HOUSING: Calgary mayor Rod Sykes, a former official of CPR's real estate subsidiary Marathon Realty, has an insider's understanding of how the property industry works. Sykes' criticisms of the industry reported in this article establish the many ways in which industry interests are protected by city hall policies, keeping housing costs high for urban residents and profits big for the property industry.

"The fact is we know how to produce the kind of housing that people 'need and want,'' he said. "The fact is we know how to produce it at a cost much lower than the average unit cost of free-market housing. We know how to solve our problem. All we lack is the will to do it."

The problem, he said, is one of deciding on priorities and he warned that any economic system that proposes to survive must guarantee people the two basics of a chance for a productive job and a decent place to live and raise a family at a reasonable cost.

"What are all the other benefits of civilization, of science, of democracy, of the free enterprise system worth to you

vide low-income housing their development plans fail to be approved.

"You don't cut red tape for them and red tape can strangle you," he said. "That sounds like coercion, and it is."

Sykes said that if unduly restrictive municipal building codes were made more flexible construction costs would be lowered.

"If unrealistic municipal services — sidewalks on both sides of the street — were eliminated costs would drop," he said. "If schools would share facilities on a community centre basis, if our segregation laws — zoning bylaws — were to allow people to live near their jobs, if we ran our

added wealth. It is easy money in the truest sense of the term. For landlords, increasing building values result from being able to charge higher rents, or from being able to sell out for redevelopment.

Property industry interests that lend money to finance the ownership of real estate don't make quite such obvious gains when the value goes up on property they've lent money on. The increase goes to the owner, not to the money-lender. But the lender does in fact make a very important gain in that the security of his loan increases. The risks attached to the loan get smaller as the value of the property increases.

The way it works is straightforward: when a life insurance company lends a developer $10 million on a first mortgage on an apartment building he calculates is worth $11 million, the insurance company can take possession of the building and sell it to get its money back if the borrower stops making payments on his mortgage. If the building increases in value from $11 million to $15 million, the developer is clearly wealthier. But the lender is also more secure. Now he knows that he has first claim on an asset worth $15 million if the borrower should default. And he knows that the borrower is much less likely to have to default if the value of his property is increasing.

Lots of people in the property industry earn their income as a percentage of the value of properties they handle, and as the value of properties increases their income for the same amount of effort goes up. There is an additional important effect: if property values are increasing by 10 per cent a year, the effect is to make everyone optimistic and to encourage property owners to do a lot of buying and selling and new construction in order to realize the gains on their holdings. That produces all kinds of extra business for real estate agents and real estate lawyers.

For the construction industry, there is no immediate gain from an increase in the value of existing properties, except that other things being equal it makes new construction relatively more competitive vis-à-vis old buildings. It also reflects a buoyant and expanding local property market, with increasing effective demand for urban real estate, and that in turn is likely to produce new construction. It creates room for new development to occur without threatening the established value of existing buildings, and of course that is essential if the construction industry is going to be allowed to add to the stock of buildings in a city.

What this means. What measures can be taken by city hall to increase the value of existing buildings and thus benefit property owners and other segments of the property industry? As it happens, there are a number of techniques available. Most of them involve simply pressing further the measures that are already implemented in order to protect existing property values in the city.

Restricting the supply of land for new development and redevelopment is necessary in order to protect existing property values. *Restrict land supply further, in the face of increasing demand for specific kinds of accommodation in the city, and the value of existing properties will not just stay stable but will begin to rise.* The whole range of land use controls like planning policies, zoning, building standards and other measures can be used to have this effect.

Ruling out innovations in construction helps protect existing property values. *Take this one step further and require higher standards of new construction than were re-quired for existing buildings and one of the effects will be to increase the value of those existing properties.* The increase may be moderated, depending on the kind of standards involved. Requiring 12 feet of kitchen cupboards in new houses rather than the previous standard of 8 feet, for instance, will make new houses more expensive than they used to be and to some extent worth more than houses with somewhat smaller kitchen cupboards. Nevertheless the general increase in house prices produced will probably lead to somewhat higher values for existing houses with the old 8-foot cupboard standard. But if fire ratings on apartment buildings are suddenly increased to raise construction costs by 5 per cent and to produce higher rent levels for new apartments, it is quite likely that old apartment rent levels will follow the increase more or less in parallel. As a result, existing apartment buildings will increase in value. Such increases in the standards of construction are always explained and justified in terms of the benefits they produce for people who use new buildings, and generally these benefits are real. But we should not forget how they operate as a help to property industry investors who own existing buildings of the same type.

Allowing demolition without regulation is an implication of the property industry's interest in maximizing land and property values. Without demolition, developers would not be able to change land use and increase densities nearly as crudely or as easily as they do at present.

Another step open to city hall to help push up property values is *encouragement of local development and business expansion and population growth.* A little growth is enough to protect property values. A lot of growth serves to produce rising property values everywhere in the city. There may not be too much that a city government can do to affect the general economic climate it operates in. Advertising for new industries in the *Financial Post* may occasionally produce some small benefits, but ultimately much bigger economic and political forces determine where growth and development will locate in the country. Nevertheless, these larger economic conditions can and are greatly affected by the actions of provincial and federal governments, where the property industry also exercises influence. Obviously growth has clear and undeniable costs attached to it, especially for the people who already live in a city that is to grow. But these costs are tiny, for the property industry, compared to the huge wealth that growth generates for it

Every year some 50,000 to 60,000 new people come to live here, and they cannot be turned away. The planning process that has coped with this influx so well in the past must be allowed to continue coping with it. Why should we now change the rules merely because some small but vociferous local groups, who have only their own narrow interests at heart, demand it? To stop development while seeking "alternatives" that may take years to find — or may not even exist — is clearly to invite chaos.

Robert L. Strom
Chairman, Apartment Group
Urban Development Institute
Don Mills

Globe and Mail Dec. 1971

by producing increases in the value of existing urban property. Ordinary citizens may ask questions about growth and development, but property investors welcome it and wait for the money to come rolling in.

Another policy city hall can adopt that will produce important increases in property values is to *improve the level of public works and services provided for privately-owned land in the city.* Persuade city council to build a new subway, and all the people who have invested money in property along its route will see the value of their investment rise sharply. Almost all civic improvements have similar effects: better roads, better bus systems, better parks, better garbage collection. Often the increases in property values are highly localized; a new subway brings major benefits to property owners downtown and along the route,

but not so much to other parts of the city. Of course these benefits have to be weighed against the costs, borne by property owners through the property tax system. A few investors will always benefit by one more new expressway, but the property industry as a whole has to weigh whether the increased costs to the industry are justified by overall benefits. Naturally, the big decisions are going to be made by the big operators in the industry, the major downtown property owners and the major property financing corporations, not by the two-bit, small-time fringe operators who make a few bucks by being insurance salesmen or real estate agents.

Perhaps the most dramatic way in which the value of land can be suddenly increased is when urban services are provided to agricultural land, thus opening it up for devel-

Continued on page 74

The glories and inevitability of growth

Property industry spokesmen like Alan Scott are firm supporters of urban growth. They argue that it is good for the city as a whole, often neglecting to point out its more specific benefits to the property industry: 1. promoting increases in the value of existing properties; 2. creating a market for large amounts of new construction.

But industry spokesmen, conscious that many people do not share their enthusiasm for growth, have a second and somewhat contradictory line of argument. They argue that growth, desirable or not, is inevitable, and that it cannot be stopped. So they allow people the view that growth is undesirable while trying to discourage them from attempts to stop it.

By ALAN J. SCOTT
Mr. Scott is president of the Urban Development Institute of Ontario.

Toronto faces one fundamental development issue — whether important planning decisions should be made centrally by elected representatives of the whole municipality or, as some ratepayers' groups are saying, on a strictly local basis by them.

By any yardstick Toronto's great recent growth, which has been centrally planned and controlled, has produced one of the finest cities of its size anywhere, with a healthy mixture of residential forms that is admired by planners, architects and other urban experts from all over the world. Growing numbers of local-interest groups are arguing, however, that we should now alter course and allow planning decisions to be made by each individual neighborhood.

This suggestion must be placed in its proper context — the fact that the city faces a continuing need to accommodate a yearly influx of 50,000 to 60,000 new people, as well as hundreds of thousands of new households the city's young people will be forming over the next few years.

The idea of local control over urban change has tremendous appeal in today's fast-paced world. But the pressures for change demand a responsibility to the needs of the overall community which, while not ignoring local desires, must take precedence if we are to cope with them. There is no way Toronto can be turned into

a private club for its present citizens to enjoy in perpetuity.

Toronto is where the action is. This means new industries will continue to be attracted, more head offices will be located here, existing businesses will expand facilities and this growth of business will continue to attract new employees and their families.

The only way Toronto's population growth could be stopped would be through a combination of four measures: strict birth controls, prohibiting other Canadians from moving here, changing immigration policies to steer away new Canadians and the redirection of all new or expanded trade and commerce.

Even this would not eliminate the coming housing needs of Toronto's present young people. So we would also have to impose strict limits on the number of new households formed within the city.

Since none of these measures would be acceptable, or even feasible, there is no question of whether Toronto's growth will continue. The only question is how best to handle it. Every Torontonian therefore has a responsibility — to himself, to his children and to the future of the city — to accept the reality of this growth and changes it may require.

Globe and Mail 9 Mar. 1972

Demolition: a key item on the property industry's political program

The right to be able to demolish any building anywhere in the city is crucial for the property industry and the way the industry currently operates.

The reason demolition is so important is that, to maximize land values and profits, developers and property owners must be free to get rid of existing buildings if they are able to build new buildings with higher densities, producing more building standing on a piece of property and thus realizing the potential profits which higher densities and higher revenues bring.

Demolition is almost as important for city hall, so the city can expropriate and tear down buildings which stand in the way of new public developments, expressways, subways, street widenings or any of the projects necessary to service new private development.

If demolition of sound buildings were made illegal, and if developers were allowed to build only on vacant land, the possibilities for profiteering would be somewhat reduced for the industry. Such a policy would put an end to the incredible waste of resources which is involved when a sound building, capable of providing satisfactory accommodation as an office, factory or house is destroyed in order to make way for something new. It would also put an end to the ravaging of a city's

---

ON THIS PAGE AND THE NEXT TWO: buildings threatened by the property industry's demolition policy. Below is the Birks building in downtown Vancouver. Its destruction is called for by a redevelopment scheme which joins Birks and Famous Players Ltd. with the Bank of Nova Scotia. Proposed is a $23 million Vancouver Centre, including a new two-storey building to house Birks, two cinemas, and a 36-storey office building for the bank.

past which comes with demolition.

Demolition is not only permitted by existing city government policies; it is actually encouraged by federal tax law.

The encouragement for demolition comes from the artificial provisions of tax laws which allow companies to deduct 5 per-cent or 10 per-cent of the value of buildings (but not land) they own each year from their income for "depreciation" of their buildings. Of course, most buildings do not really depreciate in value over time, particularly if they are adequately maintained and repaired. So the depreciation is really a tax dodge, a gift from government to property-owning businesses.

But when a company wants to sell a building it owns and move elsewhere, it finds that its property is not worth less than it was when purchased. Both the building and the land usually turn out to be worth more.

But a building valued at $1 million 30 years ago by a company will have been depreciated almost to zero by now. If the building and land are sold to someone else who goes on using the building, it obviously is worth a great deal more than zero to the purchaser. The present value of the building is calculated by the tax department, and the fictional amount of depreciation deducted from income over the last 30 years is now added on to the company's income this year. So the company has to pay tax on it, at last.

But if the company sells its land and building for demolition and redevelopment, it can argue that the building is indeed worth nothing. Only its land was valuable. The building was valueless and was torn down. The price the property is sold for is attributed completely to the land, no depreciation is considered recaptured, and no tax is paid.

So the industry's natural inclination to demolish old buildings in order to make way for bigger new ones is further incited by this federal government tax policy.

THE GRANITE CLUB: This building, belonging to an establishment Toronto social club, was sold by the club members to Four Seasons Hotels Ltd. The club got enough money to build themselves a new clubhouse farther from the city's centre, and Four Seasons plans to knock the building down in order to erect an office tower.

TORONTO'S UNION STATION: The station, erected in the 1920s, offers one of the most remarkable public spaces in Toronto. It stands on land which is owned not by the railways but by the City of Toronto. Terms of the railways' lease specify that it remains in force only so long as the land is used for railway purposes, but the CNR and CPR found no opposition amongst the pro-development majority at city hall to their Metro Centre development. The key to Metro Centre's economics is the re-use of the city-owned station site for a number of very high office buildings. The ranks of preservationists fighting the station's destruction were divided and their cause weakened when a number of them proposed a compromise whereby only the Great Hall portion of the building (shown in the photograph) would be saved, and the use of the building as a railway station ended. The building's fate is undecided.

PORTAGE AND MAIN: These buildings, standing at Winnipeg's major intersection, are scheduled for demolition as a result of a deal cooked up between Trizec, Canada's largest publicly-owned real estate company, and Winnipeg's new "unicity" council. The terms of the deal are almost impossible to believe. The city, which is expropriating this part of the site, is to lease the land to the developers for 99 years, for a rent of only 3 1/2 per cent of the cost to the city of acquiring the land. In addition the city is to build at public expense a parking garage on the site to service the new development. Finally, the city has agreed to expropriate the rest of the block for Trizec if Trizec wants the land.

opment. Sewers, water, and roads are what it takes to turn well-located agricultural land worth $3000 as farm land into suburban house lots worth $40,000 an acre.

Taking all these steps together, then, we see there is lots that city hall can and does do to help the property industry promote its second basic common interest — its interest in ensuring the greatest possible increase in the value of existing properties.

Common interest 3: maximizing new construction

A third basic interest of the property industry is that there be *the greatest possible amount of new construction*. Maximizing new construction is close to the hearts of everyone in the building industry sector, which after all makes most of its money from new construction (the rest comes from repairs and renovations to existing buildings). The construction business can be expected to do its best to ensure that its output and its profits are as large as possible. Other parts of the property industry, however, are not so committed to new construction. Investors who own existing buildings, for instance, would see the value of their buildings shoot up much more quickly if absolutely no new construction whatsoever were allowed. Here, in other words, we have come on an internal conflict, where one sector of the property industry has one interest and another has a contradictory interest.

The conflict, however, is a limited one. No one in the property industry wants absolutely unlimited amounts of new construction, because that would depress the value of existing properties and greatly disrupt the entire industry. The absolute maximum permissible amount of new construction in the eyes of the property industry would be that amount which kept existing building values steady, but did not allow them to increase. The absolute minimum, of course, would be no new construction whatsoever. In between these two extremes, factions inside the industry jostle to determine exactly how much should be allowed. Everyone agrees that there should be as much as possible; the disagreement comes over what is the maximum amount possible before the interests of existing building owners are jeopardized.

Many property investors do benefit from new construction. For speculators who buy up vacant land just outside the built-up area of the city, new construction is essential if they are to realize the value of their land as building lots and not be stuck with a lot of unwanted farmland. For owners of existing buildings, new development is the source of a new kind of demand for their property. Not only can they sell or rent their property to people who want to use it as it is; they also may have the possibility of selling their property to a developer who wants to re-use the site more profitably. Through development, property investors have access to a new route for making big capital gains on their holdings.

Mortgage-lenders benefit from new construction because it is the source of new customers to borrow their money. Finding good risks who will pay 9 or 10 per-cent interest is a constant problem for banks, life insurance companies and trust companies. New development provides a steady stream of eager customers who can pay 10 per cent and still make money.

All the professions that service the property industry as a whole look with favour on new construction because it

expands the amount of property requiring their services, and offers them the prospect of new business and new income.

What this means. The common interest of the property industry in maximizing new construction and development subject to the need to protect property values and allow existing properties to increase in value implies that *government should encourage and promote new development and redevelopment. Policies should be worked out to provide a regulated supply of land for development. Land should be designated for re-use, and for higher density development than it currently provides. City hall should do its best to ensure that growth takes place inside its jurisdiction and in its locality, not in other parts of the country.*

But it takes more than mere words and permissions to maximize urban development. *Government should also provide necessary public works and services, at the expense of the taxpayers as a whole rather than of the specific landowners who receive the benefits and see their land jumping in value.* This means new roads, sidewalks, sewers, hydro supplies, libraries, schools, and all the other basic works and services which are required to provide more accommodation for more people.

Common interest 4: keeping the property business for the property industry

A final common interest of the property industry, perhaps the most basic one of all, may seem so obvious it hardly needs mentioning. It is the industry's stake in *maintaining the basic political and economic status quo, and specifically retaining the arrangements that allow the industry to dominate the business of supplying urban accommodation and to make the profits it now enjoys in this business.*

As we have already seen in Chapter 2, federal and provincial law allows property investors to buy up unlimited amounts of urban property and to charge people as much as they can be persuaded to pay for urban accommodation. Property investors pretend that there is no difference between them and people like ordinary home owners who buy property not to make profit from but to use. There is an enormous difference, and — more than that — major property investors are more than willing to see governments sacrifice the interests and property rights of small home owners in order to allow the big corporate owners to become even bigger and even wealthier. The industry's interest in maintaining the political status quo regarding the industry means *violent opposition to any measures that would regulate the prices charged or regulate or reduce the profits of property investors and the rest of the industry.* The industry's interests also lead it to *propose and support government measures that sacrifice the interests of small property owners in order to increase the wealth and profits of large corporate property investors.*

Power to make the basic changes that could dramatically alter the operations of the property industry rests with the federal and provincial governments. They are the bodies that could take over the large corporations in the industry, allocate mortgage funds amongst different kinds of buildings, require public ownership of land where new development takes place, regulate house prices and rents, require that mortgage money be lent at low interest rates, and tax away a reasonable proportion of the profits made in the business.

Continued on Page 76

Committee seeks way to speed zoning system

The city's environment committee has called for a report on means of streamlining zoning procedures so that applications can be handled quickly.

But it has agreed that the zoning procedure laid down in the City of Winnipeg Act should be tested before the provincial government is asked to amend it.

The decision was reached Monday after Earl Levin, Winnipeg planning director (Metro) asked whether the committee wanted the planning division to investigate possible amendments to the act which would shorten the zoning process, or to wait until the new procedure had been tried.

As an example, Mr. Levin said the process could be shortened if an application was drafted into a bylaw for first reading by council, before it was sent to the community committee involved for public hearings.

Under the act, applications now go directly to the community committee for hearings, before a bylaw is prepared and presented to council for approval.

Mr. Levin said problems could be created by the new procedure, because if council chose to amend a bylaw after it had been through public hearings, the bylaw would then have to go back to the community committee for a further hearing, before it could be brought to council.

Coun. Abe Yanofsky (ICEC — Garden City) suggested the area of appeals could also be investigated. He said community committees under the act would be subject to a great deal of pressure when a zoning application was heard. He suggested council, rather than the environment committee, should be the body of appeal.

However, Coun. Paul Marion (ICEC — Tache) said he would hate to see the committee prejudge the ability of the community committees to deal with public hearings. He said the prescribed procedure should be tested before any amendments are sought.

The committee agreed a report should be prepared outlining alternatives to the present procedure, so the committee would have enough information

Winnipeg Tribune 1 Feb. 1972

RED TAPE AND DEVELOPMENT: Regulating the supply of 'new' land means that not every application for rezoning of every piece of land can be approved. This is in the interests of land developers as it is in the interests of property investors, but of course developers are always pressing up against the boundaries of city hall policy trying to get permissions for rezonings as quickly and efficiently as possible. Other property interest groups might prefer to see them granted more slowly.

This article reflects the feeling in Winnipeg after amalgamation that the new one-city government wasn't quite the boon to the property industry that was expected. Instead of being more organized, rational and efficient, it was proving in some ways more cumbersome than the complicated peculiar old city government system. This discovery by property industry interests led to proposals, as this article reports, that the new system be modified so as to suit the industry somewhat better.

The industry's interest leads it to demand as strongly as it can that none of these things be done. What the industry wants from senior governments is more concessions, not regulation that will reduce prices or profits.

City government is, at a lower level, also very much involved in the status quo arrangements that establish how the property industry now works. Though it does not have much scope for action, city hall certainly could make changes in the present situation. Cities could follow the example of Saskatoon and buy up vacant land on the outskirts of the city, servicing it as required for new construction and selling it either at cost (which would be far below what is currently charged for new building lots) or at cost plus a reasonable profit (which is what is done in Saskatoon). CMHC makes federal government funds available for municipalities to borrow for this purpose, but even the tiny amount CMHC has set aside is not fully used up by Canadian city governments.

City governments could restrict all new housing to buildings no more than six storeys in height. They could attempt to institute municipal rent controls. They could go into the housing business themselves, and reduce housing prices by undercutting the prices of private developers. They could provide start-up money for housing co-ops and other citizen groups that take direct action to deal with the housing problem. Measures of this kind would, certainly, have a limited impact so long as basic federal and provincial policies regarding the property industry remained unchanged. But they would have some effect, and they would illustrate — as Saskatoon's municipal land assembly program does — that there are practical, effective alternatives to the way the property industry does things. It is very much in the industry's interests that all such innovations and changes not be made.

Conflicts inside the property industry

On the basic issues of principle — protecting property values, maximizing the values of existing property, maximizing new development, and protecting the property business for the industry — there is agreement amongst the diverse sectors of the property industry. These are common interests everyone shares, and if some groups (like property investors) have more at stake in one issue than in another, nevertheless all gain when all four interests are being properly protected and promoted for the industry.

Still, there is room for tremendous conflict and for bitter disputes and fights inside the property industry. Investors already have an enormous amount of wealth tied up in the present property system. Huge profits are made every year inside the property industry, and tremendous capital gains on property ownership are taken for granted by everyone involved. The disputes usually centre around who is going to make the money. Will it be downtown property owners or suburban shopping centre developers, competing to provide the limited amount of commercial accommodation for department stores, shops and supermarkets the city can profitably support? For years in Toronto there was a running battle between suburban property owners and politicians on one side and downtown land owners and politicians on the other over where the new CBC headquarters in the city would be located. The CBC purchased a site in the Don Mills suburban office area, but in the end announced it would locate on downtown land owned by the CN-CP railways.

Every time a major transportation investment is pending, conflicts between property industry people erupt over attempts to control who gets the benefits. Nowhere is this clearer than in Vancouver, where enormous public expenditure is being proposed to build a new bridge from the city to the north side of Burrard Inlet. The real importance of this crossing is that it will make land on the north side of the city jump tremendously in value, so that new development which might otherwise go elsewhere locates there. Battles over whether to build a third crossing are inevitably (at least in part) battles between property investors who are competing over whose land is going to be developed next. If the money that would be spent building a third crossing in Vancouver were to be spent building expressways east out

House building by public bodies is opposed

Government has no place in the large-scale housing development field and any move in that direction should be resisted, the president of the Housing and Urban Development Association of Canada told the Toronto Home Builders Association last night.

Harold Shipp said at a THBA dinner in Toronto he is concerned Canada's federal Government will follow the lead of the United States and provide special funding for provinces and cities to engage in large urban projects.

The U.S. program also allows local housing agencies to select the builder-developers, the locations and types of projects.

He fears that agencies in Canada could be given grants for programs that would lump together housing markets to achieve economies of scale.

"I very much object to a concept that proposes to create any agency which will aggregate a market," he said, ". . . a matter which we believe to be in the province of private decisions.

Globe and Mail 16 Nov. 1971

of the city, it would make speculators to the east rich. If it were used to put in a subway system, it would make owners of land suitable for redevelopment near the subway route rich.

The property industry's understanding of the city

The city as a money-making machine. The four common interests of the property industry discussed above lead the industry to see the city in a very special way. For the property industry, a city is a money-making machine. It offers a particularly attractive and secure way of making profits and capital gains for investors.

People have different ways of seeing the city they live in. The way a trucker's wife who lives in the Lord Selkirk Park public housing project sees Winnipeg, her neighbourhood, and her street will of course be quite different from the way a banker's wife living in a very comfortable Tuxedo house sees Winnipeg, *her* neighbourhood and *her* street. Nevertheless, both (and city residents in general) tend to share a view of the city as a place to live, as their home town, as the location of their own home. They have memories, associations, neighbours, groups that are based on the existing patterns of city life.

Seeing a city as a place to live is fundamentally different from the viewpoint of the property industry, which sees the city as a source of profits and as a way of making money. For the industry the city is nothing more than a collection of investments, one beside the other, with new investment possibilities emerging all the time. Decisions by the property industry that affect the city enormously — where to build new housing, which neighbourhood to destroy, when the old hodge-podge downtown must go to be replaced by high-rise office buildings — are made solely in the light of money-making considerations. Anything else is "emotionalism."

City hall and the property industry. One of the clear and important lessons of spelling out the basic interests of the property industry and their implications for government policy and for city hall is that we can see the very tight links that exist between the powers and activities of city hall and the basic interests of the property industry. When it comes to the industry's basic interests, such as protecting existing property values or maximizing the amount of new development and construction, the role of government — particularly city hall — is absolutely crucial. Protecting property values means, among other things, regulating very carefully the supply of new land and the standards to which new buildings must be built. The power to regulate these things rests in the hands of the provinces, who delegate most of it to city hall. So do the powers to provide many of the other basic services required by the industry, and to set the basic regulations of its operations.

The property industry's program for city hall

With the information we now have on the property industry and its interests, we can make a very precise list of what the industry wants from government, particularly from city hall. It is their program for the bureaucrats and the politicians, and it is based on the political principle that city government should preserve and foster a vigorous, healthy, growing local property industry. The basic list is as follows:

— Respect for the basic system of land ownership, and for the rights of property investors (though not home owners)

— Protection for property values, and the investments of property owners

— Provision of new public works and services like expressways, subways, parks, sewers, etc., that enhance property values

— Encouragement for new development and growth

— Low property taxes.

You can run for office at city hall on a platform like that, and get elected. Many city politicians have. They have taken the view that what is good for the property industry is good for the city as a whole, and they have often pointed out as virtues the advantages to the industry of some of their platform planks.

When one particular version of a political principle of the industry begins to meet serious opposition, the industry may press forward with it regardless. Or it may shift the formulation a bit, so that it goes on arguing that what is good for it is good for everyone. For instance, property industry representatives are learning that expressways have become extremely unpopular in many Canadian cities. In Vancouver, Edmonton, and Toronto, aroused citizens have actually succeeded in stopping specific expressway projects. But it won't take long for the industry to learn that it can live almost as snugly (and profitably) with subway systems, which have the same effect of improving general accessibility and assisting property values downtown and along the route. The industry will be able to go on arguing for new public works and services — but not, as its spokesmen would have it, because they are desirable for people or because urban residents will be happier with them; the property industry wants them because they make property investors wealthy.

What they want vs. what we need

Years of exposure to the viewpoint of property industry spokesmen have convinced most people that, in some respects at least, they are right. What is good for the property industry at city hall and with other governments — respect for property rights, new public works, development, low taxes — is usually thought of as what is good for the rest of us too.

Before we get down to details, we need to be clear about one basic issue: there is a fundamental, overriding conflict between the interests of the property industry and the interests of ordinary citizens. The industry's basic desire is to have land values, building prices, and rents as high as possible at all times, and to see property values going up as quickly as possible, rents going up just as fast, and only as much new construction and development as is consistent with their desire to maximize their profits and wealth. The basic interest of ordinary people is exactly the opposite. They want to have land prices as low as possible, housing and other kinds of accommodation as cheap as possible, and rents low. Any deviation from this arrangement of low land values and low rents takes money out of their pocket and puts it into the coffers of the property industry. It makes the Bronfmans and the Eatons even richer, and it turns sleazy fast operators who get into the development business in every Canadian city into rich men. Remember that we are talking about big money here. This is not a case of someone monopolizing the match industry, so that all consumers have to spend $2 a year instead of $1 on matches. The property industry touches us everywhere — in our housing expenses, as a component in the prices we pay for virtually every domestically-produced commodity, in the expenses of every public agency and so in our taxes. No reliable statistics are available, but it is not at all unreasonable (in view of the capital invested in urban property) to think that the average Canadian family, with an income of $7,000 a year, pays out $1,500 to $2,000 a year to the property industry. That is $15 or $20 billion a year.

For what we pay we get accommodation. And to a limited extent, though people are paying more for accommodation now than they used to, they are getting better quality shelter and more of it. Nevertheless, *most* of the increase is accounted for simply by people paying higher and higher prices for the same thing. The property industry gets richer, and the rest of us are poorer than we would be if we weren't lining the pocket of the industry.

Where I used to live, there is a row of six wood frame cottages built in the mid-1800s, which have been rented to tenants ever since they were erected. In the lifetime of one lady who has always lived there, rents have gone up from $12 a month to $95. The construction costs of the cottages were of course paid for long ago. Some repairs and improvements have been made, but a year's rental income would more than pay for all the work that's been done in the last ten. What is the result of those rent increases? It is simple. The old lady and the other tenants have less money available to spend on things they need, and the property investor who owns those cottages is getting richer.

As far as the property industry is concerned, the wealthier it gets the better. As far as the rest of us are concerned, the less we have to pay for the accommodation we need, the better off we are. That is the basic conflict of interest between the property industry and the people.

Home ownership: the people's property industry?

The only serious counter to the view that there is a basic conflict between the interests of ordinary people who need urban accommodation and those of the property industry who sell accommodation is the argument that a very high proportion of people in the country are really in the property industry themselves. They are property investors, because they own (or are buying) the house they live in. As purchasers of shelter they might be losing as rents and housing costs go up and up; but as owners of real estate, and as suppliers of housing in the form of the property that they own and that they themselves use, they gain as rents and housing costs go up. And so when the property industry spokesmen argue that property values should be protected and should go up, thousands of home owners silently nod their head in agreement. Cadillac, Trizec and the other big developers and property owners win by this arrangement, but so — it is argued — do all the small-time property investors who own their own homes.

In effect, the argument is that we have a people's property industry. Lots of people own real estate. They all gain when property values go up.

The first difficulty with this analysis is that not everyone in Canada is a property owner. In Canada in 1966, there were 5,180,473 dwelling units. Of these, slightly more than 3 million were owner-occupied. That leaves 1.9 million families and individuals, or about 40 per cent of the total, as tenants; and that is a pretty substantial number of people to be left out of any kind of people's capitalism.

A second difficulty, and one which has been mentioned before, is that this analysis assumes that ordinary home owners have the same primary motive as property investors — an overriding desire to make profits. This is rarely the primary concern of home owners. They have other reasons for buying a house. And only in very special circumstances do they give up on all their concerns to make decisions based on a single overriding concern for profits and capital gains.

But we also need to examine carefully the assertion that home owners can make profits and enormous capital gains from their houses when big property investors are clearly doing this.

Most people who buy houses do so because they need accommodation, and they see long-term advantages in buying rather than renting their shelter. There is a long-term advantage because usually, with an investment of only a few thousand dollars in cash, you find yourself with a mortgage to pay off that (along with other housing expenses) costs little if anything more than rent would cost for the same house. But a mortgage payment includes an element of forced savings, and after 20 or 25 years — conveniently, and not by accident, the time when most people who bought their house when they were starting their family are nearing retirement and facing much lower retirement incomes — a home owner finally pays off his mortgage so he owns his house outright and pays only municipal taxes plus maintenance and repair costs for his housing. If during the mortgage period the value of houses falls drastically, he has not much to lose beyond his initial down payment because he has never paid more in mortgage payments and other expenses than he would have paid as a tenant for the same accommodation. If during the 20-year period the value of houses rises (and of course it has been rising steadily since 1945) he appears to be better off. The new house he bought for $15,000 becomes worth $45,000; he has made a capital gain of $30,000, or so it appears.

In spite of the apparent monetary gain, the home owner is in fact no further ahead in housing terms just because his $15,000 house has, along with all other $15,000 houses, increased in value to $45,000. His $45,000 now buys nothing more and nothing less *in housing terms* than his $15,000 did 20 years ago. He might, of course, decide to take his $45,000 and spend it on other things, but he will still have to have shelter of some kind and he will have to pay today's prices for it.

Home owners are, however, much better off in housing terms than are tenants. That is because tenants face, over the years, steadily increasing rents for the same accommodation. A home owner, on the other hand, buys into the housing market at the price level current when he makes his purchase and his shelter costs, mainly his mortgage payments, are more or less fixed for the next 20 years. At the beginning of the period both tenant and home owner might have been paying $150 a month for identical new houses, the tenant's $150 being rent, the home owner's $150 mortgage payments and taxes. Ten years later, the home owner will still be paying his $150. But the tenant is likely to be paying $200 to $250. The difference between them is not the home owner's gain; it is the tenant's loss. *It is the measure of the extra exploitation and profiteering to which the tenant is open because of his status.* The original $150 a month was a price that already provided the property industry with its usual high profits. The developer who built the house the home owner bought made handsome gains when he sold it for $15,000. The tenant who at that time was paying $150 a month to his landlord to rent the house was paying the market rent, which was enough to cover the cost of that house. But the home owner, because he had the few thousand dollars for a down payment which is the

entrance fee to the home owner category, provided profits for the property industry just once, in this initial transaction. The tenant made possible all these profits originally, and then increases them each time his rent goes up. Because his landlord can continue to increase his rent as the market rises, he goes on losing more and more every year. Home owners escape this exploitation, but to consider their escape a positive gain is to be obtuse; it is in fact only a loss that they manage to avoid.

Rent increases across the country

The economic and political climate created by activism has worked against apartment unit starts in Metropolitan Toronto, which has Canada's most acute housing problem, according to William Hignett, head of Central Mortgage and Housing Corp.

Apartment units newly completed but unoccupied declined to 2,887 in October from 3,349 a year earlier in the Metropolitan Toronto census area. In the City of Toronto, completed but unoccupied units dropped to 160 from 784 a year earlier.

This growing shortage of units will place upward pressure on the rents of existing units.

Harold Shipp, president of the Housing and Urban Development Association of Canada, and also president of Shipp Corp. Ltd. of Mississauga, says the 900 units his company owns will have rent increases varying between 5 and 10 per cent.

MEPC Canadian Properties Ltd. of Toronto has also withdrawn from the residential field. Last year it sold two of its three apartment buildings and would like to sell the third.

Peter Anker, MEPC president, says:

"If current political trends continue, it is my personal belief that in a few years time, private enterprise may have no alternative but to move out of the rental portion of the residential industry . . ."

Vancouver, however, is not suffering a shortage of apartment units except in certain areas. The rent increases are attributed solely to a need to keep pace with rising costs. Newly completed but unoccupied apartment units declined in November, however, to 752 from 777 a year earlier.

In Halifax, the apartment market is recovering from an almost complete no-vacancy state. The vacancy rate has risen from less than 1 per cent a year ago to about 4 or 5 per cent this fall.

As a result, rents in Halifax are still reasonably high, having been raised during the low-vacancy period.

Eugene Mattatall, general manager of the eastern division of Cummings Properties Ltd. of Calgary, expects a 5 per cent increase in rents in Halifax in 1972. The increase is necessary to keep pace with property taxes and escalating maintenance costs.

In November, CMHC says newly completed but unoccupied units were virtually unchanged. Totals show 67 for November, compared with 65 a year earlier.

In Montreal, an increase in November completions

has raised the number of newly completed but unoccupied apartment units to 1,731 from 1,439 a year earlier.

But in spite of this recent flurry of activity, there is still a low vacancy rate in most areas, according to Westmount Realty Ltd. of Montreal, which manages about 1,000 units for various developers.

A company spokesman says he anticipates rent increases of 7 to 8 per cent next year to help offset rising taxes and maintenance costs.

"This is a tricky business. If vacancy rates are high, then rents are too high and if vacancy rates are low then rents are too low. Right now our vacancy rate is less than 1 per cent, so you can see what kind of position I am in."

Toronto has its own special problems. One of those is that unless developers raise rents they will not be able to afford any new buildings, according to Valerie Van Iterson, director of marketing for Goldlist Property Management Ltd. of Toronto.

In Western Canada, Calgary has its own special problems. Earlier this year that city had one of Canada's highest apartment vacancy rates — about 15 per cent. The situation is improving, however, but newly completed and unoccupied units rose in November to 348 from 285 a year earlier.

Leon Snider, general manager of the property management division of Calgary-based Paragon Properties Ltd., says the several thousand units his company has in Calgary can probably look forward to only minimal increases.

Competition is still stiff in Calgary, but not so stiff as it was earlier this year.

"The vacancy rate is slowly tapering off but there's still strong competition. It just isn't as bad as it was earlier though.

"There isn't that much of a cost-price squeeze just now. The real trouble is in maintaining high standards in maintenance and service. I think we've done it and that has kept us in a good rental position."

In Edmonton, however, newly completed but unoccupied apartment units are down to 936 units from 1,097 a year earlier.

A Central Mortgage and Housing Corp. spokesman says this is not a very valid indicator of trends but suggests Edmonton might find itself suffering from the same problems as Toronto later in the year.

Globe and Mail 17 Dec. 1971   Reprinted with permission

Property ownership does not mean the same thing for owner occupants that it does for property investors. For owner occupants property ownership is a strategy that enables them to escape a certain measure of exploitation by the property industry. For property investors, property ownership is a device whereby they can use spare cash of their own to make extremely high profits and capital gains. Of course people who are reasonably well off are far more likely to own their own home than are people with a low income. That is because the property industry in collaboration with government, particularly the federal government and CMHC, has set up the housing market and the mortgage system so you have to have a certain amount of available cash to buy in, enough to make a down payment. Accumulating cash is always extremely difficult for low-income families, and many are never able to manage it. But everyone is quite clear on the advantages of being a home owner, and many working-class families go to great lengths to be able to change from being tenants to being home owners. Their reason for doing so is not to become small-time capitalists, to own a little real estate so they can make profits and capital gains just like Cadillac and Trizec and the others. Their reason for doing so is to avoid going on having to provide these property investors and others like them with their accustomed high profits every year.

The property industry is not a fine example of people's capitalism at work. Individual home owners are in general not part of the industry. They have quite different interests from those of the industry, and what is good for them and other ordinary people is quite different from what the industry considers to be good for itself.

Their program and ours

The property industry's program for government is to protect the investments and increase profits for the owners of the corporations in the industry. The industry is a large one, certainly, and there are a lot of small-time co-adventurers who ride on big-time coattails and make a little money themselves. Lawyers, real estate agents and insurance agents are in that category. But the property industry's program is basically designed for the benefit of big property investors, the mortgage lenders, the real estate and development companies, and the construction companies.

Even though there is a basic conflict of interest between the property industry and ordinary people, however, that is not to say that specific items on the industry's platform always contradict items that might reflect the interests of ordinary city residents. Thus for instance it is important for the property industry that municipal property taxes be kept fairly low, because high property taxes reduce the values of their properties. It is also in the interests of ordinary city residents that taxes be kept low, because high taxes increase people's housing costs.

For the property industry, civic investments in major works and services are highly desirable because they increase real estate values. The industry may prefer sewers, sidewalks and expressways, but they gain from subways as well, and from parks and playgrounds too. City residents may feel that they have had enough of widened streets and new expressways, but they usually want far more parks and playgrounds. On this specific matter too, their program and the property industry's coincide.

In general, though, there is a tremendous divergence between what is in the best interests of city residents and what suits the property industry. But we are all so used to seeing the city more or less through the property industry's eyes, we are so used to approving of what is good for the property industry, that it is rather difficult to grasp the extent of the conflict. The industry holds as basic principles, for example, that property values are sacred, that property rights come first, and that existing arrangements about land ownership and land tenure should not be interfered with. We have all heard millions of times how important are the basic rights of property owners. Many of us have fought for the rights of small property owners, as for instance in cases where home owners are expropriated for ridiculously low prices by city governments who want their land for dangerous and harmful projects. We are all aware of some specific advantages of the status quo. It is, for instance, a great boon to Canadian cities that downtown land is still mostly divided up into small parcels with lots of small-time property owners, because that creates a far more diverse economic life in the city than any pattern of large tracts of land held by a few wealthy owners would.

Yet the fact is that land ownership is used as a device for wealthy corporations to skim off a big chunk of everyone's earnings in the form of rents and interest on mortgages every year. If city hall owned all the land in its jurisdiction, at the very least those same amounts of money would be going to city government to pay its expenses and the tax load could be reduced. Until January 1972, virtually every penny made in capital gains by property investors was completely tax-free. Now at least some tax will be paid on these gains, at half the marginal income tax rate of the investor. Yet the British government administered for several years a 100 per-cent "betterment levy" which meant that every dollar made by a property investor in capital gains on land went to the public treasury. A measure like that would make possible pretty substantial cuts in income taxes on average income earners.

Even though the plank calling for protection of property values and property rights still goes largely unquestioned by people, other parts of the industry's platform are being challenged. No longer do people who have lived through the last 10 or 15 years of growth and expansion in Toronto or Vancouver believe that it is the most wonderful thing possible. No longer are public works of any kind, including expressways, considered progress, and automatically desirable. No longer does the whole city applaud when they send in the bulldozers to knock down another working-class neighbourhood, falsely labelled a "slum" by the politicians.

On specific matters, people have been realizing how different their interests are from those of the property industry. In general, though, the remarkable thing about the industry's political program is that every government in Canada every day including every city hall is busy occupied in implementing exactly the program the industry has ordered. What is good for the property industry is what politicians and bureaucrats are busy doing. To discover why this is, and to explain why politicians resist ferociously any suggestion from citizens and voters that things ought to be different, we have to look closely at the links between the industry and government.

ST. BONIFACE IS DEAD: When St. Boniface, the predominantly French-speaking city was abolished by an act of the Manitoba provincial government and made part of an amalgamated city government in the Winnipeg urban area, some anonymous St. Boniface residents showed their disapproval by flying the flag upside down, at half mast, in front of the city hall.

Reprinted with permission Winnipeg Free Press

PART 2

Government and the property industry

CHAPTER 6

The property industry and the "senior" governments

What is most striking about the property industry's political program is how simple and how commonplace it is. On paper, it is just the list of ideal demands we would expect the industry to make of governments at all levels; but it is much more than that — it is an outline of the actual policies being implemented every day by virtually every government, municipal, provincial and federal, in the country. That is not to say that the property industry has no complaints about government policy. Some, like the long-standing complaint about the imposition of federal sales tax on building materials, have been around for a long time and have received widespread publicity. Others, like the industry's recent unhappiness over the federal income tax change that narrowed the scope for artificially reducing income tax by charging phoney "depreciation" on real estate investments as a business expense, are less easily understood by outsiders. On the whole, though, apart from these minor irritations and a long list of ways in which government could treat the property industry even better than it treats it now, the industry knows what it wants from government — and gets it.

A lot of what the property industry wants concerns the small but highly-important powers of land-use regulation and servicing held by city hall. We will see in the next three chapters how the property industry has arranged at city hall to get its way, even at the expense of the public interest and often contrary to the explicit wishes of large numbers of people. But before we look closely at how the industry succeeds in controlling city hall, we need to look at the relationships between the industry and the "senior" levels of government, the federal and provincial levels. It is at these higher levels that major policy decisions are made which establish the basic framework in which the industry operates, and where the power resides to determine whether the industry is to be allowed to exist in its privately-owned, highly-centralized form in the first place, how it is to be allowed to operate, and what profits it is to be allowed to make. So long as a basic framework satisfactory to the industry is maintained, the industry is free to focus most of its attention on the detailed regulation done by city hall. But the busyness of industry representatives in keeping things going their way in municipal governments across the country should not obscure the enormous importance to them of having federal and provincial policies that make their operations possible and keep them as highly profitable as they are.

Why does the property industry receive such good treatment from senior governments? To answer the question, we need to look at the links between industry and government.

Personnel

The most obvious link is that out of the property indus-

try come personnel who get themselves jobs as elected politicians, and then place themselves in positions where they exercise considerable influence over government policy affecting the property industry. So, for instance, residential house builder Paul Hellyer, after a stint in the cabinet as defence minister and then an unsuccessful attempt at running for the federal Liberal leadership, becomes the de facto federal urban affairs minister and draws together a group of outsiders, many of them directly involved in the property industry, to develop new federal government housing policies. James Gillies, dean of administrative studies at York University and a director of two major Toronto-area developers, Markborough Properties and Fidinam (Ontario), gets himself a Conservative nomination in the 1972 federal election with the knowledge that a Conservative victory would propel him into a senior financial ministry where policies important to the property industry as well as to other major industries would be made. Robert Kaplan, a young lawyer and son-in-law of Max Tanenbaum who, together with other members of the Tanenbaum family, controls large amounts of developed and undeveloped land in the Toronto area, spends enormous amounts of money to beat Dalton Camp and get himself elected to the House of Commons in 1968. Former Ontario municipal affairs minister Dalton Bales turns out to have a small land speculation on the side in vacant land northeast of Toronto, close to where the new Pickering airport planned jointly by Ontario and Ottawa is scheduled to be built. A second former municipal affairs minister in Ontario, Darcy McKeough, proves to be general manager of the family plumbing supplies firm and a shareholder in a company developing a residential subdivision in his hometown of Chatham. In the absence of adequate detailed studies of the business interests of federal and provincial politicians, examples like these serve to indicate that it is quite common for politicians at these levels to have close links to the property industry. We should expect that cabinet members whose official responsibility is to make policy affecting the industry are quite likely to have personal and business interests in the industry.

Influence

The links of influence between the industry and senior governments are more difficult to trace, and even less information is available about them. What we know is that all governments take very seriously the views and concerns of powerful corporations and families. With the exception of NDP governments, there is a close similarity if not an identity between the way the corporate elite see the world and the way the people running government see it. While the federal cabinet may not pay much attention to ambitious small-time entrepreneurs busy trying to make their fortune with other people's money in real estate development, it certainly pays very close heed to the views of families like the Bronfmans and the Eatons, and listens carefully to the chairmen of the boards of Bank of Montreal and Canada Life. The involvement of the major financial institutions in the property industry is a guarantee that some of the most powerful and influential people in the country are going to be concerned about the industry's welfare, and are going to urge on provincial governments and the federal government the kinds of policies that will allow the industry to continue on its present course, to expand and to increase its profits. Any drastic change would be a very serious blow to these institutions and their investments.

Political parties

Another link between the senior governments and the property industry exists through the business-oriented political parties, the Liberals, the Conservatives and (where they are a significant force) the Socreds. Property industry people who are active at the high levels of political party organizations make the contacts with politicians that can serve them and their business associates extremely well when the party is in power, and they are able to help exercise some influence over party policies and the selection of party candidates. Other major industries, of course, also have representatives and friends involved in the business-oriented political parties, so the property industry is by no means alone in this arrangement.

An excellent example of this kind of link exists in the person of Eddie Goodman, whom we have already encountered in his capacity as a director of Cadillac Development. Goodman is past national president of the Conservative party, and fund-raiser and friend to both the powerful Ontario Tory party and to its federal counterpart. Goodman is a Toronto lawyer, and among his many clients are important property industry companies besides Cadillac whom he represents in their dealings with municipal, provincial and federal authorities. Goodman has formal links to Brascan and John Labatt, to the Eaton family and to the Bassetts, as well as to Cadillac. He represents other property developers like the Fairview-Eaton joint venture proposing redevelopment for Eaton's downtown Toronto land-holdings in 1971-72. He also takes a fatherly interest in city politics in the Toronto area, and has been involved in raising funds for developer-oriented mayoralty candidates.

Money

Along with the personnel that the property industry provides both to political party organizations and to government, money in the form of donations and campaign contributions is another link that greatly helps solidify the connections between government and the industry. We know very little about the sources of political parties' funds, apart from the NDP, which relies on members' contributions, small donations, and funds provided through labour unions. But Liberal and Conservative party representatives have often admitted that a considerable amount of the funds they receive to run election campaigns comes from large corporations, and given what we know about property industry contributions to city election campaigns it is certainly safe to assume that amongst those big contributors are many property industry corporations. The reported practice of corporate donors is to divide their money up between the two business-oriented political parties, which helps ensure that all the industry's eggs are not placed in one basket. The collapse of the Trudeau government in 1971-72 over mild reform proposals affecting big business — tax reform, the Competition Act proposed by Ron Basford, and the "takeover policy" to deal with foreign ownership — clearly indicated its unwillingness to take steps that would offend these campaign contributors. For their part, business representatives make no bones about the connection between their contributions and "acceptable" policies from parties in power.

Careers for civil servants

Complementing the links that connect the property industry to the cabinets and elected politicians of federal and provincial governments are similar links between the industry and the civil service, which of course develops and implements the policies that concern the industry. The most revealing of these is the pattern of bureaucrats' careers, whereby many of the most successful and able civil servants use their professional familiarity with the industry and government regulation to advance themselves by moving out of government and into industry.

So we find David Mansur, former chairman of the powerful federal government agency CMHC, now in the employ of private mortgage lenders. Mansur is chairman of Kinross

---

HOUSING REPORT CITED
'No land pressure'

LONDON, Ont. (CP) — Don Mathews, a London land developer and president of the national Conservative party, said Thursday he knows of no political pressure being exerted by developers to stop plans for public land-assembly projects.

He was commenting on a report prepared for the federal government and released Wednesday by David Lewis, national leader of the New Democratic Party.

Mathews, one of London's largest land developers, said that although he did not know of any pressure by developers against land-bank schemes, he does not believe public land banks or government land development is the best method of keeping down building lot prices.

Vancouver Sun August 1972

Big-time operators

There are a number of people in this town—Eddie Goodman, for instance, or Robert Macaulay, or Keith Davey—who owe their livelihoods to the fact that they can pick up the phone any time and get through to a bank president or a cabinet minister or a newspaper publisher and settle large matters in five minutes flat, including three minutes of chummy banter about hockey. But nobody is better at this game than Alan Eagleson.

Toronto Star 1 Sept. 1972

— *Toronto Star* columnist Alexander Ross explaining the way people like Eddie Goodman operate. Interestingly enough, Ross's list of Toronto operators includes both Goodman and another developers' lawyer, Robert Macaulay, a former Ontario cabinet minister in charge of housing and now a director of Victoria Wood, a Toronto-based development firm owned by U.S. interests.

Mortgage Corp., a subsidiary of the Bank of Commerce and a large-scale source of mortgage funds for builders and developers; chairman of the Royal Insurance Group; and a director of Consumers' Gas, Guaranty Trust and Markborough Properties, all property industry corporations.

We find Graham Towers, former head of the Bank of Canada, which supervises financial institutions and particularly chartered banks, as a director of Canada Life.

Or we read about how the Campeau Corporation, Canada's second-largest public real estate company, only really began to move when Jean Paradis left his job with CMHC, where he was administering federal government money being lent to developers, and moved over to Campeau, where he worked at getting those same funds (and other money) to finance Campeau projects.

And we note Paul Goyette, former vice-chairman and managing director of Ontario's public housing agency Ontario Housing Corporation, leaving his job there to work for a house builder in Ottawa.

Most of the movement between property industry firms and government appears to be in one direction — civil servants moving out into the more lucrative world of the corporations. The long-standing work relationships they have developed with their fellow government employees help cement close relationships and a sense of basic common interests between the industry and the government agencies the industry deals with. The possibility of making a move of this kind must act as an incentive for many government employees to take a kindly attitude towards the businessmen they deal with, in the hopes that they too will soon be able to move out and up.

The payoff: friendly government policies

The many links between the senior governments and the property industry suggest why government policy regarding housing and urban affairs is almost exactly what the industry would like it to be. The politicians who have been involved in the property industry and the civil servants who may have hopes of getting into it combine to develop and administer programs that honour the status quo and make it possible for the industry to continue operating as it does, and even to continue expanding its activities and its profits. What is more, the links between industry and government are such that if a politician, a cabinet minister or even a government proposes a policy the industry doesn't like, the industry can usually bring enough pressure to bear to get that decision changed. A brief look at the major policies and programs of federal and provincial governments is enough to indicate how favourable they are for the property industry.

Housing policy

Both federal and provincial governments have an interest in housing policy, though most of the major powers belong to Ottawa. The federal government has created a crown corporation, Central Mortgage and Housing Corp., which administers government programs and implements federal housing legislation. Ever since its creation, CMHC's main function has been to support the private housing industry by providing mortgage insurance to guarantee mortgage lenders against loss and to make it easier for mortgage borrowers to find lenders. CMHC officials often explain that they think they should act simply as "bankers," taking lit-

tle interest in what is done with money borrowed directly from them or through their insurance scheme beyond ensuring that it is used to construct some kind of housing. Bankers they have been, and their activities have made it easy for private developers and house builders to carry on the kind of building that serves that part of the market where the greatest profits are to be made. Only very recently has CMHC come under wide attack for its failure to implement any kind of housing policy other than that of allowing the property industry to pursue maximum profits as it thinks best.

CMHC also administers a number of federal government housing programs, such as the old people's housing program and the public housing program, which attempt to operate outside the private housing market to provide adequate accommodation for people who manifestly lack it. None of these programs has been very large in scale compared to the total amount of new residential construction, though in some cities subsidized housing built under federal programs has been a noticeable factor in the supply of reasonably priced housing for people with modest incomes. But CMHC, along with parallel provincial agencies, has managed to devise a structure for the public housing program whereby the property industry can build this kind of housing as well as housing for the private market and make profits both ways. And CMHC has been notorious in the way it discourages attempts by ordinary people to establish organizations like citizen-owned, non-profit housing companies and housing co-ops in order to take concrete steps to provide at least a little new housing at reasonable prices independent of the property industry.

Fiscal and monetary policy

With its overall powers to regulate economic activity, the federal government is in a position to make decisions about how much money is to be invested in new construction every year, what kinds of construction are to be allowed, and what the interest rate will be on funds used for these purposes. The two senior levels of government have the power to regulate property industry prices, to regulate rents, to control profits made on land, and to supervise the prices of existing properties. If it chose to do so, the federal government could for instance direct the chartered banks to lend one tenth of their total assets on mortgages at 2 percent interest for low-priced owner-occupied housing.

The federal government does take a certain interest in housing conditions, and tries to ensure that what is considered a reasonable level of new residential construction takes place every year. But, apart from the token subsidized-housing policies, it has done nothing to regulate the price of housing or profits in the property industry. It has always allowed mortgage lenders to charge higher than prime interest rates on mortgages, and these interest rates have risen dramatically in recent years. Over the ten-year period 1961-1971, the cost of borrowing mortgage money *doubled*. This is a direct result of federal government monetary policies. This rise in interest rates has been by far the largest factor in the rapidly increasing price people have to pay for housing. Even though higher prices narrow the potential market for new housing, they are extremely profitable to the property industry, particularly to the financial institutions involved in the industry through the money they lend. There is no doubt that government policies in

Continued on Page 89

Federal housing policy and the property industry: the 1972 NHA package

The close relationship between federal government policies and the activities of the property industry is well illustrated by a package of amendments to the National Housing Act which were proposed by the Trudeau government in June 1972.

The newspaper article excerpts on these four pages report on the amendments themselves, and the public reactions of a number of interested people.

Newspaper accounts (like the article quoted here from the Toronto *Globe and Mail*) repeated uncritically the descriptions of the new programs offered by the federal housing minister, Ron Basford, and his public relations men. In some cases in the *Globe* story, the reporter has copied word for word from the government's press release.

One obvious weakness of the government's proposals, as many critics pointed out, was that the new legislation had been introduced so late in the 1972 sitting of the House of Commons that it was unlikely that any concrete action would be taken before mid-1973.

What did not emerge from the accounts and criticisms, however, was how small the proposed federal effort would be in terms of the housing markets or the housing needs of Canadians. The proposed changes were so tiny in scope that they left the property industry free to carry on exactly as before.

To illustrate:

The proposed *Neighbourhood Improvement Program* very closely resembles the old urban renewal program, suspended by Ottawa in 1968 as public criticism was mounting and (perhaps more important) more and more municipalities were rushing to take advantage of the federal funds available to pay for planning expenses and then for implementation of wholesale redevelopment in both residential and commercial areas. The 1972 program still would allow expropriation and demolition, though it would restrict new housing to "medium low density" housing, whatever that might turn out to mean. It would limit urban renewal to residential areas, which was the original intention of the policy of the 1950s and 1960s, so that the federal government would no longer subsidize downtown redevelopment projects as they have in cities like Hamilton.

Estimated total cost of this urban renewal program is $80 million a year. That is enough money to buy up and tear down 6000 houses a year at $15,000 each; or enough money to build 4500 new houses at the 1971 average cost of construction for NHA houses of $18,000. If the money is used both for expropriation and for new construction, it could pay for the demolition of 3400 houses and their replacement with 3400 new houses per year. This is a tiny program to spread across the country, considering that in 1971 total new house construction was 201,000 units.

The *Residential Rehabilitation Assistance Program* is intended to provide grants and loans up to $4,000 for owner-occupiers or landlords in urban renewal areas, to cover costs of rehabilitating houses.

The first point to note about this scheme is that $4,000 is a very small amount of money to make available for repairs and renovations, and pays for relatively little work on a house. Given that the replacement cost of an old house is something like $33,000 (the cost of buying the existing house, tearing it down, and then putting up a new house in its place) a $4,000 maximum on public assistance for renovation costs is returning to the pre-1969 situation where all the pressures of federal programs were towards expropriation and demolition.

The second point about rehabilitation grants is that it takes extremely sophisticated administration to ensure that the money is not used by landlords for profiteering, or by small-time developers who buy a house, renovate it with a grant, and then sell it to a new (and usually much higher-income) purchaser. The British government, which has had a rehabilitation grant program for some time, has permitted abuses of this kind. None of the program descriptions issued by the government give any evidence that things would be better administered in Canada.

The most important thing about this rehabilitation

NEW FEDERAL HOUSING PROGRAMS AS PROPOSED JUNE 1972	ANNUAL FEDERAL INPUT, GRANTS AND LOANS COMBINED	NUMBER OF HOUSING UNITS AFFECTED
PROGRAM	(IN MILLIONS)	
Neighbourhood Improvement	$80	3400
Residential Rehabilitation Assistance Program	$6	1500
Assisted Home Ownership Program	$155	6500
Non-profit housing corporations	$142	12,900
	not specified	not many
	$383	24,300

grant program, however, is the federal cost estimate. It is $4 million for loans and $2 million for grants a year. This is enough to provide $4,000 grants to rehabilitate exactly 500 houses a year, and $4,000 loans to rehabilitate another 1000. Compared to the number of low-income owner-occupiers who could use such grants, the number of old houses needing rehabilitation and repairs, the number of old houses being demolished by private developers every year for high-rise apartments financed under other sections of the federal government's legislation, or the number of new houses being built every year, the program is so minuscule it would be unfair to describe it as even a drop in the bucket.

The *Assisted Home Ownership Program* would offer low-income families mortgages at 7 5/8 per-cent instead of 9 1/2 per-cent — not exactly what one would call a bargain — and extend the repayment period over 40 years instead of 25 — which would be discouraging, rather than encouraging, to most people although it reduces monthly payments somewhat. A scheme of this kind has been operating since 1970 and has financed 10,000 houses — 5000 a year.

The 1972 proposals would provide $155 million in mortgage money and subsidies a year for this program. At the Canada-wide average cost of a new NHA house in 1972, $23,500, this means that the number of families able to buy homes at these reduced rates would increase from 5000 a year to 6000 or 6500. These figures are still tiny given that families with average or below-average incomes cannot afford to buy NHA houses at market prices. For most people, this program reduces house costs by such a small amount that they are still unable to afford to buy a new house.

Non-profit Housing Corporations built 50,000 housing units in 1964-71, about 7000 a year. The 1972 proposals would call for $129 million a year in mortgages for these units, which could produce 12,900 units a year if they were very small and cheap apartment units, fewer if they were row houses or detached houses. The housing produced by non-profit housing corporations costs somewhat less than usual market prices because of the lower interest rate paid by these corporations on their mortgages, but it is still beyond the means of many families. More important, the size of the program is a tiny part of total new house construction and meets only a tiny fraction of the housing needs of families.

Somewhat more useful, but still tiny in relation to spending on other matters or need, would be the proposed $13 million in grants which CMHC would provide to non-profit corporations to cover their administrative costs and expenses.

Land Assembly programs have always been possible for municipalities, and since 1950 municipalities have been able to borrow money for this purpose from CMHC. Very few Canadian cities have, however, chosen to use this simple and obvious way of cutting the cost of new housing by eliminating speculators' profits in the development of vacant land. The total federal government investment in land assembly from 1950 to 1971 was $63.9 million, about $3 million a year. This program

has been of no help to the residents of almost all Canadian cities. The 1972 proposals would do nothing to start up large-scale land assemblies and land bank programs in every major Canadian city, except in the unlikely event that city councils decided themselves to get into this field.

So these proposed programs, some of which are only expansions or rewritings of old programs, would add up to very little in terms of impact on the housing market or on housing costs. In total they might affect 24,000 housing units a year. In comparison, the property industry is in total producing more than 200,000 units of housing a year. In 1971, loans totalling $139 million were made to developers for "limited-dividend" projects. In 1970, the figure was $241 million. The ordinary public housing and old people's housing program, which does not allow tenants to be homeowners and in many cities puts low-income families into high-rise apartment buildings, produced 34,000 units in 1971 and cost $414 million. Much of this $414 million was spent through private developers, who have learned that they can live with the existing federal government housing program and make money from it by doing the development and construction.

The 1972 package of proposed National Housing Act amendments carried on with the same basic policies regarding housing and the property industry which the federal government has followed for some time. Overall the government supports and organizes the private market, helping with devices like mortgage insurance and CMHC direct lending. With this support, the property industry goes unimpeded about its business of making the maximum possible profits from the housing and property business.

At the margin, though, the federal government institutes programs which mitigate to a small extent the worst effects of the actions of private industry, for instance providing a small stock of public housing with lower than market rents, and subsidizing housing for old people and students. These programs are not large enough to have any great effect on the private market, except to insulate it somewhat from pressure for large-scale reforms. In addition, they are usually designed to provide new ways for the property industry to make money, so that while some "social" demands are being met the industry's profits are being enhanced.

None of the changes involved in the 1972 amendments amount to a serious challenge to the property industry, a serious effort to solve the continual shortage of housing in urban areas, or a serious threat to the enormous profits being made by the property industry. The only program which could make major inroads on property industry profits and could achieve substantial reductions in housing costs, the public land assembly program, is one which has existed since 1950 and which the federal government has designed to rely on initiatives from municipal governments. Everyone knows from experience that municipal governments are the last people to get involved in public policies which threaten property industry profits.

Ottawa announces NHA amendments

OTTAWA — Urban Affairs Minister Ronald Basford indicated the Government is prepared to increase the $1-billion annual budget of Central Mortgage and Housing Co. by almost 50 per cent to pay for several new social housing schemes unveiled yesterday.

He made the comments at a press briefing following introduction in the House of Commons of a bill to amend the National Housing Act. The bill seeks parliamentary approval for seven new low-income housing programs the projected cost of which, if in full operation for a year, would be $457-million.

In addition, the bill increases CMHC's continuing lending authority by $2.1-billion: from $8-billion to $10-billion in the case of CMHC's regular mortgage lending activities; and from $200-million to $300-million in the case of financing for municipal sewage treatment projects.

The seven new programs unveiled yesterday have been under consideration for well over a year and have been widely touted for the past several months. They follow by a few weeks introduction of the Residential Mortgage Financing Act. This bill, also Mr. Basford's, is aimed at improving the flow of private mortgage money available to middle-income Canadians able to purchase and finance on their own.

The seven new programs (and their estimated maximum cost to the federal treasury after one full year of operation) included in yesterday's amendments to the National Housing Act are:

—A Neighborhood Improvement Program (involving $80-million in federal loans and grants) to replace the bulldozer-type urban renewal schemes of the past. It will make available loans and giants for planning, land acquisition and development activities related to the rehabilitation of urban areas. It includes financing for social and recreational opportunities and for day care and multi-use centres as well as the upgrading of municipal services.

—An Assisted Home Ownership Program (i n v o l v i n g $155-million in loans and grants) that will provide low cost federal mortgage loans geared to the income of the recipient. Also involved are matching federal and provincial grants. Both aspects of this program are designed to permit low-income families to become home-owners as an **alternative to continued reliance on public housing.**

— An easing in the terms of **CMHC's lending to non-profit corporations that sponsor housing projects** (involves **$129-million in loans and $13-million in grants**). These changes will provide up to 100 per cent Government financing for housing projects sponsored by these groups for the benefit of senior citizens, families or special purposes. It

also provides for a 10 per cent **capital grant from Ottawa when matched by provincial grants toward the projects.**

—A Land Assembly Program ($70-million in loans and grants) to help provinces and municipalities assemble land for a wide variety of uses related to residential housing development. The aim is to **facilitate larger scale land-banking activities for long-term planning and the development of new communities.**

—A Residential Rehabilitation Assistance Program ($6-million). This will provide matching federal and provincial grants and federal loans that are geared to the income of the recipient. Such funds will be available to both home-owners and landlords, primarily in NIP project areas, for the rehabilitation of substandard low-income housing. They will also generally be available to non-profit housing corporations.

—New measures to permit co-operatives to acquire existing housing and become eligible for all assisted home-purchase and rehabilitation grants and loans that are geared to the income of individual members ($4-million).

—An expansion of CMHC's mandate to participate in experimental housing projects and provide funds for development costs. It will also make "starter" funds available to individuals or groups planning low-income housing projects (no financial estimate provi-

ded).

Mr. Basford said that if yesterday's NHA amendments were passed by Parliament in 1972, the programs could be in operation in 1973. There is almost no possibility of the bill's being dealt with before the summer recess, which is generally expected to begin at the end of this month.

Globe and Mail 13 June 1972
Reprinted with permission

Plan called developers 'fortune'

By HELEN WAINMAN
Star staff writer

QUEBEC — Private developers could make a fortune from government proposals to spend an extra $457 million a year on low-income housing, a Montreal

architect warned yesterday.

Professor Joseph Baker of the Montreal School of Architecture at McGill University said amendments to the National Housing Act, introduced last week in the House of Commons, still favor the developer although they are aimed at low-in-

come families.

Baker said the proposed amendments, while an improvement o v e r previous legislation "are not going to get to the really low-income people," unless the government introduces tighter controls to prevent speculators from making a profit.

Toronto Star June 1972

Mayors' federation president finds weaknesses in Ottawa housing proposal

By GEORGE RUSSELL
Globe and Mail Reporter

OTTAWA — The federal Government's amendments to the National Housing Act do not come to grips with the problems of decaying city cores, Desmond Newman, newly elected president of the Canadian Federation of Mayors and Municipalities, said yesterday.

Interviewed after the legislation was tabled in the Commons, Mr. Newman said the proposed changes, although providing welcome attention to some problem areas, had basically handed the problem the cities. And the cities do not have the funds to handle it, he said.

Mr. Newman lauded the Government for giving attention to the need for medium density, low-income housing in Canada's cities, but said Urban Affairs Minister Ronald Basford seemed to have overlooked the need for commercial rehabilitation—in effect, old-style urban renewal —in older cities.

"There's nothing very formidable for urban renewal here at all. There was a lot of outcry about urban renewal in the past, but that was largely a result of the fact that it did not include any rehabilitative aspect at all. Now they seem to have gone to the other route entirely."

Globe and Mail 13 June 1972.

Builders don't like land bank proposals

By TERRENCE BELFORD

While some elements of the house building industry are privately expressing doubts about the speed with which the new federal housing programs will be implemented, Urban Affairs Minister Ronald Basford claims he is committed to pushing legislation through the Commons by the end of the year—at the latest.

There appears little hope, however, that the amendments to the National Housing Act, which he introduced last Monday, will be approved before the House rises for its summer recess at the end of this month.

Blair Jackson, executive vice-president of the Canadian Real Estate Association, is one of those who regard the amendments with some skepticism.

"I'd be a whole lot more enthusiastic if I could divorce from my mind the fact that all this anticipated social legislation comes just before an election.

While builders like Mr. Hurlburt say of the legislation and its programs "we must make it work," they also question aspects such as federal loans for provincial land assemblies.

In fact, some builders are hostile to government land banking, claiming it usurps a traditional role of private industry and puts tax money into projects that are not necessary since the money could be spent to better advantage by servicing privately held land.

Both Mr. Hurlburt and Mr. Morley support the view that the money could be better spent elsewhere, although they are not among the hostile faction.

Mr. Hurlburt says: "While we agree with federal objectives, we don't necessarily agree with federal methods. Land banking is not what we need. A surplus of serviced land is. We'd rather see the $70-million go to construction of services."

The thought behind servicing rather than land banking

is that massive servicing programs would bring a surplus of land ready for use on to the market and thereby depress prices.

"All land banking does is provide us with a reservoir of raw land and I'm afraid we have more than enough raw land now. Unfortunately you can't build on raw land," Mr. Morley adds.

"It's a further intrusion into private enterprise," says Mr. Jackson.

Federal officials do not meet the question of land banking head-on in their answers. Instead they point to the fact that CMHC has, for some time, made land banking and servicing funds available to provinces and municipalities. Neither level of government has put a strain on these funds.

"For the 15 years we have had funds available for land assembly, I think all we have put out is about $115-million," says one federal housing official.

"We also offer money to

municipalities and provinces for servicing and I don't think it has all been snapped up in any one year.

"We really can't come along to a developer and say 'here's some money to service your land'. Maybe the local municipality or the province doesn't want that land to be brought on stream just yet I don't think we can interfere like that."

Globe and Mail 16 June 1972

Reprinted with permission

this area pay great attention to industry interests, and virtually no attention to the interests of housing consumers.

Tax policy

If governments are determined to allow the property industry to charge high prices for accommodation of all kinds and to make enormous profits, there is still the possibility that some or all of this money could be recouped for public purposes by tax policy. If revenues from taxes imposed on the property industry allowed the state to reduce its tax load on ordinary taxpayers, then there would be at least some indirect gain to average citizens from the tremendous expense they bear in order to provide the property industry with its profits.

Very little detailed independent research has been done on the impact of federal and provincial tax policies on the property industry, but even the briefest examination suggests that here again the industry is receiving incredibly privileged treatment. In fact, it appears that the property industry is virtually tax-free, apart from the property taxes it pays to municipal governments. Even the taxes paid by other businesses (at least paid in the first instance, though of course a large proportion is passed on to the consumer) are not imposed on the property industry. Property industry corporations are liable in theory for corporation income tax, at the rate of about 50 per cent on every dollar of profit for big firms. Yet, as we have already seen in the case of Cadillac, an incredible and indefensible fiction that buildings "depreciate" allows most major property owners to escape virtually all taxation on profits made from real estate investments. There was a feeble attempt at changing this situation in the Benson tax reforms, but by 1971 even this mild change had been scotched except in the case of small-time property investors who were, it seems, willingly sacrificed by the big-time property industry lobby in order to keep its own favoured treatment.

Sales tax, another kind of taxation imposed on most industries by federal and provincial governments (and a tax that appears usually to be passed on directly to the consumer), is not paid on most property industry transactions. Instead of a substantial sales tax on sales of existing land and buildings, a tiny land transfer tax is usually imposed. Federal sales tax is imposed on materials used in new construction, but the property industry is apparently so used to its privileged no-tax position and so unaccustomed to the normal burdens of tax-paying that it is constantly agitating to have even this tax removed. The argument used by industry apologists is that the reduction in the cost of new housing would be passed on directly to the consumer, but given the industry's present performance and willingness to take profits there is little reason to think that the consumer would realize any of the benefits gained by the removal of this tax.

A tremendous amount of the money made by the property industry is in the capital appreciation of land and buildings. Until 1972, absolutely no tax whatsoever was paid on capital gains in Canada. In 1972 capital gains tax was finally implemented, though at only half the rate for every dollar earned through capital gains that is paid on dollars earned from wages, salaries and other sources. The tax is paid only when an investor actually sells the asset he owns and realizes the appreciation, so it will be some time before property investors find themselves in the unaccustomed position of actually paying out to the government some share of the money they make from real estate. If they manage to get along without ever selling their real property assets, they may be able to avoid this tax forever. In the interim, there will be lots of opportunity for industry lawyers and tax specialists to devise inventive ways of avoiding this tax, and indeed some schemes to do this have already been proposed.

Regional planning

Moving from policy areas that are predominantly federal to those that are predominantly provincial, an area of rapidly-growing importance to the property industry is regional planning. This involves broad decision-making about basic land-use patterns and about the location of economic growth and expansion. Government policy has always had implicit regional planning embodied in it; deciding to locate the country's capital in Ottawa is an early and illuminating example of a government decision with regional planning content. So were all the major decisions about the construction and location of transportation facilities. Most major government economic policies like tariff policies have direct implications for both the nature and the location of economic growth.

Given the enormous size and power of the federal government, it follows that a wide range of its decisions has regional planning implications. Its most recent explicit ad-

Let industry build housing for poor: MPP

OTTAWA (CP) — The Ontario Housing Corporation should let private industry take over the task of providing housing for poor families and old persons, a Conservative member of the Ontario Legislature told the Ottawa Real Estate Board yesterday.

Claude Bennett, MPP for Ottawa South and parliamentary assistant to provincial treasurer Darcy McKeough, said the housing corporation filled a gap in the past when private industry was unwilling to become involved in public housing.

"But the Ontario Housing Corporation has gone just far enough. I'm a firm believer that private industry should control development in the province."

Globe and Mail 19 Apr. 1972

venture in regional planning is the regional economic expansion program, where large grants of public funds are ladled out to corporations (many of them foreign-owned) on the naive and unproven hypothesis that this is the most efficient and effective way of influencing corporate decisions and the location of new jobs and economic growth.

Provincial governments are also heavily involved in regional planning, and along with the federal government's grant technique they are able to use their powers to develop regional planning policies when they decide where to locate new roads and other transportation facilities, where to permit or install sewage treatment plants and trunk water mains, and where to enact land-use legislation which permits or rules out new land uses.

Government regional planning policies have many fascinating complexities, but their overall tendency seems to be quite straightforward. Unlimited economic growth and expansion are taken for granted, and the major choices made by public authorities concern where the growth is to be located. The overall preference appears to be clearly on the side of centralization of all kinds, whether this is consolidating tiny outports into small towns in Newfoundland or choosing one town amongst the many in an area and designating it — and only it — as the "regional growth point." The most rapid growth is promoted for the largest cities, and usually this is described as highly desirable. When people object to the mindless growth mentality and the embracing of all growth as good, proponents are quick to slide to a second line of defence and argue that desirable or not it is inevitable. This position is as specious as enthusiasm for growth is empty.

We should, however, note that the action by government to make regional planning an explicit part of policy-making means that this area of decision-making is no longer to be quite so accidental or makeshift, with regional growth implications being an unexpected result of decisions taken on other grounds. With governments developing the capability for setting policies in this area and carrying them out, we should expect that the property industry will be doing its best to ensure that the decisions made are those best suited to its interests. Indeed it appears that the overall thrust of regional planning, particularly in its strong orientation towards centralization, is far more desirable for the property industry than any of the obvious alternatives. It is particularly desirable for the large integrated corporations, which are quickly coming to dominate every area of the property industry. As Vancouver increases in population from 1 million to 2,400,000 by 2001, Winnipeg from 500,000 to 1,614,000, Toronto from 2,000,000 to 6,510,000, who is expecting to build the necessary accommodation and have these new city residents as their tenants? Should we be surprised if it turns out to be Trizec, Campeau, BACM, Cadillac and the other largest and strongest corporate developers?

Local government

Local government, as we have already noted, is entirely the creation of provincial governments, which have the power to decide how local government is organized and indeed the power to alter as they see fit individual policies and actions of municipal councils. As we will see in the chapters that follow, the usual structure of city governments is one that is not at all conducive to detailed control over the decision-makers by the electorate, but rather one that is well suited to domination by a powerful special interest group such as the property industry.

The key to the policy of provincial governments in their approach to local government can be seen in the kinds of changes that they support and those that they refuse to make. Take for example the much-applauded move towards metropolitan city government in cities like Toronto and Winnipeg in the 1950s which were, it was said, suffering from a kind of municipal balkanization because of the large numbers of independent local councils, each governing their fraction of the total city. While rationality and efficiency were the usual justification for two-level metropolitan government (with an overall metro council making up a second layer of local government, above the existing municipal councils in the metro region), in fact the main impact of this reform was to make possible the construction of major public works programs, particularly trunk sewers and water mains, major roads, expressways, and bridges, which the property industry considered necessary to sustain the kind of urban growth the industry wanted to see.

Much the same thing has happened again in Winnipeg, this time ironically promoted by an NDP government (and without pressure from the local property industry), where a single city government was created out of a set of 13 city, suburban, and metropolitan councils at the beginning of 1972. The government promotion of this reform stressed the way in which it would encourage greater citizen involvement and participation in city government, and a little was

Developers seen to benefit

Two North Vancouver district aldermen have launched an attack on proposed changes in the Municipal Act that they say will benefit only developers.

Aldermen Don Bell and Gordon Rose Monday called on municipal councils and residents to oppose amendments proposed by Municipal Affairs Minister Dan Campbell to reduce the present two-thirds majority required to approve zoning bylaw changes to a simple 50 per cent majority.

Campbell introduced the proposal in an extensive list of amendments to the act given first reading March 10.

The proposed changes would affect all B.C. municipalities except Vancouver which already has a simple majority requirement for zoning approval under its city charter.

Bell said the proposal would mean, for example, that developers in North Vancouver district would only need four affirmative votes instead of five from the seven-member council.

"This means it will be easier for poorer prososals to be approved," Rose said. "Any good proposal should have no problem convincing at least two thirds if not all of council of its merits."

Vancouver Province

Unification's full benefit may not be felt for years

Unification of the 13 local governments into one city will be a boon for businessmen but the benefits of centralized administration won't be felt at once, according to Mayor Stephen Juba.

Even though the new government will be feeling its way this year, the mayor sees 1972 as a good year for local business. There should be improvement in all sectors of the local economy with the announcement of some major new developments for the downtown area sparked in part by the decision to proceed with the convention centre. This should mean a good year for local construction firms and this will contribute to a better year for local merchants. There should also be an increase in the productivity of manufacturing but this may not include much new employment.

Tourism, however, should be the area the city concentrates on promoting in the near future. The convention centre may never make a profit on its operations but in combination with the new hotels either built or under construction in the city, it will attract large numbers of tourists who will leave some dollars behind to the benefit of the entire community.

The future of investment in the city never seemed brighter. The mayor said his office has been swamped by inquiries from investors and developers since the civic elections in October and some of the proposals are for the location of completely new industries in the community.

Investors seem to be attracted by the fact that they have only one local government authority to deal with rather than the split jurisdictions of the past with their delays and bickering, Mayor Juba said.

The mayor apparently relishes his role as promoter of investment. At this point in the interview, he began to rummage through the papers on his desk for examples of the type of inquiries he has been receiving. Within moments, he had produced a request from two chief officers of a Toronto-based international firm for an interview and a letter from a company in Osaka, Japan, thanking him for his prompt reply to its inquiries and informing him that some of its executives would be coming to Winnipeg.

Probably, there will be more emphasis on dividing the city into specific use areas, with industry located in industrial parks away from residential areas, said Mayor Juba.

In this respect, the community committees, with their responsibility to screen zoning applications, are important. They will give the citizen a much greater voice in determining the nature of his neighbourhood than he ever had in the past.

Winnipeg Tribune 28 Jan. 1972
Reprinted with permission

Reform for whom?

At the beginning of 1972, Winnipeg's 13 municipal governments were abolished by the province and replaced with a single amalgamated "unicity" government.

The change was presented by the NDP government which brought it about as a positive step towards more rational local government. The politicians stressed changes which they said encouraged citizen participation. What the provincial government wanted, said one pamphlet, was "decentralization of the political processes of government . . . to permit more community participation and identification."

Wrote two of the chief government advisers and architects of the scheme, Meyer Brownstone and Lionel Feldman: "The city of Winnipeg . . . represents a first attempt in Canada to provide formal, statutory requirements and opportunities consistent with the concept of participational representation."*

What the NDP government didn't talk about much was the way in which their changes would benefit Winnipeg's property industry by bringing together the administration of the powers of local government into a single big operation where they could ensure that their interests would be properly taken care of. Whether the final scheme the NDP worked out would make any real contribution to the power of citizen groups was not clear.

What was being done for the property industry, however, was clear.

One small indication that the industry saw the opportunities the new city-wide government provided was given in comments by a director of Cadillac Development, T. H. Inglis, vice-president of North American Life Assurance. At the time when the NDP's proposals were being debated in Winnipeg, he said that he was sure they would encourage development and growth in the city.

The same view of the benefits to the property industry of this new structure are clearly put by Winnipeg's mayor Stephen Juba, in the quoted passages from a newspaper article. Juba, himself a Winnipeg businessman, was long a proponent of amalgamation, and it is clear from what he says that he thought it would be good for the property industry — as well, of course, as for the people of the city.

*Canadian Forum, May 72
p.61

done to encourage this. A great deal was done, however, to create the kind of powerful and centralized city government that could mobilize the resources necessary to provide the public works and services necessary to encourage large-scale development and that could easily be dominated by property industry representatives. Early experience with the new Winnipeg structure has been inconclusive insofar as its impact on public involvement in city politics is concerned, but it is already quite clear that the new city government is going to be an enormous boon to the property industry, particularly to large corporate developers and investors.

Another example of the local government policy of provincial governments is contained in an apparently minor legislative change made by the Bennett government in British Columbia shortly before its surprise defeat at the polls in August 1972. The change was an amendment in provincial legislation, which reduced the city council majority required to approve a municipal rezoning from two-thirds of the local council members to one half. This was done just before a municipal election period at the end of 1972, when many people were expecting anti-development candidates to do very well. The property industry could see the likelihood of the size of its reliable majorities in some British Columbia city halls being substantially reduced, and in some cases even eliminated. The effect of Victoria's change was simply to reduce the number of votes a developer had to line up in order to get a project approved. It was a quiet attempt by the British Columbia cabinet to make life a little easier for property developers under attack from organized citizen groups.

Provincial governments are on occasion found to be in-volved in decisions that appear to go in the opposite direction, and to sacrifice the interests of the property industry in order to protect those of an organized, informed and angry citizenry. This safety-valve function is one of the main jobs of provincial municipal boards, in the provinces where they exist. By holding public hearings and having the power to alter the decisions of municipal councils, these municipal boards are able to modify or soften the tendency of city governments to ignore and violate the interests of the citizenry in order to serve the property industry. By doing this every so often on particularly controversial or blatant issues, a municipal board helps preserve the existing structure of local government and to blunt the force of public demands for substantial reform in how city hall works. The need for a totally different kind of city government is reduced if organized citizen groups know that, in some of the worst cases where city hall has been too subservient to the wishes of property industry operators, they can get the decision reversed. Though virtually all provincial governments are basically sympathetic to the property industry and have strong and important ties to the industry, nevertheless they can afford to take a somewhat more detached and longer-range view of the industry's interests and insist on policies and decisions which, though they may sacrifice the interests of a particular developer or property owner in the short term, are in the long run beneficial to the industry as a whole.

Though we have no way at the present time of knowing what really went on, it is certainly reasonable to speculate that considerations of this kind were in the minds of Ontario's premier William Davis and his cabinet when they decided to cancel the Spadina Expressway in the summer of

Provinces and their cities — Winnipeg

The provincial government's white paper on urban reorganization said Winnipeg's unified city council "would be the exclusive law-making body responsible for all programs under its control, for budgets and for relationships with other jurisdictions."

But, in reality, city council isn't the final authority in two important areas — civic construction programming involving long-term loans and planning.

The Manitoba municipal board, a six-member body appointed by the provincial government, has the final say on matters relating to planning and civic construction programs in Winnipeg.

In effect, the municipal board has the power to overrule city council's decisions.

Section 296 of the new City of Winnipeg Act outlines the power of the municipal board to control the borrowing of money by the city.

The section states that subject to the approval of the municipal board, city council may pass bylaws for the borrowing of money for the purposes of the city by the issue and sale of debentures. An application for the authorization of the board for the city to borrow money must be made between the first and second reading of the bylaws.

The municipal board also continues to have the final say on zoning and planning matters in Winnipeg.

If any objections are submitted against development plans or proposed zoning bylaws, the municipal board is required to hold a public hearing before handing down a decision.

The board's decision "is final and binding on all persons and is not subject to appeal," according to the city act.

Metro, which previously was responsible for zoning and planning matters in Greater Winnipeg, was subject to similar control by the municipal board.

But some city councillors would like the powers of the board reduced. They feel elected representatives should make the final decisions.

Because of the councillors' views, it is only a matter of time before a clash occurs between the board and city council.

1971. They probably felt it better to abandon (at least temporarily) this particular expressway project than to press on with it and further enrage the large numbers of organized Toronto residents who had been fighting it. This must have been a particularly important consideration for the Davis cabinet in mid-1971, since Davis himself had only just taken over from John Robarts and the government was gearing itself up to an election. At one stroke, Davis was able with the Spadina decision to establish the fact that a different man was running Queen's Park now, and he was able to neutralize if not convert a large, organized group of Toronto residents who would otherwise have caused Conservative candidates considerable trouble in the Conservative-held, mid-Toronto ridings in the October 1971 provincial election.

What this brief survey of the relationship between senior governments and the property industry shows is that there are strong links between industry and government, links that help create and guarantee a basically sympathetic attitude in both political and administrative circles towards the property industry and its interests. These links, such as the tendency of property industry people to become elected politicians and cabinet ministers making decisions about the basic interests of their industry, also create a kind of control of government by the industry, which would make it virtually impossible for a government formed by a business-oriented political party to violate any important interests of the property industry.

What must be kept in mind, as we examine at close range in the next three chapters the way that the property industry has captured control of city hall, is that this is all taking place in the context of an arrangement that has been set up by provincial and federal governments, an arrangement they could change almost at will. If the senior governments wanted regulatory agencies for the property industry that were genuinely independent of the industry, it is completely within their power — theoretically — to create them.

Provinces and their cities — British Columbia

Dan-Dan the municipal man does his super-mayor act

By BOB McCONNELL
Province Victoria Bureau

VICTORIA — The annual Dan Campbell show hit the boards again Thursday. As he does every year, the municipal affairs minister spent a noisy 90 minutes in the legislature, alternately picking up B.C.'s municipalities and knocking them down again

He produced his usual set of figures showing that B.C. municipalities, no matter how much they may complain, are better off than any others in Canada. He also produced his usual rowdy attack on municipal governments, making it quite clear that while they may be elected to govern, they had better govern as he sees fit.

For years Campbell has been quietly building his political power base through a series of legislative changes that have made him a sort of super-mayor of B.C., a court of last resort for anyone dissatisfied with the decisions of a municipal or regional government. He is now in a position to change or veto a wide range of decisions that were formally under the control of municipal governments alone.

The line he has been developing over the last year or so is a simple one — municipal governments are too often ruled by bureaucrats who lack the wisdom of practical men like the municipal affairs minister. The main targets of his attack are municipal planners, whom he refers to in the same tones of scorn that Rehabilitation Minister Phil Gaglardi, one of the other leadership hopefuls, uses to describe social workers.

To Campbell these men are not merely planners, they are "way-out super-planners" and "airy-fairy dreamer planners" who seek to stifle progress by a maze of rules and regulations that get in the way of men of action. A few random selections from Thursday's speech make the drift of his comments quite clear:

"It is the job of political people and not the job of bureaucrats to chart the course a municipality is going to follow. We need positive proposals and not a ring of negative bylaws."

"I get complaints every day from developers and individuals who are not able to meet some ridiculous regulation or some ridiculous zoning bylaw."

Vancouver Province 28 Jan. 1972

If, on the other hand, city hall were somehow wrested out of the hands of the industry, senior governments who did not sympathize with this change would have the power to switch things around enough to put the property industry back in control of its regulatory and servicing agency. The property industry's power to protect and promote its interests and its political program clearly does not begin, and does not end, at city hall.

Creating a company town

VICTORIA — Municipal Affairs Minister Dan Campbell vigorously denounced Tuesday the NDP member who had accused Campbell of "knuckling under" in the establishment of the municipality of Dufferin.

Campbell's' attack was in response to statements made in the legislature last week by Williams regarding Dufferin, on the outskirts of Kamloops.

Williams had charged that Campbell knuckled under to supporter of Rehabilitation Minister Phil Gaglardi in setting up the municipality.

Williams called it the gerrymander of the century.

He charged that the district boundaries included industrial complexes which have been addded to Kamloops assessment and included a controversial development linked with Gaglardi's two sons.

The president of the development company which bought the land, Charlie Bennett, was later appointed mayor of Dufferin by the provincial government, the MLA said.

Bob Strachan (NDP—Cowichan-Malahat) said that no matter how much "invective" is used by Campbell to defend his government's position, "the map speaks for itself."

Strachan brandished a map showing Dufferin in two blocks, some of which is completely surrounded by Kamloops city, and joined by a thin line along CPR tracks.

Gaglardi called out that he will answer the NDP criticism later.

"That shows you called the shot," retorted Opposition leader Dave Barrett.

Campbell didn't explain why Bennett's development was included in the municipality of Dufferin, even though Williams had observed that Bennett complained he was having trouble getting desirable zoning approval from Kamloops council.

Vancouver Sun 9 Feb. 1972

CHAPTER 7

The property industry and city politicians

Vancouver's mayor Tom Campbell in 1969, swinging on a wrecking ball ready to start demolition for the downtown Block 42 project.

City governments are just as faithful as the senior governments in carryng out the political program of the property industry, and they are generally even less independent-minded about it. Provincial and federal cabinets can see that there are other interests besides those of the property industry which demand their attention, and they can also often see the need for making a minor short-term sacrifice of property industry interests in order to serve long-term interests of the industry and of other influential groups. Rarely does this kind of thinking show up at city hall. City politicians generally do whatever is best for the property industry at all times, and then say they are acting for the good of the citizenry and the city as a whole.

Before we look at how city politicians act, we must look at the links between the politicians and the property industry, because it is here we find the key to understanding the way the politicians act.

Property industry people at city hall

The most direct link occurs when industry businessmen and professionals combine their private interests in the property industry with the job of sitting on a city council as representatives of "the people." The number of property industry people in city politics is astonishing. Rarely are fewer than one third of a city's elected council members property industry people. The usual proportion is a third to a half, and in some cities people with property industry business interests form an absolute majority at city hall.

As of 1972, 12 of Toronto's 23 city politicians were property industry businessmen or professionals. In Vancouver the industry had an absolute majority — 7 of 11. In Winnipeg, where the new city government structure provides for a large number of elected city councillors, 50 plus a mayor, the property industry has apparently had no trouble in producing the requisite number of bodies to hold their usual share of the seats. Of Winnipeg's 51 elected city politicians, 24 were property industry people.

These three cities are not extreme examples; they are typical of city governments across the country. The property industry has no shortage of willing recruits ready to get themselves elected to city hall to protect and promote their own business interests, and those of the industry as a whole.

Usually these politicians are not big operators in the industry; they are not major local property owners in person; nor the presidents of the biggest local development firms; nor the directors of life insurance companies or chartered banks. Rather they are people whose personal economic interest is very tightly tied to the property industry, but who are small-time operators. Canada's city councils are full of insurance agents (who make a lot of their money selling property insurance of one kind or another), real estate agents (who make their money on commissions on sales of property, and who usually have some small real estate investments of their own), and real estate lawyers. The next most prominent group of occupations is connected to the construction industry: architects, small contractors, building supply company people, engineers. People involved in the industry in other ways may also be found at city hall. Construction trade union officials sometimes get elected to civic office; occasionally a developer (like Vancouver's mayor Tom Campbell, who boasts that he is worth $6 million in real estate), gets into the act; utility company management people (like Toronto alderman Horace Brown) are encouraged to run for office; major property owners like the local university or the downtown department store may have a middle-management person at city hall.

Very often it is property industry people who acquire key roles at city hall. In Winnipeg, the very powerful post of finance committee chairman of the 1972-74 council was held by Richard Wankling, also comptroller of Monarch Life, a Winnipeg-based insurance company. In Vancouver, the mayor himself from 1967-72 was a local developer. In Toronto, the leader of the government group at city hall, deputy mayor and budget chief for 1970-72, David Rotenberg, was an insurance agent.

The academic literature on city politics has paid a good deal of attention to the fact that many politicians have "business" connections or are businessmen. Unmentioned is the predominance of the property industry as the business most city politicians are in. Citizens interested in city politics, however, are usually very well aware of the fact that many of their city politicians are involved in the real estate and construction business in one way or another.

Sometimes the nature of a city politician's business interests is not easy to discover. In the case of a real estate agent, his place in the property industry is perfectly obvious. In the case of a lawyer, the question is not quite so simple because lawyers do not always have practices where real estate matters are an important source of income. Corporation lawyers, for example, work in a quite separate and special branch of the law, although it is hard to imagine a corporation lawyer who wouldn't have tremendous sympathies for the interests of property industry corporations. Labour lawyers, however, are likely to be very unsympathetic to the industry. One Toronto lawyer-alderman, Reid Scott, is reputed to specialize in divorce law. Specific information is needed in cases like this to identify a politician's interests positively.

In other situations, an occupation or business that seems to have no connection with the property industry at all may hide some direct participation in the industry. One Vancouver alderman, Ed Sweeney, is a partner in the family cooperage business. That may seem remote from the property business, but as it happens the family firm owns a large chunk of land in an area of Vancouver that has been designated for eventual redevelopment as a new industrial area. Perhaps this interest makes Sweeney as much of a property investor as a cooperage business operator, and indicates that he is very close to being a direct industry representative.

Another important fact about city politicians is that a great many of them seem to have small investments in real estate of one kind of another. Information like this generally emerges by accident; politicians don't make a point of talking about the property they own. When I was col-

Continued on page 104

OCCUPATIONS AND BUSINESS INTERESTS OF VANCOUVER CITY COUNCIL 1971-72

Table 7-1

PROPERTY INDUSTRY OCCUPATIONS

Earle Adams	Credit agency, insurance agent (retired)
Ernie Broome	Insurance agent
Brian Calder	Construction equipment salesman; real estate agent
Tom Campbell	Developer
Marianne Linnell	Partner, real estate agency
Art Phillips	Investment brokerage house
Halford Wilson	General contractor

OTHER BUSINESS OCCUPATIONS

Ed Sweeney	Manager, family cooperage business

OTHER PROFESSIONALS

Walter Hardwick	University professor
Harry Rankin	Trade union lawyer

OTHER

Hugh Bird	Fire chief (retired)

Politicians with property industry occupations: 7
Total politicians: 11

OCCUPATIONS AND BUSINESS INTERESTS OF WINNIPEG CITY COUNCIL 1972-74

Table 7-2

PROPERTY INDUSTRY OCCUPATIONS

ICEC	Baker, Charles	Construction equipment salesman
ICEC	Coopman, Al	Real estate agent
ICEC	Cropo, Joseph	Self-employed plumbing contractor
ICEC	Dennehy, Michael	Lawyer
ICEC	Galanchuk, Kenneth	Lawyer
ICEC	Ducharme, Albert	Construction estimator
ICEC	Gee, John	Real estate agent
Ind.	Hudson, Norman	Insurance agent
ICEC	Kaufman, Morris	Lawyer
ICEC	McGonigal, Pearl	Housewife; married to real estate lawyer
ICEC	McKenzie, Dan	Management, telephone utility
ICEC	Mercier, Gerald	Lawyer
ICEC	Minaker, George	Heating equipment company sales engineer
ICEC	Norrie, William	Lawyer
Ind.	Rebchuk, Slaw	Insurance agent
ICEC	Sasaki, William	Real estate and insurance agent
Ind.	Smith, James	Lawyer
ICEC	Stapon, Norman	Management, telephone utility
ICEC	Steen, Robert	Lawyer
ICEC	Steen, Warren	Life insurance company employee
ICEC	Wankling, Richard	Comptroller, insurance company
ICEC	Westbury, June	Housewife; married to lawyer
ICEC	Wolfe, Bernie	Insurance agent
ICEC	Yanovsky, Abe	Lawyer

COUNCILLORS WITH OTHER BUSINESS INTERESTS

ICEC	Dixon, Geoffrey	Printing salesman
ICEC	Dowhan, Stanley	"Manufacturer"
ICEC	Enns, Harry	Farm implement dealer
Ind.	Juba, Stephen (Mayor)	Manufacturer
ICEC	Kotowich, Ed	Customs broker
ICEC	Leech, Lorne	Business magazine publisher
ICEC	Marion, J. Paul	Catering firm executive
ICEC	McGarva, William	Taxi company executive; "semi-retired"
ICEC	Parkhill, Roy	Securities firm salesman
Ind.	Rizzuto, Phil	"Semi-retired businessman"
ICEC	Ross, Eldon	Owner, electronics supply firm
ICEC	Stanes, Douglas	Manufacturing firm executive
ICEC	Wilson, Bob	Manager, travel agency, collection agency

COUNCILLORS WITH OTHER PROFESSIONAL OCCUPATIONS

ICEC	Hallonquist, William	School principal
NDP	Johannson, Robert	Free-lance writer
NDP	Munroe, George	Social agency director
ICEC	Penner, Alfred	School teacher
ICEC	Pierce, Florence	School teacher (retired)
NDP	Skowron, Alfred	Credit union adviser
LEC	Zuken, Joseph	Labour lawyer

OTHERS

NDP	Cartwright, R. G.	Mailman
NDP	Cherniack, Lawrie	Full-time politician
ICEC	Fuga, Olga	None
NDP	Klym, Adam	Electrician, Ohl Systems
Ind.	Perry, Don	Electrician, CNR
ICEC	Taft, Robert	Police chief (retired)
NDP	Wade, Alan	Painter, CPR

Councillors with property industry occupations: 24 (47%)
    ICEC affiliation: 21
    NDP affiliation: None
    Independents: 3

Councillors with other business interests: 13 (26%)
    ICEC affiliation: 11
    NDP affiliation: None
    Independents: 2

Councillors with other professional occupations: 7 (13%)
    ICEC affiliation: 3
    NDP affiliation: 3
    LEC affiliation: 1

Councillors with blue-collar occupations: 4 (8%)
    ICEC affiliation: None
    NDP affiliation: 4

Others: 3 (6%)

OCCUPATIONS AND BUSINESS INTERESTS OF TORONTO CITY COUNCIL, 1970-72

Table 7-3

PROPERTY INDUSTRY OCCUPATIONS

William Archer	Lawyer
Fred Beavis	Roofing contractor (now retired)
William Boytchuk	Real estate agent
Horace Brown	Management employee, public utility
Hugh Bruce	Lawyer
Ben Grys	Insurance agent; property investor
Ying Hope	Civil engineer
Allan Lamport	Insurance agent
Tony O'Donohue	Civil engineer
Paul Pickett	Lawyer
David Rotenberg	Insurance agent
Karl Jaffary*	Lawyer

OTHER BUSINESS OCCUPATIONS

Tom Clifford	Variety store proprietor
Art Eggleton	Accountant
Joseph Piccininni	Newspaper publicity man
Thomas Wardle	Toy manufacturer

OTHER PROFESSIONALS

David Crombie	University professor and administrator
William Kilbourn	University professor
Reid Scott	Lawyer (specializing in family law)

OTHER

Archie Chisholm	Stationary engineer, union member
William Dennison	Speech therapy school operator (retired)
John Sewell	Community organizer
June Marks	None

Politicians with property industry occupations: 12
Total politicians: 23

*In the three city councils reported on here, Toronto alderman
Karl Jaffary is a special case with respect to his occupation and
his political activities. Lawyers on city councils who form part
of the opposition group (as Jaffary does on Toronto city
council) usually practice criminal law or labour law, or they
specialize in civil rights matters and legal aid counselling. This
is particularly true of lawyers who are, as Jaffary is, strong
NDP party activists. Jaffary is a partner in a law firm which
carries on a broad practice, and he deals with the real estate
transactions of his clients as well as with other matters.
Jaffary has the expertise which makes him a very competent
lawyer on real estate matters as well as in other fields (he is,
for example, the lawyer for the publishers of this book)
which, in a sense, places him in the property industry. But
he often uses this expertise against rather than with the property
industry as it is now organized, so that for example he is the
lawyer to a co-op housing organization which is building small
co-op housing projects in Ontario. Nevertheless, because of his
involvement in normal real estate transactions as well, it seemed
best to include him amongst the Toronto city council members
with property industry occupations. What distinguishes Jaffary
from the others is that he alone in his politics takes a strong
and consistent anti-property industry line (see the Toronto
city council voting record, page   ).

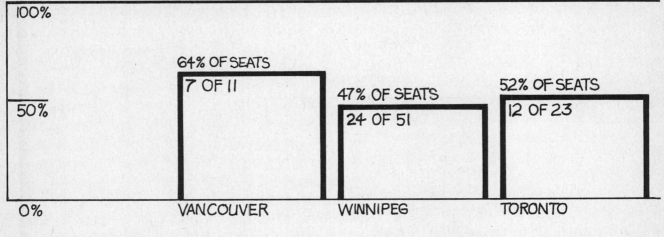

PROPERTY INDUSTRY PEOPLE AT CITY HALL

100%

50%

0%

64% OF SEATS
7 OF 11
VANCOUVER

47% OF SEATS
24 OF 51
WINNIPEG

52% OF SEATS
12 OF 23
TORONTO

Table 7-4	PROPERTY INDUSTRY PEOPLE IN ONTARIO CITY POLITICS, 1971				
City	No. politicians	No. in property industry	% in property industry	No. in businesses of all kinds	% in businesses of all kinds
Milton	9	2	22%	7	78%
Stratford	11	4	36%	6	55%
Thunder Bay*	13	6	46%	10	77%
Borough of York	11	5	45%	10	91%
Peterborough	11	7	64%	7	64%
North York	17	9	53%	15	88%
Scarborough	15	4	27%	10	66%
Kitchener	11	7	64%	7	64%
	98	44		72	

*As of October 1971.

NOTE: These tables are compiled on the basis of the main occupations of politicians in the places listed. The count of property industry politicians is a minimum figure because all doubtful cases were excluded. Also excluded are politicians who had a secondary business interest in the property industry as, for example, property investors, but a primary interest outside the industry.

lecting material for a series of articles on the five members of Toronto city council's executive committee in 1971, I discovered that three of the five had small property investments. Owning an extra house or two was the customary form of investment. The possible effect of such involvement in the property industry by city politicians was well illustrated by Ben Grys, the Toronto alderman discussed in Chapter 4, who proved to own two houses in an area where a consortium of development firms, Cadillac and Greenwin, were attempting to get city permission for high-rise apartments.

Industry representatives in office

When people in the property industry get themselves elected to city councils, they do not abandon their business interests and forget the special concerns of their industry. Usually they carry on their private business activities and remain firmly inside the property industry. Often a major reason for their getting into city politics is to improve their private business. For lawyers, a period at city hall teaches them a lot about the real procedures of municipal law and how to act as developers' lawyers. For insurance agents, it brings them into contact with lots of new potential customers, including people who build and own new buildings and who may well have reason to be grateful for favours received from municipal politicians. For real estate agents, a seat on a city council provides them with a tremendous amount of valuable information about the local real estate market.

Virtually without exception, property industry people at city hall look at every issue that comes before them and at every question of city government policy from the point of view of the property industry. They usually assume without question that what is good for the industry is good for the

Continued on page 104

Property industry politicians: Tom Terrific

One of the apartment buildings owned by Vancouver mayor Tom Campbell.

As these extracts from newspaper articles show, Vancouver's mayor Tom Campbell is an extraordinary character even in the amazing world of city politicians.

Campbell, himself a property owner and land developer heavily involved in real estate in Vancouver, has been a friend of development interests at city hall along with the governing majority of aldermen.

But his conduct as a politician is so outrageous that almost no one can take him seriously. He is constantly abused and attacked — and, as this material shows, for very good reason — by virtually everyone who comments on Vancouver city politics.

Campbell himself is not short on abuse. His powers of invective were at their height for his 1971 counter-attack against Vancouver citizen groups opposing the construction of the Third Crossing, a project close to the hearts of both powerful downtown property owners headed by the CPR and of speculators and developers on Vancouver's North Shore, the area to be served by the new crossing.

It's a plot

'Maoists, Communists' and the 'hamburgers' endanger crossing, Vancouver mayor says

VANCOUVER (CP) — Mayor Tom Campbell yesterday branded opponents of the proposed third crossing of Burrard Inlet linking Vancouver with the North Shore as "Maoists, Communists, pinkos, left-wingers and hamburgers."

Mr. Campbell, who defined hamburgers as people without a university degree, said the crossing will founder unless City Council rallies to support it and said its scuttling would be a victory for the Communist Party of Canada.

Globe and Mail 10 Feb. 1972

From law to real estate to mayor of Vancouver — Tom Campbell

"Tom Campbell's father was a policeman who rode a horse around Stanley Park. Tom Campbell is a plain man. . . . He worked his way through law school. In 1956, after a few years of practicing law successfully, he decided to 'sell space instead of time' by getting into real estate.

Today he owns about 500 apartment suites, about 100 offices '20 or 30' stores and about $1 million worth of raw land.

Campbell could probably sell out today for $8 million. He made it all himself by speculation in and development of a non-expandable, irreplaceable resource — the land.

Mr. Campbell also worked his way up in city politics, from alderman to mayor. In 1970, he was re-elected mayor in Vancouver on an anti-hippie law-and-order campaign.

Financial Post 21 Nov. 1970

★

His Worship Tom Fumble, QC, displaying more than his usual quota of disinterest, is yawning by 10:10,

Vancouver Sun 15 March 1972

It is all very fascinating, but the festivities—and the hosting by the lord mayor—do not commence until Wednesday. The dates of May 10-13 have been laid on very specifically. Why then, did His Worship suddenly flee Vancouver a week ago, in the midst of a civic workers' strike and just two days after he had led his council in voting a pay increase for themselves? Why did he refrain from telling all he had left until after he had left? Where is our wandering boy tonight?

Vancouver Sun 9 May 1972

When Tom Campbell is away, an alderman occupies the mayor's office and, more often than not, the city gets a rare sample of leadership.

For example, if Campbell had been away, Vancouver council would have had an acting mayor at an important meeting of the Greater Vancouver Regional District. The GVRD was studying various transportation matters.

The day before the meeting, Tom Campbell made a number of statements related to it.

But the mayor didn't go. Instead, he opted to attend an official "topping off" ceremony for Royal Centre, a public relations party that carried a little more glamor than a dull working meeting.

In the afternoon, the mayor went to Gastown for another opening ceremony of a development project. Following the ceremony, in which he performed for the television cameras, Campbell went back to Royal Centre for another party.

A day in the life of His Worship T. J. Campbell.

Vancouver Sun 3 April 1972

★

OUR JUNKETING CITY COUN-cil, the greatest boon to travel agents since flight bags, has not stopped yet. The mayor's Amsterdam jaunt is over. His inspection of Japan's Expo is over. The Odessa Odyssey, featuring the Tom Terrific Troika, is over. The Milan boondoggle, featuring Ald. Sweeney and Ald. Adams, is just over. The mayor is preparing for the summer trip to the Munich Olympics. But first, as a warm-up jaunt, London. The mayor and his wife leave next week, May 10, to attend the Lord Mayor's Parade. Strangely enough, he hasn't announced it yet. Little wonder. It will make it, along with Munich, four council trips to Europe alone in less than 12 months.

Vancouver Sun 4 May 1972

City politicians in the property business

There is a steady stream of news from all over Canada about city politicians who are in the property business, and who often are getting caught mixing their politics and their personal business together too closely. Many times it is only through such controversies that information about the property interests of civic politicians becomes public. The number and widely-spread distribution of cases is further evidence of the extent of direct property industry involvement in city government, and it also confirms the close relationship between the property industry's business and the powers and policies of city hall.

Surrey seeks advice in attack on alderman

A charge that Surrey Ald. Ed McKitka should be disqualified from holding office — made at Surrey council meeting Monday night—was referred to the council's solicitor.

"I am sure you will find I have broken no laws in this municipality," Ald. McKitka told reporters after the meeting. He said he was glad the matter had been turned over to the lawyer.

The claims were made by loader operator Robert McEwan who said Ald. McKitka signed a five-year lease, dated May 8, 1968, for land in the Port Kells area. He did this, said McEwan, two months before the company he represented was registered with provincial authorities.

Because Overland Limestone Products Ltd., was not registered until July 11, 1968, according to McEwan, Ald. McKitka is personally liable for contractual debts the company later incurred.

Surrey was granted a judgment against the company on Oct. 2, 1970 for $1,166.10 in back taxes plus $80 costs.

McEwan said the taxes were not paid until July 21, 1971.

He claimed Ald. McKitka contravened a Municipal Act section that disqualifies anyone from holding office who has an account in dispute with the municipality.

Ald. McKitka was first elected in 1968.

McEwan also claims, because McKitka was an alderman when he signed the contract, he contravenes a section of the act preventing elected officials entering into direct agreements with the municipality.

Ald. McKitka is a registered director of Overland Limestone Products Ltd. as of April 19, 1972," he said.

McEwan said rent on the land was paid for 1968 and 1969, but is still outstanding for the period between May, 1970 and August, 1971 when Surrey terminated the lease. He said McKitka still owes that money and is therefore again disqualified from holding office.

Toronto insurance agent, property investor and alderman Ben Grys, shown here on the left talking to fellow insurance agent and alderman Allan Lamport. In mid-1971, Grys was accused of conflict of interest by fellow alderman John Sewell after he actively promoted rezoning for a development where he and his wife had sold two houses, originally purchased for about $30,000, to the developer. The Grys family received $195,000 for their houses. At the time Grys was promoting the rezoning, the Grys family was holding mortgages of $125,000 on the two houses.

Vancouver Province 25 April 1972

RATEPAYER DEMANDS P ROBE

Vancouver Sun 14 March 1972

Council irregularities alleged

Special to The Sun
SURREY — An investigation into alleged municipal council irregularities over awarding construction contracts has been called for by a Surrey taxpayer who has named Ald. Ed McKitka in his charges.

Robert McEwan told council Monday that McKitka was the manager of the Surrey Concrete Co. when council awarded contracts for projects for which the company supplied the concrete.

McEwan quoted Sections 50 and 51 of the Municipal Act, which he said were contravened when McKitka voted on awarding contracts to firms which were prepared to buy their concrete from Surrey

'Licence to pick-pocket':MLA

Sun Victoria Bureau

VICTORIA — Properties owned by the former provincial-government-appointed mayor in Dufferin are assessed at one per cent of market values for school purposes, compared with the 41-per-cent assessment on properties nearby, the legislature was told Tuesday.

Bob Williams (NDP Vancouver East) launched an attack on the government's tolerance of the assessment system at Dufferin, on the outskirts of Kamloops, during the debate on the estimates for Premier W. A. C. Bennett

"What the minister of finance (Bennett) is doing is issuing a licence to pick-pocket in some municipalities in the province, and the prime example is in the district of Dufferin," Williams declared.

The properties were identified by Williams as those held by Del Cielo Heights Ltd., a company which bought land formerly held by the two sons of Rehabilitation Minister Phil Gaglardi at the junction of the Trans Canada and Merrit Highways.

Principal of Del Cielo is Charlie Bennett, the man who was identified as leader of a demonstration in support of a recently-resigned highways minister Phil Gaglardi in 1968, and the man appointed by the government as mayor of the new district of Dufferin in 1971.

Williams has already charged that the Dufferin boundaries were drawn to benefit Charlie Bennett — "The developer-Mayor" — and that the Dufferin council —"Dominated by a real estate office" — has been allowed to subvert B.C. statutes regulating highway access and zoning, to give access to land held by Bennett's companies.

Vancouver Sun 23 Feb. 1972

Four aldermen unseated

THUNDER BAY (CP-Special) — Four city aldermen were unseated yesterday when a court ruled that their business dealings with the city were a contravention of the Ontario Municipal Act.

In a 15-page judgment, District Court Judge W. T. Hollinger said Aldermen Edgar Laprade, Hubert Badanai, George Lovelady and Thomas Jones "are not entitled to sit or to vote in the council . . . by reasons of contracts entered by their companies with the corporation (city)."

He ordered that new elections be held to fill the vacant seats on the 13-member council.

Judge Hollinger said in his judgment he felt the aldermen "acted openly, in good faith and, I believe, honestly, in what each considered to be the best interests of the municipality."

The court action, brought by department store president Lloyd Hurdon, was sparked by council's awarding of a $285,000 contract for a municipal storage building to a construction firm operated by Mr. Jones. He, along with Mr. Badanai, a car dealer, and Mayor Saul Laskin, was out of town and unavailable for comment yesterday. Mr. Hurdon refused comment on the decision.

Former mayor must return $72,197 to city

CALGARY (CP) — The Alberta Supreme Court has awarded the city of Edmonton $72,197 in a suit against its former mayor, William Hawrelak.

The court said that was the amount of profit Mr. Hawrelak made from a land deal that was facilitated by zoning changes made after he became mayor in 1963.

Mr. Justice W. J. C. Kirby said that Mr. Hawrelak violated the laws governing persons in positions of trust when the deal was being made.

The mayor had a 40-percent interest in Sun-Alta Builders Ltd. which agreed to sell land, before he was elected mayor, to Chrysler (Canada) Corporation.

But the project for which the land was to be purchased could not proceed until the area was rezoned and this occurred after Mr. Hawrelak became mayor.

Globe and Mail 25 Jan. 1972

Globe and Mail 16 Feb. 1972

Logan Lake mayor quits

LOGAN LAKE — A special meeting of the Logan Lake village council will be held Wednesday to appoint a replacement to council for Mayor John Aldrich who resigned.

Doug Henderson, village clerk, said today Aldrich resigned because his job as townsite manager for Lornex Mines Ltd. developers of the Logan Lake village was phased out.

Aldrich was the main architect for the Logan Lake development from its beginnings at the Thompson Nicola regional district in early 1970 to the last stages of construction which are now underway.

Vancouver Sun 17 April 1972

city as a whole. When this is manifestly not so, they nevertheless take care of their real constituency — the property industry — first. The evidence is clear that politicians with property industry connections vote together as a bloc on all issues affecting the basic interests of the industry. This means they are together on major questions concerning planning, development, zoning, public works and services, and similar property-oriented matters. Apart from factionalist fights, they afford themselves the luxury of disagreement only on irrelevant matters that have no impact one way or another on the property industry.

Indirect recruiting: the political parties in city politics

A less direct but nevertheless quite efficient way in which the property industry gets its people onto city councils is through control of local political party organizations. The major political parties are involved in local politics in every Canadian city. This is sometimes done explicitly, with candidates running on party tickets, as Liberals or NDPs. Sometimes it is done without anyone quite admitting it publicly, either with ostensibly no parties at all or with special municipal parties with their own name (like NPA in Vancouver and ICEC in Winnipeg), which pretend to have no connection with the major political parties.

Most cities have at least one municipal party oriented towards "business" interests. In Vancouver, this has traditionally been the NPA, the Non-Partisan Association. In Winnipeg, it is the ICEC, the latest in a series of names for an organization that goes back to the Committee of 1000, which was the organization of the Winnipeg bourgeoisie and their middle-class supporters who fought the workers in the Winnipeg General Strike of 1919. In Toronto, there is no formal municipal party devoted to business interests, but the Conservative party machine has traditionally played a very large role in local politics and so, to a lesser extent, have the Liberals. These two business-oriented parties have not been forced to coalesce in Toronto and develop a municipal party in order to fight and win city elections.

Along with the basic "business-oriented" party, cities where people are beginning to express dissatisfaction with city hall sometimes sprout new local parties which develop a moderate "reform" image without seriously challenging the policies that the fuddy-duddy old "business-oriented" group supports. Vancouver's TEAM group is this kind of reformist-business party. Toronto's CIVAC party was in this category from the time it was set up in 1967 until 1970. In 1970 the two prominent CIVAC members moved up to the most powerful positions at the head of the majority of aldermen in Toronto city council. Once they were there, they had no further need for the CIVAC organization, which had tried to create some sort of distinction between these politicians and the old-guard aldermen. As it turned out, the political styles of the two groups were different, but their basic policies and their voting records were the same.

The NDP is involved in city politics in most Canadian cities. Usually this is explicit, with candidates running on the NDP label. Where the NDP fits into the civic political structure depends on who controls the local party organization.

Municipal political parties are set up to seek out and recruit candidates for office, to provide the candidates with some funds to pay for their campaign, to provide an organization to run the campaigns, and to give candidates a label by which their politics can be recognized. These parties are often an extremely important intermediary in the process of getting elected to city hall. A potential candidate badly needs money and an organization in order to run a successful campaign, and the parties can provide them.

In this situation, the property industry is usually to be found right in the centre of things, controlling the business-oriented political party apparatus. This ensures that the candidates whom the party runs and supports are acceptable to the property industry — which means that they must represent the interests of the industry. A relatively senior, powerful property industry representative usually places himself in a position of control over the political party structure. Of course he is a member of the local business elite, but almost without exception his particular line of business activity places him squarely in the property industry. In Toronto, the most influential local party "bosses" in the late 1960s were Eddie Goodman, Robert Macauley, and Keith Davey. Goodman and Macauley are both senior members of the Conservative party; both have held important offices in Conservative governments or in the party structure; both sit on the boards of directors of development firms operating in the Toronto area (Macauley at Victoria Wood, Goodman at Cadillac); and both are themselves developers' lawyers who often appear pleading for favours for their clients at city hall. Not only are they trustworthy, intelligent, high-level representatives of the property industry; they are also close enough to both the industry and city hall to know what is going on and who is doing what. Senator Keith Davey, whose senate committee produced a three-volume report on the media, is an altogether more minor character. Unlike Macauley and Goodman, he does not even rate a listing in the 1971 *Directory of Directors*. He attempted to get Toronto Liberals into city politics explicitly in 1969, with a slate of aldermanic candidates and a candidate for mayor. He failed to line up a strong slate, however, and didn't find a strong enough mayoralty candidate, so only two self-declared Liberals got themselves elected to Toronto city council in that election. In a perfect expression of the futility of Davey's effort, these two Liberals subsequently managed to vote against each other on every major issue that came up in the next three years.

Most of the financial support for "business-oriented" municipal political parties can be presumed to come from the property industry. Little information is available on this score, of course, but it would seem likely that the people to hit for contributions to the cause would be those with something at stake at city hall. Certainly the formal membership in these organizations is very heavily loaded with property industry representatives.

With effective control by means of money and leaders of these municipal political parties, the property industry has a valuable indirect way of placing its supporters at city hall. The candidates whom these parties back may themselves be involved in the property industry or they may have some other business interest completely. The fact that they are initially recruited and then financed and supported organizationally by these parties means that they are highly likely to be industry representatives at city hall. One strong pressure in this direction would come from the knowledge that, if they refused to give the industry the support it expected,

Continued on page 107

Winnipeg's property industry party

Ever since 1918-19, when Winnipeg witnessed a confrontation between labour and the owners of business and industry, there has been a business-oriented political organization which has recruited candidates for civic political office and helped fund their campaigns.

The internal affairs of this party, which has changed its name many times since 1918-19 and which is currently known in Winnipeg as the ICEC, are obscure. It is, however, quite clear that property industry interests have been prominent and perhaps predominant in its operations. It brings together the Conservative and Liberal parties for the purpose of running in municipal elections.

The organization grew out of the Committee of 100, set up in 1918 by business interests to combat a threatened general strike. The same structure was used a year later in the Committee of 1,000 when a general srike did occur. Chairman of the committee was A. K. Godfrey, president of Monarch Lumber.

At a meeting chaired by Godfrey in August 1919, an audience of more than 3000 people approved a proposal to establish a Citizen's League. By September that year, the organization was looking for candidates to run in the forthcoming civic election. At a September meeting, attended by 1500 people, Conservative Party organizer and lawyer R. A. C. Manning said, according to the Winnipeg Tribune: "There was a definite plan of the Reds to seize control all over the country." He did not specify how electing a labour majority on Winnipeg's city council would further that plan.

Labour candidates had done well in the 1918 Winnipeg elections, and if they did as well in the 1919 election they would capture a majority on the city council. The threat was barely beaten off by the Citizen's League. In order to reduce the chances of a labour majority, the Manitoba legislature then changed the electoral boundaries and electoral system used in Winnipeg elections.

How the organization raised its election war chest is obscure, but some financial data available suggests that it allocated quotas to be raised from members of Winnipeg's various trade and professional associations. In 1920, for instance, manufacturing firms were expected to contribute $5000, an average of $23 per firm. Banks were expected to contribute $95, insurance companies $75.

In the 1920s the name of the group (and its internal structure) changed twice, and from 1925 to 1928 there was no overt organization. By 1929, however, a formal organization had been revived.

This latest group, called the Civic Progress Association, was established at a public meeting in October 1929. The president, H. G. Tucker, was an insurance agent with the large brokerage firm of Osler, Hammond and Nanton. The group's mayoralty candidate that year was to be William Hurst of Hurst Construction, but Hurst refused the request. The group captured six of nine aldermanic seats and the mayoralty. One of their candidates elected for the first time was C. E. Simonite, a real estate agent and later long-time chairman of the City of Winnipeg finance committee.

The Civic Progress Association officially took itself out of civic politics in July 1932, when it became the Civic and Provincial Progress Association. The purpose of this new group, set up in the depths of the Depression, was to cut civic and provincial spending and to reduce taxes. Its honourary president was James A. Richardson, of the Winnipeg Richardson family, and its advisory board chairman was A. K. Godfrey, the chairman of the first meeting of the original Citizen's League. Nothing was heard of this new group after its initial meeting.

The death of the Civic Progress Association gave rise to the Civic Election Committee. The CEC may have been established as early as 1932, but its first mention in the press came in 1936. That was after labour candidates had captured control, first of the Winnipeg school board in 1933, then of Winnipeg city council in 1934.

This first labour majority on the city council had been in office for almost two years when the CEC declared its existence publicly for the express purpose of defeating the labour majority, members of the Independent Labour Party. The CEC won the civic election in 1936, and the school board election of 1937. Since that time, it has always had a majority on both bodies.

Active membership in CEC has always been small, numbering perhaps 50 to 100. Its two major tasks were recruiting candidates, and raising funds to contribute to their election expenses. CEC chairmen, once elected, tended to hold office for a number of years. These included J. Elmer Woods, then president of Winnipeg-based Monarch Life Assurance, now president of Woods Investments and a director of National Trust. Another long-time CEC chairman was Peter Curry. He was himself a CEC member of the Winnipeg school board. Curry is now chairman of Great West Life Assurance, the Investors group and the Greater Winnipeg Gas Company, and he is a director of many property industry firms as well as serving as chancellor of the University of Manitoba. Great West Life and Investors are now controlled by the Power Corporation. A third long-time CEC chairman was W. J. McKeag, president of McKeag-Harris Realty, a large real estate agency and property investor. A forth, Archie Micay, is a lawyer with real estate and financial interests.

New life came to the CEC and its successor-group, the Greater Winnipeg Election Committee, when the NDP government restructured Winnipeg's municipalities and amalgamated them into a one-city government structure in 1971. There was vague talk in Winnipeg about NDP hopes to control this new city government, since NDP candidates had taken a majority of Winnipeg seats in the previous provincial election. The GWEC re-named itself the Independent Civic Election Committee (ICEC) and won 37 of the 50 seats on the new council, thus keeping the control the party has enjoyed steadily since 1937.

— Based on "Class conflict in Winnipeg Civic politics: the role of the Citizens' and Civic Election Organizations" by Paul Barber. Mimeo., 1970.

A property industry reformist party in office: the CIVAC case

Soon after the December 1966 elections for Toronto City Council, a city hall outsider, Ryerson Polytechnical Institute lecturer David Crombie, organized a new municipal political party which was called CIVAC. CIVAC's membership include a changing group of politicians in office, plus a number of interested ordinary citizens.

CIVAC ran a large number of candidates on its label in the 1969 elections, and five (Rotenberg, O'Donohue, Eggleton, Hope and Crombie) were elected to the 23-man council. Perhaps more important, two of the five were elected by their fellow aldermen to the five-man executive committee of the council.

Once having achieved this electoral success, the CIVAC group lost what little internal coherence it had, and the organization almost dissolved. Meanwhile, an analysis of the voting record of the five elected CIVAC politicians for their first year in office, 1970, shows that the party did not function as a group of politicians who consistently voted together on major issues.

Of the 32 crucial issues decided that year, CIVAC aldermen voted together 17 times. They split 15 times, almost as often. Much more significant, however, is the fact that when the CIVAC votes were crucial in deciding the outcome of a vote, individual CIVAC politicians were much more liable to split off from their colleagues than when their votes didn't matter. There were 14 cases where CIVAC's vote was crucial. *On 11 of those 14 occasions, enough of the CIVAC aldermen went with the property industry majority to ensure it a victory.* On 8 of those 11 occasions when CIVAC gave the property industry majority the votes they needed to win, the CIVAC politicians were splitting from their CIVAC colleagues in order to do so.

On four of the 32 votes, the anti-property industry group won. On two of these four occasions, the CIVAC group was united. On the other two occasions, some of its members voted with the property industry bloc but that side went down to defeat in spite of having this support. Both the issues where CIVAC was united against the property industry position were minor matters which affected the local interests of residents of the north Toronto middle-class areas where CIVAC gets most of its electoral support.

The net result of the CIVAC organization was that, once its members were in a reasonably influential position inside city council, they replaced some of the older property industry politicians. Then they carried on with policies which were, on the whole, just as industry-oriented. The CIVAC members who were slightly less favourably inclined towards the property industry found their group dissolving as adherents took up positions of leadership in city council.

Toronto executive alderman David Rotenberg was an early member of the CIVAC group. It was the support of fellow CIVAC caucus members that propelled him onto the city's powerful executive committee and made him budget chief after the 1969 election. Having achieved the power he was looking for, and acting as the real leader of the property industry's majority on Toronto city council, Rotenberg had no further need for the CIVAC label and dropped it.

they would be cut off from the funds, endorsement and organization they depended on to get re-elected.

Property industry controls on elected politicians

Both directly and indirectly, then, the property industry has placed its recruits and its representatives on city councils all across Canada. These property industry candidates are tightly linked to the industry in one way or another, and are very likely to represent the industry's interests at city hall. This recruiting technique in itself is a highly effective way of controlling city councils. But it is reinforced and supported by other measures by which the industry exerts further pressure on city politicians to act as it wishes.

Money. The first measure is *financial support.* Even if a party organization puts up some of the funds required for an election, usually a candidate has to raise a substantial chunk of money himself to pay for his election expenses. Relatively little information is available publicly on where this money comes from in the case of candidates who represent the property industry at city hall. In fact, the candidates are generally extremely reluctant to say anything whatsoever on this subject. A Toronto alderman running for re-election in 1969 who admitted to having received $5,000 from "his friends" in the construction business who were, he said, interested in "good government" had this admission thrown in his face through the rest of the campaign. Another 1969 candidate in Toronto, sign company vice-president Frank Paznar, was spotted in a post office paying $500 for postage with a cheque from Greenwin, a Toronto development firm. Other developers have admitted that they regularly contribute to election campaigns, though without specifying which ones. A politician who relies on this source of financing is obviously going to be careful not to offend the property industry people who give him the money.

Mentality. A second kind of control on city politicians springs from the *property industry mentality.* Virtually all city politicians, city officials, development and real estate people who show up at city hall, and news media people share a common understanding of the city and city government. They have a common view about what is good for the city and what is appropriate policy for city hall. Of course there is room for tremendous disagreement on specific matters, but a common basic viewpoint persists, to wit: growth and development are good; major new public projects like new roads and bridges are desirable; citizen groups are not to be taken seriously; no one should stand in the way of progress. The basic view of the property industry, that a city is a machine for making money for the industry, is taken for granted. Most city politicians accept this premise without question. They have little choice, of course, because in many cities no alternative viewpoint has been clearly formulated. Moreover it is the way all their colleagues and associates see the world. But they are imprisoned by it. Understanding things this way, they will never be able to grasp the alternative viewpoint, which takes a city to be something more human and more complicated than a machine to generate wealth for the property industry. The property industry mentality is, however, an important control on the behaviour of individual politicians. This is so even though it was obviously not consciously created by the property industry or anyone else; it

is an unintended result of the circumstance of property industry domination at city hall.

Friendship. A third control of the property industry over city politicians is *friendship.* City politicians make up a special kind of social group, and a certain minimum kind of social interaction takes place amongst them. A politician who takes a consistent stand different from what the industry wants is going to be frozen out, then harassed and pressured by other people at city hall. It is one thing if he has his own constituency of friends and supporters not aligned with the property industry, if for instance he was elected by citizen groups whose background is fighting developers and real estate interests. Otherwise he must quickly learn that the social relations amongst city politicians act as a powerful restraint on any "deviance" from the city hall "norm."

New careers. The controls on the conduct of city politicians by the property industry listed so far are all sticks that the industry wields. It also has its carrots to dangle. These all have to do with offering a friendly politician new ways of making money. This can mean a little money on the side in well-placed property investments. A city politician, acting on a tip from a friendly developer, can buy property in an area where a development is planned and then make a big capital gain by selling it later. There are countless examples of this.

Or it can mean the offer of new business. This is particularly easy for a politician who is already in the property industry, particularly if he is some kind of independent operator offering services the property industry can use. This carrot seems generally expected by the engineers, architects, real estate agents, insurance agents, real estate lawyers, small contractors and others who get into city politics.

The carrot can also be a leg up into a better line of work. City politicians sometimes find that, after a career at city hall, they can move into senior positions with big-time property industry corporations. Before he went into city politics, William Allen was quite an ordinary Toronto lawyer. He moved up through the city hall ranks to become chairman (the equivalent of mayor) of Metro Toronto, elected by his fellow city politicians. Allen then moved out of Metro Toronto to become president of the Kinross Mortgage Company, a very large first-mortgage lending firm owned by the Bank of Commerce with holdings of about $200 million. Later Allen was also appointed president of Dominion Realty. So he was able to move out of city hall into the plush comfort of corporate boardrooms.

Fill in the blanks
1. In the 1966 civic elections in Toronto, the chief fund-raiser for the developers' mayoralty candidate Philip Givens was developers' lawyer Eddie Goodman.
2. In the 1969 civic elections in Toronto, the chief fund-raiser for the developers' mayoralty candidate William Dennison was developers' lawyer Robert Macaulay.
3. In the 19__ civic elections in _____, the chief fund-raiser for the developers' mayoralty candidate _____ was developers' lawyer

The property industry and campaign funds

Very little direct reliable information is available on the sources of election funds for city politicians, except when the politicians choose to reveal it. Usually the only people to do so are opposition candidates who publish lists of campaign fund contributors who publish lists of campaign fund contributors and expenses in order to make it clear that they are not receiving support from the property industry, and to show up the secretiveness of the industry's elected politicians.

Since the 1969 election in Toronto, when a small group of opposition candidates were elected to Toronto city council, the election contribution issue has come up in the city several times and, as these news article quotations show, a little information revealed.

Conflict law urged to include donors to campaign funds

By N. JOHN ADAMS

North York Controller Mel Lastman said yesterday most long-time municipal politicians across Metro get "90 per cent if not more" of their campaign contributions from developers and related interests.

He will move at North York Council in two weeks that elected officials declare a conflict of interest whenever one of their campaign donors is affected by Council business.

Mr. Lastman gave an unusually candid report of his own campaign donations and what he believes are those of his fellow politicians across Metro in an interview.

In the interview, Mr. Lastman said developers hand out election contributions, sometimes before they are asked because they seek a favorable, not a fair, hearing on rezoning applications and other matters of municipal business.

Mr. Lastman declared he wants the rules of North York council changed and the Ontario Municipal Act amended to remove this form of political favoritism.

He said citizens often grow angry at municipal politicians whose comments and voting behaviour they cannot understand. The explanation is often in knowing who paid to help their election and re-election.

He said two or three of the big five developers contributed to his campaign without being asked and he did not find out about it until afterward.

He received $7,000 to $8,000 in contributions, mostly from major appliance manufacturers with whom his chain of Bad Boy discount stores do business. The self-made millionaire said he did not seek funds, although one man did solicit on his behalf without approval.

"In my just over two years on Council," Mr. Lastman told the seminar, "I don't know of a request from a major developer that has been turned down."

Mr. Lastman, who also sits on Metro Council, said his figures and his criticisms apply across all Metro municipalities, based on what he has been told by other politicians.

The controller said he decided to speak out as a result of a request by a middleman not to oppose a developer's request because the developer had helped finance his election.

"This got my back up," Mr. Lastman asserted. "I fought that one just because of that. I know that is wrong in itself because I didn't really care whether it was a good or a bad development . . . It's the fault of the system."

He refused to identify the middleman, the developer or the project.

Globe and Mail 25 March 1972

8 of 12 got campaign funds from developer

By JAMES MacKENZIE and MICHAEL MOORE

Alderman Karl Jaffary charged last night that at least eight of the 12 City Council members voting for a controversial extension of high-rise St. James Town accepted campaign funds from the project's developer, the Meridian Group.

Mr. Jaffary said he believed that aldermen receiving the funds were David Rotenberg, Fred Beavis, June Marks, Allan Lamport, Hugh Bruce, Ben Grys, William Archer and Mayor William Dennison.

He said he was satisfied that Aldermen Tom Clifford, Horace Brown and Joseph Piccininni had not received contributions from the firm.

Mr. Jaffary's allegations, which plunged City Council into silence near midnight, came after council had given final approval to another controversial high-rise project in the Bloor Street-Gothic Avenue area, near High Park. His comments came as he tried to put off final council approval for the controversial St. James Town West project, which would add 2,000 more apartment tenants to the area.

Mr. Dennison said later he did not know whether such funds had been given to his campaign, because funds were collected without his knowledge.

Mr. Beavis said he received no contribution of more than $50 from Meridian and did not know details of contributions smaller than this.

Mr. Rotenberg walked out of the council meeting after the charges were made.

Council members sat quietly and tensely during the incident.

Mr. Jaffary said he did not have any tangible proof that the members he had named had received campaign funds, other than that he had asked them and they had neither denied receipt nor discussed the question with him.

Mr. Jaffary said he was not charging bribery and was not saying "strings" were attached to the contributions. But he said the developers had built up intimate relationships with those aldermen, had family-like access to their offices, and were watching those members trying to get special considerations like higher densities for their apartment projects.

Mr. Jaffary said continued friendships between developers and such council members would lead to the exchange of "hundreds of thousands of dollars" between the developer and different campaign funds.

Globe and Mail 30 Sept. 1971

Ex-Metro chairman Bill Allen
is new chief of Dominion Realty

Former Metro chairman William Allen, now president of Kinross Mortgage Corp., has been appointed president and chief executive officer of Dominion Realty Co. effective Feb. 15.

Dominion Realty is a wholly owned subsidiary of the Canadian Imperial Bank of Commerce. It manages, operates and administers all properties owned by the bank, including the new Commerce Court. Kinross is partly owned by the bank and handles placement of mortgage funds across the country.

Allen said the bank will be giving more emphasis to the management of its own properties. His new job would be "much broader in scope and I'm looking forward to it."

Toronto Star 27 Jan. 1972

WILLIAM ALLEN
Broadens his scope

Photo reprinted with permission Toronto Star

Allen's career came up in an interview I had in the summer of 1971 with David Rotenberg, then budget chief and effective leader of the majority at Toronto city council. Rotenberg is an insurance agent, but he allowed as how he hoped that when he left city politics he would not find himself remaining an insurance agent. I brought up Allen's experience, and Rotenberg said he hoped he would be able to do the same thing. "Billy wouldn't have been able to do that without his experience at Metro," said Rotenberg, illustrating yet again how the property industry can reward diligence and service in office.

Servicing the constituency and styles of city politics

According to the theory of democratic city government Candian-style, the device of elections is the principal mechanism by which citizens are able to ensure that politicians represent the interests of the people in their actions at city hall. Clearly civic elections function as a kind of filtering device, allowing some hopeful candidates to obtain office and keeping others out. But the success of the device obviously depends greatly on who those candidates are. Moreover there are a number of factors that determine the outcome of elections, only one of which is the record of a politician in office to prove he represents the interests of the voters as opposed to the promise of a novice candidate that will do so.

Continued on page 113

WHAT'S NEW

The real owners of neighborhood aren't the people

The real corridor of power at City Hall is the aldermen's lounge, a tastefully decorated area behind the council chamber that is separated from the public by a set of ornamental iron gates. Here, amid the potted palms and low-slung chairs, the aldermen and their guests can sip coffee from porcelain cups, watch the hockey game on television and, free of the restraints of parliamentary procedure and political alliance, talk things over like gentlemen.

Last night, as on all nights when a big development issue is on the agenda, the place looked like a convention of the Urban Development Institute. There was a blue-uniformed attendant on duty at those wavy iron gates to keep the public out, but he opened them with deference as the developers, in their Florida tans and Mr. Ivan sideburns, strolled in and out—almost, you might say, as though they owned the place.

On the other side of the wall in the council chamber itself, the debate was turning ugly. Council was about to give final approval to a proposal by two of the city's biggest developers to destroy a green and venerable neighborhood on Quebec and Gothic Aves. near High Park, and erect townhouses and high-rise towers its place.

It was much better to be back there in the aldermen's lounge, where people could relate to each other like human beings. Over there by the window, you could see Philip Roth of the Meridian group, deep in conversation with William Archer. Right next to the potted palm, the Green brothers of the Greenwin group could be seen sharing a joke with Graham Emslie, the city's development commissioner.

"It's okay, any old time," laughed Emslie, and one of the Green brothers held up his thumb and index finger in a comradely "O."

Toronto Star 16 March 1972

Ward boundaries and civic elections

Winnipeg, Toronto and Vancouver have three widely-different electoral systems which have quite different implications for how a city politician operates and how he can get elected.

Vancouver has city-wide elections and no smaller wards for its aldermen, though in 1971-72 there was public discussion of a 10-ward system which would have operated very much like Toronto's strip wards.

Winnipeg has 50 tiny wards, with populations of about 10,000 people each, which with very few exceptions contain single neighbourhoods and do not cut across major community boundaries.

Toronto now has 11 large wards with two aldermen elected from each. These wards are generally like Winnipeg's in their social and economic characteristics. More interesting is the previous Toronto arrangement and the plan that the city council tried very hard to have adopted in 1969, the strip plan, which carried on the traditional Toronto practice of lumping together quite disparate neighbourhoods of the city into single wards.

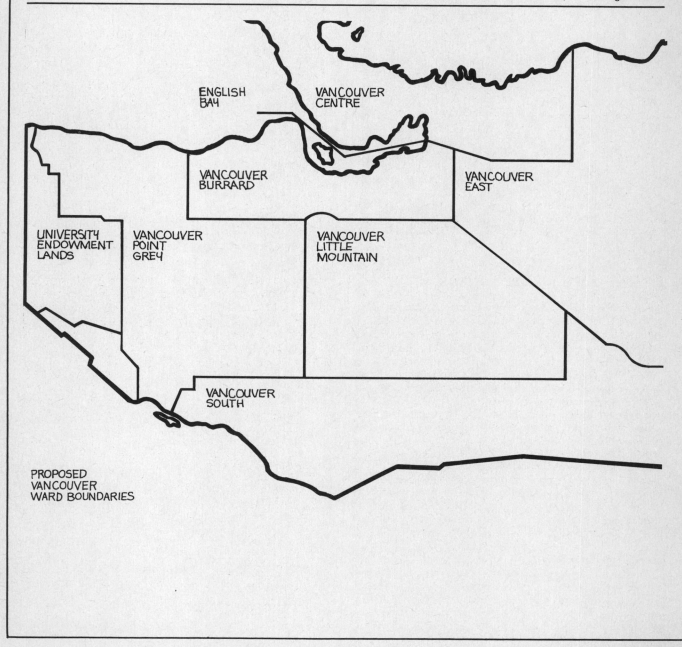

ENGLISH BAY

VANCOUVER CENTRE

VANCOUVER BURRARD

VANCOUVER EAST

UNIVERSITY ENDOWMENT LANDS

VANCOUVER POINT GREY

VANCOUVER LITTLE MOUNTAIN

VANCOUVER SOUTH

PROPOSED VANCOUVER WARD BOUNDARIES

VANCOUVER: FROM ONE GERRYMANDER TO ANOTHER? Vancouver's electoral system involves city-wide elections for all 10 aldermanic posts, as well as for mayor. This arrangement greatly favors sitting aldermen, who are more likely to have city-wide reputations, and candidates with large election budgets for advertising and promotion purposes.

In 1971 B.C. minister of municipal affairs Dan Campbell took up a long-standing proposal of citizen groups and suggested that Vancouver city government be reorganized by having 12 aldermen elected from 6 wards and another 6 elected from the city as a whole.

The motive behind his proposal was unclear, though it came just after Vancouver city council had been heavily under attack for the Four Seasons hotel scheme to be built on the waterfront at the edge of Stanley Park and for other controversial pro-developer decisions.

Campbell's proposal put city politicians under some pressure, while attracting many citizen groups into a discussion of the kind of structural issues which politicians can handle so well.

Vancouver's city politicians reacted badly to Campbell's plan. Citizen groups, however, took it up and urged a ward system on Vancouver.

In fact, however, an analysis of the details of Campbell's suggestion leads to the conclusion that his new wards would lack most of the advantages of a well-designed ward system.

The six wards used for the election would be the six provincial constituencies lying in the City of Vancouver. Two of these are strip-shaped, and lump together solid middle-class communities with working-class areas (Vancouver South, and Vancouver Little Mountain). The upper-income residential area of Shaugnessy is neatly divided in two and split between two constituencies, Vancouver Point Grey and Vancouver Little Mountain. Only one of the six is clearly homogeneous in its makeup, and that is predominantly working-class Vancouver East.

Wards with boundaries like this would have few of the advantages of a well-constructed ward system, and in fact would probably operate much like city-wide aldermanic elections.

As public debate on the proposal originated by the municipal affairs minister continued, citizen groups who supported the idea pointed out that the minister had the power to impose the system if he so chose. Up to that time, he had been "suggesting" it to the Vancouver politicians.

The politicians were continuing to object, probably on the grounds that any change in the system could only do them harm. Campbell's real interest in the change was, however, placed in great doubt when he refused to order the change, and refused even to order a plebiscite on the topic.

WINNIPEG: The last major revision in the City of Winnipeg's electoral map was made in 1919-20 when business interests and the provincial government were worried about the strength of labour candidates. At that time a three-ward system was set up, with each ward electing three aldermen using a complicated preference-voting system.

When Winnipeg's new one-city government was being established, the architects of the scheme wanted to have a large number of constituencies. One of the reasons for this was that it would provide lots of opportunities for sitting municipal politicians in the Winnipeg area who otherwise would be done out of political office by the changes. A second factor in determining exactly how many constituencies there should be was a desire of the provincial politicians not to have civic ward boundaries which corresponded too closely to provincial boundaries. Their fear was that in this kind of situation civic politicians would find it too easy to compete with their provincial counterparts. Perhaps an unspoken worry was the fact that such an arrangement would make it easy for an alderman to move up and run in provincial elections.

Critics of the one-city government plan argued that a 50-man council was unwieldy. Supporters argued that it was a major reduction in the number of elected municipal politicians in the Winnipeg area — from 112 to 51.

What no one disputed was that, in large measure, the new wards did follow the real boundaries of neighbourhoods in Winnipeg.

TORONTO: THE STRIP VS. BLOCK WARD DEBATE:

Up to 1969, Toronto had long used a ward system with 9 wards spread across the city. East end, west end and north end wards were squarish in shape, and because of the city's geography contained areas that were broadly — though only broadly — similar in ethnic makeup, incomes, occupations and social class. Central-city wards, however, were quite different because they combined a slice of the central-city working-class neighbourhoods with a slice of the upper middle-class and upper class north Toronto areas of Rosedale, Moore Park and (after 1967) Forest Hill.

One important political implication of this arrangement was that, unlike east end, west end or north Toronto aldermen, central-city aldermen could safely pay little attention to their working-class constituents of their wards and still get re-elected. This resulted partly from the higher turnouts in middle-class neighbourhoods, and partly perhaps from the relative volatility of the middle-class vote. In these circumstances, many of these central-city aldermen acted exactly this way.

In 1969, Toronto had to redivide itself into 11 instead of 9 wards. The city council asked the city clerk to prepare a new electoral map, and the clerk came up with the strip plan illustrated. The thin, narrow strip shape is used for wards 4-8, while extreme east-end, west-end and north-end wards are block shaped. When this boundaries map is superimposed on a map showing income, occupation and ethnic background data, all five central city wards include widely-disparate neighbourhoods. This is especially true with 6, 7 and 8 which are drawn in extremely awkward shapes in order to keep to the strip principle.

The city clerk prepared a second map, the block plan as illustrated. This time the wards in the central-city area were drawn using Bloor Street as the major dividing line. This practice had much logic behind it because Bloor Street functions, in a rough way in the centre of the city, as the dividing line between working-class and middle-class parts of the city. It works roughly the same way as does Portage Avenue in Winnipeg, Main Street in Vancouver. The boundary is rough, but it is there and its existence is well-understood in the way people talk about the city.

The political implication of the block plan was that central-city aldermen were no longer going to have the kind of fragmented constituency they were used to. Central-city neighbourhoods would find themselves with the same sort of control over their aldermen as other wards had traditionally enjoyed.

A more immediate, but no less important, implication of the block plan was that it changed the map around completely and left all the sitting politicians with the job of finding new constituencies where they could get elected. For the 1969 election, they would not enjoy quite the same traditional advantage over challengers.

A hot debate over ward boundaries was sparked by demands from central-city citizen groups that city council adopt the block plan rather than the strip plan. The politicians refused to do so. Later the issue went to the Ontario Municipal Board for a hearing, and the city clerk had a very difficult time justifying the strip plan. The OMB's decision on the matter was to impose the block plan on a reluctant city council. Its adoption and use in the 1969 election was an important factor in the election of a small number of aldermen who were opponents of the property industry's majority at city hall.

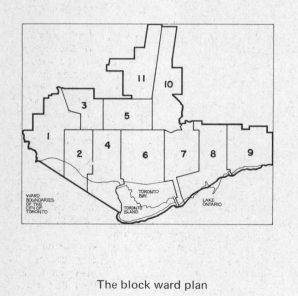

The block ward plan   The strip ward plan

The property industry has several ways of short-circuiting elections. One is controlling who it is who actually present themselves as serious candidates with the necessary organization and funds to run successfully, and then by exercising continuing post-election control over those who win.

In theory, the constituency of a city politician is the voters who have the power to elect him or someone else in his place. In practice, the constituency for the ordinary city politician is the property industry. Charges that he does not represent the people may be true, but charges that he does not represent his real constituency are usually false. His real constituency is the property industry, and he does his best to serve it.

Part of the job of serving the property industry well is ensuring that you have enough electoral support to get elected at the polls. Re-election may be a basic interest of most city politicians, though it is obviously not of quite such great concern to the property industry. In the eyes of the industry, most city politicians friendly to them are expendable. If one has to go, he can usually be replaced.

But a city politician who represents the property industry must nevertheless also pay some attention to the voters in his constituency. What this involves depends on what kind of constituency he has. The basic distinction to be made is between working-class and middle-class constituencies, though this cannot be done in a simple-minded way. Just because the majority of residents in a city ward are working-class does not necessarily mean that the ward's representative depends on working-class support to get elected. Very often city constituencies are gerrymandered to cut across natural boundaries between neighbourhoods and communities within the city in order to place both working-class and middle-class communities into a single constituency. In such a situation, even when the middle-class element is in a minority, a city politician can often get elected by paying attention to middle-class voters only. This is partly because middle-class voters seem to be somewhat more volatile in their conduct, more likely to vote against a sitting alderman if he has a habit of paying no attention to neighbourhood interests. You have, therefore, to be careful in deciding whether a politician has middle-class or working-class voters to worry about.

A property industry politician with a middle-class constituency typically pays careful attention to the local interests of his ward. He protects his neighbourhood from offensive development, he steers expressways away towards other parts of the city, and he captures a substantial portion of the parks budget to increase the supply of parkland in his area. When ratepayers' organizations ask him for attention and support at city hall, he gives them what they want so long as it affects only the local area and does not threaten any major property industry interests. Usually he lines up his colleagues in the property industry majority at city hall to get his voters what they want. With that, he has satisfied the organized voters of his ward. They do not ask of their

MIDDLE-CLASS WARD POLITICS: TORONTO'S PAUL PICKETT

Since winning the executive committee post, Paul Pickett has been an almost perfectly reliable member of the majority bloc which controls Toronto city government. But his performance since December 1969 has served only to sharpen the internal contradictions between the way he votes on issues affecting his own ward and the way he votes on similar issues affecting the rest of the city.

Thus for instance he opposes expressways inside his ward and supports them outside. He is a strong supporter of the completion of the Spadina expressway, and unlike David Rotenberg (whose ward Spadina was to pass through) he consistently voted in favor of it at City Hall. But he is just as strong an opponent of the crosstown expressway — which is planned to go right through his ward. At Metro council in September 1970, for instance, it was Mr. Pickett who revealed publicly the strategy of Metro Toronto officials who want to build the crosstown in disguised form as an extension of St. Clair Avenue across the Don Valley, to link up to O'Connor Drive in East York. Officials were at that time trying to get Metro council to start go get committed to this project by voting for an innocuous-sounding feasibility study for the high-level bridge across the Don Valley.

On development matters, Mr. Pickett pays close attention to citizens' groups inside Ward 10, supports them when they oppose developments, and tries — often successfully — to get them what they want. Thus for example he pushed through a downzoning of land in Rosedale where a small developer named Otto G. Pal wanted to build an eight-story hotel. Downzoning land is generally considered by the majority group at City Hall to be a horrible and unfair measure. For Mr. Pickett and Rosedale, it was done.

On controversial development projects outside his ward, however, Mr. Pickett shows little of the same concern for citizens' groups and their views. His voting record on controversial development projects in 1970 compiled by City Hall newsletter was nine votes in favour of developers, two in favour of citizens' groups. One of the two votes which matched what citizens' groups wanted concerned a development inside Mr. Pickett's ward. None of the nine votes favourable to developers was for a Ward 10 project.

Much the same thing is true regarding road widenings. Mr. Pickett voted against widening Summerhill Avenue in his ward in March 1970, but he voted in favour of money to widen Wellesley Street East, in favor of widening St. Joseph Street in Ward 6, and in favour of widening Caroline Avenue in Ward 8.

In he eyes of CORRA, Mr. Pickett's voting record has deteriorated badly since the 1969 elections. The 1970-71 CORRA record shows him voting eight times against citizens' groups, three times on their side. Two of the three votes favourable to citizens' groups were on projects in Mr. Pickett's own ward.

Globe and Mail 31 Jan 1972

representative that he pay the same careful attention to similar demands from people in other parts of the city for his protection and attention.

One simple way to prove that this pattern is in operation is to look at two kinds of information: (1) the pattern of privately-financed redevelopment in older residential areas close to the centre of the city; and (2) the pattern of land acquisition by city hall for parks.

As for privately-financed redevelopment, it usually turns out that it has taken place mainly in working-class and lower middle-class neighbourhoods, and has not been allowed in solid middle-class and upper-class areas even though they might be similarly located. In Toronto, high-rise redevelopment has gone on in St. Jamestown but not in Rosedale. In Vancouver, it has been concentrated in the West End, and has not touched Shaughnessy.

Park acquisitions work the other way around. Money is spent for land that serves middle-class neighbourhoods (which usually have a fair share of parks already, and lots of private green grass around). Money is not spent for new parks in working-class neighbourhoods, which have little parkland and little area in the way of private gardens and yards.

Relying on middle-class voters makes a politician somewhat flexible in his position on issues touching the interests of the property industry. When his voters are directly affected, he may support their interest over that of the property industry in a specific instance. This gives him an air of some flexibility in his voting record.

A property industry politician with working-class voters to worry about operates quite differently. He is not really expected to protect his area from city hall; residents rightly assume that little such protection can be expected anyway. Often they are not as effectively organized as middle-class areas to define their local interests and to demand that city government respect them. But this kind of city politician — the old ward politician — is expected to come up with occasional plums from city hall: a paved street here, a new recreation centre there. One such civic plum every few years is anticipated, and from the politician's point of view

Continued on page 120

WORKING-CLASS WARD POLITICS: TORONTO'S FRED BEAVIS

An old ward politician pays a lot of attention not to the political views but to the practical problems of his constituents. People bring him these problems, usually matters arising out of the day-to-day administrative routines of City Hall and other public bureaucracies, and the politician acts as an informal advocate of his constituents' interests.

Mr. Beavis described this process at a meeting in his ward, Ward 8, in 1971: "They come to me with their problems, and I tried to solve them, and I've been trying to solve the problems of the area for quite a number of years."

From time to time an old ward politician gets a highly-visible civic facility built in his ward — a swimming pool, arena or community centre. Mr. Lamport got his new ward an artificial skating rink; Mr. Wardle recently got his ward a new recreation centre. The politician then talks about the things he has done for "his people."

Mr. Beavis did this at that same 1970 public meeting: "I got you Pape Avenue Recreation Centre," he told his constituents. "I had $15,000 taken from the city budget to bring you up to the $25,000 plus the repairs to ry to put the (WoodGreen Community Centre) building back in order."

Generally these politicians find their working-class constituents are not much involved in political organizations, not even ratepayers' and residents' groups. The politicians prefer that things remain this way.

So the bargain that an old ward politician makes with his constituents is this: he provides them with a minimum level of services at City Hall and the occasional civic plum. They leave him alone to act as he wants on matters of civic policy, apart perhaps from those that have direct and immediate impact on the ward. They usually do not expect even to know what his real political position is on these matters.

Globe and Mail 24 Jan. 1972

Voting records: How the scoring was done

These voting records were compiled by rev ewing all the formal votes of where voting was recorded by the city clerk, during the period of time covered by each of the three sets of tables. Selected from all the recorded votes were those chosen which were considered relevant to the main concerns of city politics and where there was a split amongst the city politicians. In all three cities, most of the recorded votes during the time period covered have been included in these tabulations. For Toronto the initial selection of votes was done by a group of researchers working for City Hall, the newsletter published by four Toronto opposition aldermen. For Winnipeg and Vancouver, I did the initial selection.

Each issue was then analyzed to determine on which side the property industry's interests lay. In development matters, for example, the industry's interests lies on the side of approving a controversial development over the objections of citizens. On transportation matters, the industry's interest lies in pressing on with new expressways, new road widenings, new bridges and other new expenditures particularly when these are car-oriented.

In the detailed tabulations of voting in Winnipeg and Vancouver, a black dot means a vote on the side of the property industry. A white dot means a vote against the property industry, and — usually — for the people. For Toronto detailed voting records using this same format of black and white dots are available in *City Hall* newsletter and in *Inside City Hall*, a compilation of material from *City Hall*.

In the voting record summaries where each politician's voting is represented by a score, the figure on the left indicates the number of votes cast on the property industry's side and the figure on the right, the number cast against the industry. So Vancouver mayor Tom Campbell's overall score of 16-0 means 16 votes on the property industry's side, 0 votes against the industry.

Voting record problems: Absenteeism, ambiguity, and the Grys trick

There are a number of problems which come along with the information you can get from formal city council voting records.

One is absenteeism. City politicians often miss votes on major issues. Sometimes this is unavoidable, because for example they are occasionally sick. Often it is very intentional. By missing a recorded vote, a politician can avoid having to declare himself on an issue and make enemies of the people (usually citizen groups) who wanted him to vote the other way. Toronto alderman and mayoralty hopeful Tony O'Donohue seemed to make a habit of this kind of absenteeism. After O'Donohue managed to miss an important recorded vote on the controversial Eaton Centre project for downtown Toronto in mid-1972, his colleague (but perhaps not his friend) Paul Pickett called out into the lounge area behind the city council chamber once the vote had been taken: 'All right, Tony, you can come out now.'

A second problem with voting records is ambiguity. On certain issues a few politicians will waffle, voting one way and then the other, leaving everyone a bit confused about where they really stand. On the astonishing give-away deal between Winnipeg city council and Trizec for land at Portage and Main, for instance, there were 8 councillors who opposed approval in principle of the deal on June 7, 1972. When the detailed agreement came before city council for final approval on June 28, 1972, the arrangements spelled out there were no better for the city than they had been earlier, and some of the provisions of the agreement — for instance, that the city was committing itself to Trizec but Trizec was making no commitment to the city that it actually would proceed with the development on the terms the city was agreeing to — were revealed for the first time on June 28. When the vote was taken, however, two councillors who had previously opposed the deal voted in favour of it. They were Dowhan and Pierce. The voting was not close at all — the development commanded a majority of 30-5 that day, so the votes of these two politicians who usually vote with the property industry majority were not needed. Nevertheless they switched sides on the issue. As a result, in the voting record their position on the matter is recorded as a question mark, and is not included in tabulating their overall voting score.

A third problem with voting records is the Grys trick, named for Toronto alderman Ben Grys who often performed this way. The Grys trick involves voting one way on an issue when you really want to vote the other way, but when you find yourself in a situation where you will anger your constituents greatly by following your natural bent — *and when you know for sure the side you secretly support will win even without your vote.* There is a certain amount of this kind of voting at city hall, though the consistency in voting patterns indicates that it doesn't happen all that often. There is no sure way of identifying it, apart from knowing a politician's overall voting record. When you know someone's voting record, it is not difficult to pick out the occasions when he votes contrary to his usual pattern but without endangering the victory of the side he usually votes with.

Vancouver city council voting record

VANCOUVER CITY COUNCIL VOTING RECORD 1971-72   TABLE 7-5

Issue key:

1. Reaffirm Four Seasons
2. Rezoning freeze
3. Four Seasons plebiscite
4. Four Seasons vote wording
5. Cambie-Georgia land sale
6. Point Grey road
7. Third Crossing preference
8. Third Crossing meeting
9. Third Crossing funds
10. Third Crossing plebiscite
11. Third Crossing plebiscite
12. Publish plans
13. Jericho Park
14. Youth group kiosk
15. Enforcing sign by-law
16. Grant to Visitors Bureau
17. Arbitration for tenants
18. Pigeon Park
19. Garbage pickers
20. Aldermen's salary hike
21. Staff holidays
22. Strike negotiations
23. Aldermen's salary hike
24. Help with welfare cheques
25. Welfare enquiry
26. Police riot shields

GOVERNMENT GROUP

Hard-line

Name	1	2	3	4	5	6	7	8	9	10	11	12	13	14	15	16	17	18	19	20	21	22	23	24	25	26
Tom Campbell (mayor)	●	—	●	●	—	—	—	●	●	●	●	●	●	●	—	—	—	●	●	—	●	—	●	—	●	●
Earle Adams	●	○	●	●	—	●	●	●	●	●	—	—	●	●	●	●	●	●	●	●	●	—	—	●	●	●
Hugh Bird	●	●	●	●	●	●	●	●	●	●	●	●	○	○	●	●	●	●	●	●	●	○	○	●	●	●
Ernie Broome	●	●	●	●	●	●	●	●	●	●	●	○	●	●	●	●	●	●	●	●	●	○	○	●	—	—
Ed Sweeney	●	●	●	●	○	○	●	●	●	●	●	●	○	●	●	●	●	●	●	●	●	○	—	●	—	—
Halford Wilson	●	●	●	●	●	●	●	●	●	●	●	●	○	●	●	●	●	●	—	●	●	●	●	—	—	●

Soft-line

Name	1	2	3	4	5	6	7	8	9	10	11	12	13	14	15	16	17	18	19	20	21	22	23	24	25	26
Brian Calder	○	●	○	○	—	—	○	○	○	○	○	—	—	—	○	○	●	○	●	●	●	●	●	○	●	●
Marianne Linnell	—	○	●	○	—	—	—	○	○	○	○	—	—	—	○	○	●	○	●	●	●	●	○	●	○	●
Art Phillips	○	○	○	—	○	—	○	●	○	○	—	○	—	—	○	○	●	○	—	●	●	●	●	●	●	●

OPPOSITION GROUP

Name	1	2	3	4	5	6	7	8	9	10	11	12	13	14	15	16	17	18	19	20	21	22	23	24	25	26
Walter Hardwick	○	○	○	○	○	○	○	○	○	○	○	○	○	?	○	○	●	○	○	○	●	○	○	○	○	○
Harry Rankin	○	●	○	○	○	○	○	○	○	○	○	○	○	○	○	○	●	○	○	○	●	○	○	○	○	○

VANCOUVER CITY COUNCIL SUMMARY VOTING RECORD 1971-1972

Property industry occupation	Political party affiliation	Government group	Development & planning	Transportation	Citizen power	Relations with property industry	Other	Total
		Hard-line						
P	NPA	Tom Campbell (mayor)	3-0	5-0	2-0	1-0	5-0	16-0
P	NPA	Earle Adams	4-1	5-0	2-0	4-0	6-1	21-2
	NPA	Hugh Bird	5-0	7-0	0-2	4-0	6-2	22-4
P	NPA	Ernie Broome	5-0	6-1	2-0	4-0	7-0	23-1
	NPA	Ed Sweeney	4-1	6-1	1-1	4-0	6-0	21-3
P	NPA	Halford Wilson	5-0	7-0	1-1	4-0	5-1	22-2
		Soft-line						
P	TEAM	Brian Calder	1-3	0-5	1-0	3-1	5-2	10-11
P	NPA	Marianne Linnell	1-2	1-4	0-0	1-2	5-2	8-10
P	TEAM	Art Phillips	0-4	1-6	1-1	1-3	5-2	8-16
		Opposition group						
	TEAM	Walter Hardwick	0-5	0-7	0-1	1-3	1-7	2-23
	COPE	Harry Rankin	1-4	0-7	0-2	0-4	0-7	1-24

VANCOUVER VOTING RECORD   ISSUES

Planning and development

1. Sending telegram to Ottawa reaffirming the city's zoning approval for the Four Seasons project, March 16, 1971
2. Proposal that no major high-density residential rezonings be made until after the proposed rapid transit system is discussed at city hall, January 6, 1971
3. Turning the Four Seasons vote into a money bylaw requiring a 60% majority to pass and allowing only property owners to vote
4. Using a figure of $9 million as the value of the property on the Four Seasons plebiscite, June 4, 1971
5. Calling an extra-quick public tender on city-owned lands at Cambie and Georgia which a developer wanted to buy, May 16, 1972

Transportation

6. Calling a public meeting where affected residents could discuss the proposed alignment for the new Point Grey road*
7. Tabling any decision regarding a preference for a tunnel or bridge for the Third Crossing until more discussions held regarding funding with the provincial government and more information available on the proposed east-west connector, April 6, 1971. The property industry oriented position on this issue was not to delay expressing a preference
8. On the question of whether a public meeting should be held regarding the Third Crossing, December 21, 1971
9. Agreeing to contribute financially to certain elements of the proposed Third Crossing, December 21, 1971
10. Calling a plebiscite on the proposed Vancouver city hall financial contribution to the Third Crossing, December 21, 1971
11. Considering again the question of a Third Crossing plebiscite, February 8, 1972
12. Holding a public meeting of city council where the National Harbours Board consultants and others would present transportation planning proposals, February 8, 1972

Citizen power

13. Instructing the mayor to establish a committee which would proceed to negotiate with the federal government to buy the remaining 38 acres in Jericho for a park
14. Deciding on a request by a youth group for permission to establish a temporary summer information kiosk on city-owned land

City hall's relations with the property industry

15. Deciding whether to continue to allow signs violating the city's sign bylaw
16. Grant of $100,000 to the Greater Vancouver Visitors and Convention Bureau
17. Deciding on a proposal which would give tenants the right to impartial arbitration when they were unhappy about rent increases, April 6, 1971
18. "Beautification" of Pigeon Park in order to please the property investors and merchants of the Gastown area who thought that changes in the park would discourage young people and vagrants from using it, so apparently making life more pleasant for suburban shoppers and tourists, May 30, 1972

Other issues

19. Halting the activities of people at the Delta landfill operation who were salvaging things from the garbage which was being dumped, February 2, 1971
20. Increasing aldermen's salaries by 6% retroactive to January 1, 1971; July 13, 1971
21. Acting on a request to give city hall employees holidays on December 24 and December 31 because Christmas and New Year's Day fell on Saturdays in 1971, November 9, 1971
22. Instructing the mayor to enter into negotiations with striking civic workers without imposing any preconditions, April 18, 1972
23. Increasing the salaries of aldermen by 6% at the time of the civic workers' strike, May 2, 1972
24. Providing extra clerical help to the welfare department to deal with the work overload caused by the civic workers' strike emergency and threatened delays in making payments to welfare recipients, May 16, 1972
25. Acting on an offer by the United Community Services Association to investigate the circumstances behind the fact that 750 welfare cheques were not picked up by welfare recipients when the civic workers' strike made it impossible for the cheques to be mailed out as usual. The property industry oriented position on this matter was not to investigate the matter further
26. Deciding on a request by the police to spend $2000 on 50 plastic shields for use in riots, June 21, 1972

*Where dates of recorded votes are not given, this is because of a failure to record this information during the compilation of these data.

Winnipeg city council voting record

	Development		Transportation				Good relations with the property industry				Other	
	1. Kenaston Blvd. land sale	2. Trizec deal approval	3. Replacement for Arlington Bridge	4. Street widening and improvement program	5. Policy to protect city trees	6. Hiring 'independent' consultants to study works dept.	7. Spending $175,000 to promote convention centre	8. Awarding contract to non-union construction firm	9. Dividing cement contract between identical bidders	10. Grant of $100,000 to Industrial Development Board	11. General approval of City Hydro – Manitoba Hydro amalgamation	12. $2000 grant for Pollution Probe
ICEC majority group												
Juba[1] (ind.)	—	—	—	—	—	—	—	—	—	●	—	—
P Baker	●	●	●	●	●	●	●	—	●	●	●	●
P Coopman	●	●	●	○	●	●	●	●	●	●	●	●
P Cropo	●	●	●	○	●	●	●	●	●	—	●	○
P Dennehy	●	—	—	●	●	●	●	●	●	○	●	—
Dixon	●	●	●	●	●	●	●	●	●	●	●	?
P Ducharme	●	●	—	—	●	●	●	●	●	●	●	●
Enns	—	●	—	—	●	●	●	●	●	—	●	●
Fuga	●	●	●	●	●	—	●	●	●	○	●	●
P Galanchuk	●	●	●	●	●	●	●	●	○	●	●	○
P Gee	●	●	●	●	—	●	●	●	○	●	●	●
Hallonquist	●	●	●	—	●	●	●	●	—	●	●	●
P Kaufman	●	●	●	○	●	●	●	●	—	○	●	○
Kotowich	●	●	●	●	●	●	●	●	●	●	●	●
Leech	●	●	—	●	●	●	●	●	●	—	—	?
Marion	—	—	●	●	●	●	●	—	●	●	●	●
McGarva	●	●	●	●	○	●	●	●	●	●	●	○
P McGonigal	●	●	●	●	—	●	●	●	●	●	●	○
P McKenzie	○	●	●	●	●	●	●	●	●	●	●	●
P Mercier	●	●	●	○	●	●	●	●	○	●	●	○
P Minakur	○	●	●	●	●	●	●	●	●	●	●	●
P Norrie	●	●	●	●	●	●	●	●	—	●	●	●
Parkhill	●	●	●	●	●	●	●	●	—	—	—	?
Perry (ind.)	●	●	●	○	●	●	●	●	●	●	●	?
Rizzuto (ind.)	●	●	●	●	●	●	●	●	●	●	●	●
Ross	●	●	●	●	●	—	●	●	●	○	●	●
P Sasaki	●	●	●	●	●	●	●	●	●	●	●	●
P Smith (ind.)	●	—	●	●	○	●	●	●	●	●	●	○
Stanes	●	●	●	●	●	●	●	●	●	●	●	●
P Stapon	○	●	●	—	●	●	●	●	●	●	●	—
P Steen, R.	○	●	●	●	○	●	●	●	●	○	●	●
P Steen, W.	—	—	●	●	—	●	●	●	●	●	●	●
Taft	●	●	●	○	—	●	—	—	●	●	●	○
P Wankling	●	●	●	●	●	●	●	●	●	●	●	○
P Westbury	●	●	●	●	○	●	●	●	●	○	●	—
Wilson	●	●	●	●	●	●	●	●	●	●	●	●
P Wolfe	●	●	●	●	●	●	●	●	●	●	●	?
P Yanovsky	●	●	●	—	●	—	●	●	●	○	●	●
ICEC majority wavering supporters[2]												
Dowhan	●	?	●	○	○	○	○	—	●	○	●	○
P Hudson (ind.)	●	?	●	○	○	●	●	○	○	○	●	○
Penner	●	●	●	○	○	●	●	—	●	○	●	●
Pierce	●	?	●	○	○	○	●	○	●	○	●	○
P Rebchuk[3]	●	—	●	●	○	●	○	○	—	—	●	○
NDP-based opposition group												
Cartwright/Cochrane[4]	—	○	○	○	○	○	○	—	●	○	○	○
Cherniack (NDP)	○	○	○	○	○	○	●	○	○	—	○	○
Johannson (NDP)	○	○	●	○	○	○	●	○	○	○	○	○
Klym (NDP)	○	○	○	●	○	○	○	—	○	○	○	○
Munroe (NDP)	○	—	●	○	○	○	—	○	○	○	○	—
Skowron (NDP)	○	○	●	○	○	○	○	○	○	○	○	—
Wade (NDP)	○	—	●	○	○	○	●	○	○	○	○	○
Zuken (LEC)[5]	○	○	●	○	○	○	○	○	○	○	○	○

ISSUES

Development and Planning

1. Carrying on with the sale of 61 acres of city-owned land on Kenaston Boulevard to Lakeview Developments and Metropolitan Homes, March 15, 1972
2. Approving the deal between the city and Trizec whereby Trizec leased city land at Portage and Main for 99 years for a fixed and very low rent, with the city agreeing to expropriate additional land for the developer if Trizec wished and also agreeing to build a parking garage which would serve tenants in the Trizec development, June 7, 1972

Transportation

3. Approving in principle a new McGregor overpass to replace the Arlington Street bridge, January 5, 1972
4. Approving a general street resurfacing and widening program
5. Proposal from a councillor that city council adopt a policy motion emphasizing that trees are not to be cut down by the city simply to make possible road widenings which will facilitate car travel, June 21, 1972

Relations with the property industry

6. Hiring "independent consultants" to study the operation of the city works department which carries out the construction of much of Winnipeg's public works, cutting private contractors out of possible work
7. Spending civic funds of $175,000 to promote the new Winnipeg Convention Centre by giving the money to the industry organization, the Tourist and Convention Association of Manitoba, without considering submissions from advertising agencies or looking at alternative ways of spending the money, March 1, 1972
8. Awarding a Convention Centre contract to Baert Construction, when the low bid was well over the estimates for this portion of the work, March 23, 1972
9. Proposal to divide up equally the city's cement purchases between the two available suppliers, Canada Cement and Inland Cement, because as in many previous years they had submitted identical tenders, 5 April 1972
10. Proposal to grant $100,000 to the Industrial Development Board, a property industry-dominated private group with some city council members

Other

11. Approving in principle a proposed amalgamation of the city-owned hydro utility, City Hydro, with the province-owned utility, Manitoba Hydro, a move which was universally expected to lead to higher electricity bills for consumers in some parts of Winnipeg now served by City Hydro, January 5, 1972
12. Deciding on a grant of $2000 to a citizen group, the Winnipeg branch of Pollution Probe, March 1, 1972

WINNIPEG CITY COUNCIL SUMMARY VOTING RECORD 1972   TABLE 7-8

Property industry occupation	Political party affiliation	Government group	Development & planning	Transportation	Relations with property industry	Other	Total
		Hard-line					
	Ind.	Juba (mayor)	0-0	0-0	1-0	0-0	1-0
P	ICEC	Baker, Charles	2-0	3-0	4-0	2-0	11-0
P	ICEC	Coopman, Al	2-0	2-0	4-0	1-0	9-0
P	ICEC	Cropo, Joseph	2-0	2-0	4-0	1-0	9-0
P	ICEC	Dennehy, Michael	1-0	1-0	3-0	1-0	6-0
	ICEC	Dixon, Geoffrey	2-0	3-0	5-0	1-0	11-0
P	ICEC	Ducharme, Albert	2-0	3-0	5-0	2-0	12-0
	ICEC	Enns, Harry	0-0	1-0	0-0	0-0	1-0
	ICEC	Fuga, Olga	2-0	2-0	3-0	2-0	9-0
P	ICEC	Galanchuk, Kenneth	2-0	1-0	3-1	1-0	7-1
P	ICEC	Gee, John	2-0	2-0	3-1	2-0	9-1
	ICEC	Hallonquist, W.	2-0	2-0	4-0	2-0	10-0
P	ICEC	Kaufman, Morris	2-0	2-1	2-1	1-1	7-3
	ICEC	Kotowich, Ed	2-0	3-0	4-0	2-0	11-0
	ICEC	Leech, Lorne	2-0	2-0	4-0	0-0	8-0
	ICEC	Marion, Paul	0-0	3-0	3-0	2-0	8-0
	ICEC	McGarva, William	1-0	2-0	3-1	2-0	8-1
P	ICEC	McGonigal, Pearl	2-0	2-0	5-0	1-1	10-1
P	ICEC	McKenzie, Dan	1-1	3-0	5-0	2-0	11-1
P	ICEC	Mercier, Gerald	2-0	2-1	4-1	1-1	9-3
P	ICEC	Minakur, George	1-1	3-0	4-0	2-0	10-1
P	ICEC	Norrie, Bill	2-0	3-0	4-0	2-0	11-0
	ICEC	Parkhill, Roy	2-0	3-0	2-0	2-0	9-0
	Ind.	Perry, Don	2-0	2-1	5-0	1-0	10-1
	Ind.	Rizzuto, Phil	2-0	3-0	4-1	2-0	11-1
	ICEC	Ross, Eldon	2-0	3-0	3-1	2-0	10-1
P	ICEC	Sasaki, William	2-0	3-0	5-0	2-0	12-0
P	Ind.	Smith, James	1-0	2-1	5-0	1-1	9-2
	ICEC	Stanes, Douglas	2-0	3-0	5-0	2-0	12-0
P	ICEC	Stapon, Norman	1-1	2-0	4-0	1-0	8-1
P	ICEC	Steen, Robert	1-1	3-0	3-2	2-0	9-3
P	ICEC	Steen, Warren	0-0	2-0	4-1	2-0	8-1
	ICEC	Taft, Robert	2-0	1-1	3-0	2-0	8-1
P	ICEC	Wankling, Richard	2-0	2-0	5-0	1-1	10-1
P	ICEC	Westbury, June	2-0	2-1	2-1	1-0	7-2
	ICEC	Wilson, Bob	2-0	3-0	4-0	2-0	11-0
P	ICEC	Wolfe, Bernie	2-0	3-0	5-0	1-0	11-0
P	ICEC	Yanovsky, Abe	2-0	2-0	2-1	2-0	8-1
		Soft-line					
	ICEC	Dowhan, Stanley	1-0	1-2	1-3	1-1	4-6
P	Ind.	Hudson, Norman	2-0	1-2	3-2	1-1	7-5
	ICEC	Penner, Alfred	2-0	1-2	2-2	1-1	6-5
	ICEC	Pierce, Florence	1-0	2-1	3-2	2-0	8-3
P	Ind.	Rebchuk, Slaw	1-0	2-1	0-3	1-1	4-5
		Opposition group					
	NDP	Cartwright / Cochrane	0-1	0-3	0-3	0-2	0-9
	NDP	Cherniack, Lawrie	0-2	0-3	1-3	0-2	1-10
	NDP	Johannson, Robert	0-2	1-2	1-4	0-2	2-10
	NDP	Klym, Adam	0-2	1-2	0-4	0-2	1-10
	NDP	Munroe, George	0-1	1-2	0-4	0-1	1-8
	NDP	Skowron, Alfred	0-2	1-2	0-5	0-2	1-11
	NDP	Wade, Alan	0-1	2-1	1-4	0-2	3-7
	LEP	Zuken, Joseph	0-2	1-2	0-5	0-2	1-11

Toronto city council summary voting record

TORONTO CITY COUNCIL SUMMARY VOTING RECORD 1970-71

TABLE 7-9

Property industry affiliation	Known political party affiliation		Planning and development decisions	Transportation decisions	Citizen power decisions	Total
		Government group				
	NDP	Dennison	25-0	14-0	20-0	59-0
P	Cons.	Rotenberg	22-2	11-4	19-2	52-8
P	Lib.	Beavis	25-1	16-0	18-2	59-3
P	Lib.	O'Donohue	20-3	7-5	15-2	42-10
P	Cons.	Pickett	18-5	12-2	19-1	49-8
P	Cons.	Lamport	22-0	10-0	11-0	43-0
P	Lib.	Bruce	23-0	10-0	14-1	47-1
	Lib.	Marks	25-0	15-0	17-3	57-3
P	Lib.	Grys	22-0	13-1	15-1	50-2
	Lib.	Piccininni	24-0	12-2	14-1	50-3
	Cons.	Wardle	21-2	8-1	17-2	46-5
	Cons.	Clifford	25-0	13-0	17-4	55-4
P	?	Boytchuk	19-0	11-1	13-2	43-3
P	Cons.	Archer	17-2	11-4	6-11	34-17
P	NDP	Brown	16-4	5-7	6-12	27-23
P	Cons.	Hope	9-11	5-9	5-9	19-29
	Lib.	Eggleton	13-10	6-6	8-10	27-26
		Opposition group				
	Cons.	Crombie	2-17	4-6	3-12	9-35
	NDP	Scott	7-10	2-5	2-12	11-27
	NDP	Chisholm	3-20	5-9	0-16	8-45
P	NDP	Jaffary	1-21	1-13	1-18	3-52
	none	Sewell	0-26	0-16	1-19	1-61
	Lib.	Kilbourn	0-26	0-15	1-19	1-60

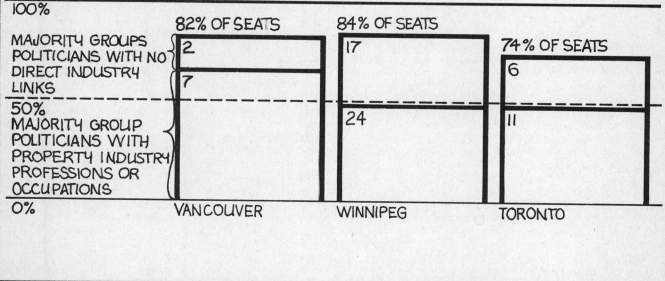

THE PROPERTY INDUSTRY CORE OF CITY COUNCIL MAJORITY GROUPS
VANCOUVER, WINNIPEG & TORONTO 1972

100%

MAJORITY GROUPS
POLITICIANS WITH NO
DIRECT INDUSTRY
LINKS

82% OF SEATS — 2 / 7
84% OF SEATS — 17
74% OF SEATS — 6

50%
MAJORITY GROUP
POLITICIANS WITH
PROPERTY INDUSTRY
PROFESSIONS OR
OCCUPATIONS

24
11

0%   VANCOUVER   WINNIPEG   TORONTO

impresses on the voters the value of having a man on the right side at city hall. More important, though, voters expect their representative to act as an informal advocate of their interests in day-to-day dealings with city hall. He can be appealed to for help if the city housing inspector is being particularly vicious. He can get people into senior citizens' apartments, from time to time. And he can be relied on to show up at local tea parties, church bazaars, and similar events. Unlike the middle-class administrator servicing middle-class voters, an old ward politician is not required to perform much (if anything) in terms of the way he votes on issues concerning his ward at city hall. Nothing is expected of him on non-ward issues. As long as he deals with his voters' problems, he is free at city hall to follow the policies desired by the property industry.

Performance

Given the way the property industry recruits city politicians and succeeds in getting them elected to office, given the means it has to control them while they are in office, and given the way city politicians are able to avoid paying much attention to the real interests of voters without jeopardizing their chances of re-election, what kind of performance does the property industry get from the politicians?

The answer is simple: the industry gets almost everything it wants. It can count on the votes of a solid majority at any city hall in Canada, and often on the votes of every council member, for virtually any policy or program that it considers to be in its best interests. City councils act as the political arm of the property industry.

The evidence for this is abundant. In Vancouver, Winnipeg and Toronto, for example, there is a serious and well-defined opposition group to the property industry's majority at city hall. In these cities, the voting records on issues important to the property industry are clear. There is a bloc of aldermen who generally vote together, who are the controlling majority at city hall, and who vote in favour of proposals the industry supports and against proposals the industry opposes.

The voting records of city politicians are, unfortunately, often not as complete or as clear as they might be. In the case of Toronto, however, city council minutes do contain recorded votes on a large number of controversial issues, which cover the entire range of subjects covered at city hall and which include a large number of matters where property industry interests are directly involved. Tabulating the votes on planning and development issues, transportation issues and citizen group issues for the 24 months of 1970 and 1971 shows that there were two voting blocs on council which consistently voted as blocs and consistently opposed each other in these areas, all major concerns to the property industry. For 1970-1971, there were 17 aldermen in the property industry's majority group, and 5 aldermen in the opposition group.

In the case of Winnipeg, a study of the first seven months of the new one-city council, which took office at the beginning of 1972, yields a relatively small number of recorded votes on significant issues. Particularly lacking were votes on major development issues, where independent-minded property industry supporters usually return to the fold and vote along with the rest of the industry's supporters. Nevertheless there was a very clear division between the property industry's majority group and the small opposition bloc. A group of nine politicians, including the seven NDP councillors, the one Labour Election Committee councillor, and a single renegade ICEC councillor, voted together on almost all issues and opposed the property industry's position. Thirty-five voted just as consistently on the property industry's side of these issues. Six split their votes between the two blocs, though with sufficiently obvious preferences for the property industry that they amount to part of the industry's effective majority.

In Vancouver, a study of all the recorded votes of the council that took office at the beginning of 1971 up to the end of July 1972 shows that again there were relatively few recorded votes on issues of great importance to the property industry. Votes go unrecorded because no city alderman asks to have the voting officially recorded in the minutes. I was able to locate voting records on only four major development issues, six major transportation issues, and four other matters where the property industry's interests were directly touched. There were, however, a number of other votes where Vancouver's politicians revealed their basic attitudes to citizen groups and the property industry. There were three voting blocs in Vancouver. One consisted of the mayor and the five NPA aldermen, who voted solidly and consistently in favour of the interests of the property industry and against those of citizen groups. The second voting bloc consisted of two of the three TEAM aldermen, Calder and Phillips, plus the NPA alderman Linnell. These three usually supported property industry interests in their voting, but they were somewhat less rigid about it than the NPA group — though of course they could afford to vote occasionally in favour of citizen groups and against the property industry because the industry had a majority except on the odd occasion when everyone ganged up against it and one of its regular supporters was absent. The third voting bloc, TEAM alderman Walter Hardwick and COPE alderman Harry Rankin, voted together and were the solid and consistent supporters of citizen groups and opponents of the property industry. In Vancouver, the property industry's majority was a coalition of hard-line supporters and somewhat more flexible supporters.

To complete our analysis of the way in which the property industry controls city politicians, we must now put the data about how different city politicians vote alongside information about the municipal political party affiliation of the politicians (if they have one) and their business or profession. Though we have identified several links between the property industry and the politicians, including campaign contributions, friendships, personal payoffs and advancement, political party involvement, and business or profession, hard data is available only on the last two listed. What we discover, however, is a pattern of remarkable consistency. City politicians with business or professional interests in the property industry are almost invariably industry supporters at city hall. These politicians form the nucleus of the industry's majority in each of the three examples we have looked at. Almost as consistent is the association between affiliation with a "business-oriented" municipal political party (likely to be controlled and funded, as we have already seen, by the property industry) and a voting record supporting the industry. To put the matter in a different way, someone running for local office who is involved him-

Performance from the politicians: Toronto

These headlines tell the story of the performance the property industry expects — and gets — from Toronto city politicians. They record the debate and inevitable approval of three major Toronto developments discussed in 1972. The Metro Centre approval amounted to a blank cheque to the developers, the CNR and CPR, ignoring all the planning arguments of the city's own planning bureaucracy. The project was later not approved by the Ontario Municipal Board, and was sent back to city hall for further consideration.

The West St. Jamestown approval permitted the developer to extend an already-enormous central-city high-rise residential project. Included in the city approval was permission to count as open space land the developer had to sell to the city to use for road widenings made necessary by the project.

The Quebec-Gothic project attracted absolutely no support from any interest group in the city apart from the developers. It too was proposed for an area already densely populated with high-rise apartments. And it was the project tainted by the revelations that an earlier council approval had been promoted by Alderman Ben Grys, whose family had owned two houses in the project area purchased by the developers for $195,000.

A fourth example of the performance obtained by the property industry from its city politicians is the refusal in February 1972 by the industry's majority to vote for a motion calling for Grys to resign.

This came after Grys (who had long denied any conflict) had reversed his view and admitted a conflict. It also came after a court hearing on the Grys issue had led to a verbal agreement where the judge had found Grys in violation of the conflict of interest provisions of Ontario's Municipal Act. The Act contains no mechanism for removing from office an alderman with such a conflict.

Plan amended, Metro Centre gains approval

By ALDEN BAKER and THOMAS COLEMAN

Globe and Mail December 1971

Council votes 9-7 to refuse to ask Grys to consider quitting

Globe and Mail 3 Feb. 1972

High-rise approved in St. James Town

Globe and Mail 18 Sept. 1971

City Council approves high rise rezoning in Quebec-Gothic area

Globe and Mail 16 March 1972

Performance: Vancouver

This brief summary by *Vancouver Sun* columnist Allan Fotheringham details the performance the property industry gets from its majority in Vancouver's city council.

The simple fact is that the four anti-NPA aldermen — aided now and then by the shifting vote of Ald. Marianne Linnell — control the initiative on council. The tired NPA men, who essentially represent the reactionary real estate interests, now fight only a holding action. They are a discredited force. The fact of their age and their predictable background forces them into desperate, defensive attitudes on most issues — any dolt who sits in on council week after week, year after year can testify to that.

self in the property industry or who is affiliated with a property industry political party is virtually certain, whatever he himself says about his political views, to turn up as a reliable member of the industry's majority at city hall.

This kind of absolutely reliable performance from city politicians on important issues is what the property industry expects — and gets — from its politicians at city hall. So industry does not just recruit politicians from its ranks, and arrange to find outsiders who sympathize with its interests. It does not just try to exercise some control over what the politicians do. It does not just isolate city politicians from much control by voters. All this could be true, and city politicians could still be quite free to act as their conscience dictated in the best interests not of the industry but of the city and its citizens.

For its investment in manpower and time, the property industry gets direct control of the powers of city council. The links between the industry and city politicians add up to real power at city hall. The industry uses this control to get decisions from city governments that are consistently the decisions it wants. City hall takes care of the property industry before it takes care of anyone else, because a majority of the politicians there are in the property industry's pocket.

Renegades

The analysis of sample city voting records establishes that not all city politicians are property industry representatives. There seem to be two quite different kinds of property industry opponents in city councils — renegades and opposition politicians. Most cities have known occasional renegades who base their political career on fighting for the rights of the citizens and of ordinary people, and opposing developers, real estate investors and other kinds of vested interests. Generally these renegades get into city politics by an unusual route, and not by recruitment by the property industry. The most common route is from involvement in a major fight between city hall and a citizen group of some kind. But these renegades are always a tiny minority, swimming constantly against the stream. Naturally enough they

are often very popular with the voters, because they soon develop a public reputation of standing up against the property industry in its worst offenses against the public interest.

The usual fate of renegades is not defeat at the polls. Rather it is absorption, gradual or sudden, into the property industry's city hall majority. For Toronto's alderman June Marks, the process took no more than three or four years. Mrs. Marks made her reputation as an opponent of developers, speculators, block-busters and slum landlords in east central Toronto when she challenged them and city hall in the mid-1960s. She was elected alderman in 1964, then controller in a city-wide vote in 1966. By 1969 she was showing only flashes of her previous anti-property industry stand. In the 1970-72 Toronto city council, her voting record was as solidly pro-property industry as anyone's. She gave strong and consistent support to many of the developers she had challenged so strongly only five years before. The developers had not changed their policies. June Marks had switched sides.

For Toronto's mayor William Dennison, the process of absorption into the property industry majority took 25 years. Dennison was for a long time an opposition alderman at city hall, and was elected controller on the strength of the reputation he made for himself in the mid-1950s in a fight against the developers of the St. Jamestown apartment complex and their "beanpole apartments" which "sometimes rise as many as 12 storeys off the ground." Dennison was the only strong opponent of a proposal made at the time that the city expropriate land for the development and turn it over to the developers. He strongly criticized the fact that W.W. Gardiner, son of the then chairman of Metro Toronto Fred Gardiner, was one of the principals in the development company. He also criticized the astonishing apparent conflict of interest by which the then Metro Toronto assessment commissioner, W.J.B. Gray, was hired as a consultant and public relations man by the developers. Ten years later, however, Dennison was proposing that the city be empowered to expropriate land for developers. And, after his surprise election as mayor in 1966, Dennison was

Continued on page 127

Renegade mayors for Calgary and Victoria?

It is difficult to be certain whether Calgary mayor Rod Sykes, re-elected in October 1971, or Victoria mayor Peter Pollen, elected in December 1972, belong to the pattern of renegade city politicians who mount one-man campaigns against the property industry's majority at city hall.

Both have received enthusiastic press coverage. Both have challenged the policies of local developers. Pollen has defeated a downtown high-rise redevelopment project, and is pushing for a 14-storey height limitation on high-rise buildings. He has also promoted an end to traditional city transportation policies calling for expressways, bridges, and road widenings.

Pollen, himself the owner of a large Victoria car dealership, defeated a department store management man for the mayor's job.

Calgary's mayor Rod Sykes has battled with some Calgary developers, and has strongly criticized the property industry for some of its housing policies. In 1971 he defeated a businessman candidate for the job. Yet development, particularly downtown office development and industrial construction, proceeds unabated and Calgary is recording new high levels of construction.

Sykes himself is very familiar with the land development business. He was previously a Calgary-based official for the CPR's real estate arm, Marathon Realty.

As one-man operations rather than leaders of municipal political groups capturing control of city hall, the powers of these mayors to implement their views are of course limited. So is their ability to mount a serious challenge to the property industry, or to develop alternative structures for providing housing and other forms of urban accommodation.

What they can do, however, is call for some moderation of the extreme policies of the industry. Limiting high-rise buildings to 14 storeys instead of 30 is not going to put an end to high-rise development by property industry firms. Demanding inclusion of low-rent family units in every new housing project, as Sykes has done, is only a minor problem for developers.

Token reforms in the property industry could well reduce the political opposition which the industry is generating for itself now in most Canadian cities. Moves of this kind are certainly in the industry's long-term interest, because they will blunt the edges and reduce the power behind demands for major and radical restructuring of the property industry. Sykes is not pushing municipal rent control, and opposes municipal land banks.

At present the evidence is not clear. But obviously it is possible that these "renegade" mayors, now so bitterly opposed by local property interests and so enthusiastically supported by many citizen groups, may point the way to a new accommodation by the property industry to the demands of citizen groups which leave its structure basically unchanged and its representatives and supporters as firmly in control of city hall as ever.

The power of Mayor Sykes' people policy

By REG VICKERS

CALGARY — With his walk-away civic election victory here Wednesday, Mayor Rod Sykes demonstrated how successful an anti-establishment, pro-worker campaign can be. By capturing nearly 60 per cent of the vote, the Mayor showed how strong an appeal his "people policy" had with the citizens.

Even as he savored the delights of his victory over businessman Frank Johns, the Mayor didn't waver from his theme. He said he was delighted that "a couple of angry little millionaires have lost a substantial investment in this campaign."

His cutting comments were levelled at the Calgary businessmen who led a campaign for Frank Johns. They aimed their election pitch directly at Mr. Sykes and the turmoil that has plagued City Hall for the past two years, pointing out that there were five vacancies in senior city positions and hinting that this was due largely to Mr. Sykes' handling of his staff. The effect of their campaign was to put the business community (establishment) against Mr. Sykes.

For his part, the Mayor concentrated on ethnic group dinners and roadside promotions. He also stressed that he was able to keep the taxes down in the past two years and passed off the continual shake-up at City Hall as necessary house-cleaning.

Globe and Mail 16 Oct. 1971

The tragic career of William Dennison

The career of Toronto's mayor from 1966 to 1972, William Dennison, is an object lesson in what usually happens to renegade city politicians. The account is tragic because Dennison spent 20 years, in and out of city hall, fighting the property industry and land development interests in Toronto and making a reputation for himself with working-class voters. Finally, with their support and fighting property industry candidates all the way, Dennison won the mayoralty and, because of the way the 1966 election went, found himself in a pivotal position between down-the-line developers' supporters and more independent-minded (though still property industry-inclined) politicians. Then, after a campaign of intensive pressure from fellow-politicians and the media, Dennison finally went over to the other side and began supporting policies and projects identical to those he had fought in previous years.

Dennison's radical past was hard to believe, in the light of his strong anti-citizen group stand as mayor. But it was real, and his political about-face was a testimony to the difficulty of mounting a one-man opposition to the property industry and its majority without the support of strong citizen organizations.

In 1969, JUST BEFORE the civic elections in which William Dennison was re-elected mayor of Toronto, a Toronto labor council official said of him: "He's a good socialist, a good friend of the labor movement, and all trade unionists should be happy that we have a socialist mayor."

Socialist mayor? No one looking at Mr. Dennison's record in office from 1966 to 1969 would ever think of describing him that way. People who do are not referring to Mr. Dennison in his office after the 1966 mayoral tion. They are referring to his record from the time he was first elected to public office in 1938 as a Toronto school trustee to a point, difficult to pin down precisely, when in the early Sixties Mr. Dennison abandoned his 20-year-old position as a radical at City Hall.

Up to that point, Mr. Dennison was indeed an opposition politician in City Council. He spoke for working-class interests and at one time took on most of the vested interests in Toronto from the Bell Telephone Co. to the three newspapers, the University of Toronto and real estate developers.

From the beginning of his political career Mr. Dennison faced attacks charging that he was dangerous, a doctrinaire leftist or Communist, and that he advocated policies which were a threat not just to "the boys" at City Hall but to every citizen.

When, for instance, the CCF ran a slate of candidates for city office in 1942, challenging the practice of candidates not declaring party political affiliations in civic politics, *The Globe* denounced Mr. Dennison and his colleagues: "Here is shown in plain language how this Socialist body hopes to destroy the freedom of the voters and place the city in the grip of party bosses . . . Every elector should make it his duty in the remaining 10 days to round up his neighbors and scotch this bald attempt to grab control of the city."

Behind these strong public attacks directed at Mr. Dennison and the CCF there was apparently a real concern among vested interests about the power of this opposition group and about the appeal of the alternative version of city government which they were proposing.

The CCF does appear to have had quite a strong and clear view of how City Hall should operate that was different from the view of the business-oriented aldermen in power.

Rather than having a city government functioning as a fairly passive agency, the CCF was talking about how the city could use its corporate powers to implement new programs which, while offending specific private business interests, would be of clear and direct economic benefit particularly to working people by reducing the cost of basic economic necessities.

One concrete proposal was for a municipal coalyard which would, Mr. Dennison said, save people $1 a ton on their coal. The coalyard was to be run as a municipally-owned public utility.

Another CCF scheme was for a municipal milk delivery system which would produce, Mr. Dennison told the public, cheaper milk. In 1944, the CCF municipal program included a call for city-owned, low-cost housing, when public housing was widely thought of as a dangerous idea and a potentially serious threat to private landlords.

The issues Mr. Dennison was involved with during the Fifties where citizens challenged City Hall were extremely important. The battles which took place then over urban renewal in Regent Park North and private redevelopment in St. James Town were the prototypes of the major conflicts between citizens' groups and City Hall through the late Fifties and Sixties. The fact that these first crucial fights were won by City Hall and lost by the citizens allowed the city administration to establish precedents which neighborhood organizations have continued to challenge with very limited success until now.

The plan to carry out Canada's first urban renewal scheme, involving the demolition of a low-income working-class neighborhood and its replacement with public housing in Regent Park North, was developed at Toronto City Hall while Mr. Dennison was at Queen's Park. The Regent Park project, of course, established a pattern which was later repeated in four other neighborhoods in Toronto, seriously threatened in three more, and imitated in many other working-class areas in other Canadian cities.

Established residents of the Regent Park area criticized the original plan and organized themselves to try to get it changed. Mr. Dennison listed for me the criticisms they raised. They pointed out that the compensation being paid expropriated homeowners was inadequate. Many homes in good condition in the area were to be demolished unnecessarily. Factories that provided jobs for people were being expropriated even though they would probably not be able to relocate successfully. Rents in the new public housing were far higher than rents had been previously in the area. Expropriated homeowners were unable to return to the area as owners because none of the new housing was offered for sale but rather was for rent only.

Mr. Dennison was involved in the unsuccessful opposition to the Regent Park scheme on these grounds. Supporters of the scheme, led by social workers and people in the social welfare establishment, got it approved. Later, as the Regent Park project was repeated in other Toronto areas and elsewhere in the country, these same objections were raised.

The second major fight Mr. Dennison was part of in the Fifties was over the private development of the St. James Town area, which was also to prove a prototype of City Hall policies right up to the present.

Developers and real estate agents -- prominent among them was W. W. Gardiner Real Estate, the firm of the son of Fred Gardiner who at the time was the chairman of Metro Toronto — were taking options and assembling property in the area. In 1956 a group called the Parliament Street syndicate claimed to control about 50 per cent of the land in the area, and they asked City Hall to expropriate the rest and then to turn the land over to them for redevelopment.

One of the consultants to the developers was A. J. B. Gray, at the time the civil servant head of the assessment department in Metro Toronto. Mr. Dennison attended public meetings of area residents, attacked the developers for asking for expropriation and criticized Mr. Gray for getting so involved in the affairs of the developer. When assessments on homes in the area jumped sharply in 1956, Mr. Dennison charged that Mr. Gray was doing this vindictively because many homeowners in the area were refusing to sell out.

Mr. Dennison took a strong stand against expropriation by the city on behalf of the developers. "I've never before heard of democratic government that takes land from one private party and gives it to another," *The Globe* reported him saying. "The city should stay clear of this, let private enterprise develop the area if it can, and let it go at that. I'm sure the intention of the law was never to bail out private companies that start on a money-making project, then get bogged down."

In 1958, an election advertisement on Mr. Dennison's behalf urged: "VOTE against the tyranny of expropriation for the benefit of speculators." It was in this election that Mr. Dennison succeeded in moving up from Ward 2 alderman to controller.

Mr. Dennison's criticism of downtown redevelopment went further than complaints about developers'

tactics and a enunciation of expropriation. He also opposed the high-rise form of apartment construction. One undated election ad on his behalf says: "Fought to stop 'beanpole' apartments."

In December, 1963, Mr. Dennison ran against Mr. Beavis for a seat on Metro Toronto's executive committee. He lost 17-6. Mr. Dennison's first major public move which was out of character with his past occurred in 1965. He originated a proposal that the city obtain the powers needed to expropriate land for private developers.

His suggestion was that the city should stand ready to expropriate the last 10 per cent of a redevelopment site.

Even though Mr. Dennison's political position appears to have been softening before the 1966 election, it was very much Dennison the opposition city politician who ran for mayor against Philip Givens, the incumbent, and Controller William Archer. Both Mr. Givens and Mr. Archer strongly favored more development, more high rise apartments and more of what they called progress.

Mr. Dennison ran the campaign of an opposition politician. In October, he promised "a strong voice for labor in city affairs." In November, he referred to the strength of establishment interests arrayed against him: "We will have powerful forces ranged against us," he told an audience of about 100, "but if everyone does a little missionary work, we will win."

Mr. Dennison was the underdog in the 1966 campaign. Few people in the news media regarded him as a serious threat, but he had his election organization, the people he had helped in fights against City Hall or with problems with the city bureaucracy, their names recorded on index cards. He had 1,200 election workers. He won that election mainly from votes in the working-class areas of the city — the east end, the west end, and central Toronto south of Bloor Street. It seems clear that he won as an anti-establishment candidate, a politician with a long record of standing up against the old guard fighting for the interests of neighborhoods, citizens' groups and working people.

If the majority group at City Hall had been comfortably in charge after the 1966 election, this might have happened. But the new Board of Control proved awkward. The controllers were a testy bunch when they got together. More serious, there was the possibility of an opposition majority on the Board of Control. Like Mr. Dennison, June Marks had a record of opposition to City Hall on the crucial issues of development. Margaret Campbell was no opposition politician, but she was independent-minded and was often opposed to the council majority on major issues. Together, they were a Board of Control majority and could have caused trouble for the majority of aldermen on Council.

What happened in this situation was that tremendous pressure was exerted on Mr. Dennison to change his political position permanently. He was urged to take on the job of speaking not for himself but for the Council majority, and to concern himself with the corporate interests of the city as a whole as defined by the majority at City Hall.

The Dennisons have since talked about the way this pressure got to them in 1967. Even though the mayor's political position had been shifting in the early Nineteen Sixties, it seems to have been this situation which prevented him finally and completely from following the policies he talked about in his election campaign.

The result was that Mr. Dennison bought the argument that he should, as mayor, speak for the city as a whole rather than for himself, and this meant speaking for the majority at City Hall. His subsequent public statements, his speeches and his voting at Council confirmed this.

In 1969 Mr. Dennison topped polls in all parts of the city, but still received his most solid support from working-class neighborhoods in the west and east ends. That was the strength of Dennison as a pro-administration, pro-development candidate. He was still able to command the support from his election organization and from working-class voters who had supported him previously on the basis of his record as an anti-administration politician at City Hall.

Since the 1969 election, even the flashes of Dennison the opposition city politician — seen, for example, in his opposition to the Lakeshare raceway scheme backed by the Bassett and Eaton families have disappeared.

In the voting on the 32 major issues before Council in 1970, tabulated by the four opposition aldermen who write for City Hall newsletter, Mr. Dennison voted on 29 occasions. On all issues, he voted with the old guard politicians — Allen Lamport, Fred Beavis, Ben Grys, Thomas Wardle, Hugh Bruce, Joe Piccininni and the others. On every controversial development issue which split Council in 1970, Mr. Dennison voted on the developers' side. On every controversial matter concerning City Hall's relation to citizens' groups, he voted against the citizens' groups.

Not only is Mr. Dennison a solid member of the majority group at City Hall, he takes an active part in the counter-attack mounted against citizens' groups and the five aldermen — William Kilbourn, John Sewell, Karl Jaffary, Archie Chisholm and David Crombie — who form the opposition at City Hall.

In 1970, for instance, Mr. Dennison charged that the Riverdale Community Organization had misused their $14,000 civic grant. This accusation proved to have an extremely obscure basis in facts, if it could be said to have any basis at all. He accused the same group of promoting violent confrontation, but when its members challenged him to specify exactly what constituted their violence, the best he could do was to point to a statement made by the group which he said was "getting pretty close to violence." Yet, months later, he was still making this charge.

Mr. Dennison disputes the view that he is fighting citizens' groups. In a newsletter called The Mayor Reports published in May 1971, he wrote about the kind of public involvement he supports. The group mentioned is the Redevelopment Advisory Council, an organization made up of representatives of major Toronto downtown landowners, businessmen and real estate people. Mr. Dennison wrote about this organization: "This is the kind of citizen participation that is listened to, appreciated and respected."

During an interview when I was collecting material for this series, I asked the Mayor whether he saw a contradiction between his present position and his earlier work when he was supporting residents' and ratepayers' groups, opposing developers and redevelopment schemes and urban renewal plans, as Mr. Sewell and Mr. Jaffary are doing now. Why is he now on the other side of the fence?

If Mr. Sewell were a real socialist, Mr. Dennison said, "he would get my support. But he is no socialist. He is either a left-wing Communist or an anarchist."

Surely, I responded, "that is exactly what your opponents were always saying about you. You were always being called a Communist." "That is true," he said, "but I wasn't a Communist. I proved that by fighting hard against the Communists, who were always trying to take over the CCF."

I pointed out that Mr. Sewell too has fought against the influence of militant leftist groups in citizens' organizations. Mr. Dennison smiled, said nothing, and waited for me to go on to another subject.

Mr. Dennison is left with all the trappings of the mayoral office. His situation is a bit like that of the Governor-General, lots of dignity but little power.

He seems to have little energy left — he told me how much he regrets not having the energy he used to have — and many people think that he has slipped into dull and incomprehending old age.

It is ironic that a man who began his political career in Toronto on socialist soapboxes being harassed by police, and by challenging the civic administration, should end it by serving exactly the interest groups he fought for so long. It is sad that this should be going on without William Dennison himself seeming to have any conception of what has happened to him.

absorbed with a vengeance into the property industry's majority at city hall. He became an absolutely faithful supporter of the industry's interests.

Opposition politicians

Not all city politicians in Canada are property industry controlled or individualistic renegades. There are also some city politicians who have backing from either labour unions or citizen groups, and who oppose the property industry in their voting at city hall.

A labour-backed opposition has on occasion been strong in Vancouver, Winnipeg and Toronto as well as other Canadian cities, and has captured control of city hall for short periods. On many occasions ratepayer groups from middle-class areas have produced candidates who have been successful. Politicians from ratepayer groups, however, are not difficult for the property industry majority to absorb. The job is not so easy with labour-based aldermen, although there are countless examples of CCF and NDP city politicians who have come to share almost completely the property industry's outlook, until their voting record is as solid as the industry's best council representatives. This is the case with Toronto mayor William Dennison, but it also applies to another Toronto alderman with NDP affiliations, Ontario Hydro employee Horace Brown. Because of the closeness of interests of construction unions to the property industry, city politicians with construction union backgrounds are likely to prove the easiest candidates for absorption into a property industry majority.

Only politicians with a strong and clear link to labour unions or citizen groups are likely to be able to withstand the pressures and controls set up by the property industry and its city hall spokesmen. Organizations of this kind are moreover necessary to provide the manpower and resources required to run and win election campaigns. They are also the only feasible long-term source of the resources necessary to help establish more citizen groups and so to broaden the base and increase the power of the opposition to the property industry.

In Vancouver, only Harry Rankin has links of this kind to organizations outside the property industry's magic circle. Fellow opposition alderman Walter Hardwick is affiliated with the TEAM group.

The 1972-74 Winnipeg city council has seven NDP aldermen, and two others who regularly vote against the property industry majority at city hall. The NDP politicians have some labour union links; amongst the others, Lawrie Cherniack and George Murphy have some experience with urban citizen groups. But Winnipeg has yet to experience the development of tough, strong, independent citizen groups who will mount the kind of challenge Vancouver's city hall has faced over expressways or the Four Seasons project.

In the 1969 elections, Toronto elected a small number of aldermen who went on to form an opposition group at city hall. Two — Karl Jaffary and John Sewell — were elected by a predominantly working-class ward where there had been a considerable amount of citizen group activity during the previous three years fighting private developers, school board expropriation, and city urban renewal. Sewell, who had worked as an organizer for many of these groups during the previous three years, was completely citizen group based. Jaffary had also been involved to some extent in citizen group activity, and was at the same time very active in the NDP. He had a double base for his candidature. A third, Archie Chisholm, was an NDP labour union candidate who had been somewhat active in citizen group activities but whose main constituency was in the unions. A fourth, William Kilbourn, was elected by the middle-class Rosedale area. Kilbourn, a historian and a Liberal, followed the traditional pattern of middle-class aldermen and carefully protected his ward from undesirable civic policies and decisions. But he voted for the same kind of protection for all other areas of the city where people were organized to demand it, and thus found himself voting reliably with the opposition. But Kilbourn's basic political position was conservative and moderate; he was voting against the excesses of the property industry, rather than advocating radical changes in the structure of the industry. Nevertheless Kilbourn's allegiances were to the citizen groups of his ward, and he was a solid opposition alderman for the 1970-72 period.

Another alderman representing a middle-class ward, David Crombie, also formed part of the 1970-72 opposition group. Crombie was a founder of the short-lived CIVAC party, a reformist property industry grouping which also included the politicians who led the property industry majority in the 1970-72 council. Crombie got into city politics through the traditional route of ambition and interest in political parties, but he too took a more moderate line at city hall than the property industry's majority. At the same time, he deplored the attempts made by Sewell and Jaffary to draw a clear line between the property industry's aldermen and the opposition. He voted more or less consistently with the opposition group, but — even more than Kilbourn — for quite different reasons.

Experience to date suggests that it takes more than an independent attitude towards the property industry to create an opposition politician. It also takes a firm organizational base, one that has the strength to support its politicians, to get them elected, and to keep them in line once they get into city hall. As the career of William Dennison clearly indicates, having your heart in the right place is not nearly enough.

Opposition politicians: the case of John Sewell

John Sewell is one of the small number of opposition politicians, drawing their strength from citizen groups or labour unions or both, who challenge property industry majorities in some of Canada's city governments.

This is partly because his political background is solely a citizen group one. He has no parallel ties to political parties, and no business or professional interests apart from his community organizing. A lawyer by training, Sewell has practised only in a small way, and generally on matters arising directly from his organizing work. So his constituency and his political commitments are completely citizen group oriented.

Another important fact about Sewell's background is that his organizing has been done almost completely with working-class people, and most of the groups in the district he now represents are also working class. Their experience (and his, as an organizer, then as a politician) is constantly more brutal and more direct than is usual for middle-class areas and organizations.

This background explains a good deal of Sewell's success as an opposition politician at city hall. The 1970-72 opposition group, of which he and Karl Jaffary were the strongest members, managed to create a clear public awareness of the existence of the property industry majority at city hall, and to formulate the major differences in political principle between the property industry group and the citizen opposition group. Sewell operated constantly to push other members of the opposition group to take very strong public stands, to challenge every major policy of the property industry majority, and to reveal publicly the strength and the arrogance (as in the Grys affair) of the property industry group. The inoffensive newspaper label for the property industry's majority, the "old guard", came to sound inadequate. Obviously there was more to distinguish them and the opposition group than the simple difference between old faces and new.

Sewell's primary achievement was one of public education, mainly through the news media. He and the other members of the opposition group developed a style of politics which could be communicated via the news media, in spite of a lack of real sympathy on the part of the media for the fundamental political principles Sewell espoused. The information which got through helped spark more citizen activity in Toronto. Perhaps even more important, it helped inform organized citizens of the real nature of their opponents at city hall. The citizen group movement expanded in size and power during these three years, particularly in middle-class areas of the city.

Sewell's strength, especially in comparison with the other opposition politicians, was in the consistency of his position. Not only did he challenge the content of the decisions and policies of the property industry majority; he also challenged the whole structure and style of their operation.

He refused, for instance, to get involved in the normal socializing that goes on amongst city hall politicians, and which creates club-like loyalties amongst the elected which often prove stronger on many crucial issues than differences of political position.

His willingness, on occasion, to talk publicly about the fact that aldermen were drinking heavily and were unable to participate normally in debates and discussion is an indication of this. So, in its way, is the not particularly sympathetic portrayal in the Macpherson cartoon reprinted here from the *Toronto Star*.

It is instructive to compare Sewell the opposition politician with Karl Jaffary, Sewell's fellow alderman from Toronto's Ward 7. Jaffary has some background in citizen groups in the ward, but he has an even longer background in NDP party activities. Jaffary is also a practising lawyer.

Jaffary's political positions vary little from Sewell's, and his voting record is virtually identical. Jaffary is just as tough-minded as Sewell on all major issues including those affecting the property industry, and he has the advantage of having an extremely inventive and probing legal mind.

But he is much closer to the traditional political style of city aldermen than is Sewell. This has operated as a limiting factor on the power of his activities as an opposition alderman. In the absence of someone like Sewell, however, Jaffary would certainly emerge as a tougher and stronger opposition politician than most of the others in that category across the country.

Reprinted by permission Toronto Star

CHAPTER 8
The property industry and independent local agencies

The Toronto Harbour Commission, an independent local agency set up by the federal government in conjunction with the other levels of government, built this administration building on land-fill stretching out into Toronto's harbour. The first photo, taken in October 1920, shows the commissioners' yacht, the Bethalma, moored in front of the building.

From the beginning the Commission was as interested in land development as in harbour administration, and within a few years had filled in a vast part of the harbour including a large area in front of its own building. Designed to stand confidently at the end of its own pier, the building was marooned in the middle of vacant land which the Commission tried to develop for industrial and commercial uses.

Fifty years later, its fine office building still stood, facing onto a vacant field hundreds of feet away from the water's edge.

Surrounding almost every city government is a bewildering array of boards, authorities, commissions and other official bodies which exercise certain limited powers of city government. Most cities, for example, have semi-judicial boards that have the power to allow minor violations of city zoning laws. In Vancouver, this body is called the Board of Variance; in Toronto, it is the Committee of Adjustment. Its power to make illegal land use legal is of course tremendously important to the property industry. Winnipeg is a major exception to this generality about independent civic boards. With the reorganization of the city government at the beginning of 1972, all these powers were returned to city council and its committees.

One of the main functions of this independent civic board structure is that it helps isolate the functions of city government from too close control by politicians who are answerable — in theory, at least — to an electorate. Most of these independent bodies have a variety of kinds of members, often including elected city politicians, people nominated by other public authorities, and "independent citizens" appointed by city hall itself. Non-elected members are able to exercise their powers with even less concern for the views of the public than are elected city politicians.

Because the powers of city government focus on regulating and servicing urban property, the powers of independent civic boards are also usually directly connected to property and the property industry. Take Vancouver as an example: The Downtown Parking Corp. provides parking facilities for the downtown area. The Greater Vancouver Visitors and Convention Bureau encourages tourist and convention business, important for hotel owners. The Industrial Development Commission promotes new industrial development in the city. The Traffic Commission deals with administering the traffic system. The Town Planning Commission develops city planning and land-use policy in the first instance, passing on its views to city council. The Board of Parks and Public Recreation, composed of elected commissioners, administers the parks and recreation facilities. The Greater Vancouver Regional District brings together representatives of the 14 municipalities and three electoral areas in the Vancouver region to deal with major regional planning and development matters. The Port of Vancouver Authority, a federal government body funded by the National Harbours Board, does the day-to-day running of Vancouver's port.

Continued on page 134

Council squelches Sewell bid to change Bruce appointment

City Council yesterday stood firmly behind Alderman Hugh Bruce as a 1972 member of Planning Board and new chairman of Council's powerful Buildings and Development Committee in the face of charges by Alderman John Sewell that Mr. Bruce represents developers rather than the public.

Mr. Sewell had said that Mr. Lamport, who came to Mr. Bruce's defence, had been involved in deals with land developers in his role as an insurance agent. Mr. Sewell said Mr. Bruce, a lawyer, does legal work through the firm of DelZotto, Zorzi, Andrews and Applebaum, which does much legal work for developers.

Mr. Sewell refused to re-tract the charge against Mr. Lamport, until Mr. Dennison threatened to invoke Council's rules of procedure to eject Mr. Sewell. Then Mr. Sewell replied, "If those remarks were offensive, I'll withdraw them."

After Mr. Sewell asked that Mr. Bruce not be on the planning board, Mr. Lamport charged that Mr. Sewell was biased against revelopment.

"Lawyers have to be able to take cocktails with friends and enemies," Mr. Lamport said in apparently defending Mr. Bruce's mixing with developers. Mr. Lamport and Mr. Bruce have a father-and-son type of friendship.

Mr. Bruce remained silent during both attacks by Mr. Sewell, at the Buildings and Development Committee caucus and at Council.

Mr. Bruce said between meetings that he is an associate, not a member, of the DelZotto law firm. This means he finds and serves his own clients, works out of offices in the DelZotto location on St. Clair Avenue West, and pays the firm a percentage of his earnings.

Mr. Bruce said he does handle some development cases referred to him by the firm. He said he gets no part of profits of the law firm, and has no interest in the DelZotto group of construction firms, whose head is the brother of the head of the legal firm.

Globe and Mail Feb. 1972

Rathie's back with big ideas for harbor

By NEALE ADAMS

Bill Rathie is back again.

The ex-mayor of Vancouver, elected in 1962 and defeated in a close race by Tom Campbell, has returned to the fray as a Liberal party appointee. He's chairman of the new Vancouver port authority.

No view from any new skyscraper in downtown Vancouver is as grand as Rathie's vision of Vancouver's "potential." He uses the word often.

He's the same man who brought Vancouver Pacific Centre and Project 200.

The project that Rathie is really excited about is closer to the centre of the waterfront, Centennial West. By filling in from Centennial Pier almost to Pier B-C, as much as 110 acres could be added.

The NHB promised CP Rail five years ago, during a land trade, to build a new pier east of Pier B-C. Rathie would rather fill in the area than build a pier.

Here the third crossing comes in. Rathie figures if a tunnel is built, sand dredged in the excavation could be pumped into this area.

The land created would be worth five to 10 times the cost of making it, he said, a gleam in his eye.

This land could be used for other than waterfront uses. It would sit beside the CP Rail's Project 200 over the railroad tracks. As in Toronto's waterfront scheme, possibly hundreds of millions of dollars worth of new buildings could go up.

What Bill Rathie says isn't as fashionable today as it was once

The first Pacific Centre tower earned the nickname "the tower of darkness." A majority of ratepayers voted against the Four Seasons project near Stanley Park. Polls show voters concerned about pollution and in favor of rapid transit.

But Bill Rathie believes the gospel as firmly as ever. He's convinced he'll win. The critics are a noisy minority of misled "knockers." The people are still for progress.

Vancouver Sun 5 Feb. 1972

Andrews overrules aldermen in setting up design panel

By LEW THOMAS

North Vancouver district has set up a seven-member advisory design panel over the strong objections of three aldermen.

Aldermen Don Bell, John Denley and Gordon Rose said Thursday in interviews they object to Mayor Ron Andrews' selection of the panel's seven members without discussions with council.

Rose and Denley in separate interviews confirmed their objections to the selection of W. K. Paulus as a building contractor representative.

"I selected Mr. Jaulus because I wanted an experienced building contractor on the panel," Andrews told The Sun.

The Mayor said the design factors in multiple dwellings would likely provide the panel with most of its work and he considered Paulus a good choice.

"Paulus is the biggest contractor in North Vancouver. Under the terms of reference for the design panel he won't be allowed to discuss or vote on his developments, because of the conflict of interest involved," said Bell.

"This means that there will be no contribution from a building contractor to panel discussions on some of the big Paulus developments. He is the only builder on it," said Bell.

Paulus is president of Dunhill Developments. The firm recently took over United Provincial Investments, another large development firm, and also owns W.K.P. Construction.

The Dunhill company is presently into the second phase of a multi-million dollar development of townhouse and condominium buildings on Lillooet Road, north of the Coach House Motor Hotel.

Vancouver Sun 5 May 1972

Property industry people and Vancouver's local agencies

These tables and graphs present details of the membership of Vancouver's most important local agencies and boards as of July. 1972.

TABLE 8-1 BOARD OF VARIANCE

Members with property industry occupations

W. Orson Banfield — Insurance agent (retired)
J. Frank Watson — Insurance agent, J. T. O'Brian & Co.
George D. Wong — Branch manager, Commonwealth Trust

Other members

Tom McDonald — Secretary-treasurer, Community Planning Association of Canada (retired)

Property industry people: 3 of 4

TABLE 8-2 VANCOUVER CITY PLANNING COMMISSION

Members with property industry occupations

A. D. Barnes — Manager, Helyar Vermeulen, firm of land surveyors
A. R. Cowie — Managing director, Canadian Environmental Sciences, a firm of architects
Roy Lisogar — President, Lisogar Construction
T. T. Manrell — President, Tenmar Construction
C. R. Widman — President, Cooper Widman, lumber dealers (retired)
H. D. Wilson — General contractor (apparently retired), long-time Vancouver alderman

Other members

D.H.A. Bellamy — Managing director, Canadian Restaurant Association
P. S. Bullen — Professor, UBC
Hy Corday — President, Corday's Ladies Wear
Everett Crowley — President, Avalon Dairy
R. Gibson — President of firm of manufacturers' agents
Mary F. Kelly — Wife of school principal
J. MacD. Lecky — Teacher
Hilda Symonds — Planning commission employee

Property industry people: 6 to 14

TABLE 8-3 VANCOUVER POLICE COMMISSION

Members with property industry occupations

Tom Campbell — Land developer and Vancouver mayor
G. Dawson — President, Dawson Developments Ltd.
A.J.F. Johnson — Lawyer, partner in Davis & Co.

Other members

Allan M. Eyre — Dueck Motors

Property Industry people: 3 of 4

TABLE 8-4 VANCOUVER RENTAL ACCOMMODATION GRIEVANCE BOARD

Members with property industry occupations

W. Orson Banfield — Insurance agent (retired)
Teresa Galloway — Widow of Bertrand Galloway, President of Howe Construction

Other members

Reg Rose — Manufacturers' agent

Property industry people: 2 of 3

TABLE 8–5 BOARD OF PARKS AND PUBLIC RECREATION

Members with property industry occupations

Arthur Cowie — Architect
E.A. Sandy Robertson — President, Robertson Kolbeins, construction engineers

Other members

D. Helen Boyce — Wife of salesman, Evergreen Distributors
A. J. Livingstone — Shift supervisor, Shell Oil (retired)
J. E. Malkin — Personnel manager, W. H. Malkin, wholesale grocery etc.
George D. Puil — School teacher
George Wainborn — Sales manager, Coca Cola

Property industry people: 2 of 7

TABLE 8-6 VANCOUVER CIVIC AUDITORIUM BOARD

Members with property industry occupations

W. Orson Banfield — Insurance agent (retired)
E. J. Broome — Insurance agent and Vancouver alderman
M. L. Gutteridge — Real estate agent

Other members

D. A. Baxter — Employee, B.C. Packers
W. G. Rathie — President, Transport Holdings; Port Authority chairman
G. A. Sutherland — Western general manager, Odeon Theatres
Norman Young — Professor, UBC

Property industry people: 3 of 7

TABLE 8-7 PORT OF VANCOUVER AUTHORITY*

Members with property industry occupations

W. Hamilton	Vice-president, Murzo Holdings: president, Vancouver Board of Trade; Chairman, Fidelity Life Assurance Co.; Chairman and president, Century Insurance Co. of Canada etc.
J. N. Hyland	Director, North American Life Assurance; director, MacMillan Bloedel; chairman, Pacific Press
G. L. Draeseke	Council of Forest Industries of B.C.; former vice-president, Rayonier

Other members

J. S. Broadbent	Vice-president, PGE Railway (represents B.C. government on this board)
H. O. Buchanan	Canadian Marine Transportation Administration
Donald Garcia	President, Canadian area, International Longshoremen's and Warehousemen's Union
G. W. McPherson	Former chairman, Okanagan Helicopters
W. G. Rathie	Transport Holdings; full-time chairman of the Port Authority; former Vancouver mayor
E. M. Strang	President, Maritime Employers' Association
Ed Sweeney	Manager, Sweeney Cooperate, family firm

Property industry people: 3 of 10

*As is apparent from the membership, this is quite a high-level body whose members represent the various interests involved in the operations of Vancouver's port. It was set up in 1971 by the federal government, which appoints its members.

TABLE 8-8 VANCOUVER PUBLIC LIBRARY BOARD

Members with property industry occupations

J. D. Bell-Irving	Real estate agent
Walter K. Davidson	Sales manager of a lumber company
Peter Kitchen	Manager, General Paint

Other members

Peter Bullen	University professor
Walter Hardwick	University professor and Vancouver alderman
Alan MacMillan	Management, CBC
J. E. Malkin	Wholesale foods, food manufacture etc.
Herbert McArthur	President, British Acceptance Corp.
F. Turnbull	Physician

Property industry people: 3 of 9

Property industry people on Vancouver's civic boards

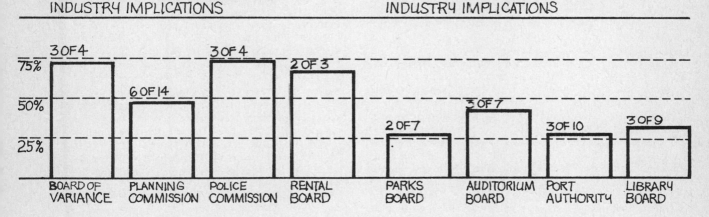

This graph summarizes the data on the number of members of Vancouver's various civic boards and commissions who have property industry occupations and commissions. Note that, while the industry has substantial representation on every one of the bodies reported on here, industry people are far more prominent in the group of boards with functions directly and immediately touching on industry interests (like the Board of Variance and the Planning Commission) than those of less immediate importance (like the Library Board).

TABLE 8-9   PROPERTY INDUSTRY REPRESENTATION ON TORONTO'S PLANNING BOARD

Property industry people: 'independent citizen' members

David Cowper	Insurance agent
Richard Frost	Lawyer
Richard Horkins	Management, Toronto Hydro
Alexander Main	Business manager, construction unions' council
Harry O'Neill	Chairman, Metropolitan Trust
Frank Paznar	Planning director (!), E. L. Ruddy Co. (signs)
Gerald Robinson	Architect
Eberhard Zeidler	Architect

Politician members

Fred Beavis	Roofing contractor (retired)
Hugh Bruce	Developers' lawyer
Horace Brown	Management, Ontario Hydro

Others: 'independent citizen' members

Stanley Buchanan	Sales manager, Coca-Cola Company
Juanne Hemson	
John Kucherapa	Physician

Politician members

Joe Piccininni

Property industry people: 11 of 15

There are occasional instances of independent civic boards whose powers have less relationship to property. One example is municipal library boards, which administer local library systems.

It should be no surprise that most of the members of the property-oriented independent civic authorities are property industry representatives. This is true of both the elected politicians who find their way onto these bodies and the "independent citizens" appointed by the city council majority. The exact number of property industry representatives varies from one board to another, but usually it is a solid majority of the "independent citizens."

The situation in Vancouver is no different. On city hall boards and agencies with little direct connection to the property industry, the number of property industry people is somewhat lower — 33 per cent on the library board, for instance, and 43 per cent on the civic auditorium board. But on the Board of Variance it is 75 per cent, three of the four members. On the Vancouver Rental Accommodation Grievance Board, a body where tenants can take their complaints about landlords, two of the three members are property industry people. One, W.O. Banfield, is an insurance agent, now retired. The other, Mrs. Teresa Galloway, is the widow of Bertrand Galloway, who was the president of Howe Construction. Of the 14 members of the Planning Commission, five are directly involved in the property industry. They include T.T. Manrell, president of Tenmar Construction; A.R. Cowie, managing director of a firm of architects called Canadian Environmental Sciences; A.D. Barnes, manager of Helyar Vermeulen, land surveyors; C.R. Widman, of lumber dealers Cooper Widman; and finally Roy Lisogar, president of Lisogar Construction. Evidently the "independent citizens" aren't quite so independent as one might think.

One of the ironic things about this situation is that, at least in some cases, independent civic boards were established specifically to remove the subjects they deal with from "politics" and from the petty personal and political interests that municipal politicians were often thought to put first. This is particularly true for "independent" civic planning boards, a structural innovation that arrived along with the emergence of city planning as a specific activity in city government in Canada. The evidence is clear, however, that "independent" planning boards are heavily populated with citizens who have direct business and professional involvement in the property industry.

Most independent civic boards have limited but nevertheless quite important powers. Often they act as land developers, for instance harbour boards which fill in harbours in order to create new building sites, which are then sold off or leased to developers. They are very often intimately involved in the provision of certain basic municipal services, like sewers and water or electricity. For the property industry, domination of these relevant boards by industry representatives helps greatly to ensure that the industry is serviced and regulated by city government in its own best interests.

CHAPTER 9
The property industry and the civic bureaucracy

WHEN WORK STOPS: When Toronto's garbage collectors went on strike to demand — successfully, as it turned out — a raise of at least 15 per cent over two years, the city turned its parks into temporary garbage dumps. Behind the garbage bags is the Allan Gardens conservatory.

In the case of elected councils and appointed civic bodies with "independent citizen" members, property industry control is exercised in quite direct ways. People with business and professional interests inside the industry become members of these bodies, and usually dominate the majority group, which controls decision-making and policy. The industry in general knows that it can count on city councils to do the right thing for the industry as a whole almost all the time, and to take care of individual developers and big property owners, because it is industry people and industry supporters who are making those decisions.

Things are different with the civic bureaucracy. City employees do not rely on the property industry for their income. They have no obvious connections to the industry themselves, except that most of them like most of the rest of us are paying the high prices the property industry sets for housing and rents.

It is quite conceivable that a civic bureaucracy could assume the interests of citizens generally and of organized citizen groups, and pose an enormous challenge to property industry domination of city government. At present, however, that is not happening. As things stand now, the property industry controls the civic bureaucracy as effectively as it does the other parts of city government. The only difference is that, instead of being direct, this control of the bureaucracy is exercised indirectly. It arises out of a number of extremely important links that have been developed to join together the interests of the civic bureaucracy with those of the property industry. Together, these indirect links have virtually the same effect as the direct links between city councils and the industry. Their result is that for the bureaucracy as for the politicians, what is good for city government is what is good for the property industry.

Council control

The first link between the industry and the bureaucracy is via the politicians. Formally, almost all the powers of city government belong to the elected city officials, the mayor and the council. It is they who ultimately make all the decisions about civic policies and priorities, and about how the administration will run. Nor is that ultimate authority the sham it is often made out to be.

Often people inside city hall confide knowingly that the real power rests in the hands not of the politicians but of the bureaucrats. They are described as the people who really run the show. If you want to get something done, you go to the head of the streets department or to the city's chief planner, not to a mere politician. All the elected officials do, it is suggested, is nod their heads wisely at council meetings, approving the recommendations and decisions already made by the bureaucrats.

This is indeed the way things work in many city halls. What must be kept in mind, though, is that this arrange-

ment of bureaucracy-directed city government depends almost completely on the willingness of the politicians to maintain a certain benign disinterest in what city government is up to. The politicians may appear to have little say, and to have abandoned their policy-making functions to city employees, but firm and determined action by the politicians can bring a quick end to this situation. If they should decide that they don't like what their officials are doing, they have the power to reassert their ultimate authority over the civic administration. And should an administrator find that he has suddenly lost a lot of his power and influence because it has been reappropriated by the city council majority, there is little he can do about it. He had his power on sufferance. Once the politicians didn't like what he was doing with it, they had the power to take his away.

There is tremendous variation from city to city in the actual allocation of responsibilities between bureaucrats and politicians. During the start-up period of Winnipeg's new one-city government in 1972, for instance, the new senior administrators appeared to be very much in control of what was going on. This arrangement was reinforced by the administrative set-up imposed by the NDP provincial government on Winnipeg, whereby the heads of the city departments were answerable not directly to the politicians but rather to a senior administrator, a chief commissioner. The existence of this office made it more difficult for the politicians to keep each department head relatively weak by playing him off against his rival department heads.

Toronto city politics offers a good comparison between a politician-directed city hall and bureaucracy-directed government. In the Metro Toronto government, the overall regional government for Toronto whose council members are all members of the councils of the cities and boroughs that make up the Metro area, the administrators have been very influential ever since this second-level government was instituted in 1953. In contrast, in the City of Toronto proper, city government is much more politician-directed.

Although bureaucracy-directed city government exists only on the sufferance of city politicians and can be brought to an end by the politicians if they are sufficiently determined to do so, it is of course true that the bureaucracy has some interests of its own, which are different from those of the politicians. Naturally the bureaucrats make use of whatever powers they are allowed to exercise to advance their own interests, as well as those interests the politicians want to see them promote. How much support they can get for their own interests will obviously depend on how much latitude they feel they can extract from the politicians.

As an establishment inside city government, the bureaucracy's primary interests concern its own care and feeding. It has a stake in increasing its size, in increasing the scope of its operations, in adding more employees to its roster and so on. The self-interests of bureaucracies are well known, and they are strongly felt by civic establishments as they are by all others. Politicians who delegate a substantial

> "[The] civil service . . . is entrusted with the task of actually administering the services and enforcing the regulations as the council directs by by-law or resolution."
>
> —Plunkett, *Urban Canada*, p.9

share of their powers to city employees have to accept that those employees will use the opportunity to promote their own interests as well as to do what the politicians want. Obviously there is a bargain to be struck somewhere, because if the politicians judge that the bureaucrats have gone too far in feathering their own nest and increasing their own civic empire, the politicians will take back the powers and authority they gave away to begin with. Knowing this, bureaucrats will be careful not to go too far.

There are many ways city politicians can keep their bureaucracy in line and ensure that it does what they want. The first is via the *city budget*. With a given amount of money to spend, the politicians decide what jobs and what departments to allocate it to. A department head who is doing a particularly fine job for the politicians can expect to see his budget go up, his empire expand, his range of activities increase. If he asks for an extra $1 million for a new program, he knows he can expect to get it. A department head who displeases the council majority, on the other hand, may see his budget slashed, his staff reduced, and his general administrative importance diminished.

A second method of control used by politicians to deal with the civic bureaucracy is through their power to *hire and fire*. The politicians will do their best, when they hire new people for relatively senior posts, or promote men out of the junior ranks, to choose individuals who will regard them with the proper respect and treat their interests with suitably tender concern. The power to fire has to be wielded discreetly, for civil servants at any level are rarely openly fired. But the threat of firing is used often and to great effect inside the city bureaucracy. A serious threat of being fired is often enough to persuade civic employees to quit, because by quitting they at least do not get the reputation of being dangerous. Members of Vancouver's planning staff at the middle level are constantly quitting their jobs, and several who have quit were threatened that they would be fired if they didn't leave voluntarily. After a monster blow-up between Toronto's two competing planning departments in 1967-68 and a demand from a citizen group that city development commissioner Walter Manthorpe be fired, the city politicians talked only sweetness and light and confidence. But over the course of the next year or so, both the planning commissioner and the development commissioner departed.

A third method of control at the disposal of the city politicians is *promotions*. Most city employees are anxious to move up in the bureaucracy, to get the higher salaries and greater power that come with more senior positions inside the bureaucracy. Most senior-level promotions are controlled by the politicians, and employees know that they have to keep the politicians happy if they are going to be moved ahead. More than that, they know that a good way to promote their own interests is to take initiatives that will particularly please the politicians.

Another way in which bureaucrats are controlled by politicians is through decisions the politicians make about the *structure of city government* and the powers of particular departments and officials. Over the years, City of Winnipeg politicians gradually permitted the development of a tremendously strong city works department headed by W.D. Hurst. Hurst was therefore able to run a very large portion of the city's business through his department, whereas in other cities, where the head of the works department was not so persuasive and suitable, city politicians set up several departments to do different aspects of the work Hurst cornered for himself. Structure was used in the opposite way by Toronto's city politicians in the early 1960s, when they were faced by a chief planner, Matthew Lawson, who did not take a growth-is-good attitude towards all proposed developments. Somewhat hemmed in by provincial government requirements that Toronto have a planning board partly autonomous of city council, the politicians did their best to put their uncooperative planner in his place by setting up at city hall a second city planning department called the development department, and appointing another planner to head the new department.

All these devices by which city politicians can control the city bureaucracy are neutral. They can be used by a city council majority to *persuade* their employees to follow council policies, whatever those policies might be. Were a major head-on clash to occur over what the bureaucracy thought was good for itself and for the city and what the politicians wanted to do, the bureaucrats would find that they held some of the cards. But on the whole, most of the power is on the politicians' side.

In the real context of city government in Canada, however, these control devices are not at all neutral. They serve as a means by which the bureaucracy is made into a tool of the property industry, protecting and promoting the industry's interests. That is because the politicians take the industry's interests as their own, and then use their ability to control their bureaucracy in order to ensure that city employees take an equally friendly attitude towards the industry.

Property tax revenues

There are several other ways in which the interests of the civic bureaucray are linked to those of the property indus-

"Metro [council], collectively, thinks that it is ridiculous to question the opinion of a senior official. . . . That brings up the question of who is minding the store. I have come to the conclusion that such store-minding as takes place is done almost single-handedly by Albert Campbell [the politician who is chairman of Metro Council and Metro government]. I think that he is powerful enough to tell most of the commissioners [the officials who are heads of departments] to do something and have them generally do it. If that is so, that is when the political element is injected into the day-to-day operations of Metro, and not at any other time; because once a Commissioner writes his report about something, Metro will do it."

—Toronto opposition alderman Karl Jaffary, describing the overall operation of the Toronto metropolitan government, on which politicians from the City of Toronto and the five suburban boroughs sit, in City Hall newsletter, Sept. 70, p.3.

try. There is for instance the system by which city hall raises a good deal of its current revenue — the property tax system.

Property taxes have a very bad reputation generally, and most people consider them an even worse way of raising government money than other kinds of taxes like income taxes and sales taxes. They are a rather unusual kind of tax, because they are in effect an assets tax. Property owners are taxed a small percentage, perhaps on the average about 1 per cent every year, on the value of the real property they own. Most other taxes fall on current income and spending. People pay 20 or 25 per cent of their income in income taxes, and then when they spend their income they pay a further 15 or 18 per cent in sales taxes on many kinds of goods and services. But these taxes don't touch existing assets, if you happen to have any. The capital gains tax, instituted for the first time in 1972, takes the tax system a small step in this direction by taxing not the value of the assets you own but rather increases in their value. But even with the present capital gains tax, for every dollar a real estate speculator earns when the value of his lands goes up, he pays only half the tax he would have to pay if he had earned the same dollar by working. *And only if a wealthy man holds his wealth in the form of real property does he have to pay an annual tax based on a percentage of its real value. If he holds his wealth in the form of diamonds, stocks, shares, bonds or mortgages, no tax of this kind is paid.*

The problem with the property tax system — and the reason it can't properly be called a "wealth tax" — is that it is imposed on most real property including housing. Ordinary home owners are by no means wealthy because they own the house they live in, and the property tax simply increases the tax burden they have to bear. Given the structure of the market, tenants have property taxes passed directly on to them, so the system serves simply to increase rents and their tax burden as well. In contrast, a tax of 1 per cent a year on stocks and shares people own would be paid almost exclusively by well-off individuals, because most Canadians own no property of this kind. The property tax on commercial and industrial property is mostly passed on to consumers in the form of higher prices, and so operates no differently from other kinds of taxes.

Quite simple reforms could, however, turn the property tax system into a true wealth tax. One change would be to eliminate property taxes on the first several thousands of dollars' value of a residential property, and to increase the tax rate beyond that point, turning it into a progressive asset tax. People living in ordinary homes would pay no property tax, and people well enough off to live in relatively expensive properties would pay more. Coupling this change with a graduated property tax rate would mean taxing the rich even more.

But city government does not finance itself by the property tax system because this is the most equitable and reasonable way that can be devised to produce the revenues it needs. Rather the property tax is the traditional method for financing local government. The reason this form of taxation is considered appropriate is, I think, that most people understand quite well the link between real property and municipal government functions. It is clear that the activities of city hall are necessary in order to make possible urban land use and to create urban property values. The greater the services and works provided by city hall, the more valuable the land in its jurisdiction will be. It is therefore perfectly appropriate that this link be recognized by a tax on property values, whereby property owners have to pay a small percentage of the total value of their holdings every year for the civic services that greatly contribute towards creating that value.

It isn't necessary to believe that a connection is clearly perceived between city government and property values to see that the property tax system forges a second important link between the property industry and the city bureaucracy. For the bureaucracy, increased city revenues are highly desirable because they make a bigger city administrative operation possible. Other things being equal, the bureaucracy would have nothing to lose by pushing the tax rate up and raising more money from existing property owners. This policy is not welcomed much by the property industry, because increases in the property tax rate tend to reduce the net profits produced by property and hence market values. It isn't much appreciated by politicians either, largely because of its unpopularity with the property industry but also because it causes politicians difficulties with voters. Nevertheless local property tax rates have been in-

---

Council rejects plan to unite departments

City Council, informally refusing to approve the proposed merger of the Streets Department with the Works Department, last night called for better and wider studies of possible administrative changes to cut costs.

The man behind the merger proposal, Alderman Anthony O'Donohue afterwards said the council decision is "proof that the commissioners run the city, not the politicians."

The Council also decided to support, in principle, departmental mergers "or any other way" to increase efficiency.

Streets Commissioner Harold Atyeo continued his vehement opposition to Mr. O'Donohue's scheme, which would place him under the authority of Works Commissioner Ray Bremner while maintaining his present salary of $29,500.

In early 1972 Toronto city council came close to abolishing one of its departments, the Streets Department, and integrating it into the Works Department. The effect of the change would have been to increase greatly the power of then Works Commissioner Ray Bremner, known at city hall as an extremely ambitious civil servant. And it would have in effect demoted Streets Commissioner Harold Atyeo, making him a subordinate of Bremner whereas formerly he had been Bremner's equal.

Apart from the obvious motive of promoting Bremner, the real reasons for the proposal were never clear. The cost argument used by Toronto alderman Tony O'Donohue who promoted the change proved to have little substance. And, in the factional fight which took place, Bremner's ambitiousness and O'Donohue's anxiety for change didn't succeed.

creasing steadily.

A much more satisfactory technique of increasing city revenues through the property tax — one where interests of the industry, politicians and administrators all coincide — is by "increasing the tax base." This is another way of saying increasing the quantity of real property in the city. Sometimes this can be done by adding more land to the city's territory, but usually the way of achieving it is by development and redevelopment. New developments that increase the total stock of real property in a city from $10 billion to $15 billion over a few years will produce a 50 per-cent increase in civic revenues without any increase at all in the property tax rate. This consequence of the property tax system gives the civic bureaucracy a vested interest in supporting growth and development as it is promoted by the property industry. Not only does new development produce greater tax revenues for a city government; it also provides a larger borrowing capacity for city hall. The city can float bond issues and obtain funds for capital investments on the basis of this increased total assessment. It forms another indirect link between the interests of the bureaucracy and those of the property industry.

New public works programs

A third industry-bureaucracy link is created by the responsibility of city hall for providing the necessary new public works and services needed to support new development, redevelopment and changes to more intensive land use. Expanding the city's population and its built-up area requires tremendous public investment in roads, sewers, sidewalks and utilities. Private real estate development and public works programs are complementary; one requires the other.

Each city government has some departments that are involved in providing these new public works. Obviously this creates a vested interest on the part of this segment of the bureaucracy in continued private development, because only with local growth and expansion will there be substantial public works investment programs.

Job possibilities

Traditionally, the city bureaucracy was based on promotion up the hierarchy of each department from within. Generally there was a single uniform set of requirements for every member of a specific department, and so everyone was equally eligible for advancement. The fire chief would usually be a former fireman; the chief city clerk would be someone who had joined the city clerk's office as a junior just like everyone else. The only exceptions would be departments that involved professionals, like the public health department, the legal department and the works department. There, doctors, lawyers and engineers would form the top layer of senior administrators.

In many other big bureaucracies this pattern has disappeared in favour of elaborate grading and distinction systems, where people have different kinds of qualifications (usually educational) on entering, come in at different levels of the bureaucracy, move up at different rates, and have quite different expectations. This is in fact now the normal pattern in most large bureaucracies, and there are often suggestions that anachronistic public bureaucracies should change. It is suggested that the police department, for instance, should recruit some university graduates instead of taking

---

Behind the news   By Val Werier

MacDonald is Winnipeg's top civil servant

Don MacDonald is a tall man with green eyes, a loping stride and he speaks with a bit of a drawl that conjures the west and with it direct and resourceful individuals.

Mr. MacDonald, chief commissioner of Winnipeg has a reputation of being straightforward and down to earth. Associates speak of him admiringly as a perceptive individual who is able to grasp the essential issues.

It is interesting to know something of Mr. MacDonald for he is Winnipeg's top civil servant and in a position of authority not known in the makeup of the former city. He is the chief executive officer of a city that has about 7,250 employees, an annual payroll of

more than $60 million and a budget that could reach beyond $100 million.

This places Mr. MacDonald in a unique position of authority in Manitoba. Along with the other commissioners, he is responsible for the supervision of employees and operations of all departments and services, subject to the general direction given by standing or community committees.

Is there a danger in the delegated authority being abused, or of the board of commissioners becoming too powerful?

"If the council delegates authority," replies Mr. MacDonald, 'it can also take it back. Regarding the commissioners, no one can become any more powerful than the council wants them to be."

"We have a fantastic opportunity here to do something for the city," emphasized Mr. MacDonald. "The ills of urbanization haven't yet had a great effect on Winnipeg. The sights are being raised today in a manner never contemplated years ago. Now we are talking of relocating railroads and are doing something in re-shaping the heart of the city."

There are indeed great things that can be done in the new city and those who have worked with Mr. MacDonald agree that Winnipeg is fortunate in having him as chief commissioner.

Winnipeg Tribune 1 Apr. 1972

anyone who has grade 10 and is 5'8" tall.

This pattern has in fact started to change in the city bureaucracy. People with specific professions and occupations like social workers and city planners are more common in white-collar jobs at city hall. Particularly in city planning, the old advance-from-the-bottom pattern has been replaced by a situation where professionals move sideways from job to job in different bureaucracies but doing similar work everywhere, instead of staying in the department where they started and moving slowly up the hierarchy.

This horizontal movement of professionals creates another link between the property industry and city hall, where city employees move out to work in the property industry and vice versa. At present there is relatively little of this, except for the significant pattern of city planners and people in land use regulation work at city hall moving into jobs in the property industry.

City planning department heads, for instance, have a habit of leaving city hall to go into the consulting business, where they spend a good portion of their time working for developers. Metro Toronto's first chief planner, Eli Comay, moved out into the consultant business. Toronto's first development department head, Walter Manthorpe, moved over to become vice-president of one of Toronto's major developers, Meridian, after he left city hall. The pattern was wryly acknowledged by Metro Toronto deputy chief planner R.J. Brower at a conference in early 1972 for would-be developers. Brower had been asked to pretend that he was advising the president of a corporation that wanted to do some downtown redevelopment. "In my present job," said Brower, "I shouldn't find myself addressing the president of a corporation in his office. So I'm going to imagine that I have followed the pattern of all good planning commissioners, who become planning consultants when they have learned enough of the wrinkles of the business."

Brower put his finger on what is desirable from the point of view of the property industry in hiring former city officials. These people know their way around city hall, they know the politicians, and they understand very well how the city's land use regulation system operates. The time they spent at city hall gave them ample opportunity to prove themselves as friends of the property industry. The possibility of this kind of job opportunity — and the fact that moves of this kind are more and more common — is another way the interests of city bureaucrats and those of the property industry are linked at present.

City employees as developers

Out of public involvement in certain kinds of redevelopment and development projects comes another link between the civic bureaucracy and the property industry. City governments have always been in the development business to a small extent, because they always had property of their own to develop for their own purposes. Often schemes like new civic centres, new concert halls and city halls have been explicitly understood as development projects intended to spark other projects by other, private, developers. When the federal government began making funds available for public urban renewal schemes, a new opportunity was opened up for city bureaucracies to carry on development projects

Budgets and bureaucracies

These notes, by Toronto opposition alderman John Sewell, on the 1972 City of Toronto budget indicate how financial allocations are being used by the politicians to reward and punish bureaucrats. The city's Development Department was allocated an extra $1 million for 1972, a 115 per-cent increase, while its competitor in the civic bureaucracy, the Planning Board, was given only a 1 per-cent increase. The Planning Board was out of favor with the property industry majority at city hall and budget chief Alderman David Rotenberg because of its staff's tendency to raise questions about some major developments.

Development: $1,783,000
This sum is an increase of some $1,070,000 over the 1971 budget. The extra million represents the neighbourhood improvement program, which is nothing more than expanded jurisdiction of the Development Department for such things as Pedestrian Malls, drop-in centres, Metro Centre Cost Benefit Study, and generally providing services to working class areas which are normally provided to middle class areas — like paving streets and sidewalks properly, or providing adequate street lighting.

So while people like the Commissioner of Budgets and Accounts claim that the Development Department budget is not really all that much different than last year, it is much different — to the tune of over a million dollars.

Public Health: $5,760,000
(3% increase)

Public Works: $8,742,000
This sum is a decrease of almost a million dollars over last year's budget — but that comes from not including a cool million which has usually been used as a capital payment, but is now included in other budgets. In fact, if this sum is not included, then this budget has really increased by about 1%. The traffic engineering division in this department has increased by 15%.

Planning Board: $1,131,000
(less than 1% increase)

City Hall newsletter 9 Mar. 1972 p.83

Hiring and firing: The unhiring of Earl Levin

A clear example of the way city politicians use their power to hire civic employees carefully is the case of Earl Levin, formerly head of the planning department in the Metro Winnipeg government.

Levin is a young, aggressive city planner. He is full of the kinds of ambitious schemes which city planners draw up when they are given their head by their employers. As the employee of Metro Winnipeg, he often clashed with both employees and politicians from the rival City of Winnipeg government before all local governments in the Winnipeg area were amalgamated into one by the provincial government at the beginning of 1972.

Levin made many enemies while he worked at Metro. One of his major non-admirers was City of Winnipeg mayor Stephen Juba. Amongst the others were a number of NDP provincial government cabinet ministers.

When the NDP government got down to the job of restructuring Winnipeg city government, it gave the job to a group of consultants headed by University of Toronto political science professor Meyer Brownstone. Brownstone had once served as deputy minister of municipal affairs for Saskatchewan's NDP government.

Brownstone and his group of consultants were extremely impressed by the abilities of Levin. They considered him a much more desirable type of senior civil servant than most of the bureaucrats they met in the provincial government and in city halls in Winnipeg.

They pushed to have Levin appointed deputy minister of the new provincial government department which they wanted to set up to oversee the new amalgamated Winnipeg. Saul Cherniack, the cabinet minister who eventually ended up with the job of pushing the legislation through the Manitoba House and then supervising its implementation, seemed to be agreeable to giving the job to Levin.

Other cabinet ministers, however, refused to allow Levin's appointment. Some of them, apparently, had encountered Levin when they themselves were municipal politicians in Winnipeg and had no liking for that style of civil servant.

That was the first case of un-hiring Levin.

Reorganization of Winnipeg city government went ahead, the new one-city council was elected, and the new council with its property-oriented ICEC majority and its new mayor Stephen Juba began looking around for people to fill the four senior posts for bureaucrats in the new structure.

One of the four posts was that of Commissioner of Environment. The new Winnipeg Environment Department had a wide scope that included responsibility for planning, zoning, pollution control, and a number of other matters close to the heart of the property industry.

Acting Environment Commissioner was Earl Levin, who moved over from his top job at Metro Winnipeg when the amalgamation took place.

Levin was the obvious candidate for the new job. Not only was he as well-qualified as anyone else around; he had lots of experience with the Winnipeg situation, he was demonstrably competent, and he was full of plans for how growth and development in Winnipeg could be encouraged. While implementing Levin's plans obviously would have been in his interests as a senior bureaucrat, it would also have been very much in the interests of the local property industry to have this kind of aggressive and competent supporter in the Environment Commissioner's office.

But factions inside the property industry's majority in the new city government remained unhappy about Levin's style of operation.

There was a long and embarrassing pause while the politicians searched for another candidate whose qualifications came close to matching Levin's. The search was not easy, and took a long time. Two of the four new commissioners were appointed in December 1971. A third, the new Works Commissioner, was hired March 15, 1972.

That left the Environment post. It was finally filled in April 1972. Levin was passed over and the job was given to David Henderson. Henderson, an architect, had no experience in municipal planning. The closest he had come to local government was in a job as research director for a provincial government inquiry on Manitoba municipal government set up by the previous Conservative government. Neither the provincial NDP politicians nor their outside consultants had a very high opinion of this commission or of the final report which it produced. It was, in fact, their lack of confidence in this Conservative commission which led the NDP when it took office to bring in their own consultants to draw up a plan for reforming Winnipeg city government.

So, for the second time, Levin was un-hired.

Newspaper accounts of the failure to fill the Environment Commissioner's job, and then of the final decision to hire Henderson in April, managed to avoid any direct mention whatsoever of the debate between supporters and opponents of Levin. No information emerged about the rift which the issue caused amongst the property industry's city hall majority. Nor was there any discussion of the implications of hiring Levin versus hiring Henderson or someone like him.

The newspapers confined themselves to dead-pan reports of the briefest kind. The only hint of the conflict which went on came in a column in the *Winnipeg Free Press* on April 29, two weeks after Henderson was hired. Reporter Bob Lisoway allowed himself an oblique sigh of relief, coupled with an amazing booster-style plea to the civil servants and city hall majority to stop these factional fights and get on with city government.

Wrote Lisoway: "They [the new commissioners] now will be working together to make Winnipeg worthy of its position as Canada's third largest city. They will have many obstacles to overcome."

Another new opportunity came when city-controlled bodies were building public housing under federal government legislation, though public housing has now been mostly reappropriated by provincial governments.

In these situations, city employees were able to get right into the land development business themselves and operate very much as private developers. They assembled their sites, they were able to use the ultimate weapon of expropriation to get hold of land from people who refused to sell voluntarily, they had to "sell" their projects to funding agencies in order to get mortgage money, and then they carried out detailed planning and organized project building and management.

The departments of the city bureaucracy that get involved in the development business themselves are closely akin to the property industry. Public developers ape the techniques of private developers. They tend to see themselves faced with the same problems. No doubt they know that their expertise opens up the possibility of their moving into the private development business. This is a further way in which the city bureaucracy's interests have got tied up with those of the property industry.

City employees and land deals

Another way in which the civic bureaucracy gets right into the land development business comes through city land deals with private property owners. City hall always owns a very substantial percentage of the land in its jurisdiction — roads, lanes, parks, blocks of vacant land, civic buildings, etc. In new development projects, one of the major issues to be resolved is how much of what land will be turned over to the municipality for roads, parks, schools and so on. In small-scale redevelopment projects, which follow the existing patterns of private land ownership, no issues about land ownership come up. But in large-scale projects there are almost always land deals to be made between the developer and city hall. The city may sell off lanes and streets to the developer, or it may want to acquire land in order to widen roads and create parks. Closely involved in these matters are civic officials in the relevant departments, although usually politicians take an interest and make the final decision on any given deal.

The experiences and attitudes acquired by city employees involved in land deals push them right into the property industry as the agents of a major city-wide land owner. They meet property industry representatives as buyer and seller, but they are both in the same business. This activity creates a further link between the property industry and the civic bureaucracy, a link of common interest in maintaining the existing rules of the land development game in which they are both involved.

Property industry control?

It is clear that at a number of specific points, the interests of the civic bureaucracy are at present linked to those of the property industry.

These links do not amount to direct property industry control of the bureaucracy. The industry does not have the same tight hold over city employees that it has over the politicians. But the industry's political agents, the elected city politicians, do have a tight hold over the bureaucracy. Even when they do not choose to exercise it, nevertheless the potential is always there and can be realized. And in a number of other highly important ways, the interests of the industry are tied to those of the bureaucracy. In promoting its self-interest in this situation the bureaucracy very often finds that it is also promoting the interests of the property industry.

Public inquiry urged on planner's dismissal

Special to The Sun

NELSON — Two Nelson aldermen and a former director of the Central Kootenay Regional District have asked for a public inquiry into the recent dismissal of a district employee.

Aldermen Keith Lacey and Bill Freno said the inquiry should be conducted by the inspector of municipalities of the department of municipal affairs.

The two, along with former district director Basil MacAlister, have protested the district board's decision to eliminate the position of planning director.

"In my opinion, the reason dispensing with the planner was not budgetary but to impede and to allow industrial development without any controls to protect the existing residential areas," he said.

MacAlister said the board rescinded a zoning bylaw for area J, which he represented for five years, after the bylaw had been given two readings.

This was done to allow an industrial plant to acquire a building permit without any of the controls included in the bylaw, he said.

Vancouver Sun 3 Mar. 1972

Growth, taxes and public works

EDMONTON — If Mayor Ivor Dent has his way, the City of Edmonton will expand in size, but will avoid the "mess" of metropolitan government.

Certainly, Edmonton as one of Canada's fastest-growing cities, will need all the efficiency of government and revenue production that it can muster in the next decade.

Capital expenditures for the city this year are running around $89 million, and at about $84 million for current expenditures. Each is a record rate.

"If current figures are indicative, the city is going to grow at a near-phenomenal rate," Dent says.

"The rate of population growth now is running at 2%-4% per year. This is really more than the municipality can comfortably handle.

"Our indications are that the growth is going to continue and could well rise to around 5% a year. That means terrific pressure for new housing, schools, services and demand for industrial land.

"It means that one of our major problems will be capital financing. We have a good A credit rating today, and we borrow $50 million-$60 million a year."

It is when the mayor thinks of the demands from growth, and of the heavy sums of capital Edmonton is going to need for the services that must come before the new tax revenues, that he is even more determined to avoid unnecessary complications and divisions of purpose from such things as metropolitan governments.

This extract from an article on Edmonton and its mayor Ivor Dent illustrates well how population growth, civic revenues, civic borrowing, and major public works expenditures are tied together.

The Hurst empire

The Inner City engineering department is the largest municipally-owned engineering complex in Canada and the second largest in all of North America.

It owns and operates quarries at Stony Mountain, gravel pits at Birds Hill and Pine Ridge, a concrete mixing plant, an asphalt mixing plant, a stone and gravel crushing, screening and distribution plant including two locomotives, an integrated machine, welding, blacksmith, carpenter and paint shop, an equipment repair garage, a storage yard, five branch yards and all shapes and sizes of construction equipment, tools and supplies.

Winnipeg Tribune 4 Mar. 1972

Taken together, there is no doubt that as things stand now in our cities these factors add up to indirect property industry control of the civic bureaucracy. The control is no less effective or complete for being less obvious and less immediate than that of the industry over the politicians. The property industry has captured the bureaucracy just as it has captured the politicians and the rest of the structure of city government. City hall, collectively, is in the property industry's pocket.

City employees as conscious agents of the industry?

It is very important to note that this analysis, which shows how the property industry now controls the civic bureaucracy, does not involve considerations of what city employees believe in, what they think is good for the city, and what they are trying to do in their jobs. My argument is not that the property industry has propagandized civic workers and convinced them that they should serve the industry's interests rather than those of the citizens and citizen groups. Rather I am suggesting that the self-interest and the work of city employees has been linked to the interests of the property industry, so that when people at city hall are doing their normal jobs and when they are protecting those jobs and getting ahead inside the system, they are also serving the property industry. So, for instance, when a city planner tells you that he follows the policies and decisions of city council because they best express the interests of the citizens as a whole, you can believe him — *and* remember that property industry domination of city council means that the politicians are laying down policies that protect not the citizenry but the industry. You should also remember the tremendous risks he would run in defying the policies and decisions of the politicians, whatever he may think of those decisions personally.

This question of what city employees believe in, what they consider to be the public interest, and how they view the property industry is nevertheless very important. Many of them have certainly adopted the property industry's view of the world, and believe that what is good for the industry is good for city hall and for the city. They can often talk just as convincingly as developers about why new development is good for the city, why growth is desirable, and why the city shouldn't do anything to interfere with the private housing market. Of course the property industry has a lot going for it: it involves very respectable and extremely wealthy corporations, which are generally treated with great deference. It also makes a lot of people fairly well off, and that too conventionally commands respect from less well-off people. It should be expected that many city bureaucrats would regard the industry's interests with great respect, and adopt its view of the world.

We should keep in mind that there are lots of people working at city hall who take very seriously the conventional democratic theory of city government, the theory that holds that the elected politicians do indeed represent the interests of the people. These employees consider that serving the politicians *is* serving the public. It may well be, however, that as the facts of the matter become clearer and the real constituency of most city politicians becomes more obvious, these city employees will become somewhat less willing to follow without question the instructions of their city council.

There are, however, some aspects of the situation of civic employees that tend to lead them to the view that their own interests are in conflict with those of the politicians, and in some cases are very close to those of ordinary citizens and organized citizen groups. Such conflict emerges, for instance, in relations between unions of city employees and management — the city hall majority. In labour-management conflicts, city employees find that they and citizen groups have a common opponent. Strikes by city workers in Vancouver and Toronto in the summer of 1972 underlined this basic conflict.

As well, there are some city employees in every Canadian city hall who understand the difference between the interests of the property industry and those of the public. They know that serving the developers is not the same as serving the people, and they realize that the politicians are in the property industry's pocket. There is a good deal of scope in city government for people taking this position to begin to change the normal course of business, and to put obstacles in the way of the property industry. There are opposition-minded people inside every city bureaucracy, who understand the interests of ordinary city residents and who want to do what they can to promote these and not the property industry's health. Vancouver city planners feeding information to residents of the West End area were of vital assistance to a local community group that demanded community facilities for the area. One city planner single-handedly produced the city reports in Toronto that eventually led to serious difficulties for the CN and CP railways in getting final approval for their "$1 billion" Metro Centre project.

The structure of city government in general, however, is pretty well constructed to separate the intentions of city employees from the results of their work. Planners may want to help make the city better support the needs of its residents, but their work is nevertheless largely devoted to regulating the supply of land in the interests of the property industry. A city-employed lawyer may want to see the city paying fair prices to people who are getting expropriated, but nevertheless his official work is helping to clear the land for a new expressway route.

Still, city employees do not have the same direct, personal stake in the property industry that most city politicians have. The present structure of city government makes very strong links between the employees' interests and those of the industry, but it is not inviolable. As the real functions of city government become clearer, as information showing how city hall and the property industry are bound together becomes better known, as the connection between city hall activities and the profits and wealth of the property industry becomes better understood, people who work at city hall are likely to see more and more clearly how their own personal interests and those of the other residents of the city conflict with the interests of the property industry and its circle of politicians. In principle, most city employees have as much to lose as the rest of us from the power of the property industry, and from the policies it has developed for city hall. City workers are bound to understand this situation more clearly as the opposition to city hall develops outside. In their unions and professional organizations, they have a considerable amount of potential economic and political muscle, which they could well decide to use in order to reduce their subservience to the

Civic strike hits Burnaby

Warning given dispute 'could be long one'

The Vancouver civic employees strike spread to Burnaby early today as some 600 members of the Canadian Union of Public Employees Local 23 walked off the job.

Pickets ringed the Burnaby municipal hall but cheerfully allowed exempt supervisory staff to go to work.

A picket line was also set up at entrances to the justice building. Police are not affected by the strike but other justice building employees were off the job.

Municipal yards were filled with idle vehicles, including heavy street equipment and garbage trucks.

Sunday afternoon Graham Leslie, chief negotiator for the Municipal Labor Relations Bureau warned that the strike could be a long one unless the union becomes "more reasonable" and agrees to a two-year contract.

He said money is the central issue and charged the union is sticking to an impossible position.

"We feel we have gone as far as we can go as a negotiating committee and still sell our councils on the deal," he added.

The MLRB represents Vancouver, Burnaby, New Westminster, Richmond, North Vancouver city and district, Delta, the North Vancouver school board and a number of other boards and commissions.

Leslie told The Sun the reason the MLRB wants the union to commit itself to a two-year contract is that it feels it is impossible to come to an agreement for a one-year period.

Vancouver Sun 8 May 1972 Reprinted with permission

By GEORGE DOBIE

The new look in the civic workers' strike this time is the white collar group at Vancouver city hall, many of them walking a picket line for the first time in their lives.

They are a mixed bag of about 1,500 people — mini-skirted young typists on up to old pro building inspectors.

They earn an equally mixed bag of wages starting at $341 a month for clerk-typist beginners to $1,391 for planners.

They are out walking the street because they don't believe an 8.5 per cent boost in wages is enough this year to give them a catchup — an extremely controversial term.

They are packing picket signs because the boss says 8.5 per cent is enough this year to keep them around the average for comparable jobs in the surrounding community.

Because they are new to the picket lines, the 1,500 or so inside workers of the Municipal and Regional Employees Union are the most interesting part of this growing civic workers' strike on the Lower Mainland.

A visit to the picket lines around the City Hall complex at Tenth and Cambie leads an outsider to believe that probably the municipal negotiators misjudged the mood of these people, possible because they are a new element which had lain dormant for so long as an association rather than a union.

They didn't think that these former non-militants would go all the way to strike action; that their first alliance with the more hardened outside workers of the Canadian Union of Public Employees would last; or that, finally they would turn down an 8.5 per cent offer over one year, which is bigger than anything they've received and accepted in the past.

Office boy to property commissioner

Harry Rogers was 14 years old that day in 1921 when he walked up the broad steps of the old city hall looking for a job.

There were seven other applicants for the job of office boy, but Property Commissioner Danny Chisholm chose him. The starting pay was $9 per week, which he took home to mother.

She gave him $1 a week for himself. The rest went into the household, and, as he recalls it, he was "on top of the world—a job at City Hall, helping the family make its way, and $1 a week of my own."

Now, 50 years later, he's property commissioner himself, at $25,000 a year. He's one of Toronto's best known and most respected civic servants and has had a profound influence on the city of today.

Staff of 350

With a staff of 350, he's responsible for the operation of 500 city-owned buildings, from the St. Lawrence Arts Centre to the new City Hall. He's overseen the construction of many of them, and had a hand in the design of some.

Nathan Phillips pushed the idea of an international design competition that produced the striking curved towers and mushroom council chamber of Finnish Architect Viljo Revell.

Rough time

Although the showdown battle came over the City Hall contract extras, Rogers believes his "rough times" with Summerville had deeper roots.

"He had just beaten Phillips in an election, and he figured I had been on Phillips' side against him for years," Rogers recalls.

"But it just wasn't so. Phillips happened to be the man in office, and my loyalty is to the man in office, no matter who he is."

When Rogers got his first job, Tommy Church was mayor, the first of 19 mayors Rogers would serve under.

He remembers particularly C. Alfred Maguire, Church's s u c c e s s o r, because "though he was straight-laced, he was gentle and kind to a green lad."

He admired Robert Saunders as "a good politician, forceful and innovative—an outstanding personality in civic history, and the first to envisage the Civic Square development, which has played such a big part in the rebirth of the downtown core."

Toronto Star 27 Nov. 1971

---

property industry, and to demand and get city government and city programs that would serve the interests of ordinary people rather than those of the landed and the wealthy.

Meanwhile, however, the civic bureaucracy is very effectively under the control of the property industry. The ways in which the bureaucracy's interests are tied to those of the industry are no less effective for being somewhat more indirect than the links between city politicians and the industry. The industry has missed no element in its domination of city government.

CHAPTER 10

The property industry and the media

The *Toronto Star* building, in downtown Toronto. At one time proudly featured in a drawing which appeared every day on the *Star's* editorial page, the building ended its days in 1972 by being demolished — apparently for tax reasons. Even this was an achievement of a kind: it is reportedly the tallest building ever torn down in Canada. It was knocked down to make way for another office tower which, though taller, will not make any more intensive use of the land the *Star* tower stood on.

Important to the control of city government by the property industry is the role played by the mass media, the main source of most people's information about what is going on at city hall. Though there are occasions when reporters, columnists, commentators or editorial writers turn a critical eye on some aspect of the industry or of city hall, generally the media report on city politics in ways which give support and encouragement to the property industry. This orientation of the media is so familiar that usually it does not even look like a bias or a party line. The property industry would be in very serious difficulty if the news media were not sympathetic to it, its interests and its program for city government. As things stand, however, the industry has very little cause for complaint.

The present orientation of the media is no accident. The interests of the property industry and the mass media are intertwined in many ways. In some cases, the media's owners are heavily involved in the industry. In others, institutions that play a large role in property finance are crucial to the business operations of the media. A look at these and other media-property industry links provides the groundwork for understanding how the media report on city politics.

Ownership

The research of the Davey Commission on the mass media and the activities of the CRTC have produced enormous amounts of information about the media in Canada.

Ownership of individual newspapers and radio and TV stations by one family or by an entrepreneur on his own is largely a thing of the past. Of the 485 newspapers and radio and TV stations in Canada, the Davey Commission found that 251 were owned by groups. Of 116 newspapers, 77 were owned by chains.

Some of the chains are part of corporate empires that extend into the property industry as well as the mass media. The Irving family, for instance, with a stranglehold on the media in New Brunswick, has important real estate interests. The group labelled Desmarais, Parisien and Francoeur by the Davey report involves two principals, Desmarais and Parisien, who control the Power Corporation. Power in turn controls Great West Life and the Investors Group (with head offices in Winnipeg) as well as, until recently, the real estate and development firm of Robert Campeau Ltd. Power Corp. owners control four daily newspapers, 12 weeklies, five weekend newspapers, two radio stations and a TV station. The Sifton group, which owns CKRC in Winnipeg, three other radio stations, two TV stations and the Regina and Saskatoon newspapers, also owns a real estate company called Jonquil Ltd. The Bassett-Eaton group is a trust for the three sons of John Bassett and the four sons of John David Eaton. Bassett does not appear to have any substantial real estate interests, but the Eaton family certainly does, through their department store chain. Bassett-Eaton owned the Toronto *Telegram* until they killed it by selling it to the Toronto *Star* for more money than they apparently could get by selling it to someone who would operate it as a newspaper. Bassett-Eaton still own Toronto's private TV station CFTO, a TV station in Windsor, which they have agreed to sell to the CBC, and seven weekly newspapers in the Toronto area.

Where the local media are not owned by a corporation that has other subsidiaries in the property industry, usually their owners have business links with property industry corporations. A good example is FP Publications Ltd., which owns the *Vancouver Sun*, both Victoria newspapers, the *Calgary Albertan*, the *Lethbridge Herald*, the *Winnipeg Free Press*, the *Ottawa Journal* and the Toronto *Globe and Mail*. FP's directors and major shareholders are G.M. Bell, R.H.

The Irving family's media interests

	Circulation	Extent of Interest
Newspapers		
Dailies		
Gleaner (Fredericton)	16,758	control
Times (Moncton)	16,241	100%
Transcript (Moncton)	17,044	100%
Telegraph-Journal (Saint John)	29,229	100%
Evening Times-Globe (Saint John)	25,170	100%
Broadcasting		
Radio		
CHSJ-AM (Saint John)	52,700	100%
Television		
CHMT-TV (Moncton)		100%
CHSJ-TV (Saint John)	296,200	100%

Report of the Special Senate Committee on Mass Media. Ottawa: Queen's Printer, 1970. Vol. II, p.89

Media interests of Power Corp. major shareholders

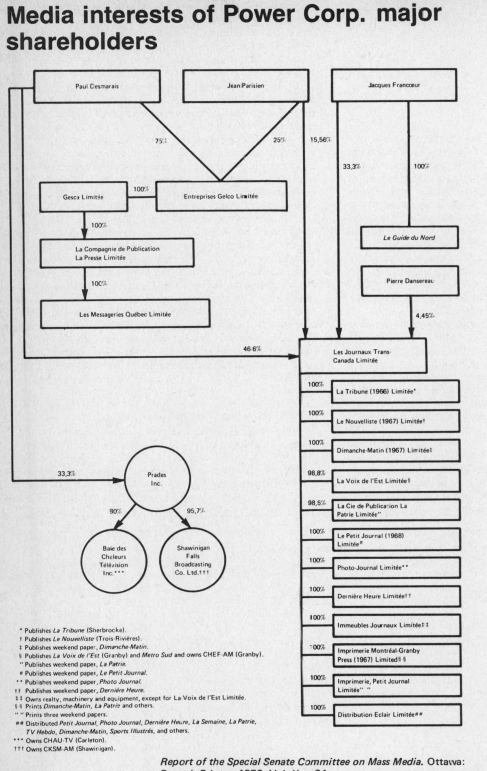

* Publishes *La Tribune* (Sherbrocke).
† Publishes *Le Nouvelliste* (Trois-Rivières).
‡ Publishes weekend paper, *Dimanche-Matin.*
§ Publishes *La Voix de l'Est* (Granby) and *Metro Sud* and owns CHEF-AM (Granby).
" Publishes weekend paper, *La Patrie.*
Publishes weekend paper, *Le Petit Journal.*
** Publishes weekend paper, *Photo Journal.*
†† Publishes weekend paper, *Dernière Heure.*
‡‡ Owns realty, machinery and equipment, except for La Voix de l'Est Limitée.
§§ Prints *Dimanche-Matin, La Patrie* and others.
" " Prints three weekend papers.
Distributed *Petit Journal, Photo Journal, Dernière Heure, La Semaine, La Patrie,
   TV Hebdo, Dimanche-Matin, Sports Illustrés,* and others.
*** Owns CHAU-TV (Carleton).
††† Owns CKSM-AM (Shawinigan).

Report of the Special Senate Committee on Mass Media. Ottawa:
Queen's Printer, 1970. Vol. II, p.84

Webster, R.S. Malone, Stuart Keate and Donald C. McGavin. Bell, who lived in Calgary at the time of his death in mid-1972, was also a director of the Bank of Nova Scotia and Canadian Pacific Ltd., both major firms in the property industry. Webster owns the Windsor Hotel in Montreal, and is the president of Imperial Trust. Malone is a director of Monarch Life, a Winnipeg life insurance firm. Personal interests of three out of five owners of the FP operation in the property industry certainly suggest a strong link.

Advertising

A second set of connections between the mass media and the property industry arises from the media's dependence on advertising for much of its revenue. About 70 per cent* of newspaper revenues come from advertising. Most of the revenues of radio and TV stations (apart from government funds for the CBC) come from advertising. Total advertising in all media in 1968 was $906 million. Of this, $118 million was spent on television and $95 million on radio.** Most of the television advertising revenue was from national advertisers, but about two-thirds of radio advertising revenue came from local advertisers. About one-fourth of newspapers' advertising revenue comes from national advertisers; the rest is from local advertisers. In 1967 national advertising in newspapers amounted to $59 million. Classified ads accounted for $54 million; retail store ads were the largest figure, $127 million.

Many big-spending local advertisers are important in the local property industry. Of these, department stores are pre-eminent, especially for newspapers, which regularly sell a very large proportion of their total retail advertising to department stores. Department stores also usually have a general stake in downtown real estate because they own a large chunk of it themselves, and because they depend for their clientele on the ability of the downtown to draw people into it. A prominent single downtown centre in a city strengthens the hand of department stores relative to their smaller neighbourhood and shopping centre competitors. And the department store business is very big business

indeed: sales of Robert Simpson Ltd. in 1970 were $302 million with profits of $21 million. Sales of Simpsons-Sears Ltd. the same year were $647 million, with before-tax profits of $25 million. Hudson's Bay Company sales for 1970-71 were $513 million, with profits of $20 million. Eaton's does not publish figures, but its annual sales are more than $1 billion.

Traditionally, classified ads in newspapers are sold to many small customers, but once a few large developers take over more and more of a city's housing market, they loom large as advertisers on the pages of classified real estate ads in the local newspapers.

When the media rely on property industry firms for a substantial chunk of their advertising revenue, there is likely to be careful attention paid to these advertisers' basic interests. Newspaper employees often argue that there is little "interference" with the news by advertisers, but at the same time they are certainly aware of the freedom with which local businessmen and advertisers contact newspaper publishers and other media executives to complain about things they don't like. One simple indication of the delicacy with which the media treat large advertisers can be found in any Canadian newspaper's clippings file on Eaton's. Stories about this particularly powerful advertiser are always very carefully written, usually to put a favourable gloss on its activities. Just as revealing (but more difficult to trace) are the stories that do not get printed, for instance of a brutal middle-management cleanout in Eaton's store in Winnipeg or of a mass firing of maintenance in Toronto in the mid-1960s.***

Continued on page 153

*Words, Music, and Dollars: Report of the Special Senate Committee on Mass Media, Volume II. Ottawa: Queen's Printer, 1970, p. 172.

**Op. cit., p. 292.

***On the latter story, and on Eaton's in general, see chapter 1 of Corporate Canada ed. by Rae Murphy and Mark Starowicz. Toronto: James Lewis & Samuel, 1972.

Eaton's and the press

. . . Elevated to the status of a native aristocracy, possessing one of the greatest fortunes in the country, close to the seats of power, the Eaton family and company were the object of a virtual conspiracy of silence by the press. And still are.

To this day, a story on Eaton's that deals with anything more than some trivia about Santa Claus parades must be passed through the highest editors of any of the English papers in Montreal, Toronto or Winnipeg. Assignments to cover Eaton events are generally assigned by the publisher or managing editor, with the addendum "Must Go".

In the Montreal Gazette, a reporter who wrote a humorous article on the Santa Claus parade of 1967 was banned by the then managing editor, John Meyer, from writing any articles not directly assigned by the editors, and from writing any features. He was informed that the article had angered Eaton's very much, that the publisher, Charles Peters, had received complaints from two

Eatons's executives the day of the innocuous article's appearance, and that "this causes the Gazette great concern." Eaton's is one of the Gazette's major advertisers. The reporter was fired three weeks later.

All Eaton's events, even the most trivial and the most blatant publicity gimmicks, are mandatory coverage, particularly in the Montreal, Toronto and Winnipeg press.

The files of the Toronto and Montreal papers on Eaton's are replete with notices of their "generous donations to charity", "sparkling party", and "the family beloved by Canadians". Last year [in 1969], to honor the 100th anniversary of the store, both the Toronto Telegram and the Toronto Star ran multi-part series on the history of Eaton's, with sidelights about the family — a sycophancy rarely achieved even in the Canadian press.

Last Post Feb. 1970

Newspapers as downtown property investors

An outstanding and revealing example of the interests of newspapers as downtown property investors — and of the way the property industry works — is provided by the *Toronto Star*.

The *Star* owned a fine 20-storey building on King Street, right in the heart of the downtown and just across the street from the big new high-rise office towers constructed by the Toronto-Dominion Bank and the Bank of Commerce. Land in this vicinity was worth about $150 a square foot in 1972. That is $6 million an acre.

Though the sale price for the *Star's* King Street property was not published, it was certainly more than the $4 million which the building cost in 1929.

As a 20-storey recently-constructed office building, the *Star* building achieved a high density on its site, certainly as high as the 12 times coverage permitted for any new building. It had much lower buildings at one side and at the back, which meant that coverage of the total *Star* site was less than 12, but a way could have been found to demolish these low buildings and erect a new building without demolishing the *Star* tower itself.

Nevertheless, in the early months of 1972, the *Star* building was demolished. It was a long, slow job because of the building's height and because of the solidity of its construction.

The *Star* building is the tallest building in Canada ever to have been demolished. Given the difficulty of carrying out this work, no one even attempted to make the usual argument that the building had to be torn down because it was so old it was worn out, and in danger of falling down. That was obviously not the case.

Why, then, was the building torn down? We might speculate that it was because the new owner of the building, an office developer called Olympia and York, simply decided that they wanted to tear it down. This, however, seems unlikely because the *Star* itself insisted on *retaining possession of the property until the building was levelled*. If the *Star* had not been concerned about what happened to the building, or if indeed its officials had hoped the building would remain, they certainly would not have insisted on demolishing it themselves.

A memorial article on the *Star* building, published by the *Star* itself and — it is interesting to note — lacking a by-line even though it was a feature article in the feature section where most articles have by-lines, laboured

The *Toronto Star* building being demolished, with only five floors left standing.

hard to give the impression that *Star* owners regretted the demolition of the building and didn't much want it to happen. Ruth Atkinson Hindmarsh, a *Star* director, is quoted as "feeling sad" that the old building was going to be demolished.

So is Beland Hondrich, now *Star* publisher and reportedly the major force behind the *Star's* policy-making. He is quoted about what a wonderful building it is, and the article closes with Hondrich saying that every day that he looks at the building from the bank across the street he feels sad that it is going to be demolished.

What this article did not say is that it was Beland Hondrich, Ruth Hindmarsh and the **Star's** *other directors who decided to demolish the* **Star** *building.*

Nor did it even try to explain why a high, recently-constructed office building should be completely destroyed only to have a new office building at no higher a density erected in its place.

The explanation suggests that *Star* sadness stopped the moment the matter became a question of dollars and cents.

The most likely explanation for the building's demolition is this: Ever since the building was constructed in 1929 at a cost of $4 million, the *Star's* accountants were slowly depreciating its construction cost on their books, probably at 2 per-cent to 5 per-cent a year. The justification for this would be that every year a building is used, it gets a little older and loses a little of its useful life. The implication is too that after 30 or 40 years, a building will be so old as to be useless.

Also important is the fact the presumably every year when the *Star's* accountants made out the corporation's income tax returns, they deducted as a business expense an amount for "depreciation" of the *Star* building. The total amount that could be deducted would be the original construction cost of the building, which might have been $3,750,000 allowing for the cost of land which *cannot* be depreciated.

Let us suppose that, over the years, the *Star's* accountants deducted $3 million as a business expense for depreciation of the building in their income tax returns. What would happen in 1972, when the building is sold and the *Star* moves over to a new building, 25 storeys high, costing $40 million?

No doubt the *Star* got more than $4 million when it sold the King Street building. If the building had been bought by an office building owner who had proceeded to fill it up with new tenants — not a difficult task, considering the building's condition, location, and quality as an office building — the income tax department might well have visited the *Star* and said that a good portion of the price received for the King Street building represented the present value of the building itself as an office building. The fact that its new owner could rent it out to new tenants at high rents would be the evidence proving that the building was not so old as to be valueless. And the income tax department might well argue, on the basis of all these figures, that in selling its old building the *Star* had "recaptured" all that $3 million which we are supposing they had deducted as a business

expense for depreciation of that building over the years. As things turned out, the tax men would have argued, the building wasn't depreciating after all.

Had the income tax department claimed the *Star* had "recaptured" $3 million in depreciation by selling the building, it would have ordered the *Star* to include that $3 million in its 1972 income *and to pay income tax on it.* The *Star's* income tax rate would have forced it to pay about $1.5 million in tax.

But what if the *Star* sold not the King Street land *and building* to Olympia and York, but simply a cleared site with no building on it? Then the matter would be obvious: the price the *Star* received was for the land only. It had to be, because the land was all that Olympia and York received. The *Star* itself ensured this, by carrying out the demolition of its own building.

How would the *Star* look at the question of whether to demolish its building or to sell building and land? First of all, it would determine whether the buyer would pay any more for the building and land than just for the land. Perhaps a company like Olympia and York might have been willing to pay a bit more for the land if the building was still standing, but from the point of view of an office developer there are considerable advantages to being able to start from scratch and to put all your available density into one big new building. Olympia and York's interest in doing that is illustrated by the fact that its plans for the site are reported to to call for an 80-storey tower, the highest yet to hit Toronto.

From the *Star's* point of view, if its buyer was prepared to pay the same price whether the building stood or not, the choice was this: sell land and building, and run the very likely possibility of being hit for perhaps $1.5 million in extra income taxes. Or, demolish the building, and avoid any possible extra taxes.

No figures have been published on the cost to the *Star* of having the building torn down, but let's assume that the wreckers offered to do it for $500,000.

That would make the *Star's* alternatives these:
— Sell building and land, and expect to pay $1.5 million in taxes; or
— Pay $500,000 to have the building demolished, sell the land only for the same price, and be certain of paying no extra taxes

A property investor interested only in profiting from his land would obviously choose the second alternative: wreck the building, and make a million dollars.

We don't know the details of the decision which faced the *Star's* directors, but we do know what they decided: wreck the building. Their responsibility for the demolition was something they neglected to tell their reporter. Instead, it was crocodile tears from Beland Hondrich all the way from the dust of the demolition site across the street to the bank.

THE DEATH OF A BUILDING

Memories of The Star at 80 King St. W

Her corridors and offices are empty now.

The presses, the heart of her being, are stilled forever and the newsroom, her soul, is cold and empty. Staring vacantly at the world through dark and cheerless windows, 80 King St. W., home of The Toronto Star for 42 years, awaits the final curtain.

Her people have all moved to One Yonge St. Soon the wreckers will come.

Beland Honderich, who has been publisher of The Star since 1966,

came to the newspaper from Kitchener in 1943 as a general reporter. He sat in his former office one day before the move to Yonge St. and remembered his first day at 80 King St. W.

"I was so thunderstruck. I was a lowly reporter who came here from Kitchener and I was overwhelmed by it. The marble in the lobby, it was very beautiful. All the bronze was polished daily in those days. It wasn't the height of the building so much that impressed me but the grandeur of the lobby.

"I will regret leaving this office most of all because this was Mr. Atkinson's office and this was his desk. It has great sentimental value to me.

"Every time I walk by the Toronto-Dominion Bank across the street, I look over at this building and I feel sad. It seems an awful shame that a building that has been standing for only 42 years has served its purpose."

Toronto Star 29 Jan. 1972

Property ownership

A third way in which the interests of the news media are linked to those of the property industry concerns the media's own real estate interests. Newspapers in particular often own relatively large and valuable pieces of downtown real estate, where their printing plants and editorial offices are located. This places them in a similar situation to that of other major downtown landowners, and gives them another reason to be concerned about the local property market in general and downtown real estate values in particular. This interest is often reflected in the newspapers' membership in the civic organization that represents downtown property owners.

Growth and development

The property industry has a basic common interest in local growth and development, and promotes this to the maximum extent consistent with maintaining existing property values and increasing them at what is considered an adequate rate. The news media share this basic common interest in the growth of cities where they are located; in industrial development, which attracts more workers; in house-building, which helps accommodate a larger population; and in all measures that increase local prosperity.

The news media's interest in growth is based on the fact that an increasing population and an increased local market can be expected to increase their circulation, boosting revenues both from subscribers and from advertisers, and increasing the profitability of their business. The media are very conscious of their circulation figures, and while they have some scope for increasing their circulation by stealing audiences away from their rivals (in cities where there are rivals), population growth is a more certain and cheaper source of larger circulation and higher profits.

The news media have another common interest with their local property industry regarding growth. For the local property industry in Kitchener-Waterloo or Moose Jaw, it is very important whether growth occurs in their territory

or in the territory of some other nearby town like Galt or Regina. The same is true for the media. In Canada the media are locally based, and growth that takes place in another locality is of no benefit either to the local property industry or to the local news media.

General performance

These links between the media and the property industry have created a situation where what is good for the interests of the property industry is generally also in the interests of the media. In these circumstances, it is hardly surprising that the media look with relative favour upon the property industry itself or upon a city hall dominated in the usual way by the property industry. It often happens that the media have specific complaints to make about the current situation in their city, which they articulate loud and long. The *Winnipeg Free Press* was always complaining about the need for one-city government in Winnipeg until the NDP government brought it about. Vancouver's newspaper columnists (not so much the city's editorial writers) are constant critics of Vancouver's mayor Tom Campbell, and columnist Allan Fotheringham has in print pointed out the domination of city hall by property interests and deplored it. Toronto's newspapers have always felt slightly uneasy about the excesses of blockbusting high-rise developers, and expressed this in editorials and sometimes even in news coverage. But these specific complaints do not detract from the news media's overall commitment to the status quo, which is expressed most clearly in the way in which city politics news reports are written.

The best example of how a newspaper is occasionally prepared to take a critical view of a property-industry dominated city government in its editorials and features — and sometimes even in its news columns — is the Toronto *Globe and Mail*. The *Globe* is in some ways an unusual city newspaper because its circulation beyond Toronto and its reliance on the nationally-oriented *Report on Business* section free it from some of the usual links to the local property industry. The *Globe* has a fairly small circulation compared to the Toronto *Star*; its readership covers a narrower range than most city newspapers, and is mainly white-collar, middle-class people; its circulation extends well beyond the Toronto area, and its *Report on Business* (which is reported to be a major factor in keeping the *Globe* profitable) has a country-wide circulation.

The overall effect of the city hall coverage in Canadian media is to lead people to accept city government by the property industry without letting on that the industry is in control. There are several ways in which this is done. First, even though the evidence about the industry's control is very clear, the news media make no consistent effort to inform their audience about this basic fact concerning who is running the city hall show. Rather they present city politicians and the city bureaucracy at face value, usually repeating with a straight face these officials' own descriptions of their policies and aims, and taking seriously their claims to being concerned first not with the property industry's interests but with the public interest. Information that would make it possible for people to understand the real state of affairs at city hall and the real implications of property industry policies for rents, housing costs, and development decisions is simply not provided. The media stay firmly on the surface, and even there are pretty selective about what they describe. The picture the media portray of how city government works is almost exactly the one city politicians and their property industry mentors would like to see portrayed. Much attention is paid to what people say, little to what they do, and even less to contradictions between words and conduct. Facts that show the status quo in a good light (decisions to build new parks, new construction projects which provide new jobs) are given careful attention, whereas facts that would have the opposite effect are played down or ignored. The overall impression given is that city hall is in the hands of a group of concerned, dedicated, honest, fairly responsible men earnestly striving to achieve the common good and to do what is best for the city as a whole. The reality is of course quite different, but the news media don't show it. The best single device still for letting people in on what is really going on is simply to sit them down at city hall and let them watch the politi-

Complaints

These two short editorials illustrate well the typical tone and content of the complaints which editorial writers often make about city politicians. Note as well how the *Province* virtually issues a public offer of support to any non-left winger interested in running in Vancouver's 1972 mayoralty race.

Picking his 'bull'

Mayor Campbell has pinned a tail, a set of hooves and a black hide on Ald. Harry Rankin in preparation for Vancouver's civic election bull ring in December. Tom's role, of course, will be that of matador and he is already making passes with his political cape and practising with his campaign sword.

The mayor says he is going to run for the fourth time rather than let Ald. Rankin, a left-winger, take the job. His worship says his private opinion poll shows Rankin would be elected if Campbell didn't save the city from such a disaster.

In all this Tom is up to his usual trick of trying to polarize opinion. He hasn't a platform or a record of achievement to run on. So he is going to run AGAINST something. Considering his previous appeals to the electors, he evidently believes Harry is the best (or the worst) thing to run against.

This newspaper doesn't hold any brief for Ald. Rankin. But if Campbell wants to play matador to Rankin's bull we'll surrender to a longfelt secret hope that the bull would sometime win. And that goes for almost any other "bull" that strays into the election ring.

Vancouver Province 22 Feb. 1972

Pipe Dream

Mayor Juba is in a huff. He is annoyed with the Free Press because it called his plan to introduce a monorail system to Winnipeg a "pipe dream." He refuses to give further information on the subject; because, he says, t h e Free Press editorial created an "environment . . . not complimentary" to the venture. He has cancelled plans to bring the principals of the European monorail company to Winnipeg "in this kind of atmosphere."

Mayor Juba considers the Free Press criticism invalid, based on insufficient information. But surely, if this is the case, his proper reaction is to provide information to prove the Free Press wrong. This he has not done. He refused to discuss the matter, to unveil his plan, or bring the interested principals to the city. It is a strange way to refute an argument.

Winnipeg Free Press 10 May 1972

Candidates for the mayor's job all fear 'Just Plain Fred' Beavis

By CLAIRE HOY
Star staff writer

There's a joke circulating at City Hall these days that television's famed Archie Bunker is really Alderman Fred Beavis in disguise.

Everybody's laughing except Aldermen David Rotenberg and Tony O'Donohue. Beavis could be as popular as Bunker has proved to be, making him something that Rotenberg and O'Donohue didn't count on —a serious threat in their undeclared scramble for the Toronto mayor's chair.

And if that isn't enough, there's always good old Bill Dennison, the Renfrew county farmboy, waiting in the wings and ready to try, perhaps, for another three-year term when the Toronto municipal elections are held Dec. 4.

Even before the 1969 municipal election, R o t e n b e r g, 42, and O'Donohue, 39, were touted as mayoralty candidates. They've spent the last three years trying to prove it.

Beavis, meanwhile, has continued to be just plain Fred, the ex-roofer with a simple, honest approach to problems and a slow, Beaches drawl. Nobody, not even Fred, thought he could be mayor some day.

Now both O'Donohue and Rotenberg admit they're worried and a close adviser of O'Donohue said the colorful Irishman might not even run if Beavis does, because they'd both appeal to the same working-class voters.

And what about Dennison? He's the only one of the bunch who has run city-wide—polling more than 50,000 votes in six consecutive elections—and he's quite possibly a candidate this time.

Beavis won't say directly he wouldn't run if Dennison does, but he concedes, "It's quite possible I wouldn't."

Rotenberg and O'Donohue are almost obligated. Rotenberg, a swift-talking, shrewd insurance salesman, without question No. 2 man in the city, has been on council 12 years and considered a mayoralty candidate for about five.

"David would have to make an excuse not to run if Dennison decides to retire," O'Donohue said.

O'Donohue, an engineer with an uncanny ability to capitalize on publicity in almost any issue, has been on council six years and for the last four has made no secret of the fact that he'd like to be mayor.

Rotenberg, who ran for Metro chairman in 1969 but finished last in a field of four, said, "the position I'm in now makes it natural that I've got to consider running for mayor. I've been on council 12 years and I'm the No. 2 man. It's too soon to make any final decision, but certainly the pressure's on me to run."

Rotenberg has another problem— David Crombie. Last time, Rotenberg beat Crombie by about 1,500 votes in Ward 11, but many people believe a Crombie-Rotenberg contest would be very close. If Rotenberg decided to run again for alderman then and finished second to Crombie, he'd become ineligible to sit both on Metro Council and the City Executive Committee.

Beavis, on the other hand, is untouchable in Ward 8 and almost a sure bet to be returned to his seat on the Executive Committee if he should decide to run for alderman again.

O'Donohue could win his own ward easily, but it would be touch-and-go whether he'd get back on the executive. "I've made a few enemies," O'Donohue concedes.

At one time, there was a chance that Alderman Reid Scott, the New Democratic Party's municipal leader, would run for mayor, but that appears remote now. Scott's second-place finish to Tom Wardle in Ward 8 last time settled that issue.

There's an outside possibility that Morton Shulman, the fiery High Park MPP, might run, but he scoffs at it, even though he's attended the last two City Council meetings as an interested spectator.

So apart from an outsider suddenly emerging, that leaves Rotenberg and O'Donohue in the almost certain category, Beavis a strong possibility and Dennison—well, who knows?

Rotenberg's weakness is his abrasive personality, his rapid-fire, nervous manner of cutting people off. His strength is his ability, his knowledge of how the city functions.

Undoubtedly, Rotenberg could poll well in the big northern wards of 10 and 11 where the people who voted in 1969 represented 40 per cent of the total city-wide vote.

But he'd draw a blank in the lower working class wards such as 1, 2, 4, 7, 8 and 9, an area where Beavis would be strong.

Dennison, like Beavis, appeals to the lunch-box crowd but always managed to rack up respectable totals in the more affluent north as well.

O'Donohue, though different in style and much more colorful than Beavis, would still have to lean heavily on the lower wards for his strength and would find tough slogging there to match Beavis.

Hence, O'Donohue's dilemma. He'd likely win a straight fight against Rotenberg on the strength of his personality, but lose if the comparatively dull, colorless Beavis entered the race.

"I'd be the last one to try to downplay the p o s i t i o n of Fred," O'Donohue said. "When you look at the various names which have been thrown about, he's got to be considered tough. It depends on whether he wants to take the plunge and risk giving up the good life or not."

Beavis faces the risk of giving up the good life as a $21,000-a-year Executive Committee member, complete with chauffeur-driven limousine service and countless social advantages. He said: "It's worth thinking about.

"But you know, I was thinking just today that if I ran for mayor and lost I could spend the summers at our family resort in northern Ontario, buy a condominium in Florida and spend the winters there. That wouldn't be too tough either."

Perhaps the easiest way to compare the styles of the four men— Beavis, Rotenberg, O'Donohue and Dennison—is to look at the way they operate at meetings.

Rotenberg, the most efficient and officious, usually sits tensely forward in his seat, waiting to jump into any wrangle, offer a solution so quickly the opposition is left boggled, then sit back smugly until the next issue.

O'Donohue, who has a nervous twitch which results in a quick glance back toward the press table, often misses key votes but is there for comment on issues he knows will get him ink.

At a s o c i a l event though, O'Donohue is liable to join the band, sing a few Irish songs and leave the folks happier for it.

Beavis normally sits, legs crossed, listening to debate while leaning back in his chair. When he wants to speak, he leans slowly forward, puts on his dark-rimmed glasses, makes obvious grammatical errors, is seldom rattled, and doesn't speak for long.

Dennison appears constantly mystified with what's going on around him. He fumbles his way from one item to another, yet somehow manages to sit back while more ambitious aldermen stick their n e c k s out.

While Rotenberg possesses a certain f i n a n c i a l wizardry and O'Donohue matches that with his public relations expertise, Beavis just keeps plodding along the way Dennison has for 30 years, looking after potholes, accumulating credits, and above all, giving the impression that his first concern is protection of the taxpayers' dollar.

"The key to the whole thing is Dennison," said Rotenberg. "Right now there are pressures on some of us to run. If Dennison runs, that will certainly change things."

O'Donohue and Beavis agree.

But Dennison just talks about his golf game. Told what the three possible candidates were saying, he remarked: "That's interesting. By the way, I played 12 games in Florida this year and my putting isn't as good as it was. But I was at the Golf '72 show at the CNE and there was this fellow there who's invented a new style putter and he said he'll give me one. . . ."

Toronto Star   13 Apr. 1972
Reprinted with permission

cians in action for an afternoon. If the news media did anything like a reasonable job in reporting what the real world of city politics actually is, the experience would not be so surprising or shocking as people invariably find it.

Facts in, facts out

Given the very little space the media devote to city politics, there is a very tight ration on how much information can be reported. Decisions are always being made, therefore, on which facts to put in and which to leave out.

Often the facts left out would be embarrassing to the city hall majority and local property industry people, or would show them in a bad light. Sometimes these omissions are on a relatively small scale. Thus for instance in a "background" article in the Toronto *Star* on three potential candidates (Beavis, O'Donohue and Rotenberg) for the mayor's job in the 1972 elections, writer Claire Hoy managed to get through his entire piece *without saying a word about the political views of the candidates or about their record based on their voting in city council.* Doing so, however, would have been rather awkward, for in spite of Hoy's efforts to show how different the three candidates were, their voting records on major issues at city hall were almost identical. And all three were extremely favourable to the property industry. Moreover all three candidates had business and professional interests in the property industry.

Sometimes the facts get left out on a much bigger scale. A good example of this was the arrangement (documented in articles in the *Globe and Mail* by Hugh Winsor) between the senior management of the *Kitchener-Waterloo Record* and local politicians and property industry people in Kitchener in the summer of 1971. Local officials and businessmen were busy cooking up a deal to sell the city hall, the city-owned farmers' market and a park to Edmonton-based developer Oxlea Investments, in which some major local investors had an interest through shareholdings in Canada Trust. The city land was to be used for a major new downtown development, which included an Eaton's store. The arrangement was that the local newspaper would not say a word about the deal until it had been approved and settled by a special meeting of the Kitchener town council. Only when the local student newspaper got wind of the story and put out a special issue on the project did the local newspaper mention it, on the morning of the scheduled meeting. But management of the news on major development projects, determining what facts get published and when, is very much a normal matter dealt with by developers. They know they can usually expect co-operation and friendly treatment from the media.

Growth is good

Another specific example of how the media in their news reporting support the property industry's control of city hall is in the way they write stories on urban growth and development. A general enthusiasm for growth is usually expressed openly in editorials and in columnists' spaces. In news columns, new projects are reported exactly as their developers describe them, with values spelled out, alleged increases in city tax revenues calculated, and so on. Nowhere is the media's orientation clearer than in the way they reproduce photographs of the very carefully contrived models that developers and architects use to sell their projects.

Usually little is made of old buildings that are to be demolished to make way for the new project, or of the businesses that will be forced to move and possibly close as a result. If the subject does come up, it will be in the form of a sentimental feature — for instance about the old Metropole Hotel, where reporters used to drink. Nowhere will there by any serious attempt to report on the real cost to the city as a whole of making available a site for the project. Usually little is said about what space will cost in new projects, and rarely are any comparisons made between costs before (in the old buildings) and after (in the new). If characteristics of the new buildings are described, it will be their venetian blinds — largest in the world! — that get mentioned.

An innocent eye on the politicians

Another specific practice of the media, which tends to support the continued domination of the property industry at city hall, concerns the way they treat city politicians. It is crazy to have to suggest that newspaper reporters cast an innocent eye on the activities of city politicians and bureaucrats, but it does appear to be true of their work — in spite of themselves. City hall reporters are always a mine of detailed information on what is really going on, on what people's individual interests are, on what the reasons are for their voting, and so on. But what comes out in the media is altogether different. There is almost never space for information of this kind. What is reported is what the politicians say they are doing, liberally spotted with quotations by the politicians and officials themselves.

When a controversial issue comes up, it is generally reported as if nothing like it had ever happened before. Newspapers rarely report city hall voting patterns, nor do they suggest that the voting blocs at city hall are such that the outcome of virtually any issue is known beforehand. Information about personal and business interests, which might begin to explain the attitudes and conduct of individual politicians, is rarely cited, and even when the data are there, no one suggests any connection between personal interests and political position.

The effect of this innocent eye is to suggest to the media's audience that it is reasonable to take city politicians more or less as they present themselves. It encourages people to think that, although there are some corrupt and some stupid people on city council, on the whole city government is in reasonable hands. What we must remember — and what the media almost never point out — is that the hands it is in are those of the property industry.

Campaigns

Another aspect of the operation of the news media is that, on occasion, they conduct campaigns to educate their readers. You think of a newspaper campaign as traditionally an all-out effort to expose a scandal or to get a dreadful wrong righted. Occasionally newspapers still have campaigns of that kind, but usually their efforts are much milder. In the field of city politics and the property industry, campaigns are important because they are often used by the media to teach people new attitudes towards the efforts of developers and the property industry.

Thus for instance in every city when high-rise housing is introduced, there is a good deal of popular resistance.

Continued on page 160

Huge waterfront development gets under way

Work began today on the | today at the foot of Bay St., | building concept involves | to ...designed pent- | driving piles into bedrock | devel...
... buildings i... | ...the residential, com- | development of ... | ... | benea... | fic...

39-storey complex to rise
on corner of Bloor-Yonge

Mayor William Dennison yesterday took part in a ground-breaking ceremony that started construction on a $20 million shopping and office centre at the north w...

Ltd. is developing a $50 million office-residential-retail

hotel and a retail ... of 40 to ...

H

Growth is good!

Taking politicians at face value

These examples illustrate one of the common rules of news reporting, which is to take seriously what city politicians say and report it uncritically.

The *Winnipeg Tribune* article quotes Richard Wankling, a senior member of the property industry majority on Winnipeg City Council, complaining that there are too many city politicians and arguing that the new Winnipeg city government structure is inefficient.

The article breathes not a hint of any other reason Wankling might have for his position. There is no mention of his property industry background. It does not talk about the potential of a small-ward system like Winnipeg for generating strong electoral pressures even on property industry aldermen, and so influencing their voting. Nor does it discuss the possibility that a 10-man council would be much easier for large property industry interests to influence than a 50-man council, even when the council is dominated by industry supporters.

The two Vancouver articles are deadpan reports on politicians' explanations of their stand on the controversial Third Crossing issue. One article suggests that North Vancouver's council does not know whether it supports a Third Crossing. All it does is report that the politicians are not prepared to act on the proposals of citizen opponents of the crossing, nor do they want to see a plebiscite on the issue. There is no suggestion that their actions indicate quite clearly that the council majority supports the crossing, but is afraid to come out openly in its support because of the strong public opposition.

The article reporting on the opposition of Vancouver area mayors to a plebiscite on the crossing takes seriously the explanation that this is, at least in part, because the questions which would have to be asked are so complex.

There is no hint of the possibility that the mayors, themselves all supporters of the project, are afraid to support a plebiscite because they are worried that it will show a majority of Vancouver residents opposed to the project.

Reduce size of council: Wankling

Winnipeg's finance committee chairman, Richard Wankling (ICEC — Wildwood), said Monday he hopes the city's 50-man council will soon be substantially reduced in size.

Coun. Wankling, addressing members of the Fort Garry Rotary Club, said the new council is "very cumbersome" at its present size. But he added a change could not likely be made until the present council has served its three-year term.

Coun. Wankling said the new council had "developed into a horrendous kind of situation" with about 23 subcommittees serving the three standing committees and the executive policy committee. H said the result was poor communications between various levels of council.

The finance committee chairman did not specify how large he feels council should be. Any reduction would require the approval of council and an amendment to the City of Winnipeg Act by the provincial government.

Coun. Wankling said the work of council since it took office unofficially last October had been "painstaking, frustrating and slow." He said he expected it would take five years to bring the new city structure into shape, but that a reasonable amount of progress should be made within about 18 months.

A council decision to post notices in all departments of all jobs available with the city has retarded appointment of department heads and other administrators, he said. "We are slowly strangling ourselves because of this."

To date, the city has been getting "increased costs without the benefits of centralization," Coun. Wankling said. "We have a new political structure but the duties, responsibilities and resources of the city have not changed."

A new fiscal arrangement with the provincial government would have to be worked out, particularly in the fields of health and welfare, to provide the city with more resources to meet its new demands, he said.

Most of Winnipeg's population increase results from a movement from rural areas to the city, and this places increasingly more demands on city funds, which are not being alleviated by the province, he said.

Winnipeg Tribune 11 Apr. 1972

Council stumped on 3rd crossing

North Vancouver city council isn't too sure now where it stands on the third crossing issue.

But council made it clear Monday in two 4 to 1 votes what it doesn't want.

It doesn't want to hold a plebiscite on the issue. And it beat back a move that called on North Vancouver city to set up a North Shore advisory transportation committee.

Ald. Stella Jo Dean, an opponent of the proposed crossing, failed to find any support for her motions to hold the plebiscite and set up the committee along the lines of an advisory planning commission or recreational commission.

Ald. Jim Warne then failed to find a seconder for a motion that would have confirmed the city's pro-crossing stand and willingness to pay its share of North Shore approach costs.

Mrs. Dean instigated the council-in-committee f i g h t over the crossing with her claim the city should take its cue from the mass of opposing briefs heard at the council sponsored public hearings in North Vancouver.

"The voice of the people was made clear at the March 22 public hearing; they want three actions, a plebiscite on the tunnel crossing, an early start on rapid transit, and a North Shore advisory transit committee," she said.

Vancouver Sun 12 Apr. 1972

PLEBISCITE VETO EXPLAINED:

Crossing issues 'complex'

WEST VANCOUVER — Three G r e a t e r Vancouver mayors oppose a plebiscite on the proposed new First Narrows crossing because they don't know what to ask.

And if they did, they don't know who should be entitled to answer it.

This version of the background behind the mayors' decision not to hold a plebiscite was given municipal ouncil Monday night by Ald. Don Lanskail.

He sat in as representative of Mayor Art Langley when mayors Tom Campbell (Vancouver), Ron Andrews (North Vancouver district) and Tom Reid (North Vancouver city) met with Federal Environment Minister Jack Davis last week to discuss the proposed corssing.

Of the no-plebiscite decision reached at that meeting, Lanskail said: "A very major factor was the apparent impossibility of wording a question that had any chance of eliciting a meaningful answer."

As the mayors saw it, according to Lanskail, the voters would have to be asked:

If they favored a crossing; if it should be for rapid transit only; or automobiles only; or a combination; if so, how many lanes for which; where it should rank in financial priority with other projects.

Said Lanskail: "Issues of this order of complexity cannot rationally be resolved through the mechanism of a popular plebiscite."

And if they could be, the question would arise who should answer them.

Lanskail said it is a myth that a crossing would serve only the selfish interests of the North Shore. In fact, he said, it would be an important highway link with Vancouver Island and Sechelt, and a probable main route to the interior via Pemberton.

So, he argued, voter interests would go far beyond the confines of the North Shore and Vancouver

Vancouver Sun 8 Feb. 1972

High-rise fires

The danger posed by fires in high-rise buildings is a subject which has received remarkably little attention so far from the news media. An exception is the article from which these extracts are taken which appeared across the country in *Weekend Magazine.*

The article, amongst other things, makes a fuss about the fire safety of the new Commerce Court office building in Toronto. The implication is, of course, that virtually no other new office building in a Canadian city has the adequate protection from fire which the Commerce Court building acquires from its sprinkler system.

ASK ANY EXPERIENCED firefighter in any city in Canada if he would live in a high-rise and he'll probably say no I asked a number in four big cities and that was usually the answer. One or two did say yes but then threw in a whole slew of "ifs". The response was the same for working in a high-rise or staying overnight in a tall hotel.

Fighting fires is a dangerous job and takes courage, so it was a surprise to learn that firemen are *afraid* of skyscrapers. But it's with good reason. They're afraid they might die if they are caught in a high-rise fire. The fear is there, apparently, because fire safety precautions in most tall buildings are inadequate. And it occurred to me that if firemen are scared . . .

As one fire-safety expert has said: "If anyone ever tried to get permission to build a one-storey building that was two blocks long and had exits at only one end, he'd be laughed right out of the permits department. And yet a high-rise is the vertical equivalent — worse really, because in a long and low building you could at least jump out the windows."

Here briefly, because it's a pretty technical subject, are some of the fire hazards in high-rise buildings:

● It isn't the structure itself that is so prone to fire but what's inside — furniture, equipment, drapes, cushions, plastics, etc. This stuff burns with great ferocity because sealed windows and fire-resistant walls designed to contain fire, create what's best described at a blast-oven, which can reach temperatures of 1,200 and 1,500 degrees Fahrenheit, twisting steel and sometimes blasting out the windows.

● Air movement in a high-rise tends to whip up flames and carry choking smoke to upper storeys. This is called the "chimney" or "stack effect".

Weekend Magazine 10 June 1972

People don't have a very high opinion of the kind of housing that high-rise apartments afford. In spite of the efforts of public relations men to contradict the obvious and call minimum high-rise accommodation "luxury housing," it is clear to people that high-rise life has many problems. People don't have front doors of their own, gardens to plant, or yards for children to play in. They lack basements, attics, and porches. Generally the apartments can't be altered to fit your specific tastes and requirements, and space is very scarce. In a sense apartment-dwellers don't have neighbours, because the high-rise arrangement proves to be one where people have an extremely difficult time getting to know neighbours in a normal way. You usually can't keep dogs, cats or birds, and often even children are ruled out.

One thing obvious to everyone about high-rise apartments is that, however well they may meet the specific special housing needs of small specific groups of people in the population (like young, childless adults looking for temporary accommodation), they are extremely unsuitable for normal family housing. Yet from the point of view of the property industry it is extremely profitable and desirable to create a housing market where large numbers of ordinary families are forced to live in high-rise apartments because alternative kinds of housing are not provided at prices they can afford.

The news media usually play a very important part in teaching people first to accept high-rise apartments — but of course not for family housing — and later to regard them as acceptable even for that. They run campaigns to teach people that it is possible to live with the disadvantages of high-rise living by showing people actually doing it. They may even try to develop the case that housing of this kind is preferable to more human-scale accommodation. Without this kind of media support, there is no doubt that the industry would have a far more difficult time persuading people to accept high-rise accommodation. It might even run into so much hostility from people that the industry would be forced to continue building less profitable but more satisfactory kinds of housing.

Newspaper campaigns vary in their subjects. They may be on the "need" for slum clearance; they may talk about the local "growth crisis" and the "need" for more development; they may explore the local "transportation crisis" and implicitly argue that expressways are necessary. The subjects vary according to the local situation and the needs of the local industry. But it is almost certain that these campaigns will have implications that the property industry likes. It would take a very strong and independent media voice to carry on a campaign the property industry didn't like.

Civic elections

At election time at city hall, newspapers are sometimes even more explicit about the position they take concerning city government and the property industry. Often local newspapers take a stand in the election campaign, recommending one of the mayoralty candidates and some of the candidates for other elected offices. Most if not all of the recommended candidates are property industry representatives or supporters, or are sponsored by local political parties controlled by the industry. In addition, a newspaper usually shows its hand and its favourite faction inside the local property industry by picking candidates who represent the downtown property owners, the suburban developers, or the big-time landed interests in the area.

Candidates for civic office attach great weight to the endorsement of newspapers at election time. How much effect an endorsement really has depends on the exact circumstances, including the reputation of the incumbent and his challengers, and the social class of the constituency. Middle-class voters seem to be more influenced by media opinion on matters like this than working-class voters.

Insofar as the media can influence the outcome of elections, however, they have open to them another way of protecting and promoting the interests of the property industry, which they make good use of.

The media's importance

If the media were suddenly to take a much more independent approach to city politics, and to abandon the practices that are so valuable for continuing the status quo and the control of city hall by the property industry, the sky would not fall in. The other means by which the industry maintains its control would continue to operate, and it could probably do without the total mass media support it now enjoys.

A much more realistic hope is that a few newspapers or radio stations might develop more detailed, serious and analytical reporting on this subject, of the kind that is usual on many subjects in some British and French newspapers. Of course this would make a difference, because it would make easily accessible to people a whole range of information previously denied them about what really goes on at city hall.

Given the situation in which the mass media operate, however, it is unlikely that there can be any dramatic change in the way they inform people about city politics. The potential lies much more in alternative media with different business structures, and hence different interests and concerns. Many Canadian cities have alternative press newspapers which do a certain amount of city hall reporting — like Vancouver's *Grape* and *Straight*, Winnipeg's *Prairie Dog Press*, Toronto's *Guerilla, Citizen,* and *Seven News*. Conventional community newspapers can also be better sources of information about city politics. When the latest scheme for an expressway combined with rerouted main railway lines was announced in Winnipeg in 1972, and residents of the Fort Garry area of the city learned that one plan called for both an expressway and a main railway line to cut through their neighbourhood, they didn't learn it from either Winnipeg paper but from the local community paper. Books, booklets and magazines — like the reports on local development and city politics published in 1972 by people in Vancouver and Toronto* — are media that are much more accessible to citizen organizations and that are therefore much more promising vehicles for conveying information about city politics than the mass media. So far, however, efforts in these directions suffer from the fact that the audiences they reach are tiny in comparison to the audiences of the mass media.

Rules of the Game (Toronto) and *Forever Deceiving You* (Vancouver).

PART 3
Civic policies

CHAPTER 11
City planning

"In that particular case, leaving his house buggers up a nice site that we could have put a good building on."

That was a Toronto city planner's explanation at a public meeting in May 1970 for the fact that this house was to be demolished as part of an urban renewal scheme the city planning board had drawn up. The house looks over a park. The planners, who were going to demolish a row of small houses behind this one, didn't claim that this house was in such bad condition it was beyond repair. But they did want to have the view of the park for one or two of their new houses.

In this chapter and the next two, we are going to look at three policy areas of city government that vitally concern citizens and their organizations. With the understanding we now have of city hall, its involvement in the real estate business and the control the property industry exercises over its actions, it should be easier to see what is actually involved in these three policy areas — city planning, transportation, and relations with citizen groups.

City planning is a good place to start, both because in its scope it touches all the functions of city government, and because it is one area of city government that is still thought to pose some challenge to property industry policies.

City planning has acquired a good image because the planners often seem to be the only obstacle in the way of the developers. If any questions at all are raised at city hall about new developments, it is usually the planners who raise them. They also speak out against the dangers of uncontrolled growth, urban sprawl, and new developments carried out with no thought to the public interest or to the people who are going to have to use them.

The profession of city planning had its origins in the work of architects and others who were concerned about the fate of cities and city life, and who had ambitions to improve the physical urban setting and thus the lives of city residents. They were often reacting at least in part to what they saw the property industry and land developers doing when they went unchecked in terms of exploiting the public and creating subhuman living and working conditions.

Planners still talk about their basic concern for urban life, and often provide concrete evidence that they won't buy just anything that some landowner or developer wants to do with his property. All of us may feel that a line should be drawn to check developers, but city planners are actually out there drawing it. And so it is quite natural to conclude that city planners are the only friends ordinary citizens have got at city hall. In many fights, that has been quite true. But it then becomes natural also to respond to bad planning, which sacrifices the public interest to benefit some developer, simply by asking for more and better planners.

However, the evidence cited in Chapter 8 — showing that property industry representatives predominate amongst the "independent citizens" appointed to the civic planning authorities that ultimately control the work of city planners and decide on what their plans will contain — should make us wonder whether the good image city planning has acquired is deserved. In fact, in spite of its image, city planning is not the only gap in the otherwise tight control of city hall by the property industry. On the contrary, it is the key element in the regulation of urban land use, a city government function crucial to the industry, which the industry has ensured will be carried out in its best interests in spite of the rest of us.

Planning and the supply of "new" land

The function of city planning in city government is quite simple. It regulates the supply of land for new uses, either for development or for redevelopment, and it attempts to co-ordinate the provision of civic works and services needed to make these new land uses possible.

The strongest form of city planning is the simplest. It is making decisions about where new water and sewage mains will be built. Since suburban development usually requires these services as an absolute minimum, deciding whether or not to expand the municipal system and whose land to service is really tantamount to deciding on the amount and location of "new" land for suburban housing.

Operations at this simple level are usually not labelled city planning. Planning as it now goes on in Canadian city halls is a much more sophisticated business, though it often deals with questions of locating new facilities like sewers, roads, and parks. But the essence of what goes on remains the same, and is just as simple.

City planning operates in the context of zoning bylaws controlling all land use. Planners gather information about

Planning the city beautiful

In student textbooks and laymen's introductions to the doctrines of city planning, we usually find the most blunt formulations of the myth that planning is devoted to creating the utopian city of tomorrow and fighting to protect and promote the public interest and the citizenry. This passage from a U.S. planner's introductory textbook illustrates these views:

"The gaudy and garish commercial areas of our cities are a disgrace to a supposedly civilized people. And there is cause for legitimate concern even in established residential areas. If we are honest, we cannot avoid asking, "Is this the best that we can do?" Obviously it is not; in some cases, it is little better than the worst we can do. I am convinced that our citizens are increasingly concerned by the all-pervading ugliness which comes with uncontrolled development. If the mental health and social well-being of our civilization are to survive, we must do a better job of community organization.

"If our communities are not to be bankrupted by wasteful and uncoordinated development, we must have practical plans for the future; if we are not to be overwhelmed by man-made ugliness, we must see to it that our plans work."

Smith, *The Citizen's Guide to Planning*, p.10

Planning and "new" land

These quotations from newspaper articles all illustrate how much of the normal work of city planners is directly tied to providing a regulated supply of 'new' land for development, land whose zoning and planning designations are altered in order to allow it to be developed or redeveloped for new uses.

District agrees on plan for Gabriola Island

Sun Staff Reporter

NANAIMO — An immediate start on a community plan for Gabriola Island was unanimously agreed to Tuesday by Nanaimo Regional District.

The decision followed rejection until the community plan has been completed, of a land use application to develop 550 lots on 244 acres flanking False Narrows. The application had been made by Gabriola Wildwood Estates Ltd.

Non-resident land owners form the mainland and Gabriola residents filled the boardroom.

Board chairman Don Beaton warned at one stage he would adjourn the session if visitors kept breaking in with questions and statements.

He said the general tenor of a public hearing on Gabriola April 19 was that a comprehensive plan of development should be done before a subdivision of such size goes ahead.

Col. W. H. Matthews, chairman of Gabriola Advisory Planning Commission, said those at the hearing were not against Wildwood Estates but were not prepared for such a large urban development, without an orderly, overall plan.

Vancouver Sun 17 May 1972

90-DAY STUDY ORDERED

False Creek plan gets a look

City planners were given 90 days by city council Tuesday to come up with proposals for implementing proposals to redevelop False Creek.

Council received a report from the consultants on the project, Thompson, Berwick, Pratt and Partners, which sees the redevelopment taking place over a period of 30 or more years with capital requirements of more than $600 million.

The report forecasts an eventual population of 30,000 living in a mixed residential and light-commercial environment on the 521-acre site.

The False Creek committee, headed by Ald. Walter Hardwick, asked city officials to consider five areas on which to make reports to council after the 90-day period;

Establish a development program, including proposals to secure developer performance;

Establish a staging plan with alternatives for components not directly within control of the city;

Establish a capital works program;

Propose a financing and income outline to include recommendations on whether to sell or lease city-owned land in the development to private developers;

Set out marketing proposals for the first stage.

Vancouver Sun 26 Apr. 1972

S. Surrey residents fight plan

Opposition to Surrey council's plan to develop the municipality's south area appeared to be growing this week.

More than 400 residents packed the Bear Creek Park Fine Arts Centre this week for council's final audio-visual presentation of the South Surrey Plan, prepared at council's request by U.S. consultants.

The plan calls for comprehensive development of the semi-rural South Surrey peninsula, which includes such areas as Crescent Beach, Sunnyside and Ocean Park.

It foresees a tenfold expansion of population, to upwards of 100,000, and would include a commercial townsite development on 450 acres of land owned by the municipality.

Vancouver Province 23 Mar. 1972

the status quo, how land is actually used and how it is currently zoned. Often land use does not conform to present zoning; that is because land being used a particular way before a zoning bylaw is introduced can legally continue in that use — be what is called a legal non-conforming use — as long as its owner wishes. The reason corner grocery stores have survived in old neighbourhoods is because the stores were there long before city hall thought of imposing a zoning bylaw on the areas requiring that they be residential only.

Planners study the status quo intensively, *because their job is to make proposals about how the present situation should be changed*. Their real function is to develop policy proposals for supplying "new" land in the city to meet the demands being made by the property industry. If, for instance, there is a market for new housing, it is via city planning that a decision will be made about which land to make available for housing developments. Planning also provides a supply of "new" land for downtown high-rise office buildings, high-rise apartments, factories and other kinds of development. In many cases, planners choose not to designate for development vacant land previously used for rural purposes. Much of the planners' activity involves rather marking off areas of land in the city currently being used one way and indicating that city hall will give permission for some different land use.

Needless to say, for every different category of land use city hall invents, there is a somewhat separate market. The market for land where you can build two-storey duplexes is somewhat different from the market for land where you are allowed to build three-storey apartment buildings.

City planning is quite a delicate matter, because it involves supplying just enough "new" land for each different use so that developers can provide accommodation to meet the increased demand for space of this specific kind, but not supplying too much, which would have the effect of pushing down the price people would pay for this "new" land and hence the value of all the land used in this specific way already.

A dramatic example illustrates this point best. In an ordinary central-city neighbourhood in Toronto, land where city hall permits high-rise apartment buildings sold in 1972 for $20 or so a square foot. That means a small lot of 1,500 square feet is worth $30,000 if its zoning permits an apartment building. But similarly-located land where the city does not permit high-rise development sells for much less, and its price reflects only the value of the house that sits on the land. An ordinary two-storey working-class house on a 1,500-foot lot would be worth on the average about $20,000.

If Toronto's city planners were suddenly to say that developers could build high-rise apartments anywhere they wanted in the city, that would greatly increase the supply of "new" land for apartments. The immediate effect would be to push down the value of land being used for high-rise redevelopment. Developers would buy their houses for $20,000, not $30,000, and no one would be willing to pay $20 a square foot when land was available for $13 or $14. Developers might be pleased to be able to get land for new projects at a lower price without having to worry about city zoning, but owners of existing high-rise apartment buildings where the land had been valued at $20 a square foot when they bought it would be very unhappy. They would find new apartments undercutting their rent levels. Mortgage lenders would also be extremely upset, because borrowers might be reluctant to go on paying off mortgages on buildings no longer worth what they were mortgaged for. So too big a supply of "new" land for apartments would cause unwanted disruption in the property industry.

On the other hand, if city planners were to go to the opposite extreme and provide absolutely no "new" land for downtown high-rise apartments, developers would be extremely unhappy, even though apartment building owners might be quite pleased. What city planning involves is trying to arrange for just the right supply of "new" land for every different urban use.

But if this is the real function of planning, then it should be clear that planning is not at all a form of protection for the citizenry against the developers. In fact it is carrying out a function crucial to the property industry: regulating and controlling the supply of "new" land for urban use and re-use. It is preparing the ground — literally — for the developers.

City planning paves the way for controlled and regulated development, and that is exactly what the industry wants it to do, because then everyone in the industry is protected and makes the largest possible profits. The planners themselves may have got into their profession wanting to liberalize and humanize the cities, to make them decent places for people to live in, but in the planning work they do they are in fact providing an essential service to the property industry.

Planners and the property industry

Everyone who lives in a city has a stake in how the city's land is used, in the regulations that are developed around the use of existing buildings and in the controls imposed on demolition and new construction. Insofar as city planners

Planning and growth

Addressing a 2-day $150-a-head seminar for property industry people interested in learning more about the practical aspects of land development, Metro Toronto deputy planning commissioner R. J. Brower addressed himself to the misconception he said many people have about the basic attitude of city planners towards development and urban growth.

"The basic philosophy of Toronto's Official Plan," said Brower, "is growth." He explained that this plan foresees the growth of the Toronto regional area from 2 1/2 million to 8 million. What it does is develop a city hall policy which will encourage this growth, and which will in particular facilitate expansion of the commercial downtown area. "The downtown is where we can best encourage further growth."

Globe and Mail Feb. 1972

have developed techniques which enable them to administrate a system of this kind, they could in principle be extremely valuable either to a city government controlled by the property industry or to one controlled by citizen groups and their allies. Most of the analysis and techniques familiar to city planners, however, have an extremely strong built-in bias towards the policies the property industry wants from government. It would require a whole new approach to the subject to develop the kind of city planning that would respond to the needs and interests of citizen groups and ordinary city residents rather than to those of the property industry.

It helps greatly to understand the present function of urban planning in city government and at other levels to note the connections between the industry and the planners, particularly those at the highest administrative levels, and also to realize how the bureaucratic set-up in which the average city planner works succeeds in separating the intentions he might have about his work in city government from the actual effects of that work.

The evidence has already been cited about how the property industry has people in the property business sitting as "independent citizens" on city planning boards where these exist. A typical independent citizen planning board member is Fred Eisen, in ordinary life the treasurer of Four Seasons Hotels Ltd., which wanted to build a big hotel project on the edge of Vancouver's Stanley Park. Four Seasons also demolished several lovely Georgian houses fronting on Hyde Park in order to build their London branch, and has gone into partnership with ITT through its Sheraton subsidiary to put up a large new hotel (its third in Toronto) opposite the Toronto city hall. Eisen takes his independent mind to the Toronto borough of North York, the location of the chain's Inn on the Park, where he serves as vice-chairman of the planning board.

The membership of city planning boards always provides a comfortable majority for the property industry. The citizens and politicians who sit on these boards usually do a careful job of supervising the work done by their staff, changing their reports and plans when necessary in order to make them conform to the property industry's interests. They also control promotions and senior appointments, ensuring that chief planners and senior administrators in city planning departments are properly sympathetic to the property industry's interests. Doing so is not always easy even at the senior level, because many people get involved in city planning specifically because they object to the kind of city the property industry is building, and want to do something to improve the situation. Finding planners with suitable attitudes for ordinary planning posts is not easy either. Vancouver, for example, has experienced a long series of resignations by middle- and junior- level planners in the city planning department who were fed up with seeing their policies and proposals altered or rejected whenever the property industry's interests demanded it. By the time planners get up to the senior levels, they have usually had to prove themselves quite sympathetic to the property industry.

One important feature of the planning profession is that there is reasonable scope for employment amongst private developers and property corporations. Senior city planners who prove their ability and demonstrate their political views in city hall jobs often move on to better-paid jobs in private industry. Both of Metro Toronto's former chief planners, Murray Jones and Eli Comay, are now consultants doing work for government and private industry. Former Toronto development commissioner Walter Manthorpe, by profession a city planner, left city hall to become a vice-president of the Meridian Group, one of Toronto's largest local high-rise apartment developers.

Since these are the circumstances in which city planners work, it is not surprising that their activities tie in so closely to the property industry.

How city planning works

The exact operations and powers of city planning vary tremendously not only from city to city but also between different political jurisdictions in the same geographic area. It is extremely important to know in detail the powers under which any given city planning takes place, in order to understand exactly what plans mean and what planners are doing. Often specific provincial legislation lays down the way in which city land use regulation will take place, and spells out the powers of plan documents and of planning bodies. Usually provincial governments retain a good deal of the power over urban land-use planning, which they exercise themselves.

There is a basic common pattern in city planning as it is done in Canada. Every city has a system for regulating existing land uses in its jurisdiction. The system is always

Property investors and city plans

From the complaints developers and property investors often make about planners and planning "red tape", the impression is given that the property industry doesn't really like the idea of official city plans which restrict their actions.

The truth of the matter would seem to be that the industry as a whole has a lot to gain from this kind of tight civic regulation, though of course individual investors and developers don't like it when they bump up against civic restrictions enacted for the good of the industry as a whole.

Some idea of the powerful support there is within the property industry for stringent city planning is given by this extract from an interview with Toronto mayor William Dennison, explaining why he devoted so much energy following his election in December 1966 to getting a new Official Plan for Toronto approved by city council:

"I wasn't mayor more than two weeks when I had a request, an urgent request, from the Redevelopment Advisory Council (an association of the major Toronto downtown property investors) under the chairmanship then, I believe, of Colonel Allan Burton (chairman of the board of Simpsons Ltd.) who urged me to proceed and get the Official Plan adopted as quickly as possible."

Would the property industry interests represented by this organization press for planning and its "red tape" like this if it did them no good?

Toronto's zoning system

This article, by Toronto opposition alderman John Sewell, explains in some detail the zoning system which Toronto uses to control city land use. Every municipality has its own variant, but the basic procedures used in Toronto are much ike those used in most other Canadian cities.

Every inch of the city is covered by some sort of zoning by-law. The zoning determines the types of uses which are permissible for any particular piece of land. There are three different types of zones:

G — areas of parks or public recreation
R — areas of residential use
C — areas of commercial and industrial uses

■ Density

There are various types of residential or commercial uses which one might put in an R or C area. It is felt that some residential uses are not compatible with other residential uses, and therefore subcategories are established in any particular R or C area. These are indicated by numbers and letters which are appended to the letter describing the general uses allowed. For example, an area designated R.1 allows detached dwellings, but does not allow a boarding house (which is allowed in an R.4 area). A general breakdown of the types of uses allowed in any particular area is set out in the following table.

These sub-categories also help to define the density allowed, that is, the intensity to which one can exercise the general use permitted. Density is based on the floor area of the structure in relation to the area of the lot on which the structure stands. In an R.1 area, the floor area of the structure can be no more than 0.35 of the lot area; in an R.3 area, the floor area of the structure can equal the total area of the lot; in an R.4 area, the floor area of the structure can be twice the total area of the lot. The floor area of the structure is determined by measuring the floor area on all floors, and adding them together. Densities allowed in any particular area are set out in the following table:

ZONE		L	V
1	0.35	1.0	3.0
2	0.6	2.0	5.0
3	1.0	3.0	7.0
4	2.0	4.0	12.0
5	2.5		

* L and V densities apply to commercial buildings.

■ The Zoning By-law

The zoning and densities which are permissible in this city are set out in *The Zoning By-law*, No. 20623. This is a rather hefty book consisting of the definitions of uses, various exceptions, and a series of about 300 maps which in detail show the zoning applicable to every block in the city. It is available from the City Surveyors' Department (telephone 367-7665) for a charge of $11.00. It is a technical book, and I only recommend it to lawyers who have a client with a specific problem. It is not generally useful to the public.

■ Non-conforming Uses

The Zoning By-law was passed shortly after World War II. Before that time, one could build whatever one wanted, wherever one wanted. This unplanned and uncontrolled use of land meant that some uses were established which were not compatible with uses generally established in any particular area. For instance, in older parts of the city one will discover a store in mid-block, or a factory on a residential street. Since these uses were established before the zoning came into effect, and since they do not conform to the other uses that surround them, they are called "non-conforming uses." The non-conforming use is allowed to exist until it ceases, but once it ceases it can no longer establish itself at that location — it must seek a location where such a use is allowed. For example, a particular small store which exists as a non-conforming use in an otherwise residential area can remain in existence indefinitely, but the same site cannot subsequently be used for a different kind of store or a factory. The site use can only be altered to bring it into conformity with the area, or to create a better use.

● Permitted
○ Permitted subject to restrictions in By-law
* Recommended; not presently included in the By-law

RESIDENTIAL DISTRICTS

	G	R 1	1A	1F	2	3	4	4A
Park—Playground	●	●	●	●	●	●	●	●
Community Centre	●	○	○	○	○	●	●	●
Church		○	○	○	●	●	●	●
Detached Dwelling	●	●	●	●	●	●	●	●
Doctor, Dentist		○	○	○	○	○	○	○
Semi-Detached Dwelling				●	●	●	●	●
Duplex			○	○	●	●	●	●
Double Duplex			○	○	●	●	●	●
Town House*					●			
Triplex					●	●	●	●
Double Triplex					●	●	●	●
Row House					●	●	●	●
Apartment House			○		○	○	●	●
Converted Dwelling			○	○	●	●	●	●
Boarding House					○	○	●	●
Parking Station					○	○	○	○
Nursing Home						○	●	
Day Nursery					○	○	●	
Children's Home						○	●	
Boys' Home						○	●	
Public School		○	○	○	○	○	●	●
Private School					○	○	●	●
Public Hospital							●	●
Private Club							●	●
Fraternity House							●	●
Public Library							●	●
YMCA, etc.							●	●
Institutional Office								●
Professional Office								●
Head Office Building								●

COMMERCIAL & INDUSTRIAL DISTRICTS

	C 1A	1B	1S	1	2	3	4
All Residential Buildings			●				
Some Residential Buildings	●	○	●				
Public Buildings	○		○	●	●	●	●
Institutions	●			●	●	●	●
Office Building	●			●	●	●	●
Hospital	●			●	●	●	●
Bank	●			●	●	●	●
Hotel				●	●	●	●
Restaurant	○			●	●	●	●
Theatre, Hall				●	●	●	●
Commercial Club	○			●	●	●	●
Place of Amusement				●	●	●	●
Retail Store	○			●	●	●	●
Personal Service Shop	○	○		●	●	●	●
Bake-Shop				●	●	●	●
Repair and Service Shop	○			●	●	●	●
Studio, Custom Workshop	○			●	●	●	●
Commercial School	●			●	●	●	●
Supermarket				●	●	●	●
Animal Hospital				○	○	○	○
Private Parking Garage	●			●			
Public Parking Garage				●	●	●	●
Service Station				●	●	●	●
Used Car Lot				●	●	●	●
Open Air Market				●	●	●	●
Restricted Industry				●	●	●	●
Warehouse				○		●	●
General Industry						●	●
Heavy Machinery Yard						●	●
Obnoxious Industry							○
Junk and Scrap Metal							○

These drawings, from a City of Toronto Planning Board report on the South of St. Jamestown area, illustrate four different ways in which a site could be developed to a density of 3.125, with 3.125 square feet of building area to every square foot of land on the site. They illustrate the fact that high-density housing can be built in many different ways, and that high density does not inevitably require high-rise buildings.

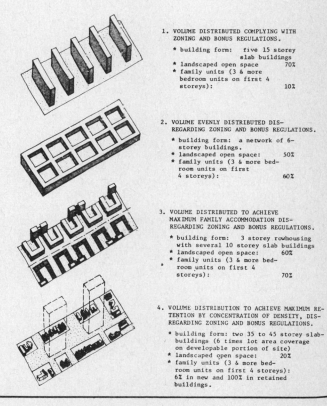

1. VOLUME DISTRIBUTED COMPLYING WITH ZONING AND BONUS REGULATIONS.
   * building form: five 15 storey slab buildings
   * landscaped open space   70%
   * family units (3 & more bedroom units on first 4 storeys):   10%

2. VOLUME EVENLY DISTRIBUTED DISREGARDING ZONING AND BONUS REGULATIONS.
   * building form: a network of 6-storey buildings.
   * landscaped open space: 50%
   * family units (3 & more bedroom units on first 4 storeys):   60%

3. VOLUME DISTRIBUTED TO ACHIEVE MAXIMUM FAMILY ACCOMMODATION DISREGARDING ZONING AND BONUS REGULATIONS.
   * building form: 3 storey rowhousing with several 10 storey slab buildings
   * landscaped open space: 60%
   * family units (3 & more bedroom units on first 4 storeys):   70%

4. VOLUME DISTRIBUTION TO ACHIEVE MAXIMUM RETENTION BY CONCENTRATION OF DENSITY, DISREGARDING ZONING AND BONUS REGULATIONS.
   * building form: two 35 to 45 storey slab-buildings (6 times lot area coverage on developable portion of site)
   * landscaped open space: 20%
   * family units (3 & more bedroom units on first 4 storeys): 6% in new and 100% in retained buildings.

incredibly detailed and complicated, and is generally carried out by zoning bylaws. These bylaws specify exactly what kinds of activities are permitted in a building. They also lay down detailed requirements about the way buildings must be laid out on their site. And they regulate the maximum amount of building that can be done on a plot of land.

Density maximums are extremely important to developers because they regulate how much building you can put on a piece of land, and therefore how much money you can make. Usually density is expressed in terms of the number of square feet of floor area of building that is permitted for every square foot of land on the lot where the building stands. These maximums are expressed as ratios, like 3:1 or 12:1. The meaning of 12:1 is that you can build 12 square feet of floor space in a new building for every square foot of land you own. Sometimes densities for housing are expressed in terms of the number of units allowed per acre of land. So 60 units/acre means that you can build 60 apartments, town houses or houses on every acre. Ratios of people per acre, like 130/acre, work the same way. The figures are based on standard assumptions about how many people live in houses of different sizes.

In addition to zoning bylaws, cities have building bylaws of various kinds, which specify very precisely how new buildings must be constructed and how existing buildings must be changed if they are to be used for a different purpose. These bylaws can have a tremendous impact on construction cost as well as building design. A height restriction of 60 feet in the building bylaw, for instance, would automatically rule out high-rise buildings. Needless to say, this particular kind of bylaw is not popular in Canada and is used usually only to protect well-established middle-class residential areas from the depredations of developers.

The zoning and building bylaw system of regulating land use is usually administered by city bureaucrats who have no pretentions to "professional" training. City planners get involved in zoning administration when there are proposals to change existing land uses.

The city planning system for regulating land use changes and providing a steady supply of land for development and redevelopment involves a hierarchy of city plans. First there is an overall city plan, often called a master plan or an official plan, which indicates broadly the changes in land uses proposed for the city and the important new public works and services whose construction will service and encourage new development. But this is not how planners describe master plans. They talk about them as proposals for the way things "ought to be" in the city. You have to look very closely at their maps to see where the planners think that things "ought to be" just the way they are now, i.e. where no change is proposed, and where planners think things "ought to be" different, i.e. where the planners are providing a supply of "new" land for development. If the planners think you and your neighbourhood "ought to be" different, watch out for the developers.

Overall master plans often show proposed new sewer systems, bridges, major roadways and expressways and other transportation and public works facilities. Co-ordinating these with new land development is essential, because often development can't take place without them, and in other cases they create a much more attractive investment possibility.

Tentative master plans drawn up by planners for the instruction of politicians are not necessarily to be taken seriously. Usually, though, there is a legal system set up by the provincial government by which city hall can adopt a master plan and make it official city policy. Once this happens, the city has taken a major step towards giving its approval to any new development the plan proposes, in whatever areas the plan indicates it should be permitted or encouraged. When politicians boast that they don't vote for development schemes that violate the city's master plan, that doesn't mean they're opposing development. It just means they're encouraging developers' projects on land the plan designates for new development and not on other sites.

A step down from the master plan in scope and a step up in detail and precision is the district, area or neighbourhood plan. In this kind of plan, details are spelled out about how things "ought to be" in a particular neighbourhood. Again, it is crucial to look for the places where the plan shows that things "ought to be" different from the way they are now. An existing low-density residential area that the plan designates as a place that "ought to be" medium-density is a neighbourhood the planners are fingering for redevelopment. Often planners muddy the water by calling for all sorts of measures that "ought to be" adopted by city hall for such a neighbourhood, but which they and everyone else know never will be adopted. The planners talk loudly about new parks, dead-end streets, better parking facilities, better street lighting and so on. Their plans often show that these things "ought to be" improved. Usually, this is a diversionary tactic away from those parts of the area — sometimes the whole area — that the planners have up for development by saying that private land use "ought to be" different from what it is now.

At their third level of operations, city planners evaluate specific proposals submitted by developers to city hall. Often a new development requires a change in the city's zoning to permit the proposed new land use. Sometimes all that is wanted is permission for the developer to vary slightly from the bylaws' requirements, or to buy the city lane that runs through his property.

In their comments and suggestions about development proposals, planners usually make some attempt at protecting what they consider to be the public interest. They talk grand and loose about the architectural qualities of the proposed buildings. But then they get down to business and inspect the project in very great detail to ensure that it meets in every particular the requirements of the city's bylaws. Usually the developer asks to be allowed to put up more building on his land than the city's bylaws seem to permit. Generally the planners approve the new project insofar as it meets the city's bylaws. Then the politicians give the developer something extra, depending on how much they like him and perhaps on how much money he contributes to their campaigns.

This detail work by city planners is the teeth of the city's policies regarding regulation of land use. From the point of view of the property industry, it is crucial to their operation. If city planners didn't do it, the industry itself would probably have to. To some extent, for instance through the detailed requirements of mortgage lending institutions about the buildings on which they are prepared to lend money, the industry does regulate its own activities. But most of the work is done through the mechanism of city

Continued on page 174

Master plans and motherhood

Planners are prone to drawing up fine-sounding lists of 'objectives' or 'goals' when they write their overall city plans. Usually they try to formulate statements which are broad enough that no one could possibly object to them. These two samples are from Toronto's implemented master plan and from a 1968 proposal for a master plan for Vancouver.

2. RESIDENCE AREAS

It is the objective of Council that the quality of life shall be improved for each resident.

Council will support the building of varieties of housing accommodation within the Toronto region sufficient to take care of the needs of various household compositions in order to reduce the pressures for family housing within the City and to maintain a balanced housing supply.

It is the policy of Council to encourage provision of suitable accommodation for families with children in *residential* buildings which are at locations and densities suitable for such families.

Residence areas will be pleasant, attractive, free of congestion and features incompatible with good living conditions, and provided with municipal services, schools, parks, playgrounds and community services, adequate for the needs of the residents.

Council will take such measures as it considers desirable and appropriate to improve and maintain the quality of *residence areas*. Such measures will include, but not be restricted to, the re-planning of streets, the provision of off-street parking space, the planting and maintenance of trees, and the acquisition and removal or improvement of buildings or uses which are incompatible with the district, the provision and maintenance of adequate municipal services, the creation of parks and playgrounds, and provision of advice and assistance in the improvement and maintenance of private dwellings.

Existing Objectives, Policies and Programs

While the City does not now have a comprehensive plan, there are a number of existing objectives which have guided decisions on the City's development. These have not always been followed consistently, and some of them are under review:

1. Revitalization of the Downtown core.
2. Acquisition of a waterfront park system along English Bay, from Stanley Park to Point Grey.
3. Improvement of the City's arterial street system.
4. Increasing the supply of housing for low-income families.
5. Clearing and rebuilding rundown sections of the Inner Area of the City through urban renewal.
6. Acquiring an adequate system of local, district and major parks.
7. Preserving the single-family areas of the City.
8. Improvement of the False Creek Area.
9. Completion of street improvements (curbs, paving, lighting, trees, etc.) on all City Streets.

District planning and high-rise development

Reading the first of these two pages, taken from a 1969 district plan proposal for the Main-Danforth area of Toronto, the last thing that a resident would think is that the planners are preparing large chunks of his neighbourhood for high-rise redevelopment. Yet the details of this plan call for approximately 100 houses to be re-zoned, permitting developers to move in, acquire and then demolish the neighbourhood. Giving the developers this foot in the door, moreover, opens the possibility that the planners or the politicians would enlarge the redevelopment area at a later date.

Reading the second of these two pages, one finds the redevelopment proposal for this section of the planning area, though it is buried in a number of far less important items and expressed in confusing language. Item 2. amounts to saying that both the vacant and industrial land included in the area marked 2. on the map *and* the row of houses just below the figure '2' on the map should be designated for high-rise development. Item 3. really says that the houses scattered amongst factories in this part of the area (and located across the street from other houses, no doubt giving residents the firm impression thaey are living in a residential and not an industrial area) should also be designated for high-rise. And, taking all these other changes into account, it is hard to believe that planners and politicians will resist the temptation to make the redevelopment area a nice, neat package by including into it the small island of houses (marked 6. on the map) which, at this stage of the plan, are supposed to be "retained" because they are "better housing".

THE FRAMEWORK OF THE PLAN

The proposals fit into a basic framework which identifies areas of "change" and "stability" for the whole area. This reflects a policy of restricting any major new developments to areas which are now essentially non-residential. "Major change" areas total approximately 78 acres.

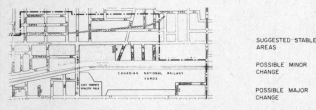

SUGGESTED STABLE AREAS

POSSIBLE MINOR CHANGE

POSSIBLE MAJOR CHANGE

It must be realized that major change is not inevitable; the present land uses could continue or be renewed as permitted under the existing zoning. By outlining "areas of major change" this means that applications for rezoning would be considered favourably in these areas. However, being dependent upon private initiative there is no way of anticipating when any changes would occur, or the exact nature of these changes. The opportunity for early redevelopment is such that the number of residents in the area might well be doubled.

SETTING OUT THE PROPOSALS

The study area has been divided into smaller local areas. Proposals are set out concisely for each of these areas. This has been done so that detailed attention can be focused upon areas with which local groups of residents and owners are particularly familiar.

1. OAK PARK-CHISHOLM
2. COLEMAN-BALFOUR
3. WESTLAKE-STEPHENSON
4. MAIN-DAWES-LUTTRELL
5. NORWOOD-GERRARD
6. MAIN-VICTORIA PARK

Public meetings will be based upon these areas to discuss both local proposals and the implications of the whole area plan.

AREA 6   MAIN-VICTORIA PARK TENTATIVE PROPOSALS

Primarily an area of railway and industrial lands, much of which is vacant, with a residential population of only 220 — to allow for large scale redevelopment for residential uses with a possible increase in population of up to 5,000.

The tentative proposals assume that the Canadian National Railways' lands will eventually be available for reuse. Even if this does not occur in entirety, the general policies set out can be applied to any development which could still take place.

1. To ensure that recreational land to be removed by the expressway is adequately compensated for, and to allow for the eventual expansion of facilities serving both the wider district and any increase in local population. Additional landscaping of the Arena would improve its appearance.

2. To recommend favourable consideration of schemes which would allow for the integrated development of this whole area for residential use at medium densities, provided that: (a) a substantial proportion of accommodation is suitable for family living, incorporating a mixture of low and high rise buildings, such as illustrated on page 6; (b) recreation facilities are provided; and (c) layouts conform to a new road pattern for the wider area.

3. To consider an eventual rezoning of the present industrial land and an incorporation of this area into adjacent residential schemes, at medium densities. To ensure that interim industrial uses are compatible with a residential environment.

4. To reserve land for an elementary school which would be needed if residential development for families takes place on a large scale in this area.

5. To recommend that a bus service be extended along Gerrard, if warranted by a large increase in population. Consideration should be given to the widening of Gerrard to accommodate any increase in traffic and to discourage the use of residential streets south of Gerrard for through movement.

6. To retain this pocket of better housing which should be satisfactorily incorporated into any adjacent new development.

7. To recommend careful landscaping of the expressway intersection and effective screening of all adjacent developments.

8. To consider the eventual provision of a covered pedestrian bridge linking any new residential development with the shopping plaza.

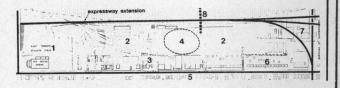

Main-Danforth Area Tentative Planning Proposals. Toronto: City of Toronto Planning Board, 1969, p.7, p.13

Planners and developers

Many city planners believe that their work contributes at least in a small way to ruling out some of the worst excesses of the property industry and creating small improvements in city life. Though the analysis in the text suggests that this is largely a misconception which fails to take account of the vital large-scale contribution which city planning makes to the property industry and to its ability to carry on with new construction, planners nevertheless often see this as their contribution. They become extremely upset when local property industry interests decide that they want a somewhat looser hand on the city hall regulatory reins and persuade their city council majority and senior city hall bureaucrats to alter planners' recommendations and proposals. In Vancouver this preference for loose city hall regulation of developers has given rise to tremendous restiveness amongst the city's planning employees.

SENIOR STAFF VOICES N O BEEFS

Planners 'tell all but obvious'

By HALL LEIREN
Sun City Hall Reporter

The advance notices said the Vancouver city planning department was going to lay things on the line and tell all.

Staff members were going to answer criticisms of the department voiced by a number of planners who have resigned — the most recent being Peter Mees, 44, a department member for eight years.

But reporters concluded by the end of the session that either all those who were discontended have resigned or, with senior staff members standing around listening to what was being said, those who may have beefs were reluctant to speak up.

Reporters attending t h e meeting Wednesday were cynical enough to suggest the latter.

The meeting with reporters, billed by planning director Bill Graham as an information session, resulted from statements made by Mees when he resigned.

Mees had said he was disappointed at "the lack of direction and leadership, the absence of courage of conviction, whether right or wrong, the politically-colored recommendations" that e m e r g e from the planning department.

He charged that certain favored developers get away with "anything short of murder, while the little man gets the book thrown at him."

★

The farce that is the City of Vancouver planning department goes on. The farce is not in the department itself, but in the way it is used— abused is the proper word. A city council, stacked with real estate and developer interests, treats it with contempt. It treats planners, in the words of one of the recent men who have resigned, "like auto mechanics." They are there, not as professionals in their field, but to service the jockeying and instant-zoning that the NPA majority conjures up in compromising votes.

★

The whole system smells. City council does not use its professional planners for planning. It does indeed use them "as auto mechanics"—to service the decisions that amateurs make in the bear-pit of compromises and trade-offs. One of the planners who has resigned says, "We don't need any more brains, we need guts. Practically every problem in the city has been analysed to death. There are studies a mile high. What is needed is guts. Someone to make a decision."

In the final sentence of his resignation, Peter Mees wrote, "It makes me sad that a city such as Vancouver, with such a fabulous natural setting, is being spoilt, by shallow, greedy developers, aided and abetted by a city administration that should know better and do better." That's a serious charge, "aided and abetted." Perhaps we do need an investigation. What is needed is someone with guts. The man we're thinking of is Mr. Dan Campbell.

planning at city hall.

City planning in perspective

The exact importance of city planning and its exact function in the context of the local property industry vary tremendously from city to city. In Winnipeg since amalgamation, land-use regulating powers have been divided between community committees and the central city government. We should expect to see efforts to further centralize planning powers, and then of course the property industry's majority on Winnipeg's city council will be able to give developers what they ask for. The decision on the Trizec development at Portage and Main already referred to is a precursor of many similar decisions.

In Toronto, planning powers are divided amongst the City of Toronto, the five suburban boroughs, and the Metro Toronto government. Yet the property industry has planning very firmly in control at all the Toronto city halls.

Whatever the details of the local situation, the overall situation regarding city planning is the same everywhere.

The powers of city planning are exercised in the best interests of the industry, supervised often by "independent citizens" drawn from the industry as well as by industry-controlled city politicians.

City planning is not the protector of the interests of the people it has so often been portrayed to be. It is on the front lines of the development industry, setting up land for development and redevelopment in the city, and administering the details of the system of regulation and control of land use and new development that is needed by the industry for its own self-protection and profitability. It does this job in the best interests of the industry as a whole, or of the faction of the industry that has captured most power at city hall. City planning is in fact the protector of the interests of the property industry, guarding the industry — developers, property investors and financial institutions — from the perils of free competition in the industry on the one hand and a citizen-controlled city on the other, where the needs of the industry would be subordinated to the needs of the city's residents.

Planner's Advice Disregarded *by John Sewell, 22 September 1970*

A developer has applied to build a five-storey commercial building and an 11-storey apartment on the south west corner of Bloor and Dundas. He requested a density of 5, which is allowed by the Official Plan. The Proposal has one interesting aspect: all of the 115 apartment units are to be junior one-bedrooms — nothing larger, nothing smaller.

The Planning Board was obviously not too impressed with the proposal, and recommended that density be no more than 3, and that no more than 87 apartment units be allowed.

The developer came before the B & D Committee and said that he had a compromise: he would build no more than 100 units, at a density of 4.

The Committee fell all over themselves at his generosity. The corner needed redevelopment, and the Official Plan allowed this type of thing to be built. Sewell's objection about the dreadful similarity of all the units was off the point: did Sewell really want families living there ? When Sewell said that he was only interested in a little diversity, the members of the Committee quickly changed their approach, and said that they couldn't tell the developer what kind of apartments he could put in.

Barker, the Chief Planner, then made a very strong speech about the position of the politicians, and the Official Plan. The Plan, he said, is a guideline as to the type and density of buildings which might be allowed. The fact that a certain density is

allowed does not mean that every building should be built to that density. Every application should be looked at in terms of planning, and the planning data should decide the maximum density. The Official Plan only describes the maximum density permitted: that density should not be allowed if the proposed development causes planning problems. Accordingly, he said, the talk that the developer has sawed off at a compromise density of 4 is ridiculous: the Planning Board has shown, by arguments not refuted, that the maximum density one should allow this particular proposal is 3.

But the Committee members didn't listen, and the developer got his way, on a vote where Sewell was the only dissenter.

Inside City Hall p.51

CHAPTER 12
Transportation

THE END? The right-of-way for Toronto's Spadina expressway. After the cancellation of the expressway by the provincial government in mid-1971, there were many proposals about what should be done with the land. The province hired U.S. architect Buckminster Fuller to develop a scheme and Fuller wisely proposed an enormous building filling up the right of way which would have been too big ever to tear down, or to go over or under. Toronto's municipal politicians were happy to let the land sit like this while they lobbied furiously to find some way of getting their expressway built after all.

Urban transportation means big money, because it deals with the gigantic expenditures required for expressways and highway systems, bridges, subway construction, parking garages and public transit systems. The vested interests involved in the urban transportation industry are familiar and powerful ones. Road-building alone is a big business, with its interests represented by "Good Roads" associations all across the country. It supports the subsidiary industries of road building equipment suppliers and road building materials suppliers, the latter including asphalt manufacturers (the oil companies) and cement manufacturers. Associated with it are the tremendously powerful auto and oil industries, who between them have an enormous stake in seeing us do lots of travelling, and as much of it as possible in cars.

Transportation planners and city politicians do their best to create a sense of mystery around urban transportation facilities. When they are explaining the reasons for the programs and projects they recommend, they say only that a proposed expressway is "needed" to "prevent congestion" or to provide "easier access to the downtown." They talk about how traffic will get more and more congested unless downtown streets are widened and one-way systems introduced. They explain that new bridges and roads are necessary to produce a "more efficient" system. Such reasoning makes it sound as if transportation planning is all for the sake of traffic and trips — to make more traffic possible and to make trips faster. Often no better explanation is offered for the tremendous public expenditures that urban transportation systems require.

What we know already about city government must make us highly suspicious of this kind of circular rationale for transportation policy. Once you note the focus of city government on servicing and regulating the urban property industry, the significance of urban transportation facilities is not hard to work out. Roads and expressways and subways are not built to make life easier and better for people. They are not even built for the sole benefit of the car manufacturers and the road contractors.

Urban transportation facilities are built by city governments because they are one of the basic, essential services required by urban property. You have to have access from one building to the others in a city just as you have to have sewer and water facilities in those buildings. Without this access, a piece of urban land would be virtually worthless. With it, the land can support a house or a factory or an office building and so becomes a valuable piece of urban property.

Property and transportation

The basic determinant of the value of a piece of urban land is the amount of money its owner can make by renting it out to someone to use. The access people have to this land, the ease with which they can get to it from elsewhere in the city, has a major effect on what they are prepared to pay to use it. Its access and the use to which it can be put according to city regulations, then, are the two factors that really determine the value of a given piece of urban land. That is where the interests of the property industry connect up with urban transportation policy; transportation policy is really policy about the access people have to specific pieces of land in the city, and that in turn is policy about how valuable that land will be to the property investor who owns it.

Improving the accessibility of all pieces of private property in a city would have the effect of increasing the value of all of them. That is because transportation costs of all kinds would diminish, the amount of money remaining in the hands of businesses and families using urban accommodation of various kinds would increase and property owners would be able to demand and get higher rents for their properties. If big property owners could persuade a provincial government to put $100 million into new urban transportation facilities (instead of, say, into pointless grants to U.S. corporations for locating in the province when they would have located there anyway), the net result would be that the whole local property industry would be better off because all urban properties would be worth more. If, however, big property owners had to pay a share of the cost of improved transportation facilities themselves in the form of increased property taxes, they would be more careful about what kinds of new facilities they supported. They would want measures that would produce gains to them much larger than the losses they would encounter because taxes had to go up.

Some kinds of transportation policy do improve the accessibility of virtually all locations in the city to most people. That seems to have been the effect, for instance, of the installation of a computer to run Toronto's traffic lights. The traffic light system runs more efficiently with the computer than it did without it, and as a result everyone's bus and car travel is somewhat faster and easier. No one appeared to lose, and lots of people made small gains from that improvement.

Other kinds of transportation policies have different effects on the accessibility of different pieces of property. A new bridge built in the south part of Winnipeg across the

It's needed because it's used?

Ald. Art Phillips told a Third Crossing expert his arguments were "ridiculous" at a Vancouver-Quadra Liberal Association meeting Saturday.

The expert, Warnett Kennedy, urban planner and consultant for the $117 million tunnel planned to link the North Shore with downtown Vancouver, said the way to prove the usefulness of the tunnel is to build it — now.

"The proof of the pudding is in the eating", he said.

Vancouver Sun 14 Feb. 1972

Red River from the bottom of Osborne Street to St. Vital greatly improved the accessibility of St. Vital houses and the vacant land beyond to the city's downtown. It did nothing for the accessibility of North Winnipeg, except to make trips between North Winnipeg and St. Vital marginally easier.

The real connections between urban property and transportation policy appear at the level where transportation decisions begin to affect different areas and pieces of property differently. Very few transportation measures are as successful as Toronto's computer for traffic lights at improving the position of all urban property in a relatively equal way. Most have very specific benefits, to specific districts of the city and specific pieces of propety in terms of increasing property values and making possible new development. And that is why transportation policy is so important to the property industry. It is at least as crucial to the fortunes of developers and property investors as are city planning policies about where new development can take place.

Transportation programs amount to decisions about which vacant land is going to be developed, which built-up areas are going to be redeveloped, and who is going to be making money from the growth and development of the city. City planning decisions about permitted land uses deal with the same issues, and often land use planning and transportation planning are systematically linked together. The important difference is that *transportation planning is much tougher*. Once you build an expressway serving the west part of the city, you can't get the decision reversed after the next election and have the expressway wheeled around to serve not the west end but the east end. Once you build a commuter rail link spreading out east and west from the city, you are not suddenly going to abandon it in favour of a rail network running north and south. Land use decisions are much easier to change and fiddle with than are implemented decisions about transportation policy.

Urban transportation policy-making involves decisions about the general ease of access between properties located in the city. It means decisions about improvements in existing transportation facilities and new facilities. *These amount to decisions about where land values will be increased and where new development will be possible*. There are also decisions about which modes of transport will be encouraged by public policy — roads (cars, trucks, buses) *vs*. rail *vs*. subway *vs*. bicycles. Such decisions about modes are very important to construction companies and equipment suppliers, but they also affect the *kind* of access which a new transportation facility provides. A suburbs-to-downtown subway, for instance, provides access to a wider range of users than an expressway along the same route, because a wider range of people can afford to use subways than can afford to use expressways.

After the benefits, the costs

The property industry greatly benefits from new transportation facilities. Property investors see land values rise, developers find new land being opened up, and redevelopment possibilities emerge. There is still room for tremendous conflicts inside the industry over the appropriate kinds of new facilities and where they should be located, since these decisions determine which and how many industry investors and developers will stand to profit. On the whole, however, particularly for big-time industry operators, the kind of new facilities that are being built in Canadian cities means only benefits, higher profits and more development possibilities.

But as well as requiring vast expenditures of public funds, which are paid by all taxpayers and not just the property owners and developers who benefit the most, these new transportation facilities produce specific costs to certain groups in the city. The costs have become more glaring as the technology of the transportation engineers has become more brutal. Widening a residential street a few feet harms the people who live on it, but not irretrievably. It does not destroy the entire neighbourhood. But pushing an expressway through usually means the demolition of hundreds of houses and commercial structures. Families are displaced; neighbourhoods disappear; businesses have to move to less well located and more expensive structures, with many of the smaller businesses dying in the process. Building a subway line is a lot more disruptive (as well as a lot more expensive) than installing a streetcar line.

These specific costs of new transportation facilities are

Subways and land development

Former Toronto Real Estate Board research director Donald Kirkup writes about the impact of subways on land values and development:

For any major urban area, mass rapid transit as the basis of a balanced transportation system creates and enhances property values like nothing else on earth.

If an urban rapid transit system never earned a dime, it would pay for itself a thousand times over through its beneficial impact on real estate values and increased assessments. . . .

The Yonge Street subway, the first subway in Canada, was completed in 1955. . . .

The total cost of Canada's first subway, including right-of-way, rails, electrical distribution system, signal system and rolling stock was $67,000,000. This small investment ignited a $10 billion development explosion along the route from Front and York Streets to its northern terminal, Eglinton Avenue.

The appraised value of all the land and facilities in Metropolitan Toronto is now $50 billion. $15 billion of this appreciation in physical value has been added in the last ten years and two-thirds of this is attributable to the existence of the Yonge Street Subway.

Properties along the subway route doubled and tripled and sometimes increased as much as tenfold in value. Land prices would have increased anyway, but sales at $50 to $100 per square foot near the downtown stations became commonplace.

Boomtown pp.56-8

usually borne by families, tenants, and small businesses. Solid middle-class residential areas are normally protected while working-class areas are victimized. It is not the bank buildings in the centre of the downtown that are demolished for expressways, but the quarters of less wealthy industries, whose survival may well depend on remaining in the same district and in cheap-rent structures.

There are also more general costs associated with decisions about transportation facilities. These have been emphasized in the debates in many Canadian cities over controversial expressways — Edmonton's Jasper Parkway, Toronto's Spadina Expressway, Vancouver's East End Expressway proposed to run along Carrall Street. People are increasingly aware that when city hall puts $100 million into an expressway, it is putting public money into that specific kind of city that comes with expressways. The expressway is, in fact, the perfect symbol of the specialized city, where middle- and upper-income white-collar workers live in housing tracts on the outer edges of the city and drive their own cars to incredibly dense concentrations of office buildings right in the centre of the city every day. This is quite a different kind of urban living from the older pattern of city streets, where neighbourhoods are fairly self-sufficient for living, working and shopping, and reasonably high urban densities result in most day-to-day journeys being walking distance trips. Many people have decided that Developer City is not the city of the future for them, and by taking a strong stand against expressways they are taking effective action to block the pattern of urban development that expressways imply.

Transportation technologies

City politicians and their transportation-policy advisers have a pretty small bag of tricks which they use over and over again in the service of the property industry. Toronto and Montreal have experienced all the major technologies of transportation policy-makers, but other cities have had their share. Winnipeg, for instance, has been treated to the expressway ring technology with the Perimeter Highway which circles the city. But instead of brutalizing the city by driving the roads through built-up areas (as was proposed, for instance, for the so-called Motorway Box in London), Winnipeg's road builders let their common sense get the better of them and built their ring miles out from the city. This may have caused the least possible harm to the city, but for local planners and the local property industry the Perimeter Highway is "too far out" to do any good. Now Winnipeg planners are pressing for another expressway ring, this time inside the edges of the city at many points and much more harmful in its overall effects.

Expressways

Of the transportation technologies best suited to the interests of the property industry as it exists now, the prize example is the expressway. Expressways are generally built not singly but in "systems," and though the effects of a given system depend on the way it is set up, usually the logic of an expressway system is to increase the accessibility of all locations in the city to trucks and workers driving privately-owned cars. But the biggest impact on accessibility is in what an expressway system does for vacant land on the edge of the city and land in the downtown area. It makes the downtown city more easily accessible to middle- and upper-income white-collar workers living in the suburbs, whose income allows them to use their own car for transportation back and forth to work.

This downtown-outer suburbs orientation is very beneficial for downtown property owners and developers, because

Bridges and property development

A revealing example of the way in which transportation decisions are decisions about opening land up for development — and which also indicates how the property industry and city politics interlock — is this account in *Forever Deceiving You* of how plans for Vancouver's third crossing across Burrard Inlet to the North Shore were first formulated:

In the early 1950s, the provincial government set up the Committee for Metropolitan Highway Planning which had government representatives from Vancouver, New Westminster, and Burnaby. This group appointed a technical committee to begin studying access to the metropolitan area of Vancouver.

At about the same time, the First Narrows Bridge Company was becoming concerned about its real estate holdings on the North Shore. They realized that Lions Gate Bridge (the First Narrows bridge) was becoming quite congested and would not provide the necessary access if development were to continue on their lands and elsewhere in North Vancouver.

By making this concern known in government circles, they eventually helped to form the Committee on Burrard Inlet Crossings in March, 1953.

The eleven-man committee was made up of representatives from the First Narrows Bridge Company, the Burrard Inlet Bridge and Tunnel Company, and representatives from the municipalities surrounding Burrard Inlet. It is interesting to note that Mayor Carrie Cates, representing North Vancouver, and Reeve Bradley, representing the District of North Vancouver, were simultaneously the representatives of the Burrard Inlet Bridge and Tunnel Company.

Their technical committee was made up of Gerald Sutton-Brown, then Director of Planning for the City of Vancouver, and W. Richardson, an engineer representing the First Narrows Bridge Company. The purpose of the technical committee was to consider how many additional lanes would be needed, where they should be built, and when.

Based on *Forever Deceiving You:* The politics of Vancouver development. Vancouver: Vancouver Urban Research Group, 1972, p.15

it means that they can concentrate new extremely high-density office developments in the downtown and create very high land values indeed. The orientation also works extremely well for the corporate land speculators developing vacant land on the edges of the city, because it means that once their land becomes accessible to the central city, the market they can capture for it is a potentially very rich one — not ordinary working-class families or badly paid white-collar workers, but the better-paid white-collar workers who can afford to spend the most on new housing. If their white-collar jobs remained downtown and transportation to them remained difficult, these people would certainly stay in older built-up areas rather than moving to new ones farther from their work. The expressway system technology also works well for high-rise apartment developers, because land around each of the exits from the expressway becomes a natural spot to build high-rise apartments with easy and fast access to the downtown. Without this kind of transportation system, there wouldn't be the same logic to concentrating large numbers of people in any particular spot outside the centre of the city.

Another thing to note about expressway technology is how easily big-time corporate capital can link up with it. It produces enormous new high-rise office buildings in the

One of the many buildings scheduled for demolition for Vancouver's proposed East End Expressway which was halted, at least temporarily, by citizen opposition.

downtown, high-rise apartments along the route, and large assembled tracts of land developed by a single developer in the suburbs. There is almost no way for small-time businessmen who own the businesses they themselves work in to hook onto a system like that. They can't set up small restaurants along the route. If there are restaurants, they're sure to be part of a glossy chain controlled by a corporate restaurant group like Versafoods. Nor can small businessmen operate little gas stations and car repair shops along the route to catch business from people whose cars break down or need repairs. The service areas and the towing business are likely to be controlled by a single public or a private franchise.

Expressways are also valuable for developers of suburban shopping centres, especially of the large "regional" variety. Most shopping centre customers come fair distances by car in order to shop. Plugging a big suburban shopping centre into an expressway system is virtually the only way to generate enough business to make it profitable. Indeed, the best explanation given for the construction of the northern end of Toronto's Spadina Expressway scheme was that the 401-Spadina interchange was considered very important by Webb and Knapp, the developers of the Yorkdale shopping centre located next to that interchange, and by Eaton's, the other major property owner involved. Eaton's and Webb and Knapp thought that the interchange was required to get cars and people into Yorkdale, and that the Spadina Expressway itself was needed to bring customers in from mid-town and north Toronto. When it turned out that Yorkdale was immensely profitable *without* the proposed Spadina Expressway but *with* that 401-Spadina interchange serving it, these important property industry interests reduced their support for the scheme.

Bridges

Bridges are a clear-cut and easily-understood technique of transportation planners and city governments. It is perfectly obvious that building the Lion's Gate bridge connecting Vancouver to North Vancouver and West Vancouver was absolutely necessary for the development of these areas as residential districts occupied by people working in Vancouver. Without a bridge or tunnel connection, that land simply couldn't have been used the way it has been for urban purposes. The enormous investment required for the Lion's Gate bridge was well justified in the eyes of property investors owning land across the Burrard Inlet, because it produced a tremendous increase in the value of their holdings.

Transportation and land development

Meanwhile District of North Vancouver Mayor Ron Andrews warned that dunking the third crossing project will hinder the district's massive east end development scheme.

"We can't put another 40,000 or more people in that area unless there is a third crossing," Andrews said in an interview.

Andrews, chairman of the Greater Vancouver Regional District, said Central Mortgage and Housing Corporation is vitally interested in the district's east end development.

"I don't know what CMHC thinks about this dragging of feet on the crossing. But there can't be any development of a significant nature in the east end without the third crossing," Andrews said.

Vancouver Sun 12 Apr. 1972

Expressways and Cadillac Development

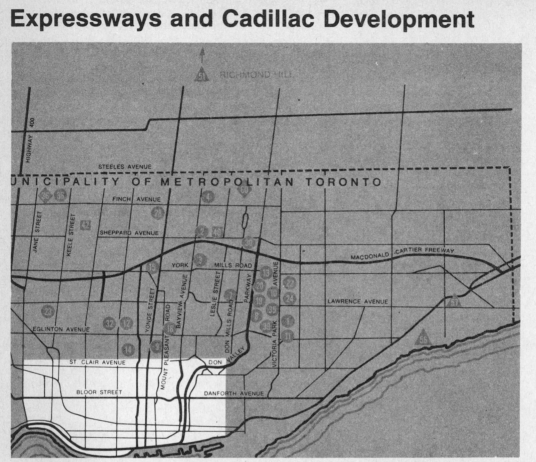

This map shows the location of Cadillac developments in Toronto. Note how many of them are clustered just to the east of the Don Valley Parkway, an expressway leading to the downtown, and along the 401 (Macdonald-Cartier), another expressway.

Winnipeg's perimeter highway, which circles the city: 'too far out' to do any good?

Every new bridge or tunnel has similar importance to property industry interests. Each time one is built, it brings capital gains for property investors and land owners whose holdings are suddenly made more accessible. The debate about the Third Crossing in Vancouver is only one example of this situation, where a major effect of the new crossing is to enhance the development prospects of land on the North Shore. While it can be argued that building new bridges simply makes it easier for people to get around the city, there are many other ways in which city government funds could be used more effectively to make movement easier on the one hand or less necessary on the other. If commercial development were less concentrated in Vancouver, for example, and most people who lived on the North Shore were able to work there as well, the issue of easy access to Vancouver's downtown would be less important and present transportation facilities might seem far less inadequate.

Subways and commuter rail

Subways and commuter rail services have a much better reputation than expressways amongst people who have confronted city government over transportation issues in Canada. There are good reasons for this preference. Subways and commuter rail systems are available to a much wider range of the population than competing expressway systems; that is because they are far cheaper to ride on, and because people don't have to be able to afford to operate a car to work in order to use them. They are also far less disruptive to existing neighbourhoods and the existing urban fabric when they are being constructed than are expressways and road systems. Subways do not require wholesale demolition of neighbourhoods, nor do they put fantastic barriers between what were once tightly-connected parts of a city. Subways and commuter rail systems are also far more economical in terms of resource use; with every driver they attract away from driving his car to work, they reduce the amount of pollution that goes into the city's air.

For suburban land developers, subways are not nearly so attractive as expressways are because they are rarely built to serve directly the vacant land where developers are working. Commuter rail, however, is a different matter; the existence of the CP commuter service west from Montreal through Dorval, Beaconsfield and Pointe Clair was obviously a major factor in permitting those areas to become middle-class suburbs for English-speaking white-collar workers commuting every day to downtown Montreal.

The subway systems built since World War II in Toronto and Montreal have served mainly already-built-up areas of the city. There are, however, some interesting exceptions. Montreal's subway was essential, for instance, in making possible intense land development on St. Helen's Island in the St. Lawrence, the Expo 67 site. Toronto's Yonge Street subway is being extended northwards almost to the boundary of Metro Toronto, and will be serving areas now in the process of being developed. On the whole, however, subway systems have not had the same attraction as expressways for suburban land developers.

For other property interests, however, subways and commuter rail transportation are very attractive. Downtown property owners and developers find them especially desirable, because the new access they provide for large numbers of people to the downtown means that the density of office development on downtown land can be increased. The result is that the number of downtown white-collar jobs (held by people who work in expensive high-rise office buildings) can increase rapidly. These workers can and will use subway facilities, though many would also use new expressways.

Another implication of subways and commuter rail systems as a transportation technology is that around subway stops and rail stations are spots of the city that have particularly easy access to the rest of the city, especially the downtown area. This pattern is quite different from the one that would exist if, for instance, the whole city were served by an efficient but evenly-spread-out bus network; then every point at the same distance from the centre would have relatively equal access to the centre and to the rest of the city. The "hot spots" created by subways and commuter rail become particularly attractive to residential high-rise developers. These developers, while they may like expressways, can do very well with subway systems.

It is important to notice that subway and commuter rail technology can have the same effect that expressways have

EXPRESSWAYS AND HIGH-RISE BUILDINGS: This cluster of high-rise apartments, standing on land where low-rise single-family houses previously stood, was built by a clever developer anticipating the completion of the Spadina expressway. Now that the expressway right-of-way sits there unused, his apartments have nothing like the locational advantage they would have if the roads were completed to the downtown.

on area specialization inside the city. Subways, like expressways, promote development that creates residential zones, industrial zones, and commercial zones within the city. This has almost totally replaced the earlier pattern of urban communities, which combined housing, offices, factories, and public spaces throughout the city.

The precise implications of the subway technology depend very much on exactly how it is used. Toronto's new subway, the Yonge Street extension, has stations every mile and a quarter at the north end, whereas at the south end there are stations every three or four blocks. That implies far less intensive land use at the north end of the route than at the south end, and implies too that people will be driving to the subway and then taking a long ride to the downtown, rather than using it for local trips as the system is used in the central city.

Road widenings

One of the very simple techniques used by city halls and transportation planners is road widenings. The point of widening a road is to make it carry more traffic, and so a general policy of road widening can improve access throughout the city for cars, trucks, and (though this seems to be usually unintended) buses.

Road widenings increase city-wide access, however, at the expense of the neighbourhoods and streets where they are carried out. On old-fashioned neighbourhood main streets, or "local shopping districts" as city planners call them, a road widening reduces sidewalk space for people and increases congestion for pedestrians as it reduces congestion for cars. On residential streets, the effects are even more serious. Sidewalks and boulevards get narrowed, and so become less desirable and less safe for kids to play on and for the neighbourhood to use. Increased traffic makes the street more dangerous. People often lose their front yards, and sometimes their porches, depriving them of the opportunity to do front yard gardening, to keep on friendly terms with their neighbourhood, and generally to enjoy neighbourhood and street life. A road widening needn't stop neighbourhood life completely, but it always makes it

Surrey, Delta councils seek third Fraser River crossing

Sun Staff Reporter

SURREY — Mayor William Vander Zalm said Thursday Surrey and Delta municipal councils will urge the provincial and federal governments to consider a third crossing of the Fraser River rather than a third crossing of Burrard Inlet.

Vander Zalm said the decision to approach the two governments was made at an afternoon joint meeting of both councils.

"There is so much controversy (over the Burrard Inlet crossing) that we agreed we would step in and take it while everyone else is arguing about it," Vander Zalm said.

"We feel we have good ammunition to support our petition," he added.

"To begin with, a bridge over Annacis Island, connecting Burnaby to North Delta, would serve a larger area and make land available for residential, commercial and industrial development.

"We also feel it would tend to keep traffic out of the city core," Vander Zalm added.

He said telegrams urging consideration of the proposal have been sent to both levels of government.

"This bridge would also be more in line with regional plans," Vander Zalm said.

Vancouver Sun 4 Feb. 1972

The Third Crossing and development

Rankin sparked the attack with charges that big interests and developers would reap most of the benefits from a third crossing.

"There's no way we can spend $400 million on freeways and then build a rapid transit system," said Rankin.

"We have turned our backs on making a freeway city . . . we should start immediately instead on planning rapid transit. The first thing we should do is beef up our bus system.

"I don't think there will be much difference in the comparative costs (between freeways, tunnel and rapid transit).

"But there will be a tremendous difference in the amount of lands that would be needed for freeways, compared with rapid transit alignments," said Rankin.

He said the argument of crossing backers that it would solve the North Shore's traffic problems "is outright nonsense."

He said big developments under way in downtown Vancouver, such as Project 200 and Block 42, would benefit from the crossing.

It would be the same story on the North Shore he suggested, with the crossing's main access routes ending up in shopping centres and major high-rise apartment projects.

Vancouver Sun 28 Jan. 1972

Works chief urges widening of 36 streets in central area

By N. JOHN ADAMS

City Works Commissioner Ray Bremner plans to make Yonge, Church, Jarvis and Sherbourne Streets one-way to expedite traffic movement in downtown Toronto.

His long-term plans, secret until today, include widening 36 streets in the central Yorkville planning district, including most of those in residential areas.

The controversial widening of Wellesley Street east of Yonge Street proposed by Mr. Bremner, is listed first in his summary of recommended widenings.

Yesterday, The Globe and Mail obtained a copy of the comprehensive plan to remodel the area's major road arteries and local residential streets.

The plan is contained in a 12-page letter Mr. Bremner sent in September, 1968, to Toronto Chief Planner Dennis Barker. Details of the plan were reaffirmed in a recent letter to Mr. Barker. In a report to his Planning Board this week, Mr. Barker termed the plan shortsighted and self-defeating.

He said growing traffic and density threaten the character of the midtown commercial, institutional and residential district.

Mr. Bremner's report said major roads should be widened to keep through traffic off residential streets. He would also widen most residential streets. He would also widen most residential streets, making many existing one-way streets two-way.

Toronto Star 12 Nov. 1972

Hidden widenings

This article reports on a common technique of transportation planners, which is to force people to accept an undesirable side-effect — street widening — in order to get something they want — regular maintenance of ordinary street surfaces.

The Inner City joint community committee has approved a capital budget of $11 million — $2.5 million more than the area's budget last year — but not before several councillors criticized the methods used to prepare the budget.

The most debated item was pavement widening with asphalt resurfacing or pavement reconstruction. Coun. Bill Norrie (ICEC — Kelvin) argued that this bound the hands of the council and presented residents of a street with an all or nothing choice. They must accept having their street widened or they could not have it resurfaced. The item should be broken down into two parts, widening and resurfacing.

Coun. Norrie's suggestion was not adopted, but after prolonged debate, in which it was repeatedly pointed out that residents and their councillors could appear before works and operations committee to have the two separated, that budget figure for such work was raised to $145,000 from $128,900.

Winnipeg Tribune 11 Feb. 1972

more difficult. Often too, a street loses its trees, generally large trees since widenings are most commonly done in older neighbourhoods, a real loss which street residents care greatly about. All this is taken as sentimental nonsense by transportation planners and city planners, but that is because they have no knowledge of the delicate and intricate possibilities of street and neighbourhood life in areas where people still have front yards, sidewalks, boulevards and porches.

One-way systems

Another quite simple technique of transportation planners is to develop one-way systems out of city streets. Like road widenings, one-way street systems improve access for city-wide traffic, but they achieve this at the cost of changing the nature of the streets involved. There can't be lots of stopping and starting, and temporary parking, and all the other normal activities of city streets on one-way streets, because one-way streets must function as sub-expressways. The local function of the street is sacrificed for a city-wide gain, at the expense of local residents (who find traffic volumes, noise, etc., increased and the road more dangerous) and people who use the buildings on the street (who find crossing the street, for instance, more difficult and dangerous).

Streetcars

It is interesting to contrast the urban transportation technologies that are now popular with transportation planners and city governments with those that they regard as "old-fashioned" and "outdated," such as streetcars. Toronto retains some of its streetcars but other Canadian cities have abandoned them. Even in Toronto, nothing remains of the suburban radial streetcar system that served commuters before automobiles took over.

Streetcar lines have a higher capacity to carry passengers than trolleybus or ordinary bus lines, but a lower capacity than subways. They are, however, much cheaper to install than subways. They are less disruptive to build, and involve no demolition or destruction of the existing city. They place no barriers into the city fabric, as expressways do. They are accessible to a wide range of people, because they are relatively cheap to use. But their operation hinders the circulation of other traffic on the street, more so than buses for instance. So the benefits of a streetcar transportation system are to some extent obtained at the expense of car transportation in the city.

Streetcar lines were used in the late 1880s and early 1900s to open up tracts of land for urban development, and their technology is associated with the suburban houses built on relatively small lots in grid street patterns of the period. Streetcar lines do not produce hot points of land easily accessible to the rest of the city as do subways (around subway stops) or expressways (around expressway exits). Instead they produce a band of land along which people can have relatively good access to the city, with this access gradually declining as you move out from the city centre or back from the streetcar tracks.

No doubt the most telling deficiency of streetcar technology for transportation planners is the sacrifice in automobile circulation that results from the use of streetcars on the streets. Subways, which in many other ways are similar in their characteristics to streetcars, do not have this drawback; transportation planners don't have to choose so

Streetcars are proving they're kings of road

Streetcars, earmarked a few years ago for oblivion by 1980, are on the verge of a major comeback in Toronto.

The huge, pollution-free vehicles, singly or in two-car trains, can churn their way through heavy downtown traffic more effectively than buses or trolley coaches.

Streetcars are ideal transit vehicles for reserved lanes as they've been proving for years in the median of the Queensway in Toronto's west end.

So the end of the line for Toronto's 394 streetcars is nowhere in sight.

And no one at the TTC, least of all J. H. Kearns, general manager of operations, is sorry.

"Pound for pound," he told The Star, "the streetcar is the best vehicle we've ever had in the transit field."

The commission last month accepted Kearns' recommendation for a major program to repair 50 streetcars a year at a total cost of $800,000.

Kearns also suggested that the commission might buy 170 new streetcars for the heavily travelled King and Queen lines.

Toronto's streetcars, built between 1946 and 1951, have operated long past their designed life-spans of 12 years and most of the units are deteriorating rapidly.

Spare parts have been scarce for years. The TTC makes many of its own or has manufacturers make them to its specifications.

A new streetcar has already been designed by Hawker-Siddeley Canada Ltd. with the help of TTC engineers.

Toronto Star 18 Dec. 1971

clearly between transit riders and car drivers when they push public investment in a subway system. One of the boasts of Toronto's traffic planners was that, after the installation of the Bloor Street subway line and the removal of the street-cars from Bloor Street, more people could move along the route by subway and car, and everyone got where they were going faster.

Neighbourhoods for walking

Another way of dealing with the problem of access in cities is to build communities where people can carry on most of their daily life within a relatively restricted geographical area, and so get around by walking. This kind of city life resembles town or village life. Old working-class neighbourhoods in Canadian cities are often of this type. You find houses on relatively small lots, so that density in the neighbourhood is reasonably high and lots of people are within walking distance of neighbourhood facilities like shops, churches and schools. A network of streets with sidewalks provides this access; they are usually laid out in a basic grid system, with short blocks and many alternate routes from one place to another. Usually too there are wide differences amongst streets in the area; some are wide and well travelled, others are quite narrow, some are on major routes and others are dead-end, leading nowhere.

In addition to houses, neighbourhoods of this kind contain a wide range of community facilities like shops, restaurants, bars, offices and so on, as well as churches, parks, schools and other public institutions. There are also buildings that accommodate businesses and industries where people from the neighbourhood can find work close to home. Next door to where I live, for instance, is an enormous peanut warehouse, which employs one or two men in ordinary times and a dozen at busy times. Around the corner is the Sleepmaster Master Mattress Factory, employing perhaps twenty people, many of them women, at very low wages and in the bad work conditions usually found in this kind of industry. The point is that local people can and often do find jobs in these places, and when they do, their $70 a week is worth much more to them in terms of money and time than if they had to travel across the city by public transit to the same job. If the only job they could get required them to have a car, they might well not be able to afford to take it at such low wages.

Neighbourhoods for walking are based on small-time capitalism, with many small property owners holding small chunks of land in the area. None of them is wealthy enough to own a large portion of the area; none is wealthy enough to own all the commercial buildings serving the neighbourhood. Everyone depends on the streets and the sidewalks, and uses that basic public framework.

Neighbourhoods of this kind were not designed self-consciously by transportation planners, but it is possible to recognize the attitude towards transportation implicit in them. Generally they minimize transportation needs and expenditures; people don't have to go very far for most of the things they do, and they can travel those distances by walking, the simplest and cheapest way of getting around the city. City-wide transportation needs are diminished in this kind of generalized neighbourhood, because most of the basic functions found in the city as a whole can also be found right in the local area. The city as a whole can then manage with relatively simple and cheap transportation facilities.

Neighbourhoods for walking are not, however built any more. The property industry has developed the techniques of specialized enclaves within the city, and with vast amounts of capital available to them they have developed architectural and planning devices that enable large tracts of real property to be owned and controlled by a single property-owner instead of a host of small ones. Thus, for instance, new towns are developed by one developer, high-rise apartments are built where hundreds of people are tenants of the same owner, and shopping centres make all the shop owners tenants of an owner who skims off a good deal of the profits of the store owners in the form of rent payments.

The property industry has apparently discovered that these techniques are more suited to the kind of capital available to the industry and produce larger profits than developments on a smaller scale, which can plug into existing basic public facilities like streets rather than internal-

Continued on page 188

WHAT A ROAD WIDENING CAN DO: These two Toronto streets were built at about the same time. They had similar houses, with similar front yards, trees, lawns and sidewalks. In the 1950s, Toronto transportation planners scheduled them both for widening. Carlton Street east of Parliament, on the left, was saved by protests of residents. Shuter Street, on the right, got its widening. Note how the Shuter houses no longer have front yards or trees.

Transportation plans for Vancouver

The Committee for Metropolitan Highway Planning, set up by the B.C. provincial government, started its technical committee gathering data for a transportation study of the Vancouver area in 1956. In July 1957, the technical group was authorized to make a final report.

For the next two years, technical reports were issued leading up to the final plan produced in 1959, "Freeways with Rapid Transit — A study on highway planning." Working mainly from present and projected traffic volume statistics, the report recommended 45 miles of new expressways. Public transit supporters were offered a proposal for buses which would travel on the expressways. Included in the package was a second crossing of the First Narrows where the Lion's Gate bridge is located. The price tag placed on the total scheme was $500 million.

The first stage was for a $340 million expressway system linking the new First Narrows crossing with a right-of-way around the west and south side of the downtown and east to the Port Mann bridge.

This plan was never officially adopted by Vancouver city council, but it seems nevertheless to have been accepted by city hall. One indication of this is that the city began buying up land in the West End along the downtown bypass route proposed in the plan, and a development freeze was placed on other properties also on this route. This action produced some resistance from citizen groups who complained both about the proposed road and about the council's secrecy.

In March 1960 a variation on the overall Vancouver plan was suggested by the engineering and consulting firm, Swan Wooster Engineering. Swan Wooster proposed a 4-lane bridge across the First Narrows and an 8-lane expressway through Stanley Park. This was claimed to be $18 million cheaper than the original proposal. No official action was taken on this alternative by the park board or by city council.

The provincial government pressed ahead with further studies of the proposed first stage of the original overall plan. The province's committee suggested that an outside consulting organization, Stanford Research Institute, be hired to consider how the first stage could be financed. There was some resistance from suburban councils because the new study did not allow for consideration of alternative routings. And Vancouver city hall, perhaps thinking that their West End land acquisitions were a bit premature, decided in 1961 to dispose of property they had acquired only a short time earlier.

A provincial government study of rail and rapid transit for the Vancouver area was released in March 1962 which concluded that there 'wasn't enough demand' to justify rail rapid transit in the area. With this evidence to support their neglect of alternatives to expressways, Vancouver city council voted unanimously to restart the Stanford study which had been temporarily halted. And, two years later, in 1964, the Stanford report was released. It repeated the original 1959 plan for a $345 million expressway system, with those same expressway buses thrown in.

In 1965, the first official step was taken towards approving a variant of the 1959-64 plan. In January of that year, the board of administration recommended to city council that a waterfront expressway be approved linking the proposed new First Narrows crossing to the proposed new East-West Freeway running east from the downtown to join up to the Trans-Canada highway which now stops at the Burnaby-Vancouver boundary. This waterfront alignment was different from the "Ocean Park" alignment proposed by the Stanford study a year earlier.

City council approved the waterfront expressway in principle. Their official reasons for preferring the new route were interesting. One was that it would help promote Project 200, the CPR's big downtown redevelopment scheme. A second was that it would cost less because the CPR might donate some of the needed right-of-way land. A third was that it would not have the same adverse affects on Stanley Park.

In 1965 another concrete step was taken towards

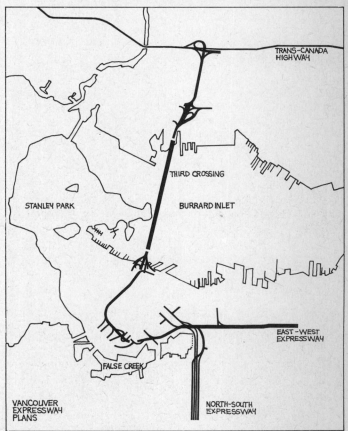

This map shows the expressways planned for Vancouver. These plans would provide a new high-speed route through the city, and would greatly improve access from the North Shore, the east and the south to Vancouver's downtown.

implementing the plan, although it was not described that way at the time. Vancouver ratepayers approved in September that year a $10 million money bylaw authorizing city hall to replace the "structurally unsafe" Georgia Viaduct. An outside firm of consultants was brought in to design a new viaduct which would be incorporated into the overall city expressway plan.

In August 1966 a new consulting firm was hired to prepare a "general" transportation plan for Vancouver, in conjunction with the work already being done on the Georgia Viaduct. In fact, however, the new consultants were hired to locate the waterfront expressway and to design a waterfront expressway running from the Georgia Viaduct east through the Strathcona urban renewal area. Consideration was to be given to route changes specifically in order to get the expressway inside the urban renewal area, to take advantage of possible extra federal government financial assistance.

In July 1967 these consultants proposed a route for the waterfront freeway along Carrall Street, and city council approved the recommendation. But this decision produced a barrage of public opposition, and the politicians staged a tactical retreat by asking their consultants to consider all alternative routes. This new directive, however, turned out to mean studying just one alternative route, along Gore Street. Finally in January 1968, city council abandoned its Carrall Street alignment but approved construction of the new Georgia Street Viaduct.

Following this decision there was further planning activity commissioned by city council. Behind-the-scenes financial negotiations were going on regarding the new crossing of the First Narrows, but these appeared not to be successful. In 1971, Vancouver city council voted to hold a plebiscite to obtain voter approval for approach roads for the new First Narrows crossing. But by 1972 the politicians had retreated from any proposal to hold a plebiscite and were planning to spend $3 million of the city's general revenue for the roads. Public protests forced city hall to delay this action for public hearings, and later there were more proposals for an area-wide plebiscite on the crossing issue.

Evidently what was happening all this time is that Vancouver's transportation planners, politicians and administrators were moving slowly but steadily towards implementation of the overall city transportation plan first formulated in 1959 and revised (but mostly repeated) in 1964. As things stand, Vancouver is in line for exactly the same kind of transportation policies that are being advocated for most Canadian cities: a small amount of new public transit, enough to blunt the force of critics, and lots of new expressways.

Based on *Forever Deceiving You:* The politics of Vancouver Development. Vancouver Urban Research Group, 1972, pp.15-21

Lion's Gate bridge, Vancouver

The Second Narrows crossing, Vancouver

izing them into shoppers' malls and high-rise apartment corridors.

Along with this basic change in the way cities are being developed have come the techniques of transportation planners, which involve moving large numbers of city residents relatively long distances by means of expensive equipment like cars, subways and commuter rail lines. The techniques involved in the old neighbourhoods for walking, which were built 60 or 80 years ago, have been largely abandoned, and are now hardly even understood by professionals.

Transportation plans

Comprehensive transportation plans, incorporating some or all of the current technologies used by transportation planners, are the final technique we should examine. Most cities have overall transportation plans, and many have more than one. Sometimes these are drawn up by city planning departments; more often, they are produced by the roads and works departments of city hall. The most common pattern, however, is for a basic comprehensive transportation plan to be drawn up by a team of sophisticated consultants who apply their formulas to a city and produce a plan that looks very much like the plans that have been produced for every other city. Most Canadian cities have had area transportation studies carried out, and most of these have led to plans known as MTARTS (Metropolitan Toronto Area Regional Transportation Study), WATS (Winnipeg Area Transportation Study) or something similar.

Typically these overall transportation plans propose a whole new network of expressways for the city. These may be linked to existing city streets, drastically "improved" by being widened or made one-way. There also may be plans for parking garages to hold the additional cars travelling on the new roads once they reach their destinations, usually in the central city. Generally a number of alternative plans are proposed, going from one "extreme" of a new total expressway system to the other "extreme" of a new total subway system. Each alternative is analysed, usually only according to simple engineering criteria like the time taken for an average trip and other indicators of engineering "efficiency." Direct construction costs are sometimes estimated, but external costs (like the cost to someone living a few hundred feet from a new expressway, resulting

from the noise and pollution it produces) are rarely mentioned. Usually no attempt is made to evaluate in a sophisticated way the real costs or real benefits of these plans, in order to see whether their enormous construction and maintenance costs are really worthwhile for the citizens of the city. That is not surprising, of course, because whether or not in the end they are beneficial to ordinary city residents, these projects are almost certain to be beneficial to the local property industry.

The comprehensive transportation planners usually recommend what they call a "balanced" transportation system, one somewhere in between the "extreme" proposals. Generally the "balanced" system involves a tremendous amount of new expressway construction, and enough subway construction to appease people who like public transit or who argue that expressways serve only well-off suburban commuters.

Where these overall transportation plans have been drawn up, they are often — but not always — made public. It is hard to take them seriously, because they are so simple-mindedly similar. According to the transportation engineers, whatever your problems are, the answer is lots of expressways, and maybe some subways too. Subway proposals are not limited to the biggest Canadian cities. Why shouldn't Edmonton have one, and Winnipeg? And why shouldn't they, according to the transportation planners, have lots of expressways too?

One of the absolutely crucial facts about city hall and transportation planning, however, is that often the real plans are *not* made public. Often the bureaucrats, in connivance with at least a few of the politicians, have secret plans which they do their best to keep secret as long as possible. They go about implementing them on a piecemeal basis, one piece at a time, without ever pointing out publicly how the pieces fit together. They get city hall to implement their plan bit by bit, so that by the time potential opponents — including people who will be directly hurt by these plans — wake up to what is going on, city hall is too far along with the project and its commitment is too great to be able to stop it.

Secret planning is extremely common in the transportation field, because of course the more information that falls into the hands of ordinary citizens the more public opposition there is likely to be to what the planners want to do.

RIPE FOR REDEVELOPMENT: These railway lands, located to the north of Winnipeg's central area, will become available for redevelopment when the plans which have been drawn up to relocate Winnipeg's rail services from the central city area to the fringes are implemented. Rail relocation has now been tied into the plan to build an extensive expressway network. In the distance is the Arlington bridge. Early in the history of the new one-city government in Winnipeg, politicians were expressing their support for the plan to replace this bridge with a new expressway-scale bridge which could be part of the proposed expressway network. Once constructed, the new crossing would function just as Vancouver's new Georgia Viaduct is functioning now, as a pressure for building the expressways which would connect into it.

WATS for Winnipeg

A general transportation plan for Winnipeg, published in 1968 and called WATS (for Winnipeg Area Transportation Study), is apparently now the effective basis of official transportation policy-making in the city.

Though its impact would be enormous, most Winnipeg residents have very little idea indeed of what WATS involves. And many people who do know of the plan's existence refuse to believe it will ever be implemented. They should take heed of the enormous persistence transportation planners and city hall officials have shown in other cities where they have spent 15 or 20 years in the slow but steady implementation of plans of this kind.

The accompanying map shows the new expressways which are part of the WATS plan. The map indicates a considerable number of bits-and-pieces expressways, which don't quite carry through to form a complete expressway network. Where the expressways on the plan end, however, they connect into major city arterial roads which would function like sub-expressways. So the network is really much more complete than the map suggests.

Though the WATS study considered a number of alternative plans, its recommended scheme was the usual kind of plan which planners call "balanced" — meaning that it included both a large amount of new expressways, and provision for some money to be spent on subway-type rapid transit. The WATS recommended scheme calls for the construction of 119 additional miles of streets and expressways in Winnipeg. It would increase the proportion of total travel done by car from the present level of 60 per cent to 70 per cent. Perhaps more significant, it would increase the use of cars for trips to and from the downtown from the present level of 47 per cent to 55 per cent. So the plan is heavily weighted towards encouraging greater reliance on car transportation.

This is even more so considering the proposed phasing for the WATS plan. The planners did write a subway into their recommended scheme, and costed it at $130 million. But they recommended that no large sums of money be spent on improving public transit until 1982, while in the period from 1968-81 they called for an expenditure of $122 million on new streets, and *$252 million on expressways*. And in the 1982-91 period when Winnipeg was spending $130 million on a subway the planners proposed the city also invest $178 million in expressways.

Should the politicians decide in the 1980s that they couldn't afford both more expressways and a subway — not an unlikely prospect, given the enormous cost of either facility — it would not be difficult to delete the subway from the plan. It would be extremely difficult to delete the expressways whose construction is scheduled for 1982-91, because they are necessary to link up to those which would already be built by that time, and which would have cost $252 million in public funds. It is hard to escape the impression that the planners were doing everything they could to guarantee that, if only part of their total plan were implemented, it would be the expressway part.

The enormous cost of these new transportation facilities may help persuade many people that they will never be built because the city cannot afford them. Perhaps Winnipeg residents would not be so complacent if they looked at the more recent plan which incorporates the relocation of main railway lines into the WATS expressway plans and which shows in detail how it all can be done. While city politicians may be vague about their position on the matter, and while provincial politicians express reservations about the suburban belt-line expressway shown on the map, officials are busy going about the implementation of the plan.

Financing the WATS plan Expenditures					TOTAL
	68-71	72-26 (in millions)	77-81	82-91	68-91
Streets	$53	$ 41	$ 28	$ 57	$179
Expressways	$22	$101	$129	$178	$429
Rapid transit	$12	$ 7	$ 8	$130	$158
TOTAL	$87	$149	$165	$364	$767
Average per year	$22	$ 30	$ 33	$ 36	$ 32

Winnipeg Area Transportation Study. Winnipeg: 1968

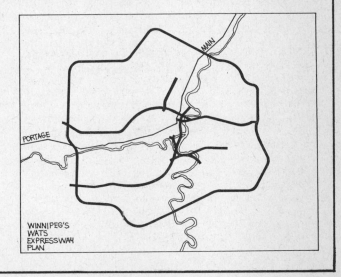

WINNIPEG'S WATS EXPRESSWAY PLAN

The whole history of transportation planning in Vancouver illustrates this point, since both planners and politicians appear to have quite a clear conception of the transportation system they are implementing piece by piece without the city council ever having formally adopted any scheme. In Winnipeg, the master transportation plan, which seems to be the basis of city decision-making, is not exactly secret; copies of the relevant documents (the 1968 WATS plan and the more recent study of railway relocation) are available to the public, for example, in the provincial legislative library. But the decisions that are being taken about proceeding with these plans are being made at secret meetings of bureaucrats, and for all that Winnipeg residents know about these plans they might as well be secret. In Toronto, the history of the Spadina Expressway is the history of transportation planning kept secret absolutely as long as possible in order to forestall possible opposition to the scheme.* More recently, it took a leak by a city planner to a newspaper to bring out into the open a plan by Toronto's works commissioner for an enormous program of street widenings and one-way systems in the central city. And it took tremendous efforts from opposition politicians to drag out even a few details of Metro Toronto's transportation planners' secret scheme to widen east-west midtown Dundas Street into a six-lane roadway crossing the city, serving as a sub-expressway and a partial substitute for the currently cancelled Midtown Expressway.

The property industry and transportation policy

When we see that new transportation facilities are directly related to new land development, redevelopment, and increasing property values, it is no surprise to look behind city hall transportation policies and find the local property industry. Nevertheless it is extremely important to do this, because it establishes clearly the fact that expressways are being proposed and built not because transportation engineers are too stupid to realize what damage expressways do to cities, *but because expressways mean money to specific powerful interests inside the property industry which now control city government.*

The common technologies of urban transportation policy are directly linked to the technologies of the property industry. New development follows the familiar lines of high-rise apartments, suburban housing developments on large lots, shopping centres, industrial parks, extremely intensive high-density office development in the downtown. The larger and faster-growing cities have more of this than the smaller and slower-growing, but everywhere the formula is being used. Canadian cities look more and more the same, more and more like Toronto and Montreal, more and more like Chicago and Los Angeles. In Vancouver, this trend is obvious and well-established. In Winnipeg, only the early signs are visible. All seem destined, if the property industry has its way, to become Developer City.

Transportation policy at city hall is a direct result of the development techniques of the property industry. Just as city planners regulate the supply of new land and zone the city so as to create special functional enclaves with industry here, commerce there and residential somewhere else, so transportation planners produce the expressways, one-way street systems, widened roads and subways necessary to support these kinds of development and to make more of them possible. These transportation plans clearly hurt many people in existing city neighbourhoods, and they are harmful to small-time property investors like store owners who see their business slashed when their street becomes a one-way throughway or when they are expropriated to make way for a widened mid-city mini-expressway. But they directly benefit the property industry, which has captured control of city government.

For the property industry the technology of neighbourhoods for walking, where communities inside the city are largely self-sufficient, is out-dated and long-gone. So long as the industry is making the decisions about how cities will develop, transportation policy will consist of plans for subways, expressways, sub-expressways and the other current techniques the transportation engineers know so well. If power at city hall were in other hands, clearly the techniques of transportation planning would change dramatically. Sidewalks would be widened instead of roads; bicycle paths would be built; lanes on roads would be reserved for buses; streetcars would probably be reinstituted; and simultaneously the way that the city is being developed and redeveloped would change so that travelling back and forth to work and to shop would become less necessary for people. While power is firmly in the property industry's hands, however, bold and perhaps irreversible transportation plans using the current techniques of the planners are being implemented slowly, steadily, and often stealthily by city hall for the greater good of the property industry and their allies in the auto industry, the construction materials industry, and the "Good Roads" associations.

---

*For documentation on Winnipeg, see *Prairie Dog Press*, issue 1, July 1972; on Vancouver, *Forever Deceiving You*, p. 15 ff.; on Toronto's Spadina Expressway, *The Bad Trip* by David and Nadine Nowlan.

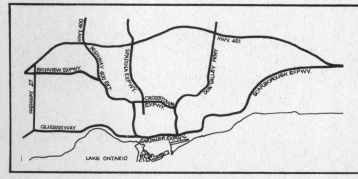

Expressways for Toronto

This map shows both existing and proposed expressways in the Toronto area. The system was originally developed in the MTARTS study, similar to Winnipeg's WATS study. A comparison of the two maps will show that the studies produced remarkably similar recommendations for expressway systems.

For the present, the only proposed expressway shown on this map which is supposed to be going ahead is the Scarborough expressway, an extension of the Gardiner expressway. The Spadina is officially "cancelled" for the present, as is the Crosstown, which threatened the powerful Rosedale neighbourhood. But with its inner and outer ring pattern, the system as shown has a clear internal logic, and it would be surprising if all transportation planners and all politicians ever abandon hope of implementing it in full.

Taken in front of Toronto's city hall, this photo was used for a citizen group poster in 1971. After everyone was assembled in front of the photographer, it turned out that there were three more letters than there were people to hold them. So three kids on the skating rink in front of the city hall were enlisted to help, which is why there are three people with skates on.

Charlotte Sykes Reprinted with permission

Dealing with citizen groups and their demands ranks with land-use planning and transportation as one of the major policy issues facing city governments across Canada. Citizen groups have been around for a long time, and politicians and officials are accustomed to them in at least one form, ratepayer groups from solid middle-class residential areas. But there are more citizen organizations today than there used to be, and from a wider range of neighbourhoods. They are making tougher demands on city politicians, their tactics are improving, and they are proving less willing to accept defeat or a token victory and to give up than they used to be. They are also often much better organized, and on occasion they even have professional organizers working for them.

The basic city hall-citizen conflict

The reason citizen groups pose a policy problem for city hall is that there is a serious divergence between what citizens think they have a right to expect from city government and what they find themselves actually getting. People expect city hall to provide democratic, responsible government. They expect their elected representatives to pay attention to the interests and wishes of the citizenry, and to protect and promote those interests in their policies and decisions. Some people believe that this is in fact the way city government usually works. Others think that city hall doesn't operate this way at all. But virtually every ordinary citizen is agreed that this is what city hall *should* do.

The conflict between city hall and ordinary city residents arises because city hall all too obviously does not put the interests of the citizenry first. As we have seen, city politicians do not respect and represent the views of their constituents, nor are they really accountable to the people who elect them. Everywhere the property industry has a comfortable city hall majority of politicians committed to representing the interests and views, not of the voters, but of the industry. That city hall majority is accountable and responsive, not to the people, but to the industry.

Given this situation, citizens usually come into conflict with city government almost as soon as they begin making requests of city hall. Whatever people may have previously thought about city government, once they become part of an organized citizen group and make proposals to city hall, they learn from immediate personal experience that city hall pays little attention to the views and interests of ordinary citizens. They see that it is the developers and other real estate interests that get the careful consideration and not the citizenry. They also begin to think that, if they want to have some influence over what city hall does, they are going to have to develop some political muscle to force the politicians and bureaucrats to respect their interests. The way things are set up now, they cannot expect it to happen automatically.

Where citizen groups come from

People come up against city hall in many different circumstances. Often the encounter is an individual one, when for instance a home owner wants to find out why fixing up his basement has increased his taxes and his assessment. On other occasions a group of people in the same area find themselves with a common complaint. They learn that their street is to be widened and the trees cut down, or they are told that city hall has marked their area for expropriation because the houses are "slums."

When people have individual problems with city hall, they usually try to deal with them on an individual basis. They talk to city bureaucrats, they ask their local politician to intervene, they write letters to the newspaper and so on. Often when people have a problem that is shared by many other people, they still try first to solve it individually. When they fail, or when the problem is obviously a serious and immediate one affecting lots of people, they form groups. Often they begin in a very informal way; someone starts talking to his neighbours, and together they decide to call a meeting. Sometimes a fledgling group gets a community organizer who works with them to get the group going. On occasion organizers arrive on the scene and start organizing a local group where no one in the area had taken that step himself.

Almost always the basis of a citizen group is some problem people find they have with city hall, with some other government body, or with a local factory or business. Problems and threats that loom up suddenly are much more likely to spark organizations than problems people have lived with so long that they have stopped being upset about them. Residents of one of Winnipeg's urban renewal areas had lived for years with junk yards and scrap metal dealers on their street, until city hall threatened them with an urban renewal plan. Once people got together to talk about the area and the city's plan, they also found themselves doing something about the junk yards. Most city neighbourhoods, apart from the most solid and well-protected, have long-standing grievances where their interests are regularly being neglected by city hall. Organizers who want to start citizen groups and who are able to identify people's problems have little trouble finding issues to organize around, particularly in working-class neighbourhoods. Everyone thought that Toronto's Riverdale area had few serious problems until some full-time organizers began working in the area. Before long, the organizers had identified two problems that concerned lots of people. One was the lack of adequate local bus service, which made it impossible for older people and difficult for many other residents to get around because they had to walk as far as half a mile to the nearest streetcar or subway. The other was the parking problem. Because most houses in the area lacked garages or back lanes, people had to park on the street overnight. This produced a regular flow of traffic tickets that cost area residents $100,000 a year. Both problems were tackled by the citizen groups established in the area by the organizers.

Citizen groups vary tremendously. Some have extremely elitist structures, with power concentrated in the hands of a few people who make all the decisions. Others are very democratic, doing their best to involve as many people as possible in the important decision-making. Groups differ according to the areas they represent; there are exclusively working-class groups, mixed groups containing working-

How citizen groups get started

These brief histories of Vancouver citizen groups, taken from *Forever Deceiving You: The Politics of Vancouver Development*, a handbook on Vancouver city politics and citizen groups published in 1972, give some idea of the ways in which these groups get going and the kind of issues they get involved in.

West End Community Council

Over the years since 1948, the West End Community Council has fought a never-ending battle to preserve life and sanity for the residents of the densest population area in Canada.

Years ago, residents fought for a new King George High School in a new location and finally won. Adult education was included for the first time in the new high school, after requests from local residents. And in the last couple of years, the school has been used after school hours as a community centre complex.

The council fought to develop Nelson Park and to save Sunset Beach as a natural park, and won in both cases, although the Parks Board may finally be getting the restaurant they wanted in the Crystal Pool complex.

They worked against street widenings and car parking on both sides of residential streets (at one time the city wanted to make many residential streets in the West End into four lanes). This linked into the Save-the-Trees campaign, which all finally resulted in the city re-thinking its concept of through streets in the West End. A plan being aired now is to re-route most through traffic through Robson, Denman, and Davie Streets.

Another fight was against freeway plans through Stanley Park and proposed widening of Nelson Street as a throughway to a new bridge. Now the fight is against the Third Crossing and its related horrors.

Strathcona Property Owners' and Tenants' Association

SPOTA formed in 1968 in response to the city's Urban Renewal Scheme II for the area. After many long months of work and negotiation with federal, provincial, and municipal governments, the emphasis in the area was changed from total redevelopment (demolition and rebuilding) to the renovation of old houses.

SPOTA continues to work on these issues. The funds for renovation have only just come through after a seven month wait, and much delay from the city.

North West Point Grey Homeowners' Association

This Homeowners' group was formed fourteen years ago, mainly to preserve the area for single family dwellings against the onslaught of apartment developments.

Lately they have been working with the Jericho Park Committee to try to keep the 38 acres between Jericho Beach and 4th Avenue as parkland, instead of being zoned for multiplex housing.

Save Stanley Park Entrance Committee

This organization was formed to fight the Four Seasons Development when the federal government was faced with the decision whether or not to allow the transfer of water leases from an old project to the Four Seasons project. The group, composed of individuals from all over the city, was unsuccessful in convincing the federal government to stop this transfer. It was successful, however, a short time later, in convincing Council to hold a public plebiscite over the issue of the city buying up the land for use as a park.

The plebiscite, although not won, did by a vote of 51 per cent in favour of buying the land for park use show that the city ratepayers supported the fight against the Four Seasons proposal (a vote of 60 per cent in favour was needed to pass the money bylaw). The federal government then withheld one vital water lease needed by the project, effectively stalling it.

Forever Deceiving You: The politics of Vancouver Development. Vancouver: Vancouver Urban Research Group, 1972 pp.61-75

class and middle-class people, exclusively middle-class groups and so on. Class makeup affects a group's understanding and analysis of its situation and the tactics its uses. Groups also differ in terms of the status of their members concerning property ownership, so there are home owners' groups, tenants' organizations, and groups that include both. Most citizen groups represent a specific community or neighbourhood, but some are built on a broader geographic base, and try to include, for instance, all public housing tenants or all people affected by a large expressway project.

The first aim of a genuine citizen group (and there are phoney ones, which pretend to be locally based while really being organized by city hall or by some welfare agency for their own purposes) is self-protection, guarding the interests of the group's constituency from harm at the hands of city hall. Most groups never go beyond articulating and defending this first aim. Some, however, go on to try to promote the group's common interests, and to get decisions and policies that not only protect the group from harm but also obtain for it some tangible benefit. Bus service for Toronto's Riverdale area was a benefit for the neighbourhood, though in fact most people saw it as nothing more than what they had an absolute right to expect from the public transit authority. A new park for an already well-served middle-class neighbourhood is an example of the kind of benefit another citizen group might try to obtain.

A challenge to the property industry

Citizen groups of all kinds are a threat to the property industry because they seek power at city hall, power to influence decision-making so that city government will take better care of their interests. That is the basis of the conflict between the property industry and citizen groups: it is a struggle for power. One side can gain only at the expense of the other. The greater the ability of neighbourhood organizations to demand city planning policies that protect the interests of neighbourhood residents, the smaller the freedom property investors and developers have to operate without restriction in that area. Any gain by citizen groups in influencing transportation policy at city hall is a loss to the property industry, which is used to having almost complete control over this process.

Pointing out that there is an inevitable conflict between citizen groups and the property industry because they both want power at city hall does not necessarily imply that on every specific issue all citizen groups and every segment of the property industry will be at each other's throats. Often interests of the two sides temporarily coincide, as, for example, when neighbourhood groups demanding subways discover that downtown property investors also support subways because they are preferable to nothing happening in city transportation spending and they benefit the downtown. Citizen groups fighting a measure like Vancouver's Third Crossing may well find as their allies land development interests from the southeast part of Vancouver who know that, if development does not go to the North Shore, it is very likely to come in their direction.

Just as there are occasions where the specific short-term interests of the property industry coincide with those of some citizen groups, so there are times when one citizen group finds itself opposing the proposals of another. A classic case occurred in Toronto in 1971, where residents of an east end dead-end street wanted a chain link fence erected at the end of their street to make it inaccessible to residents of a new public-housing project. The public-housing tenants' organization, naturally enough, wanted to be able to use the street because it was a short-cut.

These short-term alliances and conflicts should not, however, obscure the basic common interests that citizen groups share and that conflict with the basic interests of the property industry. The basic interests that citizen groups share are easy to identify.

One is that *city government actions should not harm existing communities in the city*, should not sacrifice their interests without adequate compensation in order to benefit some other group. Changes undesirable to a specific area should be made only when the benefits to other city residents (not to the property industry) are clear, real, and important. Some people would argue that existing communities should never have to experience harmful changes without being adequately compensated; they would argue that if, for example, a new streetcar line were to be laid down on an existing street, street residents should be compensated in real money for the damage to their peace and quiet. Other people in citizen groups might point out that people in urban neighbourhoods also share city-wide interests, and that they are likely to be prepared to sacrifice their local interests when this is genuinely necessary to carry out some program with real benefit for the city as a whole. But these variations never obscure the basic common interest citizen groups have in ruling out city government actions that sacrifice local neighbourhood interests without compensation. Usually city hall argues back that the benefits are for the citizens at large, while in reality the benefits are for the property industry.

A second basic interest of citizen groups is that *city hall should not make the city worse for people to live in.* On the basis of strong factual evidence, many people feel that expressway systems have the overall effect of making city life worse for everyone. Many people think that the same is true of high-rise office and apartment buildings, which provide far less commodious accommodation in many ways than do other types of building forms. Even at the very simple level of park and street furniture, there is a good case for believing that what is being provided by city hall now is in many ways worse than what was there before. On each individual matter there is room for dispute and a great need for evidence, but the basic common interest in not making the city worse for people to live in remains clear. Obviously this concern for the interests of ordinary city residents does not extend to the property industry, which certainly puts its profits and capital gains first and is willing to push for measures that make the city worse for ordinary residents if they yield higher profits for the industry.

A third basic interest of citizen groups is that *land and housing costs should be minimized.* People who have to buy housing have a common interest in paying as little of their incomes as possible for it, and in not being exploited by developers, property investors and others. Housing costs touch everyone directly, but other payments for the use of urban land also fall indirectly on consumers as an element in the prices people pay and the taxes that cover the costs of running the government.

This long-term interest in minimum housing and land costs is often obscured by short-term considerations, where, for instance, home owners whose area has been picked for redevelopment by the property industry argue in favour of the highest possible value for their land so that they will make the most money possible out of the situation. Home owners are often encouraged to regard themselves as property investors rather than housing consumers, and some owner occupiers actually act like property investors and make money doing so. But home owners pay like everyone else the indirect costs of rising urban land values, and they usually made no real gains from the fact that their home increases in value in money terms. Though the terms of house mortgages are such that owners might encounter small — but nevertheless real — losses if property values went down in money terms in absence of government measures to the contrary, nevertheless owners have little real interest in continually increasing urban property values. They share the basic common interest of citizen groups and city people generally in keeping land and housing costs as low as possible.

Every one of these basic interests of city residents and citizen groups conflicts directly with the basic interests of the property industry. The property industry uses its power at city hall to advance its own interests, and the greater that power is the more trenchantly the industry promotes its cause. Benefits to the industry are largely won at the cost of the interests of city people in general, and of residents of a specific neighbourhood in any given case. Citizen groups attempt to generate some political power which they can use at city hall to protect their interests. Usually any success they have is at the expense of the property industry.

It is the prospect of losing that control it has so long enjoyed at city hall that worries the property industry.

Developers, real estate speculators, property investors, insurance agents and all the rest understand that they have a big stake in maintaining the status quo at city hall. And they understand that at present citizen groups are the only real threat to that status quo.

Neighbourhood protection

Nothing illustrates better the kind of protection and good treatment established upper-class and upper-middle-class neighbourhoods get from city hall than these three photographs.

Shaughnessy in Vancouver has no ratepayers' association. Tuxedo residents in Winnipeg had no real need for a ratepayers' organization until recently because they had self-government, a small municipality covering just the Tuxedo area.

Rosedale, which has for some time been part of the

City of Toronto, has found it necessary to have ratepayers' organizations to protect its amenities. Rosedale residents have managed to keep their distinctive ornamental street lights, their narrow, winding streets, garbage collection from the back door rather than the front sidewalk, and pleasant city parks. Their objections were a major factor in preventing the construction of the Crosstown expressway, which would have cut through the area. They have also largely prevented the incursion of high-rise apartments into their territory.

The Shaughnessy area in Vancouver

Toronto's Rosedale

Tuxedo, in Winnipeg

Citizen groups made official

Compared to other Canadian cities, Winnipeg has seen relatively little sustained activity by citizen groups on civic issues. Along with the traditional middle-class ratepayer organizations, there have been a few groups which have challenged city hall over issues like bus routing, new bridge proposals, and urban renewal plans. Unlike most other cities, however, there has almost always been official or semi-official involvement in these groups via social workers employed by social agencies who helped set them up and continued to advise them.

When Winnipeg's new one-city government structure was drawn up by the Schreyer NDP government in 1970-71, one element which was greatly stressed in the provincial government's public relations was the 'community committee' system. Under this arrangement, aldermen from the various communities of the city would form a local area community committee' and would have local resident advisers whom they were obligated to meet with regularly. This was presented as a way of encouraging citizen participation and involvement in civic affairs.

But the new structure gave virtually no real power to the citizen advisers. Moreover it linked them directly into the city government structure at the relatively low level of the community committees. One interpretation of the effect of this innovation is certainly that it could operate to forestall the development of strong new independent citizen groups which might challenge property industry domination of Winnipeg city government and some of the major new programs of the new city council — programs like heavy public support and subsidies for downtown development, public assistance for the relocation of railway yards, and the building of new bridges and expressways through the city.

In mid-1972, six months after the new city government took over, the evidence about the impact of the community committee structure was still unclear. But there certainly had been no enormous increase in the number of citizen organizations in Winnipeg, nor any serious challenge been mounted to any major policy of the new city government.

After Chants And Shouts, Citizens Finally Chosen

A meeting of the Lord Selkirk community committee, punctuated by a lively discussion of what the meeting was all about, finally got down to business Monday night and elected 44 people as their representatives on the committee.

Later during the meeting, they decided, upon the advice of their councillors, to apply to the provincial government for a grant under the provincial employment program.

The meeting opened with a discussion on the purpose of the meeting. Councillor Ken Galanchuk of the Lord Selkirk community committee, told approximately 200 people that the meeting was called to elect representatives for the citizens committee.

Many of the audience, however, thought the meeting should discuss broader issues, and that the audience, not the councillors, should run the meeting.

Winnipeg Free Press 11 Feb. 1972

Ft. Garry Reviews Spending; No Cuts

Fort Garry community committee reviewed part of its 1972 operating estimates at a public meeting Thursday, but no reductions were made.

About 10 of the community's 48 resident advisers were present.

No total estimates figure was available, since one department — water utilities — has yet to submit its annual estimates.

The committee dealt with the police, fire, health and welfare, culture and recreation, works, and general government estimates.

Winnipeg Tribune 10 Mar. 1972

Committee debates before 3 spectators

The Inner City Joint Community Committee finished its business in less than two hours Wednesday before only three spectators.

The councillors debated several points at length but changed almost nothing in the reports from subcommittees.

The question of fees non-residents of River Heights must pay to use the River Heights indoor rink caused the most controversy.

Several speakers contended that all community centre facilities should be available to all residents of the city for the same fee. However, when it was pointed out that River Heights residents had raised $141,000 of the $153,000 to build the rink, and that it would cost the city much more to operate the rink than to have the residents run it, the committee voted to have the present policy of charging $5 per year to non-residents and $2 to residents of River Heights continued.

Winnipeg Free Press 25 Jan. 1972

City hall reaction to citizen groups

The city hall reaction to citizen groups reflects exactly the interests of the property industry in this matter. The policy required of city hall is to maintain the public image of democratic city government controlled by the citizenry, while effectively discouraging as much as possible any organized attempts by people to get together and develop power to wield at city hall. When organizations of this kind do develop, city hall is expected to respond in ways that will help break them up, that certainly will not assist them in increasing their power, and that will encourage them to go back to being happy with the previous status quo.

Citizen groups have for a long time been a minor established fact in city government, but recently in most Canadian cities their numbers have been increasing and their style of activity changing. City hall reaction to citizen groups comes in a predictable series of stages, as these organizations become more numerous and more powerful. In each stage, there are two reactions from city government: the verbal response, what politicians and bureaucrats say, and the action response, what the politicians and bureaucrats do. There are usually some extremely important discrepancies between the words and the actions.

Stage 1: a few ratepayers' groups only

In most cities there are a few communities that have traditionally had ratepayer groups. Usually these are in the well-established middle-class or upper-middle-class districts of the city. Traditionally these groups formulate small and specific requests to be made of city hall, such as arranging for garbage to be picked up from the back of the house or having a new road sign installed.

The verbal response of city politicians to this situation is always positive and welcoming. They assert their gratefulness that at least some people show a little interest in what goes on at city hall, and say that city politicians always try to do their best to take care of these groups.

Their actions are no less favourable for the organized areas. The very existence of these ratepayers' groups is enough to establish the fact that these neighbourhoods expect to be protected and not to be victimized by city hall policies. Usually the residents of these areas with long-established ratepayers' groups include politically influential individuals, often property industry people themselves. A quick tour around these neighbourhoods is enough to establish that they have indeed received protection from many of the least desirable policies of city government, such as widened through streets, truck routes, high-rise redevelopment, public-housing redevelopment, and expressways. They have also usually done very well in acquiring specific benefits from city hall, such as recreation centres, parks, and decent street furniture. The actions of politicians representing these areas generally correspond with their declared sympathy for ratepayers' groups. The local politicians have intelligently protected the interests of these groups at city hall, and have persuaded their colleagues to do the same.

Simultaneously, while expressing in general terms their enthusiasm for citizens getting together into ratepayers' groups of this kind, city politicians act to minimize the possibility that other areas will go the same route. Usually they do not tell their constituents much about what is happening at city hall, particularly things that might upset them. They encourage people to come to them individually with problems, and while they deal with some, they try to persuade people to resign themselves to civic policies on others. They attempt by their actions to forestall the possibility of many groups imitating the few established ratepayers' groups.

Stage 2: a few new, noisy groups

The second stage in the development of citizen groups occurs when a few new, noisy organizations do get going. Usually this happens because people in a certain neighbourhood find themselves victims of a civic decision that will destroy their area or cause them serious, immediate harm. Often people realize the implications of a city decision to carry out an urban renewal project or to build an expressway through their area only because they have watched the same thing happen with dire results elsewhere in the city. As development pressures increase and the pace of civic activities speeds up, the likelihood of new citizen groups forming increases.

Usually these new groups start by making noisy requests of city hall for protection, and for changes in city decisions. They want an expressway stopped, an urban renewal plan drastically altered, or a developer discouraged. Often they start by taking these demands to their local politician, but when he fails to get action at city hall or when he tries to persuade them to give up, they turn their problem into a public issue.

At this stage, city politicians usually say that they welcome these new organizations and their concern about city government. They say they want to hear the views of the citizens, and to consider them carefully. They express great concern over the problems the groups have exposed, though

---

The unrepresentatives

"While this is an association, it is difficult to be sure if the association does speak these same words for everybody [in the area], even though they may be members of the association."
— Toronto controller Allan Lamport, explaining why he did not believe that the Trefann Court urban renewal area residents' association spoke for the people of the area (Transcript, Board of Control 3 Sept. 69)

"Our study indicated that politicians, in general, disliked the [neighbourhood citizens'] groups and they, in turn, knew it. In addition, the politicians often do not see the groups as legitimate representatives of the neighbourhood. . . .

100 per cent of the politicians the Bureau interviewed for this study agreed that the groups are not representative of the neighbourhoods they purport to represent, and 60 per cent felt that the groups often act contrary to the public interest."

From a report on the views of Toronto city politicians on citizen groups. Italics added. *Neighbourhood participation in local government:* A study of the City of Toronto. Toronto: Bureau of Municipal Research, January 1970, p.11

they may voice some reservations about how "representative" the groups are and emphasize that the final decisions belong to the politicians.

In their actions, however, city bureaucrats and politicians usually carry right on with their original plans. They listen to what the people have to say, but then they go ahead and reaffirm their original decisions. If they are relatively skilled at public relations techniques and are well advised by their bureaucrats, they will attempt to make some token concessions that will persuade the public watching via the news media that city hall has taken the citizens' views seriously. This may even buy off their opponents. At this stage, then, city hall is talking sweetly but acting tough.

Stage 3: tough tactics from citizen groups

The reaction of many organizations to kind words and hard action from city hall is to halt their protests, either because they think they have won a real victory or because they understand what has happened, get discouraged and go home. The ultimate aim of city hall policy regarding citizen groups, of course, is precisely to have them get discouraged and go home. Occasionally, however, the response of a group to a stone wall at city hall is to get stronger as an organization, to develop tougher tactics, and to put more pressure on the politicians and the bureaucrats. They try to embarrass city hall; they demonstrate; they try to get their case across to the public through the news media; they look for supporters to make their side stronger.

At this stage of citizen group activity, the words of city hall get as unfriendly as their actions. Politicians and officials claim that the organizations are made up of a "tiny, vocal minority." The groups are said not to represent the people they claim to represent. They are condemned as being the voice of special selfish interests. They are accused of being a bogus group organized by a bunch of radicals and outsiders. By the time city hall is this worried, however, the citizen group has usually succeeded in getting at least part of its case across to other people, and it is becoming ob-

vious that its members *are* being harmed by city hall. The civic reaction is an attempt to undercut that outside support.

But if the words of city hall turn ugly, their actions turn even uglier. Instead of being content with the relatively passive response of refusing to take any action on requests being made by the citizen group, city hall actively attempts to undercut it. One common measure is for the city, directly or indirectly, to set up a rival group, which claims to speak for the same constituency and interest group represented by the original organization. The city may, for instance, persuade a social agency to send in a social worker to organize another group. Or a city politician may, through his political party connections, locate a local resident who is prepared to act as a front man for this new organization. Another common technique is to try to split the group by buying off one faction, or by making proposals that will set factions at each other's throats. Meanwhile city hall will not only deny the requests of the organization, but will press forward vindictively with the measures the members are protesting. All these activities have the aim of destroying the group as a political force and persuading it to give up its attempts to influence civic policy. These techniques may seem brutal, and of course

Protesters plan march on Victoria

The Citizens Co-ordinating Committee for Public Transit, now representing 35 community and labor groups, plan to march on Victoria on Feb. 21.

However, directors made it clear on Monday that they do not want a confrontation with the provincial government over the proposed third crossing for Burrard Inlet.

"We will ask that a few of us be allowed to meet with the cabinet or Municipal Affairs Minister Dan Campbell," said committee president Bruce Yorke.

Rather than oppose the crossing, the committee will support the proposal of Social Credit MLA Hunter Vogel that a Crown corporation be set up for rapid transit.

The committee also sent a telegram to Urban Affairs Minister Ron Basford asking him to arrange for public meetings in Vancouver on the crossing issue.

An earlier decision to send a delegation to Ottawa was dropped because of recent cabinet changes and the expense involved.

Yorke said more than 6,500 names have been collected on petitions. More will be sought on Saturday in Greater Vancouver.

The committee said it has $1,700 and will use some of the money to set up an office for volunteer workers to co-ordinate efforts against the crossing.

Vancouver Province 1 Feb. 1972

Citizens' group proposal rejected by Surrey council

Special to The Sun

SURREY — Aldermen Tuesday turned down a suggestion by Mayor William Vander Zalm that a 16-member citizens committee be formed to make recommendations on the future of South Surrey.

A $50,000 concept plan for the area was recently completed and has been shown to residents for feedback.

Many of them have opposed the scheme, some have joined together to form the South Surrey Study Group.

The group has pressed council for a greater citizen's voice in decision-making on planning proposals.

Vander Zalm said he thought the committee he proposed was necessary because some citizens felt council was ramming the concept down their throats.

"I must admit," he said, "that in our request to have citizens participate we no

doubt overlook the fact that if we ask people to share in deciding a plan for the area they should be given information commensurate with the importance of the decision to be shared."

Other aldermen, however, felt no decision on a committee should be made until all public showings of the plan have been completed and all comments for and against are available for study.

Vancouver Sun 5 Apr. 1972

they are, but usually the extent of their harmfulness is hidden from virtually everyone in the city apart from people directly involved because of the position taken by the news media. Given their basic friendliness towards the status quo at city hall, it is not surprising that the news media rarely if ever report accurately and completely on this kind of city hall action.

Stage 4: some victories, a little power for citizen groups

Naturally the effect of the civic reaction described in stage three is to destroy many groups and to persuade many people to give up on their efforts to influence what happens at city hall. But this is not always the case. Sometimes citizen groups succeed in winning a few victories in spite of all the opposition they encounter. An occasional development project is stopped; expressways get at least temporarily abandoned. Victories of this kind are extremely important because they establish that citizen organizations can on occasion exert some influence over what happens at city hall, though the ferociousness of the struggle makes it clear to all the participants that power at city hall will never be easily won.

If the groups survive, they may start linking together and forming coalitions so that city hall no longer engages one isolated group at a time but rather is confronted by a number of groups who understand that they have certain basic common interests. The groups may also decide to extend their activities; formally or informally they build up election machines that run candidates, get them elected to city hall, and then control their actions after they are elected.

When city hall politicians and bureaucrats find the enemy in their midst, the seeds of an organization that might wrest control of city government away from the property industry, their reaction becomes stronger than ever. They accuse citizen groups of anything that might be believable in order to discredit them: anarchy, radicalism, communism, violence, and so on. They declare them a threat to what they have always considered to be good city government, to growth, to progress, to a healthy city and so on. They respond by treating citizen groups as municipally seditious, as threats to the established order, as promoters of a revolution at the civic level.

Yet, by the time citizen groups have got to this stage, they have developed a considerable amount of power of their own. And once the civic status quo is under strong attack, the politicians and bureaucrats often find themselves on the defensive rather than the offensive in explaining their actions.

At this stage, the actions of city hall outstrip their verbal reactions in attempts to discourage the citizen group effort. There have not yet been enough occasions where citizen groups have forced city governments to this level to be able to produce documented evidence of all aspects of the city hall response, but the range of activities is likely to be wide. The politicians attempt to line up and solidify the strongest possible coalition of interests, including all elements of the property industry and related interests, that feel comfortable with the status quo. They are unlikely to pay particular attention to construction labour unions and civic labour unions in trying to enlarge the property industry coalition, since this will help mitigate the impression that the fight for control of city hall is between big rich developers and prop-

erty investors on one hand and just ordinary people on the other. City hall is likely to infiltrate citizen groups in order to get information about their activities and intentions. It may go one step further than establishing phoney rival

Communists and anarchists

Following is a catalogue made by the Riverdale Community Organization in Toronto of the charges made by city politicians against it:

"Communists."
"Their philosophy leads to anarchy."
"Using threats of violence."
"Trying to replace city government."
"Oppose city hall just for the sake of opposing it."
"By-pass elected officials."
"Stir up trouble."
"They don't represent anyone but themselves."
"Self-appointed defenders of the people."
"Organizers go around knocking on doors, creating complaints."
"If people are satisfied, organizers try to make them dissatisfied."
"They pretend to be the only solution."
"Troublemakers."
"Outside agitators."

'No more high-rise,' tenant group chants at Meridian opening

By NEIL LOUTTIT

Premier William Davis had just finished talking about a healthy urban environment when a distant chorus of voices started chanting: "No more high-rise."

It was the tenants from the South of St. James Town and they had arrived at the official opening of the Meridian Development Group's Crescent Town to present their case to Mr. Davis. But the party was a private affair and they couldn't get in.

So they chanted briefly from the sidelines, watched by Metro police and private security guards, then they left quietly.

Earlier, at a press conference at City Hall, Jeffrey Sack, lawyer for the tenants, said the latest proposal from Meridian in the landlord and tenant dispute was unacceptable. The tenants made a counter proposal to Meridian.

At the opening, Mr. Davis, flanked by municipal politicians and Meridian executives, said a healthy municipal and urban environment "has to be a way of life. It has to be our objective."

Globe and Mail 17 Sept. 1972

groups, and arrange for dummy extremist groups to discredit the citizen opposition by violence and by other tactics that will lose it popular support. The city politicians and property industry people may attempt to intimidate activists in the citizen opposition. One Toronto alderman, an opponent of the Spadina Expressway scheme, had his garage burned down and suspected arson. Another expressway opponent had his house broken into, and the evidence made it clear that the action was politically motivated. Attempts to buy off the opposition, with token political concessions or with corrupt pay-offs, will continue. So will attempts to split up the opposition and factionalize it.

Yet in spite of these tremendous efforts by people with a vested interest in the status quo at city hall to prevent any shift of power from the property industry to citizen groups,

it is conceivable that the citizen opposition might capture control of city government by electing a majority in a civic election. That would amount to stage five in the struggle for power between the property industry and citizen groups. Should this happen, or should the prospect even seem likely, it would be reasonable to expect the property industry and their city hall allies to use even stronger measures to protect their position. They would be likely to turn for help to the provincial government, which has the power to make all the rules about city government and which could, if it chose, abolish city government completely. So long as city government as it is currently set up works as an effective mechanism for the property industry to regulate itself, the provincial government is likely to remain happy. Should the property industry ever find itself losing control

Continued on page 203

City vindictiveness

There is no more shocking example of the vindictiveness of city politicians and city officials facing a strong challenge from a citizen's group that the conduct of Toronto's city hall in the Don Mount urban renewal area dispute in August and September, 1967.

· When five homeowners refused to move out of their expropriated houses, city hall used its powers of expropriation and eviction to sneak up on one man's house on a Saturday morning and to begin tearing it down while he was out shopping.

Then the city refused to delay its evictions in spite of clear evidence available at the time — and later confirmed beyond any shadow of doubt by official reports from Ontario's Law Reform Commission and by a government Royal Commission — that the city was trying to force homeowners to move out while offering them prices for their homes which were too low to enable them to buy an equivalent home elsewhere.

And these, it should be remembered, were urban

renewal area residents. This was all in the process of implementing a plan which was supposed to improve area residents' housing conditions and to improve the city.

What stopped the city eventually from evicting the homeowners was its own illegality, the fact that it was put into a situation where city officials were going to have to admit in court that they had acted illegally in the way they calculated the original expropriation prices offered the homeowners. Then, and only then, did the city cease its legal battle to evict the four remaining homeowners.

And even after that, it was only when one stalwart holdout threatened to take the city to court for yet another illegal action — this time, illegally closing a street and preventing a property owner from having access to his own property — that the city was finally backed into a corner and forced to make a fair compensation offer to that one remaining homeowner.

Giving People the Works

by William Kilbourn, 22 Sept. 1970

Should City Hall officials meet with community groups who invite them out to discuss their problems? Last week most members of the City Works Committee said, No, they shouldn't — unless, of course, the Commissioner in his wisdom decided to let them.

"I will not permit our staff to go out and be insulted," said Alderman Marks.

"Our officials are here to do a job and shouldn't go out and be ridiculed," said Alderman Clifford.

Works Commissioner Bremner gave the Committee a lecture about wasting his

staff's time and about the need for "most people" at such citizens' meetings to be better educated in what they were talking about, though the only education he suggested was for them to come down to Committee meetings (alternate Monday mornings) at City Hall.

The discussion was triggered by a letter from a neighbourhood group in the Danforth-Broadview area asking if a Works official would come and help them find a solution to problems of laneway repairs and traffic signs (for controlling speed and parking) — "both areas under the jurisdiction of your department."

"We are concerned about keeping our neighbourhood a desirable place to live. We are confident that your department shares this interest and that with representatives at our meeting we will be able to work out mutually satisfactory solu-

tions."

Bremner had refused this request and written to the group that the proper procedure was for them to send their suggestions to the Committee secretary and if they were relevant to his department he would investigate and report to the Committee, who could then consider what to do.

Alderman Lamport agreed with Commissioner Bremner about the irrelevant nature of many of the things said at citizens' meetings and the need to be precise, the need — "to put your foot on what is going on, I mean your finger . . . This floor is where business should be done." If citizens have problems, they should appear before the proper authorities and seek redress.

The hamburger classic

A classic example of the name-calling tactics often used by city politicians in an attempt to discredit their citizen opposition was Vancouver mayor Tom Campbell's attack on opponents of the Third Crossing proposal.

Campbell made headlines across the country with his description of the citizen opposition.

He also attracted a barrage of public criticism, reflected in a wide variety of critical letters to the editors of Vancouver newspapers.

The reason that the word "hamburger" may have sprung to Mayor Tom Campbell's lips when he was hassling critics of the third crossing was that he was coincidentally mulling a request from McDonald Hamburger boss George Cohon to turn up at one of the chain's stores and eat the nine-billionth hamburger served by the chain, as a publicity stunt. Campbell subsequently turned down the stunt, but by that time his "hamburger" crack was all over the headlines, and Cohon had changed his mind anyhow. . .

Vancouver Sun 24 Feb. 1972

Campbell blew it

Editor, The Sun, Sir— Vancouver citizens are fortunate indeed. Tom Campbell has blown his chances of re-election with his "hamburger" statement.

Next to Trudeau's "like it or lump it" statement Campbell's "hamburger" statement is probably Canada's greatest case of foot-in-mouth disease.

DON BARRY
Box 609, Rossland

Vancouver Sun 22 Feb. 1972

Editor, The Sun, Sir — Well now! Our wonderful mayor has finally done it. Up until now he has remained a fairly bearable — perhaps even humorous — fixture in the Twelfth Avenue m o n o l i t h. Now, however, he seems to have slipped his cogs completely; calling down the Wrath of the Saved upon the heads of the hamburgers for "wrecking" his beloved third crossing.

race will collapse in a pile of erudite rubble (no, Mr. Campbell, I am not a hamburger; I hope to get my B.A. next year). But the height of idiocy came when he declared that Bruce Yorke, who has demonstrated that he represents the opinions of a sizeable bloc of citizens, will not be allowed to speak at an upcoming public hearing on the third crossing, because he is "not an expert on anything." Perhaps we should limit Mr. Campbell to questions of renting apartments, such being what he is "expert" at and leave him out of everything else.

Please don't mistake me; I am in favor of a rapid transit crossing (I would rather see intensive development in barren North Vancouver than in arable Richmond, and I think prospective developers and residents should be encouraged), but I strongly object to Mr. Campbell's outdated and ridiculous smear tactics. I also object to his continued refusal of a plebiscite on the issue. It is the right of the people to make their views known, and it is not his function to play God in Vancouver. I hope TEAM and Mr. Rankin serve him with a lawsuit for malicious libel; he deserves it.

Oh, and good luck at the polls next time.

J. A. MORLEY
2110 West Thirty-seventh

Vancouver Sun 16 Feb. 1972

Campbell cries ruin

Mayor Tom Campbell said Wednesday that opposition and dissent could scuttle the planned Third Crossing of Burrard Inlet and that if this happens "it'll be a real victory for the Communist Party of Canada."

The mayor told reporters he can't see Ottawa or the B.C. government putting up promised funds for the tunnel system because of "the amount of hostility that is being faced in Vancouver."

He said the $200 million crossing project is in jeopardy because of opposition from "Maoists . . . communists . . . pinkos . . . left-wingers . . . and hamburgers."

(A hamburger, Campbell explained, is anyone who doesn't have a university degree. The Dictionary of American Slang also gives this definition: "A bum or tramp; anyone who is down and out.'

(Campbell's d e f i n i t i o n prompted Ald. Art Phillips to say: "If anyone without a university degree is a hamburger, I guess that makes (Ald.) Walter Hardwick, with a PhD., a filet mignon.")

Hardwick, a University of B.C. urban geographer, said that Campbell deserves a great deal of blame if the project is "sinking", as the mayor suggested Wednesday.

"If it is sinking, it is sinking because of the mayor's reluctance to discuss the impact of the project with the public and professional people during the past year."

And Ald. Harry Rankin, one of the targets in Campbell's attack, retorted: "Tom is just a pathetic buffoon. He is 15 years out of date. At one time Red-baiting would work, but now people will just laugh at him."

Vancouver Province 10 Feb. 1972

DEAD END.
(the minority ruled)

Sponsored by the "GO SPADINA" committee, P.O. Box 291, Postal Station, "T", Toronto 19

A newspaper ad run by organizers of a "citizen campaign" to get the Spadina expressway built.

Toronto Star 14 June 1972

of the mechanism set up by the province for its regulation, it would be bound to try to use its power at the provincial level and, supported by all the allies it could find, to try to get changes made which would restore the status quo of property industry control over the servicing of urban land and the regulation of its use.

Dealing with citizen groups is a much more difficult problem for city hall now than it once was in most Canadian cities. The politicians and the bureaucrats have worked out effective techniques for dealing with the challenge to the status quo and property industry control that the citizen opposition represents. In some cities, citizen groups have nevertheless been increasing in strength, but the struggle is long and hard, and they are still far from wresting control of city government out of the hands of the property industry. The industry itself and its political arm at city hall have shown little inclination to accommodate the citizen opposition. This is partly because the industry recognizes the basic conflict between its interests and those of citizen groups. But the industry could well decide that, rather than fighting the citizen opposition groups tooth and nail, it should try to buy them off. And it is of course quite possible that these efforts could succeed, finally persuading people in citizen groups to go home peacefully, and so leaving city hall in the hands of the property industry. On the other hand, attempts to buy off citizen groups might serve only to encourage people and lead them to harden their demands for real power at city hall.

St. James Town
High-rise supporters overwhelm committee

Cheering and jeering friends of St. James Town packed city hall's council chamber last night to urge final city ratification of a controversial bylaw rezoning land west of St. James Town for three 30-story a p a r t m e n t blocks.

The meeting of the Buildings and Development Committee was overwhelmed by area residents, development company employees and construction workers who had been urged to come out to support the project and denounce Alderman John Sewell, its opponent.

The committee agreed to ratify the bylaw to rezone the land between Bleecker and Sherbourne Streets, which would add three more apart-

ment buildings to the 16 now in St. James Town.

Only aldermen Paul Pickett and Arthur Eggleton voted to cut the density of the buildings. Mr. Sewell was alone in voting against any approval and asking the matter be referred to a committee of the developers and the residents. There are 11 aldermen on the committee.

Speakers were wildly cheered as they said downtown apartment developments like St. James Town would keep Toronto booming and attractive, create employment, eliminate crime in open space areas, and drive away slum alcoholics and welfare freeloaders in the Cabbagetown area.

Toronto Star 7 Feb. 1972

Protesters picket TTC chief's home 'give us a service'

By ROBERT DOUGLAS
Star staff writer

"Dissatisfied" with the Toronto Transit Commission's (TTC) refusal to extend bus service into their neighborhood, 25 Riverdale-area residents drove up to the Rosedale home of Ralph Day last night to protest.

However, the 73-year-old commission chairman was out, and after less than a half-hour's picketing the protesters packed up and went home.

And if they had tried, they soon would have found that the communications gap between themselves and Day involves more than bus lines.

"I find it a bit interesting," Day said, "that these people came up here in cars."

Said one of the baffled protesters: "How else would he expect us to get there? We don't have any buses in our area. If there'd been one, we would have taken it."

The protesters want a bus to run the length of Jones Ave. from Queen St. to Danforth Ave. Protest leader Patricia Kendall said they wanted Day to give them the kind of hearing the TTC has denied them so far.

The commission refused to allow them to attend the meeting at which the Jones line was discussed, she said.

"Unless you do something like this," she said, after the visit to Day's house, "you can't get through to the TTC."

Toronto Star 13 April 1972

Infiltration: the Lionstar case

One of the ways developers deal with citizen groups who criticize and oppose their projects is by blunting the force of the opposition, either by creating a counter-group which supports the developer or by inserting into the group developers' friends or his agents who can cause internal dissention or even take control of the organization.

Usually evidence of infiltration of citizen groups is difficult to find. One case, however, where it was done almost openly and probably with the co-operation of city politicians was in the Bloor-Dufferin area of Toronto in 1970 where a development firm called Lionstar was proposing a new high-rise apartment project.

A public meeting of area residents was called. The two ward aldermen assured residents that they wanted to have their views on the developers' proposals, and that the politician's job was to protect the interests of his constituents.

"We want to have your participation," said junior ward alderman Art Eggleton.

"We're only here as the representatives of the people," said senior ward alderman and member of Toronto's executive committee Tony O'Donohue, "to make sure that you get a fair deal in whatever's drawn up. I can assure you that we will do our best to make sure that whatever's done here is with the approval and the full knowledge and the full approval of everybody here."

The developers' architect then presented a long slide show illustrating what the development might look like. Then there were questions from the floor, not all of them hostile to the developer but indicating that there was a considerable amount of suspicion and unhappiness about what he was planning to do in the area.

Near the end of the meeting Alderman O'Donohue made a proposal which, as he said, had been planned in advance. He stood up and made a brief speech ending with a proposal for a local citizen committee: "What we did have in mind, seeing as how there's so much interest in this, was to get a committee together so people here might be able to deal with the people involved. . . . This would be my suggestion, that we should have somebody from each of the streets sit on some sort of a committee." Mr. O'Donohue, rather than have his suggestion discussed, immediately called for volunteers.

Sitting in the audience at the meeting were a group of five or six young men, a blonde woman, and an older man. The older man was Gordon Singer, the developer in the area. Though Singer was present throughout the meeting, he was never introduced to the audience.

There had been a good deal of movement centred around Singer during the meeting, and some of the young men had gone to other parts of the meeting hall drifting back occasionally for a few words.

As soon as O'Donohue made his suggestion, they moved quickly. At least two of the young men got themselves down as volunteers, street representatives for the new citizen committee. It was as if they had been expecting O'Donohue to make the suggestion, and they certainly seemed to know what to do when it happened.

One of the young men who volunteered for the committee spent some time during the meeting talking quietly to a lady sitting near me. He was evidently suggesting to her that she sell her house, because at one point she said loudly that she didn't want to sell. As he left her, he handed her a business card. I concluded that he was a real estate agent.

So, by the end of the meeting, a local citizen committee had been set up by the two ward aldermen, which indicated that they would be able to have some say in its activities. And, without anyone apparently realizing it, the developer had managed to get at least two of his men on the committee right from the beginning.

Pepin calls for peoples' committees to topple Bourassa

QUEBEC (CP) — Marcel Pepin, president of the Confederation of National Trade Unions, yesterday called for the CNTU to form peoples' committees across the province to defeat the ruling Quebec Liberal Party.

In his keynote address to more than 1,400 delegates at the opening 235,000-member group's convention, he said the committees would bring together CNTU members with those of the Quebec Federation of Labor and the Quebec Teachers' Corp.

"The spokesmen for the regime, whether they are politicians or editorial writers, never stop saying that we should give up any slight desire we may have to express our opinions on political subjects," he said in his speech entitled To Overcome.

This contrasted "with what they preached earlier when they invited us to replace the regime at the next election if we were unhappy with the current one."

Mr. Pepin said the immediate task of the peoples' committees would be to fight all provincial Liberal Party candiates and nominate or support candidates who formally endorse the economic and social positions of the three labor groups, in particular the formal condemnation of capitalism and economic liberalism.

The committees would become permanent organizations financing themselves independent of the three labor groups.

Globe and Mail 12 June 1972

CONCLUSION
Power at City Hall

No photograph has ever captured the present realities of power at city hall better than this one, taken in 1967 by Frank Chalmers of the *Winnipeg Tribune*. Winnipeg resident Mrs. Frank Birch was expropriated by municipal authorities to make way for a sewage treatment plant. When the Birch family refused to move out, the municipal authorities obtained a court order to evict them. Three bailiffs and a Mountie pried open a locked door to take possession of the house, then posted the No Trespassing sign.

Once again, the property industry and the business community are being challenged for control of city government in many Canadian cities. This happened last in the 1930s, when labour-based opposition groups mounted strong campaigns and in some cities actually won power for several years. John Queen, a labour leader who was arrested in a midnight raid and charged with seditious conspiracy at the time of the Winnipeg General Strike, later became mayor of Winnipeg at the head of a labour majority for several years in the thirties. That was also the period when William Dennison, then a young socialist making speeches supporting the CCF on Toronto streetcorners, was first elected to city hall on a platform that proposed taking milk and coal supplies out of the hands of private profit-making business and turning them into municipally-owned public utilities.

The new citizen group-based opposition to the property movement has developed quite differently in different cities. The series of stages described in the last chapter is an attempt to sketch in general terms the pattern that has been followed up to now, but there is no reason to think that every citizen opposition will follow this pattern. There is even less reason to think that progress from one stage to the next is inevitable. City hall and the property industry are busy trying to buy off or put down this most recent challenge to the status quo wherever it occurs, and it is quite possible that at least in some cities they have succeeded.

Nevertheless, in many places the property industry's control of city government is threatened. As we have seen, this is no small-time fight with small-time people. The front-runners of the property industry often are small-time speculators and entrepreneurs, but behind them are large and powerful financial institutions. Moreover their place in the property industry is rapidly being taken over by large integrated property corporations, and there is absolutely no doubt about the wealth or power of Trizec, Cemp-Fairview, Eaton's, Marathon, and the others.

And while citizen groups rarely get past city councils and the petty politicians involved in city politics, nevertheless by getting even that far they are challenging an agency of provincial governments, which provincial politicians have established for sound reasons of their own. In tougher fights with politicians, it does not take citizen groups long to bump up against big-time politicians, federal and provincial cabinet ministers, nor does it take them long to discover that these people have the same basic commitment to the status quo and to property industry dominance of city hall that the city politicians have.

Where things stand now

The present strength of citizen opposition varies greatly from city to city. As of mid-1972, Winnipeg, Vancouver and Toronto taken together demonstrated this range of var-

iation, and Toronto and Vancouver illustrated two quite different situations a developing opposition movement can find itself in.

Despite a few established ratepayer groups, and here and there isolated organizations of working-class and lower-middle-class people that emerge briefly to fight urgent local issues, Winnipeg has yet to see a well-developed citizen group movement. But then Winnipeg residents have not really suffered the pressures of large-scale change threatening many different city neighbourhoods either. Winnipeg's rate of growth has been quite slow, and local governments have not had access to the large amounts of capital necessary to effect vast urban renewal projects.

Also the local social agency establishment in Winnipeg has managed to deal with many of those situations which in other cities would probably have created strong, independent citizen groups to challenge the property industry majority at city hall. The technique has been to provide social agency employees to "work with" newly-formed groups or to set up groups from scratch. Among the agencies doing this have been the Urban Studies Institute at the University of Winnipeg (funded in part by CMHC and headed by Lloyd Axworthy, former executive assistant to Paul Hellyer when he was the federal urban affairs minister); the People's Opportunity Service, a provincial government agency; and the City of Winnipeg itself, which has helped create citizen committees in urban renewal areas. The presence of social agency employees in newly-organized groups has diluted their protests and directed them towards "more constructive" policies, which in general avoid direct challenges to the decisions of city government.

It could be, however, that a number of strong, independent citizen groups will soon be challenging the property industry's majority at Winnipeg city hall, for the new amalgamated city government is embarking on a series of major policies which, while favourable to the industry, will be directly harmful to many city residents. Proposed expressway construction threatens a large number of neighbourhoods, both suburban and central-city. Plans for downtown development call for widespread demolition of existing buildings and an amazing set of giveaways, most of which will probably go to large, already-wealthy corporations with no local roots. In the forum provided by the much-vaunted and over-sold community committees of the new Winnipeg city council, residents will quickly encounter the unwillingness of city politicians to protect neighbourhood interests, so familiar to citizen group activists in other Canadian cities.

The contrast between the present situation in Winnipeg and that in Toronto is very striking. In Toronto, citizen groups have challenged city hall on a wide range of policies. The fact that city government is controlled by developers and real estate interests has been clearly established as a result of the activities of the opposition group of aldermen in Toronto city council and of the city's citizen groups. The basic common interests of citizen groups from widely different neighbourhoods have also been established. The effort of some city politicians and some people involved in citizen groups to create the impression that a little compromising and moderation of the property industry's policies would be enough to make everyone happy has made little headway alongside the tough and imaginative tactics of the dissenting forces, including the two strongest opposition aldermen, Karl Jaffary and John Sewell, which have held up for scrutiny the basic conflicts of interest between city residents and the property industry.

Nevertheless there is tremendous pressure to make more believable the reformist middle, which could moderate some of the worst practices and policies of the property industry without challenging its control of city government. Aldermen like Ying Hope, a civil engineer, and David Crombie, a university administrator and lecturer, belong to this group. It may be in the interests of the property industry to avoid a clear-cut battle for power in Toronto by encouraging this group and puffing it up as a real alternative to the developers' boys at city hall. An indication that enlightened property industry interests see things this way is that one of the very first people to urge David Crombie to run for mayor in December 1972 was Hugh Macaulay, Premier William Davis's closest adviser, who is a smooth Conservative like Davis and the brother of Robert Macaulay, a former Ontario Conservative cabinet minister and now a developers' lawyer.

While citizen groups have been making progress on some fronts in Toronto, relatively little has been done to organize new groups in working-class districts of the city. In the absence of working-class groups, property industry candidates can still run and easily win in working-class wards. Also Toronto's citizen group movement has been suffering from a shortage of the clear-minded analysis and strong tactics of organizations from working-class neighbourhoods like Trefann Court and Riverdale.

In many respects, the situation in Vancouver is similar to that in Toronto. There is a rich, recent local history of citizen groups, which have fought city hall on parks, development projects, downtown redevelopment, urban renewal and expressways. The subservience of the NPA majority group at city hall to the property industry has been long since demonstrated, and the job of persuading people that they must organize to protect their interest has been done best by Vancouver mayor Tom Campbell with his colourful contempt for citizen groups and their views.

Vancouver's citizen group movement does not, however,

THE CITY WE ARE LOSING: Hundreds of houses like this one have been torn down to make way for property industry projects, and many more are threatened with imminent demolition. With them goes the kind of neighbourhood and the kind of city life which they have provided many people.

THE PROPERTY INDUSTRY AT WORK: The house which used to be attached to this one has been torn down, helping to destroy an existing neighbourhood — this time in the South of St. Jamestown area — to make way for yet another development project.

seem to have the same basic solidarity as Toronto's, and the political initiative at city hall has not been seized by the two politicians who are reliable supporters and representatives of citizen groups. Opposition aldermen Harry Rankin and Walter Hardwick vote consistently against the property industry for citizen groups, but they have not discredited the reformist middle group made up of TEAM aldermen Phillips and Calder and NPA alderman Linnell. This could be due at least in part to the fact that, unlike issues concerning transportation and citizen groups, major development issues in Vancouver have not been turned into the hard, bitterly fought, protracted struggles that characterized the Metro Centre, Eaton Centre, and St. Jamestown developments in Toronto in 1971-72. In fights over major development projects, opposition aldermen gain a credibility that clearly distinguishes them from reformist-middle politicians who, when it comes to the crunch, are prepared to vote in favour of undesirable developments.

On the other hand, the city hall opposition in Vancouver has stronger links to parts of the labour movement than exist as yet in Toronto. Rankin in particular has as many connections to the labour movement as he does to citizen groups.

In none of the three cities is there a citizen group coalition that is just about to wrest power from the hands of the property industry at city hall. None of these cities (and none of the other cities in the country except, perhaps, in Quebec) has a citizen group movement that is certain of not being bought off or defeated in the next few years. The success these groups eventually have depends on the internal strength they can generate, on their ability to pick the right issues on which to challenge city hall and the property industry, and on the skill with which they carry out these battles.

What next?

Citizen groups are challenging the property industry on two quite different fronts. One of these is direct action against specific projects of the industry and of city hall, attempts to halt undesirable and damaging schemes. The other front is political action against the property industry's politicians at city hall, with citizen groups developing candidates and organizations to run in civic elections and beat incumbent property industry supporters. There is room for tremendous expansion on both these fronts.

The basic need of the citizen group movement, however, is more groups, with larger numbers of people, better strategies and tactics, and firmer links to potential allies. The number of city residents directly involved in citizen groups is still very small, and even in the best-organized cities there are many neighbourhoods where no groups exist and where no organizing is being done. Middle-class neighbourhoods have been reasonably good at spontaneously organizing themselves, though often the groups that develop suffer from internal structures which concentrate power in the hands of a small elite and do not encourage real involvement from large numbers of people. Working-class districts are less prone to organize themselves. The resulting lack of strong groups from working-class areas is an extremely serious deficiency in most cities.

LIVING IN THE PAST? Hundreds of houses like these two in Winnipeg's North End are threatened with demolition for various projects — like urban renewal schemes and expressway systems — which are supposed to be benefitting the city and its citizens.

Developing more strong groups will require many more full-time, competent organizers who understand the logic of citizen groups and the political context in which they are operating. Community organizing is, unfortunately, one of those things most people think they can do whether they can or not, and where it is difficult to assess real ability. It is, however, safe to dismiss virtually all people who have taken university courses in community organizing. Universities often teach social workers how to set up safe local groups, which can be controlled by the social agencies or public bodies that employ the social worker-organizers attached to the groups. Rarely if ever do these educational institutions teach people the kind of organizing that produces independent citizen groups strong enough to challenge the status quo in the way the groups referred to in this chapter and the last have done.

Developing the basic strength of citizen groups will also require much greater effort by the groups themselves at analysing their activities, understanding where they were right and where they were wrong, why they succeeded and why they failed. Without critical self-examination of this kind, it is going to be difficult for groups to improve their tactics and match the competence of their opponents.

A more informed understanding of the political situation in which citizen groups are operating is also required for stronger citizen groups. Already there are community newspapers, periodicals, and publications of various kinds putting useful information into the hands of people who need it, but more publications of this sort will surely be needed if groups are to grow in size and strength.

The need for more groups, stronger and more democratic groups, for more competent community organizers, for more analysis of experience, and for more useful information is basic to the citizen group movement. The more progress that is made along these lines, the more confident and capable groups will be to challenge the property industry both by direct action against specific projects and by political action designed to throw the industry's friends out of government.

Direct action

How can citizen groups find new ways to use their power in order to take direct action against projects of the property industry and city hall? Some groups are already quite sophisticated in fighting individual projects, and there is a lot to be learned from the material available recording their fights.* The most promising new direction in direct action is to expand the range of attack so as to include not just the individual developer or city council promoting a specific undesirable project, but to go after the other people, whether in the property industry or in public agencies and government, who are actively supporting it. For this, analysis of the interconnections amongst different firms in the property industry is very helpful. Ways in which such an analysis can be made include:

— Taking account of the links amongst property industry firms, and attacking the more sensitive and public-relations-conscious associates of developers (like their banks and their insurance company mortgage lenders) in order to bring pressure to bear on developers

— Undercutting attempts by the industry to put on a respectable front — for instance, at conferences where de-

THE CITY OF THE FUTURE? Toronto alderman David Rotenberg, selling "total development" of a part of the city's downtown.

*Here is a short list of accounts of citizen group battles with developers and city hall. Most of the items refer to Toronto because so far most of the published material has been on Toronto:

Forever Deceiving You, by the Vancouver Urban Research Group. Includes four Vancouver case histories.

Up Against City Hall, by John Sewell. Chapters on all the major citizen-city hall fights in Toronto in 1970-72, by the strongest supporter of citizen groups on Toronto city council.

Fighting Back, by Graham Fraser. A history of the Trefann Court urban renewal battle, which began in 1966 and which still continues.

The Real World of City Politics, by James Lorimer. Includes chapters on several Toronto issues of 1969-70, the ward boundary fight, a school expropriation issue, and others.

Marlborough Marathon, by Jack Granatstein. A brief account of a middle-class neighbourhood negotiating with the CPR's Marathon Realty over a big proposed development.

The Revolution Game by Margaret Daly. Includes chapters on community groups in Cape Breton and Calgary.

All these books are available in paperback format.

velopers mingle with architects, university professors, social workers and government people and where they are unaccustomed to be challenged on the respectability of their day-to-day tactics such as blockbusting and needless demolition

— Picking on a relatively sensitive local developer about whom a fair amount of information is available (preferably a public company) and then conducting a continuing critique of that developer's operations, while seeking support amongst the more socially-conscious and sensitive businesses and shareholders involved in the company

— Investigating the economics and financing of specific development projects and then revealing details of the profits, capital gains, tax evasions and government support (often through CMHC) involved even in "normal" development projects

— Replying to an attack by a developer to your neighbours and your neighbourhood by taking the issue to his neighbours and his neighbourhood, where the developer might well be sensitive to criticism

— Establishing a monitoring system that can detect threatening public projects at an early stage, when they are still being discussed and decided on in secret, and turning them into noisy public issues

— Establishing defence organizations for major civic ameni-

ties like the waterfront, the rivers and the parks, to keep a close watch out for threatening projects

— Investigating systematically the statutes applying to public projects and city hall in general, in order to locate technicalities which can be used to delay or defeat undesirable public projects

— Investigating the careers of both city employees and city politicians to discover possible private interests in public projects

While the attack against property industry and city hall projects can be expanded along these and other lines, there is also considerable scope for citizen groups to develop counter-projects of their own, which demonstrate the difference between what is done by a profit-hungry industry and what can be done by people who have other motives and interests. There appears to be a good deal more room for innovative and experimental projects than actually exists. That is because both the government and the property industry are aware of the potential dangers of successful citizen group-inspired projects that demonstrate how much better things could be done. Nevertheless an idea ruled out as impossible by the powers that be can often develop into a powerful weapon. Possibilities of the kind include:

— Establishing neighbourhood nonprofit housing corporations to buy up existing tenant-occupied housing and turn it over to co-ops or organizations of present ten-

THE CITY OF THE FUTURE? Summerland, brought to Winnipeg courtesy of R. C. Baxter Ltd., the Bank of Montreal, All Seasons Apartments Ltd., Read Jones Christoffersen, Structural Engineers, and Foundation Pilings.

ants, who are then protected from further profiteering rent increases by their landlord, who are more secure in their premises, and who are able to make decisions themselves about how their accommodation will be administered rather than having the decisions made for them

— Establishing a neighbourhood anti-development corporation to buy up key properties in the area in a pattern that rules out assembly for redevelopment

— Setting up coalitions among labour unions, credit unions and citizen groups to build housing for working-class people on the most reasonable possible terms, and designed according to the needs and wishes of the actual occupants .

— Organizing anti-industry housing companies to mobilize private and public funds available at reasonable (i.e. low or zero per cent) interest rates and using them for new construction that is beneficial both to existing residents of areas where it takes place and to the people it accommodates

— Reviving squatting, to make use of vacant and unused urban accommodation or land

— Instigating action projects whereby people can provide for themselves those facilities (such as bicycle paths or street parks) that civic authorities refuse to provide

— Organizing design teams to produce a steady stream of constructive, practical projects for vacant and unused land (particularly city or speculator-held land being kept vacant in anticipation of a future profit)

There are some serious difficulties with positive direct action projects like these. One is that they are very attractive to people who see them as desirable projects in themselves, but who do not appreciate that the fact that they are desirable *but undone* is an expression of the true interests of the people currently possessing the power to make decisions. The point in constructing a bicycle path, for instance, is not only to create something useful for people but also to emphasize that the real priorities of present city governments lie in city-wide, automobile-oriented transportation facilities to serve the specialized-sector city the property industry is building. It does very little good indeed to build one bicycle path unless the process of implementing that project is also helping to weaken the political power of the property industry and their friends at city hall, and to strengthen the power of organized citizen groups until they could elect representatives who would make quite different decisions about transportation matters.

Any direct action taken to stop a harmful project has two goals: one, stopping the project itself and so preventing

THE CITY OF THE FUTURE? "Innovative housing", one of the experimental projects financed by the federal government and CMHC through a special $200 million fund CMHC expended in 1970. The most innovative thing about this apartment building, located in Toronto, was that after it was constructed it began to sink into the ground. That is why, in mid-1972, it was still unoccupied, and why one section of each floor has been taken out in an attempt to level up all the floors sufficiently that people would be willing to live in the building.

the harm it would cause; and two, strengthening the political power of organizations of citizens to take control of the political process itself. Stopping one expressway is better than stopping no expressway, but if the enormous amount of energy that has to go into stopping that expressway does not also contribute to weakening the hold of the property industry at city hall and replacing the industry's representatives with politicians who represent the interests of ordinary city residents, the victory is a minor one and probably short-lived.

Likewise with positive direct action: doing something helpful and useful is a relatively small achievement taken by itself, considering how much that is exploitative and undesirable is being done at the same time by the property industry and city hall. Carrying out any positive direct action project requires extremely close attention to the nature of the project and to the strategy employed, in order for it to have a real effect in strengthening the hand of the property industry's opposition.

Another major difficulty about positive direct action projects is that there is really very little scope for these so long as power remains in the hands of the property industry. This has, for instance, been the experience of urban renewal area residents in the Strathcona area of Vancouver and in Toronto's Trefann Court. In both areas, long and hard work by area residents gradually changed urban renewal plans calling for total demolition to schemes to rehabilitate existing houses and protect the existing neighbourhood. The foot-dragging reluctance of city officials and the unwillingness of CMHC to force fast action on the city for those innovative proposals contrast remarkably with the speed with which demolition-style urban renewal schemes were whipped through the bureaucracies in the "good old days" of urban renewal, when people were expropriated literally before they knew what was happening. In spite of an official commitment towards new techniques in urban renewal and the goal of improving neighbourhoods rather than destroying them, most officials and politicians did their best to block the successful implementation of the Strathcona and Trefann plans. Given the powerful impact that demonstration projects like this could have, if many other city neighbourhoods were to demand the same kind of constructive improvement in conditions and the power to make planning decisions about their future, no wonder government authorities tried hard to scuttle them. The fact that in both Strathcona and Trefann Court area residents seem (for the moment at least) to be succeeding attests to their political strength and persistence.

In general, people interested in promoting positive direct action by citizen groups are going to have to be extremely inventive and resilient in order to find ways around the opposition of vested interests at all levels. The major changes required to alter drastically the way in which urban accommodation is provided and to moderate the cost people have to pay for it will obviously have to wait until the property industry loses the extensive power it holds at all levels of government. While the industry is in control, it may make token concessions if it feels these are required to guarantee its survival, but it is not going to abandon willingly its enormous power or the profits now being made in the property business.

Political action

The goal of citizen group political activity is to wrest control of city government out of the hands of the property industry. Real progress in altering the decisions being made about urban affairs and in developing positive programs which respond to people's needs can only take place if political power rests in different hands.

In most cities, there are small groups of opposition politicians who are sympathetic to the interests and concerns of citizen groups and who challenge the property industry's representatives at city hall. At other levels of government as well, there are in the opposition parties occasional supporters and friends of urban citizen groups.

What is required is much more than simply increasing the number of citizen group sympathizers on city councils. It is necessary that politicians be more than sympathetic to citizen groups; *they must be controlled by them in formal and informal ways, just as property industry politicians are controlled now by the industry*. Without satisfactory controls, the enormous pressures that can be applied to force individual elected politicians to change their political position will be applied and will succeed. There is a small but notable group of city politicians who, once elected, switched sides; one surprising member of the group is Vancouver's Tom Campbell, who got himself elected mayor in 1966 by vigorous criticism of the Block 42 downtown redevelopment scheme which, he said, was a civic giveaway to Canada's two richest families, the Eatons and the Bronfmans. After his election, it didn't take Campbell long to get some token concessions from the developers and then become a strong supporter of the scheme.

While the property industry has a comfortable majority at city hall, an elected politician who feels sympathies with citizen groups and their politics can support them in his voting without threatening the industry. But should his vote become crucial, the industry will bring all the pressure it can to bear, and will make it as difficult as possible for that politician to express his personal feelings. A politician who is not tied very tightly to local citizen groups, who does not rely on those groups for his campaign funds and campaign organization, whose social life does not revolve around friends in the groups, whose outside professional life (if he has one) does not increase his dependence on his citizen group constituency, and whose resignation is not kept in the pockets of the groups in his ward is a likely target to be picked off by the property industry should it badly need his vote.

Citizen groups need to construct political organizations that can produce strong candidates for office and that can continue to control those candidates after they are elected. They have to be able to run campaigns for their candidates and win. They have to be able to defeat property industry politicians and defectors from their side. And they have to be strong enough to counteract the appeal of middle-of-the-road reformists who offer the appearance of change but not its substance.

Such organization is extremely difficult to achieve, but without it citizen groups cannot count on any significant long-term success. They cannot afford to stand aside from city elections, because then they cannot hope to control the politicians who are elected. They cannot afford to split off and splinter into more than one election organization and one set of candidates, because their power and support is still so limited that splits ensure defeat. They cannot afford to take a tolerant view of individual activists who want to become politicians and who all run against each other, because refusing to intervene in such situations greatly weakens their chances. Nor can they remain loyal to old friends if old friends betray their interests once they are safely in office.

Apart from the short-lived coalition of citizen groups in Montreal in 1970, there is no recent example of a city-wide citizen group election organization that has tried to run and win in a Canadian city election. In most cities, the citizen group movement is not strong enough or advanced enough for such an effort. Vancouver is a good example of the weakness that comes from the absence of such an organization. Two election organizations, TEAM and COPE, claim the support of people who are opposed to the property industry domination of Vancouver city politics and to the NPA council majority. The TEAM group is a collection of middle-class reformers, though "reformer" is really too strong a term. TEAM's strongest members have the same business and professional alliances to the property industry that NPA aldermen have, and their basic political position (apart from TEAM alderman Walter Hardwick) is identical to that of NPA. The difference between the two is one of style, not content. COPE's single alderman, Harry Rankin, is the strongest supporter citizen groups have, and he and Hardwick regularly vote together. But COPE has not succeeded in becoming the umbrella organization under which anti-property industry interests could have grouped themselves, and no other such organization has emerged. This makes it possible for TEAM candidates to siphon off much of the potential support for genuine anti-developer candidates.

Citizen groups alone will probably never generate the power and financial resources necessary to organize activities across a city and to run a winning election organization. There is only one direction in which citizen groups can hope to find reliable long-term allies with interests similar to their own, and that is in the labour movement. Most of the labour movement's political action takes place through the NDP, and often where unions retain some interest in civic politics they either support NDP candidates or pick a slate of candidates considered friendly to labour. The property industry can be expected to try to portray citizen group politicians as enemies of the interests of the labour movement, so inhibiting the emergence of any powerful labour-citizen group coalition which might win elections. These arguments are likely to have most success with construction unions, whose leaders often see their interests as being very similar to those of property industry owners.

To counteract this tendency, and to create the kind of situation in which a lasting coalition could be created between labour unions and citizen groups, citizen groups are going to have to seek out the labour movement and develop programs expanding on their common interests. One way of doing this is for citizen groups to line up in support of labour unions in disputes where the unions find themselves up against the same city hall majority that citizen groups are constantly fighting. Another is for citizen groups and labour unions to get together on the housing question, one which has traditionally concerned unions. Unions are acutely aware of the impact that housing shortages and

THE CITY OF THE FUTURE? Apparently inspired by the enormous commercial success of its towering black office high-rise building in Toronto, the Toronto-Dominion bank went across the country and built another towering black office high-rise building — this one — in Vancouver.

rising housing costs have on the standard of living of their members. Unions and credit unions have considerable financial resources, which can be used — and have on some occasions in fact been used — for anti-property industry housing projects.

Another way in which the common interests of citizen groups and the labour movement can be established could emerge in the formulation of some of the general policies about how cities should be governed, how housing and other kinds of urban accommodation should be provided, and how the provision of housing and other kinds of urban accommodation should be organized to replace the property industry's current management. At this point, what is needed are imaginative attempts to work out the general kinds of policies a citizen group-labour movement majority would have to implement in order effectively to change the kind of city that is being built around us, and in order to have a city government genuinely responsive to the interests and needs of ordinary people. We now have few ideas along these lines because the possibility of ever being in a position to implement them is so remote. The kinds of proposals made by citizen group candidates in city elections must be far more concrete, specific, and immediate. The following list of broader policies to be explored is no platform for property industry opponents running for civic office. Anyone who advocated policies of this kind *at this time* would lose my vote, because it would indicate to me that he was completely out of touch with the most pressing and urgent problems that people have with city hall. These proposals are offered for discussion and consideration, not as a ready-made platform that citizen group candidates should be adopting.

Some of the ideas that could be explored are:

— Public control over funds invested in new construction of all kinds, ensuring that resources are directed into projects that benefit people using them and people affected by them, so that urgent needs (like the need for adequate low-cost urban housing) are satisfied before less urgent needs (like an expensive new concert hall, or one more 60-storey downtown office building)

— Public regulation of interest rates charged for funds lent to finance new construction, providing money for urgently-required construction at modest rates like 2 per cent or 3 per cent rather than 8 per cent or 10

— Encouragement for nonprofit and co-op organizations, particularly democratically run groups of people with a direct interest in the projects they are involved in, to act as developers and owners of new housing and other kinds of urban accommodation

— Wholesale transfer of large-scale absentee-owned tenant housing from the corporate property investor owners into the hands of tenants now paying the full cost of these projects in their rents

— Strict limitations on the profits of property industry firms, regulation of rent levels to provide investors with a modest profit on their original investment only, and a severe restriction on capital gains

— Public control and public ownership of the supply of new land for development to regulate land values and to minimize the contribution of land costs to housing costs

THE CITY OF THE FUTURE? TORONTO: One of the world's great big cities?

THE FACE OF THE FUTURE: Top, Vancouver, Middle, Winnipeg. Bottom, Toronto. The skylines of the three cities with their high-rise buildings and their echoes of Manhattan indicate better than anything else how far along the road we are to identical Developer Cities, owned and operated by the property industry.

— Programs to create public ownership of downtown land used for commercial purposes, perhaps by means of tying redevelopment permission for private owners to the owner transferring title of his land (though not his building) to a public authority, thus guaranteeing that future increases in land value will accrue to the public rather than to a private investor
— Tax policies designed to appropriate virtually all the capital gains made on increases in land value by speculators and investors (but not home owner-occupiers)
— Severe limitations on the powers of public authorities to expropriate owner-occupied property
— Development of new governmental bodies of a decentralized, democratic type to put much of the power of city government to regulate and service urban land into the hands of neighbourhoods and communities within the city
— Development of new structures for representation of the citizens in public bodies to provide for more direct control by a constituency of its elected representatives

Whether policies like these are in fact the policies that should be implemented by a citizen-controlled city government is impossible to predict with certainty. There is no way to tell whether we will ever find ourselves in a situation where ideas of this kind could be seriously considered as urban policies in Canada. Certainly the fight to take control is going to be tough, and victory is not going to come quickly. There is absolutely no reason to be easily optimistic, to think that because citizen groups are something fairly new on the political scene and because they appear to have gained some ground in the last few years, they are the inevitable wave of the future. We should remember how, at other moments in Canadian history, for instance in 1837 and 1919, the economic and political interests that controlled the country seemed on the verge of defeat, yet emerged victorious.

But if the property industry retains control of our cities, then obviously the future of the cities and their residents is bleak. The day when power is taken out of the industry's hands by a broad coalition of citizen groups and other organizations representing the interests of ordinary people may seem a long way off. But what other hope have we got? What else is going to stop the irresistible logic of demolition, blockbusting, expropriation, high-rise apartments, enormous office towers, expressways, 50 per-cent annual profits for developers, constantly rising housing costs, and all the other too-familiar components of the identical cities owned and operated by the property industry that are being built quickly in some places, more slowly in others, right across Canada?